Applied Derivatives

To Nancy,
*whose patience in the early years helped to provide
the base from which this book was written*

Applied Derivatives
Options, Futures, and Swaps

Richard J. Rendleman, Jr.

BLACKWELL
Publishers

Copyright © Richard J. Rendleman Jr. 2002

The right of Richard J. Rendleman Jr. to be identified as author of this work has been asserted in accordance with the Copyright, Designs and Patents Act 1988.

First published 2002

2 4 6 8 10 9 7 5 3 1

Blackwell Publishers Inc.
350 Main Street
Malden, Massachusetts 02148
USA

Blackwell Publishers Ltd
108 Cowley Road
Oxford OX4 1JF
UK

Library of Congress Cataloging-in-Publication Data has been applied for.

ISBN 0-631-21589-1 (hardback); ISBN 0-631-21590-5 (paperback)

British Library Cataloguing in Publication Data

A CIP catalogue record for this book is available from the British Library.

Typeset in 10 on 12 Galliard
by Newgen Imaging Systems (P) Ltd., Chennai, India
Printed in Great Britain by MPG Books, Bodmin, Cornwall

This book is printed on acid-free paper.

Contents

List of Figures

List of Tables

Preface

Applied Derivatives: Options, Futures, and Swaps has evolved over a number of years as a product of teaching PhD, MBA and undergraduate courses in derivatives securities markets at the Kenan-Flagler Business School of the University of North Carolina at Chapel Hill. Much of the material in this book began as teaching notes. However, in an effort to provide more detail, the notes were expanded into book chapters. These chapters cover material that I have emphasized in my teaching and are presented in a way that I have found to be effective when communicating to students who, for the most part, do not have strong quantitative backgrounds.

Topics Covered

The book covers many of the same topics that have been included in other books on derivatives markets and that will continue to be included as long as books are published on this topic. However, many non-traditional topics, most of which have been a product of my research and writings, are also developed in detail. As such, *Applied Derivatives* represents the core of what I have found to be interesting and relevant in my teaching and research activities related to options, futures, and swap markets. These non-traditional topics include:

- The use of put–call parity as the starting point for developing standard no-arbitrage-based option pricing restrictions.
- An emphasis on the use of put–call parity as a means of providing insight into the individual determinants of option prices.
- A CAPM-based derivation of the binomial model (in addition to the standard replication-based derivation), the use of this derivation to gain insight into the relationship between true and risk-neutral binomial

probabilities, and more significantly, the use of this derivation to show that there can be no strategies involving options that simultaneously reduce risk and increase return.

- The effects of volatility misestimation in synthetic option replication programs involving stock and safe assets.
- Examples of how well synthetic option replication programs should work when rebalanced at discrete points in time rather than continuously.
- A chapter on the use of linear programming in options-based arbitrage to find the portfolio that maximizes anticipated arbitrage profits from price discrepancies while satisfying various risk constraints such as delta-, gamma- and vega-neutrality.
- A chapter on the use of Arrow–Debreu-type replication in combination with traditional stock/safe asset option replication to minimize the upfront cost of replication in the presence of transaction costs.
- A chapter on the relationship between the standard Black–Scholes and binomial models and CAPM-based risk-return theory, emphasizing the difference between expected and most likely returns from various option portfolios.
- A chapter on the formation of optimal portfolios using a single stock or index, an option on the stock or index and safe assets.
- A relatively non-technical chapter on pricing options when the primary source of risk is interest rate risk, including the Heath, Jarrow and Morton, Ho–Lee, and Black, Derman and Toy models, and how these models can be used in managing interest rate risk.
- The development of the spot/futures pricing relationship based on: (i) the leverage-equivalence of futures; (ii) the use of futures in riskless hedging; and (iii) the spot-equivalence of a long futures position held in conjunction with safe assets.
- Making a very clear distinction between forward, or unit-based hedging, and futures-based hedging. In many texts, hedging with futures is approached using both methods without making a clear distinction between the two.
- A detailed treatment of duration-based hedging with Treasury Bond and Note futures which carefully identifies the bond that is cheapest-to-deliver and recognizes how the wild-card play and the possibility of a change in the bond that is cheapest-to-deliver can further complicate the analysis.
- A detailed treatment of interest rate swap pricing that recognizes the market convention of tying the floating payment to the LIBOR rate and the fixed payment to the US Treasury rate.
- A detailed analysis of swap duration and an example of interest rate immunization using swaps.

The Binomial Model

Applied Derivatives employs the binomial model for developing the mathematics and economic insight into option pricing theory. The Black–Scholes model is developed (but not derived) as an extension of the binomial model without using stochastic calculus. As such, I view the target audiences for this book to be MBA students, introductory PhD students, undergraduate students (provided the reading material is selected carefully) and practitioners, and I have used sections of this book very successfully in my teaching to all of these audiences.

Emphasis on Applications

As the title suggests, much emphasis is placed on the practical implications of the theory of derivatives securities markets rather than computational details. I cannot think of anything more practical than knowing Black–Scholes and binomial-based option prices are 100 percent consistent with CAPM-based pricing, and as such, no strategy involving the purchase or sale of options at theoretical prices should provide investors with opportunities to earn excess risk-adjusted returns. This type of insight should be universal even if more widely accepted models of valuation eventually come along. I think it is very important to understand how well Black–Scholes-based dynamic option replication strategies should work when continuous portfolio adjustments cannot be made and there is the potential to misestimate volatility. The concept of using linear programming to control for all portfolio risk constraints simultaneously rather than using rules of thumb has the potential to improve the performance of options-based arbitrage and to also shed light on the potential costs associated with additional risk constraints. Given that transactions costs may make dynamic replication strategies prohibitively expensive, it is important to understand how an investor can reduce replication costs by including other exchange-traded options in replicating portfolios. Finally, I think it is extremely important to understand how options can be used in asset allocation to form optimal portfolios that maximize an investor's expected utility.

Throughout the options section, *Applied Derivatives* draws on concepts from option pricing theory to gain insight into these important issues while making minimal use of advanced mathematics. This is not a book that "dots the i's and crosses the t's" of derivatives pricing theory nor a book that develops the pricing theory associated with non-standard or exotic securities. Instead, the book is designed to take the most fundamental concepts of pricing theory and show how these concepts can be used to gain better insight into the potential risks and returns from conventional derivatives-based investing.

The Rendleman Website

References to several Excel programs are made in the Questions and Problems sections of this book. These programs, as well as additional Excel software, can be accessed at http://www.rendleman.com/book. The webssite will also be updated with additional questions and problems.

Acknowledgments

Hundreds of my MBA students have used various chapters of the options portion of this book for the last several years and provided very useful feedback. Mike Cliff has also used portions of the book and provided many helpful suggestions. Bob Connolly has read portions of the book and answered many questions regarding currencies and swaps. Stanley Kon also provided comments on the futures pricing chapter.

I am indebted to my many co-authors, particularly the late Henry Latané, my dissertation advisor, who suggested in 1973 that I do research on the new option markets. I also wish to acknowledge Patrick Dennis, whose work with me on advanced option replication techniques led to the development of the mathematical techniques described in chapter 9. I am also indebted to three anonymous reviewers who provided very detailed comments that have been incorporated into the book.

Finally, I want to thank the Executive Editor, Al Bruckner, Assistant Editor, Colleen Capodilupo, and the Copy Editor, Mervyn Thomas, of Blackwell Publishers. Al was very understanding from the outset, knowing that the pace of this project would be very slow and that the content of the book would be quite different from other derivatives texts. His willingness to allow me to work at a comfortable pace and take the risk of publishing a book that covers a number of non-traditional topics were very important factors in my choice of publishing companies. At my request, Colleen provided me with numerous gentle reminders to move the project along and made many useful suggestions during the final stages of editing. Mervyn's eye for fine detail helped to eliminate a number of technical errors that could have proven problematic to readers.

An Introduction to
Option Markets

1.1   Background

In April, 1973, the Chicago Board Options Exchange began trading listed call options on 16 stocks. Shortly thereafter, the number of stocks on which options were traded was expanded to 32. Over the next several years, additional options were added, the trading of put options was approved by the Securities and Exchange Commission, and option trading expanded to four additional exchanges within the United States.

Presently listed stock options are traded at the Chicago Board Options Exchange, the American Exchange, the Philadelphia and Pacific Exchanges within the US and on numerous international exchanges. As of March 9, 2000, the US exchanges listed options on 2,711 individual stocks and on numerous stock market, industry, and fixed income indices. Many of the major domestic and international futures exchanges provide for the trading of options on their listed futures contracts. In addition, a vast over-the-counter market has developed in specialized options with investment and commercial banks serving as primary dealers.

During the 1990s a very significant over-the-counter derivatives market developed among major financial institutions, primarily for the purpose of managing interest rate risks and selling interest rate-related products to their customers. Unlike most of the trading on listed exchanges, these products are often customized "one-of-a-kind" financial instruments designed to fit a specific need, and many of these products, such as swaptions, caps, and floors have option-like features.

Many conventional financial instruments have imbedded option features that have an effect on their pricing and trading characteristics. A home mortgage is a good example of such an instrument. Although a typical home mortgage may provide for monthly installment payments over a 15 or 30-year period, the homeowner is granted the option to pay off the full balance of the mortgage early. Presumably, a homeowner concerned with minimizing mortgage payments could be expected to pay off the mortgage balance whenever it is cost-effective to refinance at a lower rate of interest. The possibility for such refinancing would be factored into the initial terms of the mortgage and would affect the price at which it trades in the secondary mortgage market. Similarly, most corporate debt issues have call features that enable the issuing company to pay off the debt early to refinance at a more favorable rate of interest. Also, convertible corporate debt is much like a regular debt issue with a call option or warrant attached which gives the owner the right to convert the debt into a pre-specified number of stock shares. Although most of the focus of this book is on exchange-traded call and put options issued on individual stocks, indices or debt issues, the ideas can be extended to more complex securities such as mortgages, corporate debt, and many of the over-the-counter derivative securities that contain option-like features.

1.2   Let's Get Started

What exactly are call and put options? An exchange-traded *call option* is a security that gives its owner the right to *buy* 100 shares of a specific underlying stock at a set price within a set period of time. The price at which one has the right to buy the stock is called the *striking price* or *exercise price*. (Throughout this book I will use the terms *striking price* and *exercise price* interchangeably, so don't get confused – they both mean the same thing.) It is important to note that the owner of the call option has the *right* to buy the stock, not the *obligation* to buy. A call option is not a "have to" instrument. The owner of a call should only elect to buy the stock if it is his interest to do so.

A *put* option is the mirror image of a call. An exchange-traded put option gives its owner the right to *sell* 100 shares of a specific underlying stock at a set price within a set period of time. Like the call, the price at which the owner of the put has the right to sell stock is called the *striking price* or *exercise price*, terms used interchangeably in this book and among investors in option markets.

To illustrate call and put options, consider the following options on Microsoft stock as of the close of trading on March 8, 2000. A call option, expiring on July 21, 2000, with a striking price of $95 closed at a price of $11\frac{1}{4}$ per share of underlying stock. A put option, with the same expiration date and striking price, closed at a price of $10\frac{1}{4}$ per share. At the same time,

Table 1.1 Payoff table for Microsoft call
option with a $95 striking price

Stock price as of 07/21/2000 ($)	Payoff to buyer of call option ($)
130	35
120	25
110	15
100	5
95	0
90	0
80	0
70	0
60	0

Closing stock price on 03/08/2000 was 92\frac{7}{8}$.
Closing call price was 11\frac{1}{4}$.

Microsoft stock closed at a price of 92\frac{7}{8}$ per share. If one were to have actually purchased one of the call options at the 11\frac{1}{4}$ price, the amount paid would have been 11\frac{1}{4}$ $\times 100 = \$1,125$ plus commissions, since each option is issued on 100 shares of stock. Although readers should always keep the 100 shares in the back of their minds, throughout the book I will refer to option values on a per share basis without multiplying by 100.

To understand how call and put options work, it is useful to construct payoff tables for each. In a payoff table, one lays out a range of stock prices that could reasonably occur as of the expiration date of the option. Then, for each stock price, the value of the option is calculated as of its maturity date. Table 1.1 represents a payoff table for the Microsoft call and table 1.2 represents a payoff table for the put.

The payoff characteristics of a call option

Consider the situation, illustrated in table 1.1, where the stock price, as of the option's maturity date, is $130 per share. In this situation it would be in the call owner's interest to exercise the call by providing notice to his broker that he wants to buy the underlying stock at the option's exercise price of $95. Although there is no requirement that he sell the stock after buying it, if he were to buy the stock for $95 and sell it immediately for $130, he would create an immediate positive cash flow of $130 − \$95 = \$35$ per share or $3,500 per option. Because of the potential to sell the stock at $130, the option should have a value in the market of approximately $35 as of the last day of trading. Assuming the investor purchased the call for $11\frac{1}{4}$ per share, his net profit would be $3,500 - $1,125 = $2,375, ignoring commissions and other transaction costs. This would represent a return on investment of 211 percent during a time that the stock was earning 40 percent.

> One can see from this example that the call option provides a great deal of implicit leverage, or "bang for the buck," in relation to the underlying stock. One who buys the call in anticipation of a significant increase in the price of the underlying stock could earn a handsome return on investment if the stock were to make a significant move upward.

Also, consider the situation in which the ending stock price is $100 per share. In this case, the call owner could exercise his right to buy Microsoft stock at $95 and potentially sell the stock immediately for $100, bringing in $5 per share. Occasionally I have had a student who has argued that the option should not be exercised in an instance like this, since the $5 does not cover the option's initial cost of 11\frac{1}{4}$ per share. But this is faulty logic. The 11\frac{1}{4}$ is a sunk cost. The decision of whether or not to exercise should be independent of what one paid initially for the option. By exercising, the investor recovers $5 per share, resulting in a 6\frac{1}{4}$ per share loss. Not exercising would result in a loss of 11\frac{1}{4}$ per share. Most rational people would prefer to lose 6\frac{1}{4}$ rather than 11\frac{1}{4}$.

Now consider an ending price for Microsoft stock of $90 per share. In this instance it would be irrational to buy the stock at $95 per share, through the exercise of the call option, when the same stock could be purchased in the market for $90. Therefore, in this situation, and for any ending stock price of $95 or less, the option would expire worthless.

It is important to note that with an ending stock price of $90 per share, the associated value of the call option is not minus $5. Although the value of the call *would be* minus $5, if the owner were *obligated* to buy the stock, he is not obligated; therefore, the option's value is zero.

> Generalizing from this example, one can conclude that a call option will be exercised at maturity whenever the stock price exceeds the striking price and will not be exercised if the ending stock price is less than or equal to the strike. When the option is exercised, it's value will equal the difference between the price of the stock and the striking price, and when the option is not exercised, its value will be zero.

The payoff characteristics of a put option

Table 1.2 illustrates the payoff characteristics of the Microsoft July 95 put option. (The term, "July 95 put option" means the put option that expires in July and has a striking price of $95 per share.) Assume that the price of Microsoft stock falls to $60 per share as of the option's expiration date. In this situation, the owner of the put option could purchase Microsoft stock in the market at a price of $60 per share and immediately sell the stock for $95 per share by exercising the put. Together, these two transactions would produce a payoff of $95 − $60 = $35 per share, or $3,500, for a single option issued on 100 shares of stock. After subtracting the investor's initial cost of 10\frac{1}{4}$ per share, or $1,025 for the put option, his profit would be $3,500 − $1,025 = $2,475. This represents a return on investment of 241 percent. Over the same time period, the stock would have lost 35.4 percent. Thus, the owner of the put could earn a very large return on investment if the price of Microsoft stock were to decline significantly between March and July.

If the price of Microsoft stock is $95 per share or higher, as of the option's maturity date, the put will expire worthless. For example, assume the price of Microsoft stock on July 21 is $100 per share. It would make no sense to sell Microsoft stock at $95 per share through the exercise of the put when it could otherwise be sold in the market for $100 per share. Therefore, in this and similar situations for which the ending stock price is $95 per share or higher, a rational put owner would not exercise and would allow the option to expire worthless.

Table 1.2   Payoff table for Microsoft put option with a $95 striking price

Stock price as of 07/21/2000 ($)	Payoff to buyer of put option ($)
130	0
120	0
110	0
100	0
95	0
90	5
80	15
70	25
60	35

Closing stock price on 03/08/2000 was 92\frac{7}{8}$.
Closing put price was 10\frac{1}{4}$.

> Generalizing from this example, one can conclude that a put option will be exercised at maturity whenever the stock price falls below the striking price and will not be exercised if the ending stock price is greater than or equal to the strike. When the option is exercised, it's value will equal the difference between the option's striking price and the stock price, and when the option is not exercised, its value will be zero.

Writing a call option

Call and put options are not created out of thin air. For every call or put that is purchased, an equivalent option must be written. Thus, anyone who participates in the options market must be either a buyer or a writer. Often the terms *writer* and *seller* are used interchangeably.

Suppose John buys one Microsoft July 95 call and Mary writes or sells it. For now, I will assume that John and Mary have contracted with each other, although later, I will describe how the actual contractual arrangements are structured on listed options exchanges. If John is the buyer and Mary is the writer, John must pay Mary $11¼ per share, or $1,125, less commission. Mary, in turn, will have the obligation to sell Microsoft stock to John at a price of $95 per share. If John decides to exercise the call, Mary will be obligated to sell the stock. But if the price of Microsoft stock does not rise above the $95 striking price, John will not exercise the option, and Mary will have no further obligation.

Table 1.3 illustrates the payoff structure to Mary's call writing position. Comparing tables 1.1 and 1.3, we can see that all the payoffs that are positive for the option buyer are of the same magnitude, but negative, for the option writer.

Consider, for example, the situation for which the stock price is $130 on the option's expiration date. Table 1.3 indicates that the payoff to Mary, the option writer, is minus $35. How does this minus $35 come about?

There are two ways to think about how Mary would receive a negative $35 payoff. The first way is to assume that she is an uncovered, or "naked," writer. This means that she does not already own the Microsoft stock for which she has written the option. In this case, if the stock rises to $130 on the option's expiration date, John will provide Mary notice that he wants to exercise his option to buy the stock at a price of $95. Mary does not own the stock, and, therefore, will have to buy the stock in the market at a price of $130 per share and then turn around and sell it to John at a price of $95. Since buying the stock at $130 and selling it for $95 results in an immediate loss of $35, Mary will be out of pocket $35 in the event

Table 1.3 Payoff table for a writing position in the Microsoft call option
with a $95 striking price

Stock price as of 07/21/2000 ($)	Payoff to writer of call option ($)
130	−35
120	−25
110	−15
100	−5
95	0
90	0
80	0
70	0
60	0

Closing stock price on 03/08/2000 was $92\frac{7}{8}$.
Closing call price was $11\frac{1}{4}$.

Microsoft stock rises to $130. But part of this loss will be reduced by the $11\frac{1}{4}$ per share that John paid Mary when the option was written. Thus, Mary's net loss would be $35 − $11\frac{1}{4} = $23\frac{3}{4}$ per share.

A second way to think about the negative $35 payoff is to consider Mary's position as a *covered* option writer. As a covered writer, Mary would own the stock for which she has written the option. If the stock price reaches $130 per share, Mary will be required to sell her stock for $95 when it would otherwise be worth $130 if she had not written the option. Thus, Mary would have an *opportunity loss* of $35 as of the option's maturity date. Of course, this opportunity loss is reduced by the $11\frac{1}{4}$ per share that Mary received when she wrote the option.

Mary's obligation as an option writer will be minimized if the price of the stock ends up at $95 per share or less as of the July 21 maturity date. In this case, the option will not be exercised, Mary will have no further obligation, and she will be able to keep then entire $11\frac{1}{4}$ she was paid to write the call. Thus, the most money that Mary can make is $11\frac{1}{4}$. At the same time, her potential loss as an uncovered writer, or opportunity loss as a covered writer, is unlimited. In contrast, the most that the option buyer can lose is $11\frac{1}{4}$ per share, and his potential for gain is unlimited.

Looking at the positions of John and Mary, without regard to any other related positions in their portfolios, John, as the buyer, is hoping that Microsoft stock will go up while Mary, as the writer, is hoping the price will go down. Thus, we can see from this example that there are two ways to use options to bet on a decline in the stock price. One way is to buy

Table 1.4 Payoff table for writing position in Microsoft put option with a $95 striking price

Stock price as of 07/21/2000 ($)	Payoff to writer of put option ($)
130	0
120	0
110	0
100	0
95	0
90	−5
80	−15
70	−25
60	−35

Closing stock price on 03/08/2000 was $92\frac{7}{8}$.
Closing put price was $10\frac{1}{4}$.

a put. A second way is to write a call. Although both positions may be initiated with similar objectives, they are not the same thing. Make sure you understand this. *Writing a call is not the same as buying a put.*

Writing a put option

Like call options, every put option that has been purchased must also have been written. Continuing with the Microsoft example, if John purchases the Microsoft July 95 put, he must pay the writer, in this case Mary, the option price or *premium* of $10\frac{1}{4}$ per share. Mary, in turn, will have the obligation to buy Microsoft stock if John finds it in his interest to exercise the put.

Table 1.4 illustrates the payoff characteristics of Mary's put writing position. Assume that the price of Microsoft stock is $60 on July 21. In this case, John will exercise his right to sell the stock at $95, and Mary will be required to buy it. By purchasing stock for $95 that is otherwise worth $60, Mary will have lost $35 whether or not she actually sells the stock at $60. Thus, her final payoff as a put writer will be −$35 per share, $10\frac{1}{4}$ of which will be offset by the money paid to her by John when the position was initiated.

As illustrated in table 1.4, Mary's final obligation as a put writer will be minimized if the ending stock price is $95 or higher. Looking at the positions of John and Mary without regard to any other related positions in their portfolios, John, as the buyer of the put, is hoping that Microsoft stock will go down while Mary, as the writer, is hoping the price will go up.

We see from this example that there are two ways to use options to bet on an increase in the stock price. One way is to buy a call. The other is to write a put. Although both may be motivated by similar objectives, they are not the same.

Index options

US options exchanges provide trading in call and put options on various indices such as the S&P 500 Index, the Dow Jones Industrial Average, industry indices and interest rate or fixed-income indices. When S&P options were initially introduced, it was very difficult to actually buy or sell an index, or equivalently, to buy or sell the securities comprising the index in exactly the same proportions as they are represented in the index.[1]

To get around this problem, the exchanges employ a method called *cash settlement* to determine the payoffs to the buyers and writers of index options. To illustrate cash settlement, consider table 1.1 which shows the payoff structure for Microsoft July 95 call options. Assume that this same option is an option on an index, rather than Microsoft stock, and the option provides its owner the right to buy 100 units of the index at a price of $95 per unit. In this case, if the ending index value were $130, the owner of the call option would be paid ($130 − $95) × 100 = $3,500 in cash, the same amount that would be received if the index were purchased at $95 per unit and sold immediately for $130 per unit. Similarly, the writer of the index option would be required to make a cash payment of $3,500. If the option expires out-of-the-money, no cash changes hands.

The same type of cash settlement procedure applies to put options. If an index put expires in-the-money, the put owner is paid a cash amount per unit of the index equal to the difference between the striking price and the final index value. At the same time, the writer of the put is required to pay this difference. If the put expires out-of-the-money, no cash payment is made.

Most final cash settlements for index options traded in US markets are based on the opening value of the index on the last trading day. The opening value is defined as the value of the index computed using the first

1. Today it is possible to purchase shares of the S&P 500 index through S&P 500 Depository Receipts (SPDRs). However, securities of this type are not available for all indices for which options and futures are traded.

trading price for the day of each of its component securities. If a particular security does not trade, the most recent previous price is used in computing the index value.

Option investing as a zero-sum game

The preceding examples illustrate the zero-sum nature of option investing. Every dollar made by an option buyer is lost by a writer, and every dollar made by a writer is lost by an option buyer. In fact, when commissions and other transaction costs are taken into account, option investing represents a negative sum game to buyers and writers as a group. Unlike increases in stock market prices, when option prices go up, we do not get richer as a society. Although some may get richer, others become poorer, or, at least, less rich. And when the financial gains and losses of all option market participants, including brokers, are summed together, the net figure is always zero.

This does not mean, however, that society does not gain from the risk sharing provided by option markets. If the trading of options allows financial risks to be shared more optimally, society as a whole should benefit.[2] In fact, I am confident that the unprecedented high level of stock market prices in recent years may be due in part to the risk sharing that options and other derivative instruments have provided and that stock market prices would be significantly lower in the absence of options trading. Nevertheless, for a given option trade, any money made or lost by an option buyer must be lost or gained by the option writer (and brokers).

European and American options

The term *European* option is a term used to describe an option that can only be exercised on its maturity date. The term *American* option is a term used to describe an option that can be exercised at any time. There is no requirement that options traded in America be *American* or that options traded in Europe be *European*. In fact, in today's markets, most options are American, although there are some important exceptions.[3]

In analyzing the payoff structures of option positions, I treated the Microsoft options as if they were European. I did not consider what might happen to the stock and its associated call and put options prior to the

---

2. The potential benefits to society from the risk sharing provided by option and related markets is developed in Arrow (1964), Breeden and Litzenberger (1978), Debreu (1959) and Ross (1976).
3. The most significant European-style option traded in US markets is the S&P 500 contract.

July 21 maturity date. Instead, I treated the outcomes as of July 21 as the only ones that mattered.

In fact, the Microsoft options, and most exchange-traded options in the US, are *American*. Therefore, to be technically correct, I should have considered all dates between March 8 and July 21 in analyzing the payoff structure to the Microsoft options.

Fortunately, as we will see in the next chapter, little damage is done by treating American options as if they are European. In fact, as I will prove in the next chapter, it will never be rational to exercise an American call option on a non-dividend paying stock, or even a very low-dividend paying stock, prior to its maturity date. Therefore, even though such a call option may be American for legal purposes, for analytical purposes, we can treat it as a European option.

On the other hand, the circumstances that make a call option less likely to be exercised make the exercise of put options more likely. Therefore, some damage is done in the analysis and pricing of American puts on non-dividend, or low-dividend paying stocks, when we treat the options as if they are European. But as the pricing theory of this book develops, you should see that the damage is small. As you might imagine, it is much easier to analyze and price European options, since the only date that is relevant is the option's maturity date. In contrast, to be technically correct in the pricing and analysis of American options, the outcomes of the stock at every moment in time, from the time the option is purchased until the time it expires, must be taken into account. Although this may seem like a monumental task, modern methods of option pricing can easily accommodate this level of complexity. And we will learn about these methods – but not quite yet.

1.3 The Legal Relationship Between the Buyer and Writer

Prior to listed options, there was limited trading in options in the over-the-counter market. For a relatively large fee, put and call dealers were able to bring potential buyers and writers of options, such as John and Mary, together in an option contract between the two individual parties. But in such a contract, if the writer were to default on his or her obligations, the buyer would have little recourse other than litigation. Because of this potential risk of default, very few investors were willing to take on the default risks associated with options investing, and the old over-the-counter options market never became an important part of the US financial system. Fortunately, listed options trading has eliminated the potential for default risk. Here's how contracts for exchange-traded options actually work.

Assume that a trade is executed on the floor of the Chicago Board Options Exchange in which John is the buyer of the Microsoft July 95 call and Mary is the writer. This trade would then create two contracts. The first contract would be between John as the buyer and the Options Clearing Corporation (OCC) as the writer or seller. The second contract would be between the OCC as the buyer and Mary as the seller.

Leaving out the technical details, the OCC is an organization capitalized and backed by the largest Wall Street firms and many other option trading houses that readers of this book have probably never heard of. In essence, the OCC and its members guarantee all option trades. In fact, every trade that is made in listed options in the US must be guaranteed by a member of the OCC. A small portion of each option commission is paid to the clearing member for its guarantee and another small portion is paid to the OCC to help build up its capital.

From time to time defaults by option writers do occur. Generally default losses are borne by the clearing member that has guaranteed the defaulting option position. But in the unlikely event that the clearing member incurs such a large loss that it becomes insolvent and cannot fulfill the obligations of its defaulting option writers, the OCC will step in and cover the losses. Although it is possible that the OCC could default, it is very unlikely. The way the OCC's guarantee is structured, the only risk associated with a default by the OCC is a meltdown of our entire financial system.[4]

Getting back to John and Mary, even though a trade was executed between them, no specific contract is created between John and Mary. Suppose that eventually the circumstances are such that John decides to exercise his call or put option. He will provide his broker with a notification that he wants to exercise. The broker will then notify the OCC. The Clearing Corporation, in turn, will select one of its members on a random basis as the firm responsible for the writing position. The chance that a specific firm will be selected is directly proportional to the number of contracts it has written for itself or its customers as a percentage of the total contracts outstanding for the option that is exercised. For example, if Merrill Lynch has written 10 percent of all of the outstanding options in the series that is exercised, there will be a 10 percent chance that Merrill will be assigned the exercise notice. Merrill, in turn, must assign the notice to one of its accounts, either on a first-in-first-out basis, or in accordance with the same type of proportional random selection procedure. By the time John decides to exercise, Mary may have terminated her position.

---

4. In the event a large loss causes the OCC to use up its entire capital, its collective membership is required to step in and use its own capital to cover the loss. If Merrill Lynch, Goldman Sachs and similar firms as a group are unable to cover the loss, we can say good bye to our financial system as we know it.

But if her position has not been terminated, her chances of being assigned John's exercise notice are no greater than those of anyone else.

1.4   How Option Positions are Terminated

Option positions may be terminated in one of two ways. First, they may be held through the termination of the contract or until exercised. The second method of termination is to make an option trade that reverses the initial position.

Reversing the position of an option buyer is straightforward. Suppose John buys the Microsoft July 95 call on March 8, 2000 at a price of $11\frac{1}{4}$ per share. Several days later the market price of the option increases to $18 per share. If John wants to terminate his position, he can simply sell the call option that he has purchased. In this case, he would earn a profit of $18 - $11\frac{1}{4} = $6\frac{3}{4}$, less commissions. And, of course, terminating a position in a purchased put would work the same way.

Reversing the position of an option writer is also straightforward. Suppose Mary writes the Microsoft July 95 call on March 8, 2000 at a price of $11\frac{1}{4}$ per share. Later, the price of the call rises to $18 per share. Mary gets nervous and decides to terminate her position as a writer. To do so, Mary simply enters an order to buy the same option. By purchasing the option for $18 per share that she had sold earlier for $11\frac{1}{4}$, Mary loses $6\frac{3}{4}$ per share plus commissions. On the other hand, if the price of the same option were to decline to $3 per share, Mary could terminate the position profitably by purchasing the option for $3 that she had sold earlier for $11\frac{1}{4}$, resulting in a profit of $8\frac{1}{4}$ per share, less commission. Although the order of buying and selling is the reverse of that of typical securities transactions, it is still the case that Mary will make money if her selling price exceeds her purchase price and will lose money if her selling price is less than her purchase price.

1.5   Standards for Exchange-traded Options

The terms of most US exchange-traded options have been standardized. All exchange-traded equity and index options expire on the Saturday following the third Friday of their expiration month. For all practical purposes, however, the expiration date should be thought of as the third Friday, unless Friday is an exchange holiday, in which case the expiration should be thought of as the Thursday preceding the third Friday. Why? Because this is the last day that the options can trade and the last day an exercise notice can be tendered. Extending the expiration to Saturday provides brokerage firms and the OCC a short window of time to get their paperwork done.

Typically there are four expiration dates available for trading in regular equity and index options. The first expiration is the most immediate calendar month for which the expiration date has not passed. The second expiration occurs in the month immediately following the first expiration month. For approximately one-third of all contracts, the third expiration date will be in the next month, or the second month following the initial expiration month. Another third of the contracts will have their third expiration in the fourth month following the initial expiration month, and the final third will have their third expiration in the fifth month. The fourth expiration month for all contracts is three months following the third expiration month.

Sound complicated? It really isn't. Suppose it is March 8, 2000. The third Friday of March, 2000 is March 17. Thus, on March 8, all regular exchange-traded equity and index options will have a series that expires on March 17. Also, all regular exchange-traded equity and index options will have a series that would normally expire on April 21, but since April 21, 2000 is the Good Friday holiday, the second series ceases trading on Thursday, April 20. Approximately one third of the options will have two additional option series for which the expiration dates are May 19 and August 18. Another one third will have option series that expire on June 16 and September 15, and a final one third will have contracts that expire on July 21 and October 20.

In addition to fixed expiration dates, the number of striking prices available for regular exchange-traded options is also fixed. The striking price interval is $2\frac{1}{2}$ points when the striking price is between $5 and $25, 5 points when the striking price is between $25 and $200, and 10 points when the striking price exceeds $200. Generally, when a new option series is introduced, options with exercise prices immediately surrounding the stock price are offered for trading. If the price of the stock subsequently moves to the mid-point of another striking price interval, a new series of options with the next striking price is added for trading.

Occasionally one can find striking prices that violate the above price intervals. These violations reflect adjustments for stock splits. For example, suppose a stock with listed options splits 2 for 1 and call and put options with a $95 striking price are available for trading prior to the split. After the split, each outstanding option contract becomes two contracts with a striking price of $\$95/2 = \$47.50$. If there were a 3 for 2 split, the striking price would be adjusted to $\$95 \left(\frac{2}{3}\right) = \$63.33$, and each option contract would be for 150 shares of stock rather than the original 100 shares.

By limiting the number of striking prices and expiration dates available for trading, there should be a reasonable amount of trading interest in most of the available option series. Typically, most trading occurs in the near-term "near-the-money" options. The terms *near-the-money* and *at-the-money* mean that the stock price is very close to the striking price. In contrast, the trading volume is typically low for options that are way "in-the-money" and way "out-of-the-money." An option is considered *in-the-money* if exercising would produce a positive payoff. For example, if a stock is selling for $100, call options with striking prices below $100 and put options with striking prices above $100 would be *in-the-money*. In contrast, an option is said to be *out-of-the-money* if its immediate exercise would produce a negative payoff. Presumably, rational investors would never exercise *out-of-the-money* options.

In addition to regular options, the exchanges also offer LEAPS and FLEX options. LEAPS is an acronym for Long-term Equity AnticiPation Securities. These are equity and index options that are issued with original maturities of two to three years. Over time, when the maturity dates for these options coincide with the maturity dates of regular options, the LEAPS are rolled into the regular option series.

FLEX options are options whose striking prices and expiration dates are negotiated by investors at the time the options are initiated. But to initiate a new FLEX option series, the initial position must be in 250 options or more. FLEX options were introduced to appeal to institutional and wealthy individual investors with investment and hedging needs that could not be accommodated easily by regular options with standard striking prices and expiration dates. To avoid confusion, the exchanges do not allow FLEX options to expire on the same dates as regular options.

1.6   Some Common Option Investing Strategies

Pure speculative positions

Options can be used to take pure speculative positions with respect to future price movements in the underlying stock. If one is very bullish about the return prospects for the stock, one can buy a call or write a put. Or if one is very bearish, one can buy a put or write a call. But before taking such positions, remember that even if you are correct about the future direction of the stock price, if your timing is bad, you can still be right but lose money.

Table 1.5   Payoff structure to Microsoft stock held with protective put

Stock price as of 07/21/2000 ($) +	Payoff to put option ($) =	Total portfolio value ($)	Percentage return	Percentage return to stock alone
130	0	130	26.1	40.0
120	0	120	16.4	29.2
110	0	110	6.7	18.4
100	0	100	−3.0	7.7
95	0	95	−7.9	2.3
90	5	95	−7.9	−3.1
80	15	95	−7.9	−13.9
70	25	95	−7.9	−24.6
60	35	95	−7.9	−35.4

Percentage return based on total investment cost of $92\frac{7}{8}$ for the stock plus $10\frac{1}{4}$ for the put, or $103\frac{1}{8}$ total.

Buying a protective put

Suppose you own Microsoft stock on March 8, 2000 at a price of $92\frac{7}{8}$ per share. You like the stock, but cannot afford to sustain a large loss if the price of the stock declines by a significant amount. To protect against a significant loss in Microsoft stock, you could purchase the July 95 put. The cost of the put would be $10\frac{1}{4}$, bringing your total investment in Microsoft to $92\frac{7}{8} + \$10\frac{1}{4} = \$103\frac{1}{8}$ per share. Assuming the position is held until the July 21 expiration of the put option, the payoff structure to your position is as follows.

Table 1.5 shows that the worst payoff is $95 per share, representing a loss of 7.9 percent on the initial investment of $103\frac{1}{8}$. No matter how much Microsoft stock may decline, the worst possible outcome is a 7.9 percent loss. This protection does not come without cost, however. Note that when the stock increases in value, there is a significant opportunity cost associated with the purchase of the put. For example, if the price of Microsoft stock in July is $130, the protected, or insured portfolio earns 26.1 percent. But if the same stock position had not been protected, the return would have been 40 percent.

> As we will see throughout this book, there is an upside and a downside to any option-related position. The benefits associated with option investing are not free. There is always a cost.

Covered call writing

Covered call writing is a very popular strategy among option investors. With covered call writing, one either previously owns or buys a stock and

Table 1.6   Payoff structure to a covered call position in Microsoft stock

Stock price as of 07/21/2000 ($)	+	Payoff to call writing position ($)	=	Total portfolio value ($)	Percentage return	Percentage return to stock alone
130		−35		95	16.4	40.0
120		−25		95	16.4	29.2
110		−15		95	16.4	18.4
100		−5		95	16.4	7.7
95		0		95	16.4	2.3
90		0		90	10.3	−3.1
80		0		80	−0.1	−13.9
70		0		70	−14.2	−24.6
60		0		60	−26.5	−35.4

Percentage return based on total investment cost of $92\frac{7}{8}$ for the stock less $11\frac{1}{4}$ for the put, or $81\frac{5}{8}$ total.

writes a call option on the same number of shares as the stock position. Assuming that one simultaneously purchases the stock and writes the call, the proceeds from the sale of the call can be used to offset a portion of the stock's cost.

For example, assume that you purchase 100 shares of Microsoft stock on March 8, 2000 at a price of $92\frac{7}{8}$ per share and simultaneously write the July 95 call at a price of $11\frac{1}{4}$. Your net investment cost would be $92\frac{7}{8} - \$11\frac{1}{4} = \$81\frac{5}{8}$ per share. Table 1.6 illustrates the payoff possibilities to this position as of July 21.

Table 1.6 shows that the maximum portfolio payoff of $95 per share occurs if the final stock price is $95 or higher. No matter how high the price of the stock might go, the upside payoff is limited to $95, representing a 16.4 percent rate of return. Note that if the stock price stays between $90 and $95 per share, the overall return is positive and much higher than that of the stock alone. If the stock price falls significantly, the covered writer will lose, but not as much as if the call had not been written. Generalizing from this payoff structure . . .

> Covered call writing call is an attractive strategy for an investor who is moderately bullish about the return prospects for the stock but does not think that the stock price will rise by a large amount.

1.7   Spreads

Spreads are portfolios that contain two or more different options on the same stock but do not include a position in the underlying stock. Typically, the risks of at least two of the option positions in a spread are of opposite direction.

Vertical spreads

A very popular spread is a *vertical* or *money* spread. If one *purchases* a vertical call spread, one buys a call and writes the same quantity of another call with a higher striking price but the same expiration date. Note that in this case, the call being purchased should have a higher value than the call that is written. Therefore, the net investment would be positive, and an investor who buys the lower striking price call and writes the call with the higher striking price is said to *purchase* the spread. If one *sells* a vertical call spread, the positions are reversed; the call with the higher striking price is purchased and that with the lower striking price is sold.

Consider the Microsoft July 95–100 vertical call spread on March 8, 2000. The term *July 95–100 vertical call spread* refers to a vertical call spread using options with striking prices of 95 and 100 that expire in July. Assuming that the spread could be purchased using March 8 closing prices for Microsoft options, one would have paid $11\frac{1}{4}$ per share for the July 95 call and received $9\frac{1}{8}$ per share for writing the July 100 call. Therefore, the net investment cost would have been $11\frac{1}{4} - $9\frac{1}{8} = $2\frac{1}{8}$ plus commissions.

It should be noted that to buy or sell a spread, it is not necessary to enter separate orders for the options involved. All that is necessary is that a net price be specified. Therefore, in the example above, one could enter an order to buy the spread at a price of $2\frac{1}{8}$ per share without specifying the buying and selling prices of the two options comprising the spread. This same type of order can be entered for any standard spread, including all that are mentioned in this chapter.

Table 1.7 illustrates the payoff structure as of July 21 for this particular spread, and figure 1.1 shows the same payoff structure in graphical form.

Table 1.7 and figure 1.1 both illustrate that the vertical call spread has a value of zero if the final stock price is $95 per share or lower and a value of $5 if the final stock price is $100 per share or higher. For stock prices between $95 and $100, the value of the spread increases $1 for every $1 increase in the price of the stock. Generalizing from this example, a vertical call spread will have a value of zero if the final stock price is at or below the lower of the two striking prices. It will have a value equal to the difference between the two striking prices if the ending stock price is greater than or equal to the higher of the two strikes. For ending stock prices between the two striking prices, the value of the spread will increase $1 for every $1 increase in the price of the stock.

Note that with this particular spread, an investor could earn a very high percentage return with only a very modest gain in the price of the stock.

Table 1.7 Payoff structure to Microsoft July 95–100 vertical call spread

Stock price as of 07/21/2000 ($)	Payoff to long position in 95 call ($)	+	Payoff to writing position in 100 call ($)	=	Total ($)	Percentage return to spread
120	25		−20		5	135.3
110	15		−10		5	135.3
100	5		0		5	135.3
99	4		0		4	88.2
98	3		0		3	41.2
97	2		0		2	−5.9
96	1		0		1	−52.9
95	0		0		0	−100.0
90	0		0		0	−100.0
80	0		0		0	−100.0
70	0		0		0	−100.0

Percentage return based on total investment cost of $11\frac{1}{4} - \$9\frac{1}{8} = \$2\frac{1}{8}$.

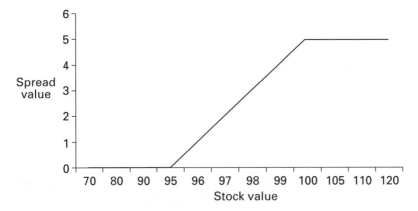

Figure 1.1 95–100 vertical call spread

At the same time, the investor stands a good chance of losing his entire investment, since the final stock price must rise from $92\frac{7}{8}$ to at least $95 before the spread will provide a positive payoff.

One can also buy or sell a vertical spread involving puts. When an investor buys a vertical put spread, he buys a put and writes a second put on the same stock with a lower striking price but the same maturity date. On March 8, 2000, the closing price of the Microsoft July 100 put was $14 and the closing price of the July 95 put was $10\frac{1}{4}$. Therefore, I will assume that one could have purchased the July 95–100 vertical put spread for a net

Table 1.8   Payoff structure to Microsoft July 95–100 vertical put spread

Stock price as of 07/21/2000 ($)	Payoff to writing position in 95 put ($) +	Payoff to long position in 100 put ($)	= Total ($)	Percentage return to spread
120	0	0	0	−100.0
110	0	0	0	−100.0
100	0	0	0	−100.0
99	0	1	1	−73.3
98	0	2	2	−46.7
97	0	3	3	−20.0
96	0	4	4	6.7
95	0	5	5	33.3
90	−5	10	5	33.3
80	−15	20	5	33.3
70	−25	30	5	33.3

Percentage return based on total investment cost of $14 − $10\frac{1}{4} = $3\frac{3}{4}$.

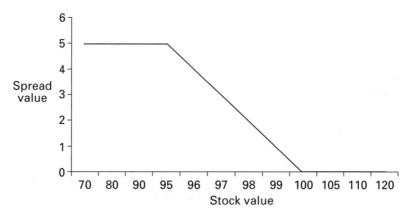

Figure 1.2   95–100 vertical put spread

price of $14 − $10\frac{1}{4} = $3\frac{3}{4}$. Table 1.8 and figure 1.2 illustrate the payoff structure of the July 95–100 vertical put spread.

Table 1.8 and figure 1.2 illustrate that the vertical put spread has a value of zero if the final stock price is $100 per share or higher and a value of $5 if the final stock price is $95 per share or lower. For stock prices between $95 and $100, the value of the spread decreases $1 for every $1 increase in the price of the stock. Generalizing from this example, a vertical put spread will have a value of zero if the final stock price is greater than or

Table 1.9 Payoff structure to Microsoft July 95–100 box spread

Stock price as of 07/21/2000 ($)	Payoff to vertical call spread ($)	+	Payoff to vertical put spread ($)	=	Total ($)	Percentage return to spread
120	5		0		5	−14.9
110	5		0		5	−14.9
100	5		0		5	−14.9
99	4		1		5	−14.9
98	3		2		5	−14.9
97	2		3		5	−14.9
96	1		4		5	−14.9
95	0		5		5	−14.9
90	0		5		5	−14.9
80	0		5		5	−14.9
70	0		5		5	−14.9

Percentage return based on total investment cost of $2\frac{1}{8} + \$3\frac{3}{4} = \$5\frac{7}{8}$.

equal to the higher of the two striking prices. It will have a value equal to the difference between the two striking prices if the ending stock price is less than or equal to the lower of the two strikes. For ending stock prices between the two striking prices, the value of the spread will decrease $1 for every $1 increase in the price of the stock.

Note that with this particular spread, an investor could earn a return of 33.3 percent, provided the ending stock price is $95 per share or less. Given that the stock price at the time the position is initiated is $92\frac{7}{8}$, there is a very good chance that an investor in the spread would earn the maximum return of 33.3 percent. However, the price of Microsoft stock does not have to rise very far before the entire investment is lost.

Box spreads

The purchase of the Microsoft July 95–100 *box* spread, illustrated by table 1.9, involves the simultaneous purchase of the 95–100 vertical call and put spreads. Note that no matter what stock price might occur on July 21, the ending value of the spread is $5 per share. Thus, even though each of the four option positions in isolation is very risky, the combination is perfectly safe.

Table 1.9 indicates that the return on investment for the box spread is −14.9 percent. Why would any rational investor pay $5\frac{7}{8}$ per share for the box spread when the payoff is only $5? No rational investor would do this. Therefore, there must be something else going on.

In all likelihood, one or more of the four option prices used in computing the initial cost of the spread is not indicative of the price at which one could trade. I took these prices from *The Wall Street Journal*. But the *Journal* does not indicate the time at which the transactions associated with these prices actually occurred. If the last trade in a particular option did not occur near the end of the trading day, it could have been a reasonable price at the time it occurred but an unreasonable price as of the close. This is a phenomenon that option researchers refer to as the *non-synchronous data problem*. Before drawing inferences about the rationality or lack thereof of option and stock prices in relation to each other, it is important that all the prices occur at approximately the same time.

Another possible source of price discrepancy in the box spread arises from analyzing the spread as if the options are European, even though they are actually American, thereby ignoring what might happen prior to the options' maturity date. Although we are not yet equipped to understand why, it is possible that a payoff greater than $5 could occur if a significant decline occurs in the price of the underlying stock and the puts are exercised prematurely. Despite this possibility, it is unlikely to account for the entire price discrepancy.

Butterfly spreads

A *butterfly* spread involves the use of call or put options with the same maturity date but with three different striking prices. To qualify as a butterfly spread, the middle striking price must lie half way between the two outer striking prices.

When an investor purchases a butterfly call spread, he buys the call with the low striking price, writes two calls with the middle striking price and buys one call with the high striking price. For example, using March 8, 2000 closing prices for the Microsoft 90–95–100 butterfly call spread, the investor would purchase one July 90 call at $13\frac{3}{4}$, write two July 95 calls at $11\frac{1}{4}$ and purchase one July 100 call at $9\frac{1}{8}$. This would result in a net cost of $\$13\frac{3}{4} - \$11\frac{1}{4}(2) + \$9\frac{1}{8} = \$0\frac{3}{8}$ plus commission. Note that the purchase of the butterfly spread is equivalent to buying the 90–95 vertical call spread and selling the 95–100 vertical call spread. Table 1.10 and figure 1.3 illustrate the payoff structure for the Microsoft July 90–95–100 butterfly call spread.

Table 1.10 and figure 1.3 illustrate the triangular payoff structure of the butterfly spread. Generally, a butterfly call spread will have a maximum

Table 1.10 Payoff structure to Microsoft July 90–95–100 butterfly call spread

Stock price as of 07/21/2000 ($)	Payoff to one long 90 call ($)	+	Payoff to writing two 95 calls ($)	+	Payoff to one long 100 call ($)	=	Total ($)	Percentage return to spread
120	30		−2(25)		20		0	−100.0
110	20		−2(15)		10		0	−100.0
100	10		−2(5)		0		0	−100.0
99	9		−2(4)		0		1	166.7
98	8		−2(3)		0		2	433.3
97	7		−2(2)		0		3	700.0
96	6		−2(1)		0		4	966.7
95	5		0		0		5	1,233.3
94	4		0		0		4	966.7
93	3		0		0		3	700.0
92	2		0		0		2	433.3
91	1		0		0		1	166.7
90	0		0		0		0	−100.0
80	0		0		0		0	−100.0
70	0		0		0		0	−100.0

Percentage return based on total investment cost of $13\frac{3}{4} - \$11\frac{1}{4}(2) + \$9\frac{1}{8} = \$0\frac{3}{8}$.

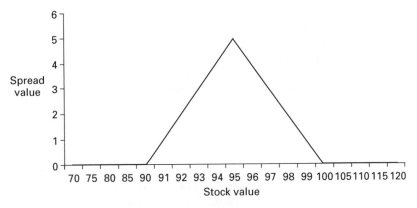

Figure 1.3 90–95–100 butterfly call spread

payoff equal to half the difference between the high and low striking prices, and this maximum payoff will occur if the final stock price equals the middle strike. The spread will have a value of zero if the final stock price falls below the low striking price or above the high striking price. Between the two striking prices, the value of the spread increase $1 for every $1 increase in the price of the stock between the low and middle strikes and then decreases by $1 for every $1 increases in the price of the stock between the middle strike and the high striking price.

In this particular example, the initial investment cost is $0\frac{3}{8}$ based on the closing prices of the four Microsoft options. This seems a bit low, based on the likelihood that an investor could earn a very high return from the spread. Although not illustrated, a butterfly put spread with the same maturity and striking prices should have an identical payoff structure at maturity, and if it were not for the possibility of premature exercise, should have an identical cost. However, using closing prices on March 8, 2000, the net cost of the butterfly put spread would have been $1, based on costs for the July 90, 95 and 100 puts of $7\frac{1}{2}$, $10\frac{1}{4}$ and $14, respectively. The fact that there is such a large difference between costs of the butterfly call and put spreads is another indication that the closing prices from the *Wall Street Journal* did not all occur at the same time.

> Typically, when option prices seem out of line with one another, it is an indication that the prices are out of synch in time rather than an indication that one could make a profit by trading the mispriced options.

Putting pricing issues aside, the purchase of the Microsoft 90–95–100 butterfly spread is essentially a bet on volatility or a bet that the price of Microsoft stock will not change by a significant amount between March and July. A moderate change in the stock price in either direction would cause the spread to expire worthless. Thus, an investor who thought the future volatility of Microsoft stock would be low might purchase the butterfly spread, while an investor who believed the volatility would be high might sell the spread.

Straddles

Another way to bet on volatility is through the purchase or sale of a *straddle*. To buy a straddle, one must purchase a call and put option, both with the same striking price and maturity date. When writing a straddle, one simply writes the same call and put. Using the March 8 closing prices of $11\frac{1}{4}$ for the July 95 call and $10\frac{1}{4}$ for the July 95 put, the cost of the July 95 straddle would have been $11\frac{1}{4} + 10\frac{1}{4} = 21\frac{1}{2}$ plus commission. Table 1.11 and figure 1.4 illustrate the straddle's payoff structure.

Table 1.11 and figure 1.4 illustrate the "V"-shaped payoff structure of the straddle. By purchasing the call and the put, the investor is hoping for a large change in the price of the underlying stock, but does not care whether his ultimate payoff occurs because the stock goes up or because

Table 1.11 Payoff structure of Microsoft July 95 straddle

Stock price as of 07/21/2000 ($)	Payoff to long call ($)	+	Payoff to long put ($)	=	Total ($)	Percentage return to straddle
130	35		0		35	62.8
120	25		0		25	16.3
110	15		0		15	−30.2
100	5		0		5	−76.7
95	0		0		0	−100.0
90	0		5		5	−76.7
80	0		15		15	−30.2
70	0		25		25	16.3
60	0		35		35	62.8

Percentage return based on total investment cost of $11\frac{1}{4} + $10\frac{1}{4} = $21\frac{1}{2}$.

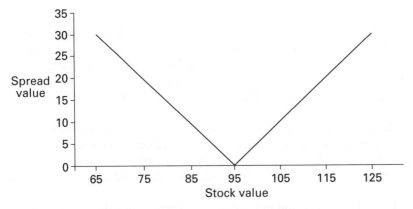

Figure 1.4 Straddle with $95 strike

the stock goes down. As with the butterfly spread, the investor is betting on volatility, but in this case, the investor is betting that volatility will be high, whereas an investor who buys a butterfly spread is betting that volatility will be low.

Time spreads

A *time* or *calendar* spread represents a more complex volatility bet. In a time spread involving calls, an investor purchases a call and simultaneously writes a second call with the same striking price but shorter maturity. A time spread can also be purchased or sold using puts. With a time spread, the investor is betting that the rate of decay in the price of the shorter-term option that is written is higher than that of the longer-term option that is purchased. This will generally be the case if the stock price does not change by a significant amount prior to the maturity of the near-term option. However, if the stock price makes a significant change in either direction, or if the market decides to price the options using a lower estimate of future volatility, the investor can lose. To construct a payoff table or graph for a time spread, we must have a method to determine what the value of the longer-term option will be as of the maturity date of the shorter-term option. At this point in the book we are not equipped to develop such a table. Later, however, we could use the binomial model of Cox, Ross, and Rubinstein (1979) and Rendleman and Bartter (1979), developed in chapters 3–5 and the Black–Scholes (1973) model, developed in chapters 5–7, to provide further insight into the payoff characteristics of time spreads.

1.8   Summary

Presently, listed options are traded on over 2,700 individual stocks and on numerous stock market, industry and fixed income indices. A call option is a security that gives its owner the right to buy an underlying asset or index at a set price within a set period of time. A put option is just the opposite of a call. It gives its owner the right to sell and asset or index rather than the right to buy.

Both call and put options can be used as purely speculative instruments. For example, an investor wanting to speculate on an increase in the price of a stock could buy a call or write a put on the stock. If an investor wanted to speculate on a decline in the stock price, he could buy a put or write a call.

Even though call and put options represent very risky securities when viewed in isolation, they can actually be used to reduce risk, or hedge, when used in conjunction with an investment in the underlying asset or index. For example, a put option can be purchased as insurance against an adverse decline in the price of a stock held in an investor's portfolio. Similarly, an investor can buy a stock and write a call on the same stock, and in the process, create a pattern of possible returns that is much less risky than that from holding stock alone.

Options can also be combined into "spreads," option positions for which the risks of one or more options are partially or fully offsetting. Some spreads, such as vertical call spreads, can be used to speculate on a moderate short-term increase in the price of a stock or index. Others, such as butterfly spreads and straddles, can be used as a means to speculate on future volatility. And finally, a box spread, consisting of a position in four different options issued on the same underlying security, combines the risks of the various options in a way that eliminates risk entirely.

Although there are infinitely more ways to invest in options that the common strategies discussed in this chapter, these strategies help to illustrate that options can be used to accomplish many objectives that could not otherwise be accomplished through more conventional investing using stock and safe assets alone. The remainder of this book will develop the theory of option pricing and the related theory of hedging that should enable readers to begin to understand the unlimited potential for options to enhance the management of risks in investment portfolios.

REFERENCES

Arrow, K. J., "The Role of Securities in the Optimal Allocation of Risk Bearing." *Review of Economic Studies* (April 1964), 91–6.

Black, F. and M. Scholes, "The Pricing of Options and Corporate Liabilities." *The Journal of Political Economy* (May/June 1973), 673–54.

Breeden, D. T. and R. H. Litzenberger, "Prices of State-Contingent Claims Implicit in Option Prices." *Journal of Business* (October 1978), 621–51.

Cox, J. C., S. Ross, and M. Rubinstein, "Option Pricing: A Simplified Approach." *Journal of Financial Economics* 7 (December 1979), 229–64.

Debreu, G., *Theory of Value*. John Wiley and Sons, New York (1959).

Rendleman, R. J., Jr. and B. J. Bartter, "Two-State Option Pricing." *Journal of Finance* 34 (December 1999), 1093–110.

Ross, S., "Options and Efficiency." *Quarterly Journal of Economics* (February 1976), 75–89.

QUESTIONS AND PROBLEMS

1. Define a call option.
2. Define a put option.
3. Is the owner of a call option required to buy the underlying stock? Why or why not?
4. Is the owner of a put option required to sell the underlying stock? Why or why not?
5. What is the difference between an American option and a European option?
6. Describe the rights and or obligations of one who writes a call option with no further position in the underlying stock or its options.
7. Ignoring margin requirements, what are the initial cash flow implications of writing a call? In other words, how much money must you invest, or how much do you receive?
8. Describe the rights and or obligations of one who writes a put option with no further position in the underlying stock or its options.

9. Ignoring margin requirements, what are the initial cash flow implications of writing a put?

10. What is the date of the last trading day for an exchange-traded call that matures in April, 2001?

11. What is meant by the terms "in the money" and "out of the money"?

12. What are the contractual differences, if any, between writing a call and buying a put?

13. What are the contractual differences, if any, between writing a put and buying a call?

14. Create a payoff table and payoff graph for the Microsoft July 90–95–100 butterfly put spread. For the purposes of computing the percentage profit for the spread, assume you could have purchased or sold the puts involved with the spread at March 8, 2000 closing prices of $7\frac{1}{2}$, $10\frac{1}{4}$ and $14 for the 90, 95 and 100 puts, respectively. The closing price for Microsoft stock on March 8 was $92\frac{7}{8}$ per share.

15. Discuss two ways involving spreads, that one can bet that the future volatility of a stock will be very high and two ways that the future volatility will be very low.

16. The Microsoft July 95–100 box spread illustrated in this chapter would have cost $5\frac{7}{8}$ per share using March 8 closing prices, a price that theoretically is too high. Assuming all the options in the box spread are European, what should the theoretical value of the July 95–100 box spread have been on March 8, 2000? For the purposes of this problem assume that the risk-free rate of interest was 6 percent per year compounded annually.

17. Table 1.6 illustrates the writing of a covered call on Microsoft stock. In this example, the price of Microsoft stock is assumed to be $92\frac{7}{8}$ and the July 95 call is assumed to be written at a price of $11\frac{1}{4}$, both prices taken as of the March 8, 2000 close.

    The net cost of this position is $92\frac{7}{8} - 11\frac{1}{4} = 81\frac{5}{8}$ per share plus commissions. If the price of Microsoft stock is $95 per share or higher on the options's expiration date of July 21, 2000, the position will earn a return of 16.4 percent over this 135-day time period.

    Some brokers would sell this position as earning an annual return of $1.164^{(365/135)} - 1 = 0.507$, or 50.7 percent. What, if anything, is misleading about this particular representation of the return from writing the covered Microsoft call?

18. The purchase of a call option is often described as being equivalent to borrowing to buy the stock with a collateralized single-payment loan that provides for no personal liability in the event that the value of the stock cannot cover the full debt obligation. Therefore, if the value of the stock falls below the final debt obligation, the lender

receives the stock, but does not receive additional funds from the borrower to make up the difference of what is owed. Use a payoff table or any other device to illustrate the equivalency between buying a call option and taking out the type of collateralized loan described above.

2

Put–Call Parity and Other Pricing Restrictions

2.1 Introduction

The pricing of call and put options is governed by a number of restrictions that must apply regardless of the method or model used to determine the option's price. If these restrictions are violated, an investor can engage in transactions that earn riskless "arbitrage" profits, or stated differently, transactions that "put money on the table" or enable the investor to "earn something for nothing." Investors who specialize in such transactions are called arbitrageurs. Since efficient capital markets should not provide regular opportunities to earn riskless arbitrage profits, we can reasonably assume that the pricing restrictions will hold.

Throughout this chapter and the remaining sections of this book that deal with option pricing theory, I assume that options are issued on one share of stock rather than 100 shares, as is the case with most exchange-traded options. If a pricing model indicates that the price of an option on one share of stock is $8, the price of the same option if it were actually issued on 100 shares would be $800. It is much simpler and less cumbersome to ignore the 100 share scaling factor for exchange traded options when developing the theory of option pricing.

I also ignore taxes and transaction costs in this chapter and in most of the remaining sections of the book, although chapter 8 specifically addresses the issue of option replication and pricing in the presence of transaction costs. Many non-professional readers of this book may face significant transaction costs when trading options, and the use of options may complicate their end-of-year tax situations. However, transaction costs can be very small for professional investors, and taxes on gains and losses for such investors are likely to be treated as an ordinary business expense, which means they are even less significant. Since these investors should have the greatest influence on option prices, very little damage is done by ignoring taxes and transaction costs when developing the theory of option pricing.

The first restrictions, shown as 2.1 and 2.2, are self-evident.[5]

$$call_E \geq 0$$

$$(2.1)$$

$$put_E \geq 0$$

$$(2.2)$$

These two restrictions indicate that the current prices of European call and puts, denoted as $call_E$ and put_E, respectively, cannot be negative. What does a restriction against negative price mean? It simply means that no one should have to pay you to own a call or put option. Since the worst possible final payoff for both the put and call is zero, neither security should have a negative value today.

The next restrictions describe the relationship between European and American options with the same striking price and maturity date:

$$call_A \geq call_E$$

$$(2.3)$$

$$put_A \geq put_E$$

$$(2.4)$$

American options, denoted as $call_A$ or put_A, can be exercised at any time, but European options can only be exercised at maturity. Therefore, an American option is equivalent to a European option with an added feature that gives its owner the right to exercise the option any time prior to maturity. As such, an American option should have a value that equals or exceeds the value of a European option with the same striking price and maturity date.

2.2 Pricing Restrictions for Options on Stocks that do not Pay Dividends

This section focuses on pricing restrictions for options on stocks or other assets that do not pay dividends or make other cash payments over the life of the option. In section 2.3 the analysis is extended to include options on dividend paying stocks.

---

5. These and all subsequent pricing relationships are based on the classic analysis of option pricing bounds presented in Merton (1973b), and the put–call parity relationship originally developed by Stoll (1969) and subsequently modified by Merton (1973a).

Table 2.1 Portfolio payoff structures illustrating put–call parity (US $)

	First portfolio				Second portfolio		
Stock	Put	+ Stock	= Total	Call	+ Safe asset	= Total
70	0	70	70	15	55	70
65	0	65	65	10	55	65
60	0	60	60	5	55	60
55	0	55	55	0	55	55
50	5	50	55	0	55	55
45	10	45	55	0	55	55
40	15	40	55	0	55	55
35	20	35	55	0	55	55

Both the put and call options are European with a striking price of $55 and maturity of one year.

Put–Call parity

The put–call parity equation is very useful for analyzing option prices without making reference to any specific pricing model. To understand put–call parity, consider the following two portfolios.

The first portfolio consists of a long position in a one-year *European* put option on a stock, currently worth $50 per share, along with a long position in one share of stock.[6] The second portfolio involves the purchase of a *European* call option with the same maturity date and striking price as the put along with the purchase of a safe asset that will make a total payment in one year equal to the striking price of the options, denoted as K. This payment includes both principal and interest. For the purposes of this example, assume that the striking price is $55 per share.

Consider the payoff structure of the two portfolios. Throughout this book, I use the term "payoff" to indicate *what a portfolio will be worth* at some specific future point in time rather than the *profit* from the portfolio. In contrast, the profit of a portfolio is the payoff less the portfolio's initial cost. Table 2.1 summarizes the payoff structure for the two portfolios contingent upon a number of different possible stock prices on the options' maturity date.

Although table 2.1 does not include all possible stock prices that could occur on the maturity date of the two options, it should be quite clear that no matter what stock price occurs at maturity, both portfolios will have identical maturity values. It should also be clear that the assumption of a

---

6. A "long" position means that the stock is being held as a regular investment.

one-year maturity in the example is not critical. Any maturity will do as long as it is the same for both options.

> The first portfolio is sometimes referred to as an insured portfolio. Notice that the purchase of the put along with the stock ensures that the ending value of the portfolio cannot fall below the striking price of $55. By owning the put along with the stock, the investor has the right to sell the stock for $55, no matter how low the stock price might fall by maturity. Thus, the put option is like a pure term insurance policy on the stock that allows its owner to sell the stock for $55 no matter how low the stock price might fall by the put's maturity date.

Although the second portfolio does not involve the purchase of stock, it is economically equivalent to an insured stock portfolio. From a practical standpoint, one of the most important messages from put–call parity is that for any portfolio involving a European put, one can construct an economically equivalent portfolio involving a European call and vice versa. Table 2.1 provides the first illustration of this very important principle. Now back to put–call parity.

Since the portfolio involving the stock and put has the same payoff structure as the portfolio involving the purchase of a call and safe asset, the *present* or current values of the two portfolios should be the same. Otherwise, there would be money on the table or an opportunity to earn a riskless arbitrage profit for a smart investor. Here is how such an arbitrage transaction might work.

Recall that the initial stock price is $50 per share. Assume that the current price of the put is $7 per share. Then the first portfolio would have an initial cost of $57. Recall that the safe asset will pay $55, the common striking price of the two options, when the options expire in one year. Assume the cost of such a riskless asset is $52, implying a one-year interest rate of ($55 − $52)/$52 = 0.0577, or 5.77 percent. Under these conditions, if the cost of the two portfolios is the same, the call option should have an initial value of $5 per share.

But to illustrate riskless arbitrage, I will assume the two portfolios have different costs. For example, suppose the stock price is $50, the price of the put is $7, the cost of the safe asset is $52, but the call option has an initial price of $6 per share which is $1 too high in relation to the costs of the other three securities. How could an arbitrageur take advantage of this price discrepancy?

In this situation, the cost of the stock/put portfolio is $50 + $7 = $57 while the cost of the call/safe asset portfolio is $52 + $6 = $58. As a

Table 2.2 Payoff structure of arbitrage portfolio (US $)

Long stock	+	Long put	+	Write call	+	Re-pay loan	=	Total
70		0		−15		−55		0
65		0		−10		−55		0
60		0		−5		−55		0
55		0		0		−55		0
50		5		0		−55		0
45		10		0		−55		0
40		15		0		−55		0
35		20		0		−55		0

Both the put and call options are European with a striking price of $55 and maturity of one year.

rule, an arbitrageur should purchase the less expensive of two economically equivalent portfolios and sell the more expensive. Therefore, in this situation, the arbitrageur should buy the stock/put portfolio for $57 and sell the call/safe asset portfolio for $58.

What does it mean to sell the call/safe asset portfolio? First, the investor must sell (or write) the call option for $6 per share. Simultaneously, he must borrow $52 for one year at the 5.77 percent market rate of interest. (Since we are ignoring transaction costs, the interest rates for borrowing and lending should be the same.) Therefore, after one year, the arbitrageur will owe $52 × 1.0577 = $55 on the loan, an amount equivalent to the common striking price of the two options. By selling the call option for $6 and borrowing $52, the arbitrageur will take in $6 + $52 = $58 today. Using the $58, he can purchase the stock/put portfolio for $57 and have $1 left over. Table 2.2 shows what the arbitrageur's position will be worth if maintained for the full term of the options.

From table 2.2 it should be clear that no matter what the maturity date of the options happens to be and no matter what stock price occurs at maturity, the arbitrage portfolio will have a value of zero in one year. However, when the position was initiated, the arbitrageur took in $58 − $57 = $1. Thus, the arbitrageur clearly got something for nothing. In this case he was paid $1, knowing that he would neither receive nor pay anything else in connection with the portfolio position. Although few readers would go to this trouble to receive a mere $1, a sophisticated Wall Street arbitrageur who recognized the same price discrepancy might attempt to put on the position in very large quantity, thereby earning a sure profit of many thousands of dollars. Moreover, in an efficient market, activity of this type should continue until price pressure from the arbitrage transactions causes the potential to earn a riskless arbitrage profit to go away.

This implies that when the market is efficient, the following equation, known as the put–call parity equation must hold.

$$put_E + S = call_E + PV(K)$$

$$(2.5)$$

In equation 2.5, the symbol S denotes the price of the underlying stock and $PV(K)$ is the present value of the striking price discounted at the riskless rate of interest. Although 2.5 is a simple mathematical equation, there is an important story behind it. The story is that the portfolio represented by the left-hand side of the equation is economically equivalent to the portfolio represented by the right-hand side. Therefore, the prices of the two portfolios should be the same. Mathematically, the put–call parity equation can be rearranged in many different forms. But when the equation is rearranged, the story remains the same; the portfolio on the left is equivalent to the portfolio on the right.

In the arbitrage transaction described above, we have implicitly seen the equation rearranged as follows:

$$put_E + S - call_E - PV(K) = 0$$

$$(2.6)$$

In this equation and others like it, a negative sign indicates a negative investment or short position. For a call option, a negative position is a call writing position. In this case the investment is "negative," since someone else pays the investor to take the position. A negative position in the riskless asset is borrowing. Again, the investor is paid by a bank or other lender to take on the obligations associated with the loan.

In equation 2.6, what does the zero on the right-hand side of the equation represent? Zero is nothing. Therefore, buying the put, buying the stock, writing the call and borrowing the present value of the striking price is equivalent to doing nothing. If the transaction is equivalent to doing nothing, it should cost nothing!

Put–call parity in other forms

The put–call parity equation can be rearranged in other ways, and in each case there is a new story behind the rearranged equation. Here are various rearranged forms of the put–call parity equation and their stories:

$$S = call_E + PV(K) - put_E$$

$$(2.7)$$

Equation 2.7 indicates that there are two economically equivalent ways to buy stock. The conventional method, represented by the left-hand side of the equation, involves buying the stock outright. The alternative way is to buy a European call option, invest the present value of the call's striking price in a safe asset, and write a European put with the same striking price and maturity date. If the values associated with the right and left-hand sides are different, an investor who wanted to buy stock might be able to obtain it at a lower cost by purchasing the portfolio represented by the right-hand side of 2.7. Alternatively, if the values were different, an arbitrageur could earn a sure profit by purchasing the cheaper portfolio and selling the more expensive.

Equation 2.8 shows the two ways to do the equivalent of purchasing a European call option.

$$call_E = S - PV(K) + put_E$$

(2.8)

The first method, represented by the left-hand side of the equation, involves buying the call in a conventional fashion. The second method involves buying the stock, borrowing the present value of the call's striking price through the option's maturity date, and purchasing a European put with the same maturity and striking price.

Equation 2.9 shows the two ways to effectively purchase a European put option.

$$put_E = PV(K) - S + call_E$$

(2.9)

In this situation, the alternative portfolio involves investing the present value of the put's striking price in a safe asset through the option's maturity date, shorting the stock and buying a European call option with the same maturity and striking price.

Equation 2.10 shows the two ways to invest in a safe asset:

$$PV(K) = S + put_E - call_E$$

(2.10)

The first method, represented by the left-hand side of 2.10, involves investing the present value of the striking price in a safe asset directly. The second method, represented by the right-hand side of 2.10, involves buying the stock, purchasing a European put with a striking price of K and a maturity date equal to that of the safe asset, and writing a European call with the same striking price and maturity.

Readers who are being introduced to option investing for the first time may find it difficult to believe that a portfolio consisting of three relatively

Table 2.3 Payoff structure of portfolio involving long stock, long put, and call writing (US$)

Long stock	+	Long put	+	Write call	=	Total
70		0		−15		55
65		0		−10		55
60		0		−5		55
55		0		0		55
50		5		0		55
45		10		0		55
40		15		0		55
35		20		0		55

Both the put and call options are European with a striking price of $55 and maturity of one year.

risky security positions can combine in such a way that the ending outcome of the combined position will be absolutely safe. To illustrate how the three securities combine to form the equivalent of a safe asset, table 2.3 shows the payoff structure of the right-hand-side portfolio.

Minimum value for a call option

Using put–call parity, we can easily establish the minimum value for a European call option. Consider equation 2.8, re-stated below:

$$call_E = S - PV(K) + put_E$$

$$(2.8)$$

We also know from 2.1 that $put_E \geq 0$. If we take put_E out of equation 2.8 while recognizing that put_E cannot be a negative quantity, we obtain:

$$call_E \geq S - PV(K)$$

$$(2.11)$$

Also, since $call_A \geq call_E$,

$$call_A \geq S - PV(K).$$

$$(2.12)$$

Let's now examine pricing relationships 2.11 and 2.12 in more detail.

For the purposes of illustration, assume $S = \$60$, $K = \$55$ and $PV(K) = \$52$. Under these conditions, pricing relationship 2.11

Table 2.4 Payoff structure of long European call vs. leveraged position in stock (US$)

	Left-side portfolio	Right-side portfolio			
Stock	Call	Long stock	+ Re-pay loan	=	Total
70	15	70	−55		15
65	10	65	−55		10
60	5	60	−55		5
55	0	55	−55		0
50	0	50	−55		−5
45	0	45	−55		−10
40	0	40	−55		−15
35	0	35	−55		−20

indicates:

$$call_E \geq S - PV(K)$$
$$\geq \$60 - \$52 \geq \$8$$

Thus, the European call option must be worth at least $8. And since an American call must be worth at least as much as its European counterpart, $call_A \geq \$8$, even though the difference between the stock price and striking price is only $5.

As with put–call parity, there is a portfolio represented by the left-hand side of 2.11 and another portfolio represented by the right-hand side. But since 2.11 is an inequality rather than an equality, the two portfolios must be interpreted differently. In this case the portfolio represented by the left-hand side of 2.11 must be superior to that represented by the right-hand side, meaning that it never produces a lower payoff. Thus, as illustrated in table 2.4, buying a European call option never produces a lower payoff than borrowing the present value of the call's striking price while taking a long position in the stock.

Table 2.4 also illustrates that a long position in a European call option is equivalent to borrowing the present value of the call's striking price to help finance the purchase of the stock, but doing so with a loan in which the investor has no liability for negative outcomes (limited liability). Therefore, the value of the call option is equal to its pure leveraged value, $S - PV(K)$, plus the value associated with being able to convert all negative outcomes from leverage to zero.

How could an investor borrow $PV(K)$ to help finance the purchase of the stock while guaranteeing that all negative outcomes are converted to zero? This could be accomplished by purchasing a European put with a striking price of K that matures when the loan becomes due. The implication is that $call_E = S - PV(K) + put_E$, and we are back to put–call parity!

Premature exercise of American call options

Continuing with the same example, the price of a one-year *American* call option with a $55 striking price must be at least $8 when the stock price is $60 and the present value of the striking price is $52. Assume that you have owned the American call option for some time but today you would like to terminate your position. There are two ways to terminate. The first is to exercise the option. In this case you would pay $55 to purchase $60 stock, netting $5 of immediate value. Alternatively, you could sell the option. Assuming the market is efficient, the sale of the option should bring *at least* $8. Therefore, the optimal way to terminate the position is to sell the option rather than exercise it.

As it turns out, this principle is not unique to this particular example; it holds for any American call option, provided the stock pays no dividend. By exercising the call, the investor obtains an immediate payoff of $S - K$. By selling the same call, the investor should receive at least $S - PV(K)$. Since $S - PV(K) > S - K$ as long as there is any time remaining until the option matures, it is better to terminate a long position in a call option by selling rather than exercising. Therefore, even though an American call option provides the investor with the additional flexibility to exercise prior to the option's maturity date, if the stock pays no dividend, it will never be optimal to do so. This implies that ...

> American and European call options with the same striking price and maturity date issued on the same non-dividend paying stock will have exactly the same value, since it never pays to exercise the American option prematurely.

Using put–call parity, we can also establish the minimum value for a European put option. Consider equations 2.9, re-stated below:

$$put_E = PV(K) - S + call_E$$

$$(2.9)$$

We also know that $call_E \geq 0$. If we take $call_E$ out of equation 2.9 while recognizing that $call_E$ cannot be a negative quantity, we obtain:

$$put_E \geq PV(K) - S \tag{2.13}$$

Also, since $put_A \geq put_E$,

$$put_A \geq PV(K) - S \tag{2.14}$$

To illustrate pricing relationships 2.13, assume $S = \$50$, $K = \$55$ and $PV(K) = \$52$. Under these conditions, pricing relationship 2.13 indicates:

$$put_E \geq PV(K) - S$$
$$\geq \$52 - \$50 \geq \$2$$

Thus, the European put should be worth at least $2. Even though the put is $5 "in-the-money," that is, the put's striking price exceeds the stock price by $5, one must wait until maturity to exercise the European put, and therefore, its immediate exercise value is irrelevant.

As with the analysis of the minimum value of a call option, pricing relationship 2.13 can be interpreted in terms of a left- and right-hand side portfolio. In this case, a long position in a European put option, represented by the left-hand side of 2.13, provides payoffs that equal or exceed those of portfolio consisting of a short position in the stock and an investment of $PV(K)$ in a safe asset.

Some readers may not be familiar with shorting stock. If an investment firm shorts stock, it borrows stock from a customer or from another investment firm and then sells the stock in the open market. In this example, with a current stock price of $50, shorting the stock would create an immediate cash inflow to the investment firm of $50. But since the firm does not own the stock, it must eventually return it to its original owner. Therefore, at some future date, the investment firm must go into the open market and repurchase the stock that it has shorted. Just like the ordinary purchase and sale of stock, the investment firm will profit if the price at which it sells the stock exceeds the purchase price. However, with a short sale, the sale of the stock occurs before the stock is purchased.

Box cont'd

An investment firm that shorts stock will have immediate access to the cash generated by the short sale. However, most individual investors who short stock will not be given immediate access to the cash, and, in fact, will be required to post margin consisting of cash or marketable securities to ensure against future default in connection with the short sale.

In this example and others throughout the book, I analyze short positions from the perspective of an investment firm that is not required to post margins and has immediate access to any cash generated from the short sale transaction. Margins and restricted access to cash make the analysis of short positions from the standpoint of an individual investor much more complicated.

Continuing with the example, the portfolio represented by the right-hand side of pricing relationship 2.13 consists of taking a short position in \$50 of stock and purchasing a safe asset for \$52. In this example, the investor could fund the \$52 safe asset investment by using the \$50 received from shorting the stock plus \$2 of the investor's own money. Thus, the out-of-pocket cost to the investor would be \$2. For the purposes of this example, assume that the investor plans to cover the short position by repurchasing the stock on the same date that the safe asset matures. Table 2.5 illustrates the payoff structure to this "right-hand-side" portfolio along with that of the left-hand-side portfolio consisting of a long position in the European put.

Table 2.5 shows that the two portfolios have identical payoffs, provided the ending stock value is \$55 per share or lower. However, at higher ending stock values, the put option has payoffs of zero while the payoffs for the right-hand-side portfolio are negative. Since the payoffs for the put equal or exceed those of the right-hand-side portfolio, the current value of the put should equal or exceed $PV(K) - S$.

Premature exercise of American puts

Continuing with this same example, since $put_A \geq put_E$, the value of the American put must also equal or exceed \$2. Thus, the minimum value of the American put established on the basis of holding until maturity must be at least \$2. However, the American put can also be exercised prior to maturity, and in this example, immediate exercise would bring $K - S = \$55 - \$50 = \$5$. Since the value from immediate exercise exceeds the minimum value associated with holding to maturity, it *could* be optimal to exercise the put immediately. But be careful in your thinking. I have not said that the value of the put based on holding to maturity is \$2. I have said

Table 2.5   Payoff structure of long European put vs. short position in stock and long position in safe asset (US$)

Left-side portfolio		Right-side portfolio			
Stock	Put	Safe asset	+	Repurchase stock to cover short position	= Total
70	0	55		−70	−15
65	0	55		−65	−10
60	0	55		−60	−5
70	0	55		−55	0
50	5	55		−50	5
45	10	55		−45	10
40	15	55		−40	15
35	20	55		−35	20

it will be *at least* $2. At least $2 could be $4; it could also be $7. Therefore, if the value of the unexercised put is $4, a smart investor would exercise to receive $5. On the other hand, if the value of the put not exercised is $7, it would be irrational to exercise immediately and receive only $5.

Here is another way to think about the possibility of premature exercise for an American put. Consider what you would do if you owned an American put and the company went bankrupt. You would exercise the put immediately; there would be no reason to wait. Since there is always the possibility of bankruptcy, no matter how small, there is always a possibility of early exercise. Of course, bankruptcy is not required to exercise early, but it clearly establishes the possibility that a put might be exercised early.[7]

At this point we have not developed the theory of option pricing in sufficient detail to determine if the unexercised put should be worth $4, $7 or some other value that exceeds $2. Nevertheless, it should be clear that ...

... there is always some possibility that an American put could be exercised prematurely, and, therefore, the value of an American put will generally exceed that of an otherwise identical European put.

---

7. The author acknowledges an anonymous reviewer for suggesting this way of thinking about the possibility of premature exercise.

2.3 Pricing Restrictions for Options on Stocks that Pay Dividends

Table 2.1 illustrates that if a stock does not pay dividends, a portfolio consisting of the stock and a European put will have the same payoff structure as a portfolio consisting of a European call and an investment of $PV(K)$ in a safe asset. But suppose the stock is expected to pay a dividend over the life of the option. In this case, the payoff to the stock/put portfolio will exceed that of the call/safe asset portfolio by the amount of the dividend plus any interest that might accrue on the dividend over the life of the option.

If the dollar amount of dividend payments is certain, it is very simple to adjust the call/safe asset portfolio to also produce a payoff structure equivalent to that of the stock/put portfolio. Assume the stock in the previous examples is expected to pay dividends of $0.25, $0.30, $0.30 and $0.35 per share in one, four, seven and ten months, respectively. In this case, if the options mature in one year, the stock/put portfolio would receive $1.20 in dividends plus interest that would not accrue to the call/safe asset portfolio. However, the payoffs of the two portfolios can be equalized if four additional safe assets are purchased as part of the call/safe asset portfolio. The first of the four safe assets would pay $0.25, the amount of the first dividend, in one month. The second would pay $0.30, the amount of the second dividend, in four months, and so on. If the entire cost of the dividend-adjusting portfolio is denoted as $PV(div)$, the put–call parity equation with dividends becomes:[8]

$$put_E + S = call_E + PV(K) + PV(div)$$

$$(2.15)$$

With this modification, the minimum values of European calls and puts are:

$$call_E \geq S - PV(K) - PV(div)$$

$$(2.16)$$

$$put_E \geq PV(K) + PV(div) - S$$

$$(2.17)$$

---

8. This same form of the put–call parity equation will hold, even if the dollar amount of the dividends is not certain, provided the present value of the expected dividends is computed properly. For example, assume a stock is expected to pay a single dividend over the life of an option equal to one percent of the price of the stock at the time the dividend is paid. This dividend-related payoff can be replicated in the call/safe asset portfolio by purchasing 0.01 shares of stock. Therefore, in this case $PV(div) = 0.01S$.

> Equations 2.16 and 2.17 show that the payment of dividends makes the minimum value of a European call smaller but increases the minimum value of a European put. These changes to the minimum values result from the fact that the payment of dividends causes an automatic reduction in the price of the stock at the time the dividend is paid, thereby making calls less valuable and puts more valuable.[9]

Dividends and premature exercise

Since American options must be worth at least as much as corresponding European options, pricing restrictions 2.16 and 2.17 must also apply to American calls and puts.

$$call_A \geq S - PV(K) - PV(div)$$

$$\text{(2.18)}$$

$$put_A \geq PV(K) + PV(div) - S$$

$$\text{(2.19)}$$

As in the previous analysis that ignored dividend payments, it would be irrational to exercise an American call option if its minimum value exceeds its value from exercising. Therefore, the call should not be exercised if:

$$S - PV(K) - PV(div) > S - K, \quad \text{or}$$
$$PV(div) < K - PV(K).$$

> Even if the stock pays a dividend, if the size of the dividend is sufficiently small that $PV(div)$ can never exceed $K - PV(K)$ over the life of the option, the American call will not be exercised prematurely. However, for larger values of $PV(div)$ in relation to $K - PV(K)$, the call *could* be exercised prematurely, but there is no guarantee.

The same type of analysis can be applied to American puts. It would be irrational to exercise an American put if its minimum value exceeds its

---

9. Actually, the price of the stock will fall on the stock's ex-dividend date, the date that a new buyer of the stock is not entitled to receive the dividend. Typically, the actual dividend payment will be made several weeks later to those who owned the stock prior to the ex-dividend date.

value from exercising, or if:

$$PV(K) + PV(div) - S > K - S, \quad \text{or}$$
$$PV(div) > K - PV(K).$$

> If the dividend payment is sufficiently large, it may be irrational to exercise the put option at the present time or at any time through the time the dividend is paid. However, between the time of the last dividend payment and the maturity date of the put, $PV(div)$, which in this case would be zero, cannot exceed $K - PV(K)$. Therefore, it is almost always the case that an American put could be exercised prematurely, even if very large dividends are expected to be paid over the option's life.

In chapter 3, the specific effect of dividend payments in the pricing of American and European puts and calls is developed in more detail within the context of the binomial option pricing model. However, even without reference to a specific model of option pricing, the preceding analysis shows several of the important effects that dividends have in the pricing and exercise of put and call options.

2.4 More Insight from Put–Call Parity

The put–call parity equation, modified for dividends and restated below, provides insight into the various factors that can influence option prices.

$$put_E + S = call_E + PV(K) + PV(div) \tag{2.15}$$

Equation 2.15 indicates that the prices of European puts and calls are functions of the stock price, S, the striking price, K and the dividend payment, div. In addition, the present value of the striking price, $PV(K)$, is a function of the risk-free rate of interest and the time remaining until the option matures. Similarly, if the dollar amount of the dividend payment is certain, $PV(div)$ is a function of the risk-free interest rate and the time remaining until each payment. However, if the dollar amount of dividend payments is not certain, the determinants of $PV(div)$ will be more complex. In summary, if it is assumed that there is no uncertainty in the dollar amount of dividend payments, equation 2.15 indicates the prices of put and call options are functions of the following:

1. The current stock price.
2. The option's striking price.
3. The time remaining on the option.
4. The risk-free rate of interest.
5. The size and time remaining until each dividend payment.

> Although an option's price may be related to other variables not captured by the put–call parity equation, the equation indicates that anything else that might influence the price of an option must have an equal influence on both the put and the call.

As we will see in the development of the binomial and Black–Scholes option pricing models, the volatility of the underlying stock's returns, a variable that is not reflected in the put–call parity equation, has a positive impact on the prices of puts and calls. However, from the put–call parity equation, the effect of volatility on option prices must be identical for both the put and the call. For example, if a higher level of volatility would cause the price of a European put to be $1.00 higher, the price of a European call option with the same striking price and maturity date must also be $1.00 higher to maintain the equality of both sides of the put–call parity equation. More generally, anything not reflected in the put–call parity equation that causes the price of one option to change must cause the price of the other option to change by exactly the same amount.

Many readers may think that option prices should be influenced by the expected return of the underlying stock. Intuitively, one might think that a higher expected return for the stock should be associated with higher call prices, since calls benefit from an increase in the stock price, and also associated with lower put prices, since put prices should fall when the price of the stock goes up. However, the put–call parity equation tells us this is faulty logic. If a higher expected return for the stock causes the price of a call option to be higher, it must also cause the price of a corresponding put to be higher by exactly the same amount. Since this is such a counterintuitive result, perhaps the stock's expected return has no influence on the price of an option at all! As we shall see later, this is exactly what the Black–Scholes and related option pricing models tell us. The price of an option is not a function of the underlying stock's expected return.

Perhaps years from now a reader of this book may develop a new option pricing model in which the prices of European put and call options are functions of the outdoor temperature in the city of Chicago. But put–call parity tells us that if the temperature in Chicago influences the price of a

European put option by a certain amount, it must also influence the price of a call by exactly the same amount. Although I doubt that such a model will ever be developed, I could anticipate readers taking other factors into account in the pricing of options that are not captured by put–call parity. If so, be consistent. If consistency in pricing seems counterintuitive, you should probably remove the factor from your thinking.

2.5 Summary

The put–call parity equation establishes the relationship between the prices of European call and put options with the same maturity and striking price. Adjusted for dividends, the put–call parity equation is as follows:

$$put_E + S = call_E + PV(K) + PV(div)$$

From this equation, it is a simple matter to determine the minimum values of European calls and puts.

$$call_E \geq S - PV(K) - PV(div)$$
$$put_E \geq PV(K) + PV(div) - S$$

These relationships, in turn, can be used to determine how the prices of European and American options with the same terms relate to each other.

Although we will be developing the binomial and Black–Scholes models to place specific values on call and put options, the put–call parity equation and the minimum values for call and put options that follow from put–call parity still must hold. In fact, these same pricing restrictions should be alive and well in the year 3000, well after the binomial and Black–Scholes models have become obsolete!

As a final note, . . .

> whenever you are faced with a question regarding the relationship between the prices or risk characteristics of call and put options, put–call parity may provide the answer. Put–call parity can provide a great deal of insight into option pricing, risk management, and options-based arbitrage. Don't forget about it!

REFERENCES

Merton, R. C., "The Relationship between Put and Call Option Prices: Comment." *The Journal of Finance* 28 (March 1973a), 183–4.

Merton, R. C., "Theory of Rational Option Pricing." *The Bell Journal of Economics and Management Science* (Spring 1973b), 141–83.

Stoll, H. R., "The Relationship between Put and Call Option Prices," *The Journal of Finance* 24 (December 1969), 801–24.

QUESTIONS AND PROBLEMS

1. For this question, assume that all options have a one-year maturity and that the risk-free rate of interest is an annually compounded rate. Also, assume that all options are European and that the underlying stock pays no dividends. Using the put–call parity equation, fill in the blank portions of the table below.

Stock price	Strike price	Call price	Put price	Interest rate
100	100	14.00		0.05
	103	11.00	10.10	0.05
50	50	9.00	9.00	
100		15.00	13.00	0.10

2. A one-year European put option on a non-dividend-paying stock is currently selling for $5. The stock price is $47, the option's striking price is $50, and the risk-free interest rate is 6 percent per year compounded annually. A European call option on the same stock with the same striking price and maturity is selling for $6. What opportunities are there for an investor to engage in riskless arbitrage?

3. The risk-free rate of interest is 5 percent per year compounded annually. What is the minimum value of a one-year European call option on a non-dividend-paying stock, assuming a stock price of $80 and a striking price for the option of $75?

4. Assume that the call option described in question 3 is selling for $7. What opportunities are there for an investor to engage in riskless arbitrage?

5. Given the same set of circumstances as question 3, determine the minimum value of an American call option.

6. The risk-free rate of interest is 3 percent per year compounded annually. What is the minimum value of a one-year European put option on a non-dividend-paying stock, assuming a stock price of $58 and a striking price for the option of $65?

7. Assume that the put option described in question 6 is selling for $4. What opportunities are there for an investor to engage in riskless arbitrage?

8. Given the same set of circumstances as question 6, determine the minimum value of an American put.

9. Explain why an American call option on a non-dividend-paying stock should never be exercised before its maturity date.

10. Explain why it could be rational to exercise an American put option on a non-dividend-paying stock before its maturity date.

11. What effect, if any, should dividends have on the market values of call and put options?

An Introduction to the Binomial Option Pricing Model

3.1 Background

Many readers of this book will be students who have had at least one course in introductory finance. Typically, one of the primary themes of such a course is the valuation of assets, both financial and real, under conditions of uncertainty. Using the standard approach to asset valuation, students are taught to estimate an asset's expected payoff and expected cash flows and then discount these values back to the present at an appropriate rate to obtain an estimate of the asset's fair value. This principle is illustrated in the following example.

Consider a common stock with a probability distribution of end-of-year values as described in table 3.1 below. For the purposes of the example, dividends are ignored.

The stock's expected payoff at the end of the year is:

$$\$150 \times 0.10 + \$130 \times 0.20 + \$110 \times 0.40 + \$90 \times 0.20$$
$$+ \$70 \times 0.10 = \$110.$$

If the stock's required return is 10 percent, the best estimate of the stock's fair value today would be $\$110/1.10 = \$100$.

Table 3.1 End-of-year payoffs to hypothetical common stock

Ending stock value ($)	Probability
150	0.10
130	0.20
110	0.40
90	0.20
70	0.10

THE BINOMIAL OPTION PRICING MODEL **51**

Table 3.2   Probability distribution for 1-year
call option with $100 striking price

Ending stock value ($)	Value of call option in one year ($)	Probability
150	50	0.10
130	30	0.20
110	10	0.40
90	0	0.20
70	0	0.10

Now, suppose an investor wants to determine the value of a one-year call option with a $100 striking price issued on the same stock. Table 3.2 shows the probability distribution associated with the option's payoffs.

Using the approach to valuation taught in introductory finance courses, the investor would first compute the expected value of the call option in one year. This value is:

$$\$50 \times 0.10 + \$30 \times 0.20 + \$10 \times 0.40 = \$15.$$

Next, the investor would discount the $15 future expected value to the present to obtain an estimate of the option's current fair value. But what discount rate should be used to get from the future to the present?

To address this issue, assume the one-year risk-free rate of interest is 5 percent. Inasmuch as the stock's expected return is 10 percent, there is an implicit risk premium in the pricing of the stock. Should the same risk premium be used to determine the required return, or discount rate, for the option?

No, because the call option is riskier than the stock. Moreover, the risk characteristics of the option are almost certain to change with the passage of time and with changes in the value of the underlying stock. Thus, it is not clear what discount rate should be used or whether it is even appropriate to price the option by discounting its expected end-of-period payoff at a pre-specified required rate of return.[10]

---

10. The method of analysis described above was employed in several papers pre-dating the 1973 publication of Black and Scholes' classic paper on option pricing. (See Bachelier [1900], Boness [1964], Sprenkle [1961], Ayres [1963] and Samuelson [1965]). The primary difference between these papers and the analysis above is that stock prices are assumed to follow a normal distribution or lognormal distribution rather than the overly simplified distribution of five outcomes shown in tables 3.1 and 3.2. Also, after determining the expected maturity value for an option, much of the focus in these papers is in determining the required rate of discount. See Smith (1976) for an excellent review of this literature.

Option pricing theory provides a way of valuing securities such as exchange-traded options whose values and risks depend upon price outcomes for an underlying asset such as common stock. Unlike the introductory finance approach to valuation, the theory of option pricing is not cast within the framework of discounted present value. Inasmuch as an option's risks cannot be expected to be constant, but instead, are related to both time and the value of the underlying asset, a fundamentally different approach to valuation must be taken.

The binomial option pricing model, originally developed by Sharpe (1978), Cox, Ross, and Rubinstein (1979) and Rendleman and Bartter (1979), employs an approach to option pricing based on simple algebra. Although the math is a little more advanced than that which one might see in an introductory finance course, most students who are comfortable with algebra can handle the mathematics of binomial option pricing. In contrast, the Black–Scholes (1973) model, which revolutionized the theory of option pricing and many other aspects of finance, is based on stochastic calculus and derived by solving a stochastic partial differential equation. Given the level of mathematical training typical of most business and economics students (and professors), one must typically "black-box" a significant portion of the mathematical detail when teaching Black–Scholes and related models. As such, it is easy for students to get lost in the mathematics of Black–Scholes and never fully understand the story behind the model and the insights to investing it can provide.

It is possible to structure the binomial model to produce option values that are both mathematically and economically equivalent to Black–Scholes prices. As such, the binomial model provides a way to understand the key elements of modern option pricing theory without having to employ advanced methods of calculus. Moreover, because of its direct relationship to the Black–Scholes model, the binomial model can be used as a powerful numerical approximation technique for computing option prices for complex options that do not lend themselves to closed-form (formula) solutions. For example, using the Black–Scholes approach, it is impossible to derive the formula for pricing an American put option. However, if the parameters of the binomial model are selected to approximate Black–Scholes pricing, the binomial model can be used to obtain approximate solutions for the prices of American puts and other complex options to any degree of accuracy under what would otherwise be standard Black–Scholes assumptions. As such, the binomial model has become the model of choice for approximating values for many types of complex options.

The binomial model has been employed in two distinctly different types of applications. Initially, the model was developed for pricing stock options and related securities whose values depend on price movements in an underlying security or asset such as common stock. In these applications, price fluctuations in the value of the underlying asset reflect improvement or deterioration in profitability rather than changes in interest rates. Later, Rendleman and Bartter (1980) developed a binomial approach to valuing options on default-free fixed income securities such as government bonds. In recent years, this framework of analysis has been extended by Ho and Lee (1986), Black et al. (1990), Heath, Jarrow, and Morton (1992), Hull and White (1990) and Jeffrey (1995) to value interest-dependent financial claims while guaranteeing that model prices of default-free securities are equal to their observed prices.

This section of this book focuses on conventional binomial pricing theory and its applications to option-like securities whose values do not depend on interest rate fluctuations. The binomial approach to valuing interest-dependent securities and related securities with option-like features is developed in chapter 11.

3.2   An Introduction to Binomial Option Pricing

Consider figure 3.1 that shows how the price of a hypothetical stock will evolve over three periods. Initially, at time $t = 0$, the stock price is $100 per share. At the end of the first period, time $t = 1$, the stock price can take on only two values, $120 or $90. Note that if the stock price goes up to $120 at time 1, the price will be 1.2 times its $100 value at time 0. In this example, 1.2 is called the "up" factor. Similarly, if the price goes down to $90 at time 1, the price will be 0.9 times its time 0 value, implying a "down" factor of 0.9. It has become common practice to denote the up and down factors as u and d, respectively.

In figure 3.1, state designations are shown in the format $\{t, j\}$ where t denotes time in binomial periods and j indicates the number of times the stock has increased in value. For example, the state designation $\{2, 1\}$ associated with a stock price of $108 indicates that as of time 2, the stock price must increase one time to reach a price of $108.

Throughout figure 3.1, the stock price is assumed to take on either an "up" or "down" value at the end of any time period. More than two outcomes are not possible. When the stock goes up, it always goes up by a factor of 1.2 times its previous value, and when it goes down, it goes down by a factor of 0.9. In typical binomial option pricing applications, constant up and down factors are assumed, although it is not necessary to make this assumption. It should be noted, however, that when the up and down factors do not change over time, the "binomial tree," or sequence of events describing binomial outcomes, is said to "recombine." In a recombining tree, an increase in value followed by a decrease will produce the same

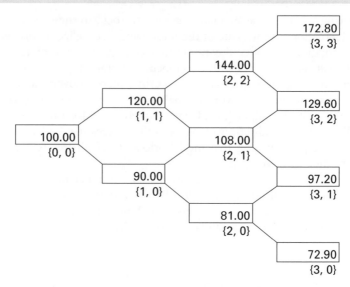

Figure 3.1   Binomial stock prices with $u = 1.2$ and $d = 0.9$

value for the stock as a decrease followed by an increase. More generally, in a recombining tree, the ordering of up and down outcomes over any number of periods is not important. If over t periods there are j ups and $t - j$ downs, the stock price will be the same, regardless of the order in which the ups and downs occur. For example, in figure 3.1, if the stock price goes up, down and then up, the resulting stock price at time 3 is $100 \times 1.2 \times 0.9 \times 1.2 = \$129.60$. Alternatively, if the stock price goes up, up and then down, the same ending price of $\$100 \times 1.2 \times 1.2 \times 0.9 = \$129.60$ results. Since order doesn't matter in multiplication, the order of ups and downs doesn't matter in determining the final stock price, just the total number of ups and total number of downs.

For now, one should not be concerned about how the up and down factors are determined or whether it is realistic to assume that a stock price can take on only one of two values from one time to the next. However, in the next chapter we shall see how to choose the up and down factors so that the distribution of stock prices will be realistic and reflect the risk characteristics of the stock.

Pricing a one-period call option

I begin with a simple example of binomial pricing to determine the value of a call option issued on one share of stock with a striking price of $110 that matures at time 1. Figure 3.2 shows how the payoffs of the stock and call

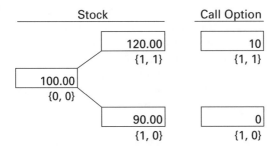

Figure 3.2 Payoffs to one-period call option with striking price of $110

option are related. The risk-free rate of interest is assumed to be 1 percent from time 0 to time 1.

In this example, if the stock price ends up at $120 at time 1, the call option will be worth $120 - $110 = $10. Otherwise, with the stock price at $90, the call option will be worthless, since it would not be to the advantage of the call buyer to pay $110 for a $90 stock by exercising the option.

The price of the call option can be determined using the principle of "no-arbitrage." According to the no-arbitrage principle, any two securities or portfolios with identical payoffs should sell for the same price. If not, it would be possible to engage in riskless arbitrage by purchasing the cheaper of the two portfolios or securities and selling or short selling the more expensive. Inasmuch as riskless arbitrage opportunities cannot be sustained in an efficient market, the prices of the two equivalent financial assets should be the same. It is this line of reasoning that causes one to expect the price of IBM stock to be the same in all markets for which it trades. In an efficient market, IBM could not sell for $170 on the New York Stock Exchange and, simultaneously, be priced at $172 on the Chicago Exchange. The stock should be priced equivalently in both markets.

In applying the no-arbitrage principle to option pricing, we will construct a "synthetic" option consisting of positions in the underlying stock and riskless security that has a payoff structure identical to that of the option. We will refer to this synthetic option position as the *option replicating portfolio*. According to the no-arbitrage pricing principle, the option and its equivalent synthetic replicating portfolio should have identical values. Otherwise, if one of the two were more expensive than the other, one could purchase the cheaper and sell the more expensive to earn a sure profit. The binomial pricing theory relies on the principle of market efficiency which ensures that price discrepancies between equivalent securities or portfolios cannot be sustained. As such, if we know what it costs to purchase the replicating portfolio, we know what the option should be worth.

In the replicating portfolio, long positions in the stock and riskless security are represented mathematically as positive quantities. Short positions are represented as negative quantities. A negative position in the riskless security also can be thought of as borrowing at the riskless rate of interest or as a reduction in an existing long position. Similarly, a negative position in the stock can be thought of as a short position or as a reduction in previously outstanding stock holdings.

> In general, when replicating a call option's payoffs, one must hold a long position in stock and borrow at the riskless rate of interest. When replicating a put, one must short the stock while taking a long position in the riskless security.

To determine the appropriate mix of the stock and riskless security in the synthetic option portfolio, let Δ denote the number of shares of stock to hold in the portfolio and B denote the amount of money to invest in the riskless security. (The Greek symbol, Δ, is the standard "street" term for the number of shares of stock required to replicate an option position.)

Assume that one can borrow or lend at the risk-free rate of interest of 1 percent per binomial period. If Δ units of stock and B dollars of the riskless security are purchased at time 0, the synthetic option portfolio will have a value at time 1 of $\$120\Delta + 1.01B$ if the stock goes up and $\$90\Delta + 1.01B$ if the stock goes down. In replicating the call option, we need to determine the values of Δ and B so that when the stock goes up, the payoff to the synthetic option replicating portfolio will be the same as the value of the call, or $\$10$. Similarly, when the stock goes down, the synthetic portfolio should have the same payoff as the call, which, in this case, is $\$0$.

This gives rise to the following two equations in the two unknowns, Δ and B, which can be solved simultaneously to determine the mix of stock and safe assets in the replicating portfolio:

$$\$120\Delta + 1.01B = \$10$$
$$\$90\Delta + 1.01B = \$0$$

Solution values for Δ and B are:

$$\Delta = \tfrac{1}{3}$$
$$B = -\$29.70$$

implying that $\tfrac{1}{3}$ of a share of stock must be purchased while simultaneously borrowing $\$29.70$ at a riskless interest rate of 1 percent. The entries in table 3.3, below, verify that the solution values are correct.

Table 3.3 Verifying the solution values for the components of the synthetic call option

State	Stock value at time 1	Call option value at time 1	Value of synthetic call option at time 1
Stock up	$120	$10	$120 × $\frac{1}{3}$ − $29.70 × 1.01 = $10
Stock down	$90	$0	$90 × $\frac{1}{3}$ − $29.70 × 1.01 = $0

The objective of this analysis is to determine the fair price as of time 0 for the call option. Since the synthetic portfolio has a payoff structure identical to that of the call option, the price of the call option should be the same as the cost of establishing a position in the replicating portfolio. This cost is $100($\frac{1}{3}$) = $33.33 for $\frac{1}{3}$ share of stock, less the $29.70 received from borrowing, or $3.63. Thus, the fair or "equilibrium" value for the call option is also $3.63.

Pricing a three-period European call option

The analysis is now extended by pricing a three-period European call option with a striking price of $100 on the same underlying stock, assuming, as before, that the riskless rate of interest is 1 percent per binomial period. By definition, a European call option cannot be exercised prior to its maturity date. As such, the possibility of premature exercise is not taken into account in the pricing analysis. Later, however, the binomial method is extended to include this possibility.

Figure 3.3 shows the price path for the underlying stock and how the value of the option will evolve over its three-period life. In the table, stock values are denoted as S and option prices as P. In addition, the table shows the composition of the option replicating portfolio in each state, with Δ denoting the number of shares of stock to hold in the replicating portfolio and B the dollar investment in bonds (or, if negative, the dollar value of funds borrowed). The analysis that follows shows how these values are determined.

I begin the analysis by determining what the option will be worth in each possible state at maturity. For example, if the stock advances three times, as of time 3 the stock will be worth $172.80, and the corresponding value for the call option will be $172.80 − $100.00 = $72.80. Similarly, if the stock increases in value two times, as of times 3 its value will be $129.60, and the call option will be worth $29.60. If the stock price falls below $100 at time 3, the option will expire worthless.

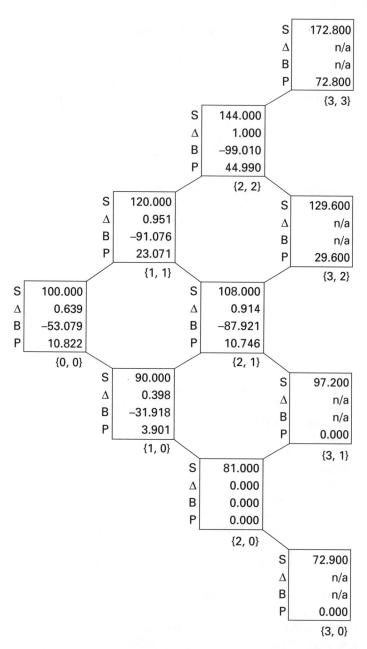

S	172.800	
Δ	n/a	
B	n/a	
P	72.800	
	{3, 3}	

S	144.000	
Δ	1.000	
B	−99.010	
P	44.990	
	{2, 2}	

S	120.000	
Δ	0.951	
B	−91.076	
P	23.071	
	{1, 1}	

S	129.600	
Δ	n/a	
B	n/a	
P	29.600	
	{3, 2}	

S	100.000	
Δ	0.639	
B	−53.079	
P	10.822	
	{0, 0}	

S	108.000	
Δ	0.914	
B	−87.921	
P	10.746	
	{2, 1}	

S	90.000	
Δ	0.398	
B	−31.918	
P	3.901	
	{1, 0}	

S	97.200	
Δ	n/a	
B	n/a	
P	0.000	
	{3, 1}	

S	81.000	
Δ	0.000	
B	0.000	
P	0.000	
	{2, 0}	

S	72.900	
Δ	n/a	
B	n/a	
P	0.000	
	{3, 0}	

Figure 3.3 Pricing a three-period European call option with a $100 striking price. Riskless interest rate is 1 percent per binomial period

Next, I back up to time 2. Assume the stock price reaches state $\{2,1\}$ where the stock price is $108. In this state, the stock price can only go to $129.60 or $97.20 in the final period. If the stock goes to $129.60, the option will be worth $29.60 at maturity; if the stock goes to $97.20, the option will have a value of zero.

As in the previous analysis, with the stock price at $108 at time 2, it is possible to form an option replicating portfolio consisting of the underlying stock and safe assets (either borrowing or lending) whose payoffs at time 3 will be identical to those of the call option. The composition of the replicating portfolio can be found by solving the following two equations simultaneously for Δ, the number of shares of stock to purchase, and B, the dollar investment in bonds:

$$\$129.60\Delta + 1.01B = \$29.60$$
$$\$97.20\Delta + 1.01B = \$0$$

Solution values are:

$$\Delta = 0.914$$
$$B = -\$87.921$$

Thus, the value of the replicating portfolio in state $\{2,1\}$ is:

$$\$108\Delta + B = \$108(0.914) + (-\$87.921) = \$10.746$$

To prevent riskless arbitrage, the value of the call option must also be $10.746. The values for the replicating portfolio and its components shown for the other states at time 2 are determined in similar fashion.

The same logic can be used to value the option at time 1. For example, in state $\{1,1\}$, in which the stock price is $120, the stock price can go to either $144 or $108. If the stock price increases to $144, the option will be worth $44.99. If the stock falls to $108, the option will take on a value of $10.746.

Again, a portfolio is formed that consists of stock and borrowing or lending to replicate the end-of-period payoffs to the option. The number of shares of stock, Δ, and the dollar investment in safe assets, B, necessary to replicate the end-of-period payoffs to the option can be found as the solution to the following two simultaneous equations.

$$\$144\Delta + 1.01B = \$44.990$$
$$\$108\Delta + 1.01B = \$10.746$$

Solution values are:

$$\Delta = 0.951$$
$$B = -\$91.076$$

and the value of the replicating portfolio is:

$$\$120\Delta + B = \$120(0.951) + (-\$91.076) = \$23.071$$

Using the same approach, the value of the option replicating portfolio is $3.901 in state $\{1,0\}$. Similarly, the initial components of the replicating portfolio are 0.63901 shares of stock and $53.079 in borrowings, implying an initial option value of $0.639(\$100) - \$53.079 = \$10.822$.

Generalizing the results

In the above example, I determined the value of the call option at maturity based on the relationship between the stock price and the option's striking price. Next, I backed up one period to time 2 and determined the components of the option replicating portfolio in each state based on the two possible values for the option at time 3. Knowing the components of the replicating portfolio and its cost, I was able to determine the option's value. Similarly, I backed up to time 1 and then to time 0, determining the components of the replicating portfolio and using this information to determine the option's price.

Inasmuch as the logic of the valuation process is the same at all times prior to the option's maturity date, a simple formula can be derived to price the option in any state as a function of its two possible values in the next period.

> To derive the formula, let $P_{t,j}$ and $S_{t,j}$ denote the prices of the option and underlying stock, respectively, in state $\{t,j\}$. Also, let u denote the total return per dollar invested (one plus the rate of return measured as a decimal fraction) in the underlying asset if its price goes up, d denote the return per dollar invested if the stock goes down and r denote the rate of return on the safe asset over a single binomial period.

To replicate the payoffs to the option, the value of the replicating portfolio should be the same as that of the option in both the up and down states. This implies the following two relationships which can be solved simultaneously for the amount of stock to hold in state $\{t,j\}$, $\Delta_{t,j}$, along with safe assets, $B_{t,j}$ for all times, $t < T$, where T is the option's maturity date:

$$S_{t+1,j+1}\Delta_{t,j} + (1+r)B_{t,j} = P_{t+1,j+1}$$
$$S_{t+1,j}\Delta_{t,j} + (1+r)B_{t,j} = P_{t+1,j} \tag{3.1}$$

In the absence of dividends, $S_{t+1,j+1} = S_{t,j}u$ and $S_{t+1,j} = S_{t,j}d$. Solution values are:

$$\Delta_{t,j} = \frac{P_{t+1,j+1} - P_{t+1,j}}{S_{t,j}(u-d)} \quad \text{for } t < T$$
$$B_{t,j} = \frac{uP_{t+1,j} - dP_{t+1,j+1}}{(1+r)(u-d)} \quad \text{for } t < T. \tag{3.2}$$

The value of the replicating portfolio in state $\{t,j\}$ is $P_{t,j} = S_{t,j}\Delta_{t,j} + B_{t,j}$. Substituting values for $\Delta_{t,j}$ and $B_{t,j}$ and simplifying yields the following pricing relationship:

$$P_{h,t,j} = 0 \quad \text{for } t = T,$$
$$P_{h,t,j} = \frac{P_{t+1,j+1}\pi + P_{t+1,j}(1-\pi)}{1+r} \quad \text{for } t < T, \tag{3.3}$$
$$\pi = \frac{1+r-d}{u-d}.$$

In equation 3.3, the symbol $P_{h,t,j}$ has been used to denote the value in state $\{t,j\}$ of "holding on" to the option for one more period. (Note that in equation 3.3, the hold value is set to zero on the option's maturity date, T, since there is no value to holding the option beyond its maturity date.) When pricing more complex American options that can be exercised prematurely, it is important to make a distinction between the hold value and the value of exercising. Within this context, we can think of a European option as having zero exercisable value at all times prior to maturity, with the investor making a choice to exercise if it is optimal to do so. Of course, with a premature exercise value of zero for a European call, it would never be optimal to exercise before maturity.

With these relationships in mind, we set the price of the option in state $\{t,j\}$ to:

$$P_{t,j} = \max\left\{P_{h,t,j}, P_{x,t,j}\right\},$$

(3.4)

where $P_{x,t,j}$ is the value of exercising the option in state $\{t,j\}$.

Denoting the option's striking price as K and the price of the underlying stock at maturity, T, in state j as $S_{T,j}$, the values associated with exercising European calls and puts are given as follows:

$$P_{x,T,j} = S_{T,j} - K \text{ for a call option,}$$

$$P_{x,T,j} = K - S_{T,j} \text{ for a put option,} \quad \text{and}$$

(3.5)

$$P_{x,T,j} = 0 \quad \text{for } t < T \text{ for European calls and puts.}$$

It should be noted that the value of a European option prior to maturity is its hold value, since the value of exercising before maturity is zero.

We will now use equation 3.3 to re-compute the option values from the examples of the previous section. Recalling that $u = 1.2$, $d = 0.9$ and $1 + r = 1.01$,

$$\pi = \frac{1.01 - 0.9}{1.2 - 0.9} = 0.3667$$

$$P_{h,2,1} = \frac{\$29.60\pi + 0(1 - \pi)}{1.01} = \$10.746$$

$$P_{h,1,1} = \frac{\$44.990\pi + \$10.746(1 - \pi)}{1.01} = \$23.071$$

$$P_{h,0,0} = \frac{\$23.071\pi + \$3.901(1 - \pi)}{1.01} = \$10.822$$

From this point on we will use equation 3.3 directly for computing option values in terms of their two possible values at the end of the period. Although equation 3.3 does not indicate the amount of stock and safe assets held in the replicating portfolio, *these amounts are embedded in the option's price* and potentially change from state to state.

Pricing European put options

A European put option gives its owner the right to sell the underlying stock at a set price on the option's expiration date. In contrast, the owner of a European call option obtains the right to purchase the underlying stock at expiration. As such, the only difference between the valuation of European put and call options is in defining the option's value at maturity (equation 3.5).

Figure 3.4 provides detailed calculations for the valuation of a three-period European put option with a striking price of $100 on the same underlying stock as in the previous example. Note that all the Δ's, which denote the number of shares of stock in the replicating portfolio, are negative or zero throughout the table. This implies that the portfolio that replicates the put option requires that a short position in the underlying stock be maintained. Note, also, that all B's are positive, indicating that the replicating portfolio requires the maintenance of a long position in the riskless asset. As with the valuation of call options, equation 3.2 is used to calculate Δ and B, and equation 3.3 is used to calculate the hold value of the put option over time. (The reader is encouraged to verify the values of Δ, B and P within figure 3.4.)

Figure 3.4 shows that the initial price of the put option is $7.881. We could have also determined the price of the put from the put–call parity equation developed earlier in chapter 2. According to the put–call parity equation, the relationship between the prices of European put and call options with the same strike price and maturity date is:

$$put_E + stock = call_E + PV(K) + PV(div)$$

$$(3.7)$$

We can rearrange this equation to determine the put price in terms of the other variables:

$$put_E = call_E + PV(K) + PV(div) - S$$

$$= \$10.822 + \frac{\$100}{1.01^3} + \$0 - \$100 = \$7.881$$

Therefore, having computed the call price, we can use put–call parity to compute the value of the put option without having to make the calculations required by the binomial model.

Maintaining the replicating portfolio

Note from figure 3.3 that the initial replicating portfolio for the call option consists of 0.639 shares of stock at $100 per share and $53.079 in borrowings. Figure 3.3 also shows that the required stock position and borrowing requirements will be different in each state, implying that one must be prepared to buy or sell stock and also increase or reduce borrowings in order to maintain the replicating portfolio.

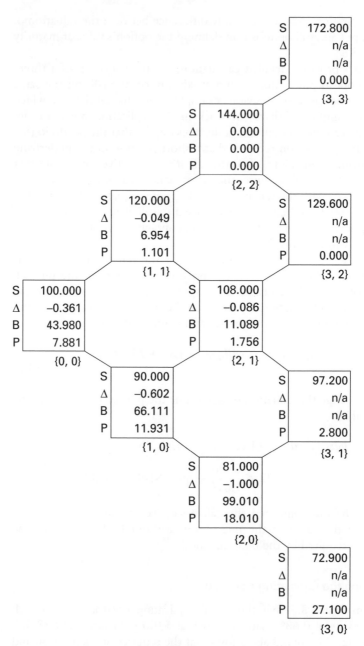

Figure 3.4 Pricing a three-period European put option with a $100 striking price. Riskless interest rate is 1 percent per binomial period

For example, assume that state $\{1, 1\}$ occurs at time 1, in which case the value of the stock will increase from \$100 to \$120 per share. In this state, $\Delta = 0.951$ and $B = -\$91.076$. Therefore, in state $\{1, 1\}$, one must hold 0.951 shares of stock and maintain a total borrowing amount of \$91.076 in order to continue replicating the option through time 2. Since 0.639 shares are held initially, $0.951 - 0.639 = 0.312$ additional shares must be purchased. With the stock price at \$120, this will require an outlay of $0.312 \times \$120 = \$37.47$.[11] At the same time, the total amount borrowed must increase to \$91.076. Before we can compute the additional amount to borrow, however, we must account for the interest owed on the initial borrowings of \$53.079. With an interest rate of 1 percent per binomial period, the total amount owed from the initial borrowing is $\$53.079 \times 1.01 = \$53.610$. Therefore, the amount of additional borrowing required is $\$91.076 - \$53.610 = \$37.47$.

Note that the \$37.47 of additional borrowing is precisely the amount needed to purchase additional stock. Thus, the funds borrowed would pay for the stock, and the investor would not be required to commit additional funds to the option replication program. In this case, the replicating program is said to be *self-financing*. Note that the program will also be self-financing at time 2. For example, if the stock price falls to \$108, $0.951 - \$0.914 = \$0.038$ shares of stock would be sold at a price of \$108, bringing in \$4.066. At the same time, borrowing must be reduced to \$87.921 from $\$91.07 \times 1.01$, requiring that \$4.066 be paid to reduce the loan balance. Thus, the proceeds from the sale of stock would exactly match the required payment on the loan, and no further investment would be necessary.

Finally, assume that the stock price increases to \$129.60 at time 3. In this case one must sell 0.914 shares of stock at \$129.60, bringing in \$118.40. From this amount, the final loan balance of $\$87.921 \times 1.01 = \$88.80$ must be paid, leaving $\$118.40 - \$88.80 = \$29.60$, which matches the option's ending value. As such, the portfolio rebalancing program allows one to make an initial investment of \$10.822 in a portfolio consisting of stock and borrowed funds which, with no further investment outlay, but with several self-financing portfolio revisions, will replicate the payoffs to

---

11. Multiplying 0.312 by \$120 gives \$37.44, not \$37.47. This and other arithmetic differences in this section are due to rounding.

the call option if the stock price goes up, down and up over the option's life. Moreover...

> it can be easily verified that no matter what sequence of price movements occurs, the mathematics of option replication ensure that the replicating portfolio will be self-financing, and the ending value of the replicating portfolio will match that of the option.

Readers who are not convinced should pick any arbitrary stock price path to verify that this is the case. Using figure 3.4, readers are also encouraged to verify that the principle of option replication will hold for a put option, no matter what sequence of price movements occurs for the price of the underlying stock.

Risk-adjusted or risk-neutral probabilities

> An interesting feature of the binomial model is that probabilities and investor preferences do not enter the valuation equation. In the pricing examples, one does not need to know the probability that the stock price will go up or down or make an assumption about the risk aversion of investors. The probability associated with an increase in the stock price could be 99 percent or 1 percent, or investors could be extremely risk averse, moderately risk averse, or even risk-neutral, and the same option price would still be obtained.

It is tempting to think of π in equation 3.3 as the probability that the stock price will increase in value. After all, the option value in the up state is weighted by π and weighted in the down-state value by $1 - \pi$, two pricing weights that sum to one, just like probabilities. Although it can be shown that π is related to both the probability of a stock price increase and the market's aversion to risk, for the purposes of pricing stock options, it is not necessary to specify either of these two amounts.

The analysis in Appendix A shows that if the Capital Asset Pricing Model (CAPM) governs the returns of the stock and option, the relationship between π and the true probability that the stock will increase in value, denoted as θ, is given as follows:[12]

$$\pi = \theta - \lambda_i \sqrt{\theta(1 - \theta)}$$

$$\lambda_i = \frac{\rho_{j,m}(E[r_m] - r)}{\sigma_m}. \tag{3.8}$$

---

12. This idea is developed further in Rendleman (1999).

In equation 3.8, $\rho_{i,m}$ is the correlation between the returns of stock i and the market, $E(r_m)$ is the expected market return, r is the risk-free rate of interest, and σ_m is the standard deviation of the market return, all measured over a single binomial period.

The easiest way to see how π relates to investor preferences is to think about how the stock would be priced if investors were risk-neutral, that is, if they did not care about risk. In this case, the expected return for securities or portfolios would equal the risk-free rate, implying that $E(r_m) = r$, $\lambda_i = 0$, and $\pi = \theta$. Thus, if investors were risk-neutral, π would equal the true probability associated with an increase in the stock price. As such, π is often referred to as a "risk-neutral" probability. π and θ will also be the same if the correlation between the returns of the stock and the market is zero (or if the "beta" of the stock is zero). In this case, even if investors are not risk-neutral, the stock and its options will be priced without adding a risk premium to their expected returns.

Typically, the correlation between stock and market returns will exceed zero, in which case π will be less than the true probability, θ. Under such circumstances, investors would tend to price securities as if the probability of a favorable outcome for the stock (an up movement) is less than the true probability and the probability of an unfavorable outcome (a down movement) exceeds the true probability.

To shed more light on this issue, in our pricing example $\pi = 0.3667$. It is entirely possible that investors might arrive at this pricing weight in the following way. Hypothetically, investors might estimate the true probability of a stock price increase as 0.50. But being risk averse, for pricing purposes they adjust the probability of a favorable outcome down to 0.3667 and the probability of an unfavorable outcome up to 0.6333. If they were more risk averse, they would adjust the probabilities further, resulting in a lower stock price, and if they were less risk averse, they would make a smaller probability adjustment, resulting in a higher price. For our purposes, however, all we need to know is that $\pi = 0.3667$; we need not know the true probability and how it was "adjusted" to arrive at 0.3667.

Pricing American options

Unlike European options, American options can be exercised at any time. When valuing European options, exercise values of zero are assigned to the option at all times prior to maturity. But for American options, the valuation procedure must be changed to allow for exercise at any time. This results in the following general valuation relationships for American options:

For a call option:

$$P_{x,t,j} = S_{t,j} - K \quad \text{for } t \leq T.$$

For a put option:

$$P_{x,t,j} = K - S_{t,j} \quad \text{for } t \le T.$$

For a call or put option:

$$P_{h,t,j} = 0 \quad \text{for } t = T,$$

$$P_{h,t,j} = \frac{P_{t+1,j+1}\pi + P_{t+1,j}(1 - \pi)}{1 + r} \quad \text{for } t < T,$$

$$P_{t,j} = \max\{P_{h,t,j}, P_{x,t,j}\} \quad \text{for all } t \le T.$$

In the pricing relationships above, prices denoted with a subscript of "x" denote exercise values, those denoted with "h" are hold values, and those with no designation represent prices after taking into account the optimal decision to exercise.

In chapter 2, it was shown that it would be irrational to exercise an American call option prematurely, provided the stock pays no dividends or a very low dividend over the life of the option. The basis for this assertion is that the option should always be worth more "alive" (or unexercised) than "dead" (exercised). We can see this principle at work in figure 3.3, which provides detailed calculations for pricing a European call option. One can verify easily that in every state prior to the option's maturity date, the option is worth more than if it were exercised. For example, in state $\{2, 2\}$ with the stock price at \$144, the price of the European option is \$44.99. If given the opportunity to exercise the option in this state, the investor would obtain \$144 − \$100 = \$44 upon exercise, an amount slightly less than \$44.99. Accordingly, a rational investor would find it optimal to hold the option, or at least sell the option to someone else who should be willing to pay \$44.99, rather than exercise and receive only \$44. This same logic would apply in every state; if given the opportunity to exercise, the smart investor would refuse. This leads to the conclusion that the value of the American call will be the same as its European counterpart. Therefore, figure 3.3, which provides pricing detail for a European call, also provides the detail for an equivalent American call option. It is important to note, however, that this line of reasoning does not apply if the stock is expected to pay a large dividend over the option's life. This principle will be illustrated in the next section. But before dealing with dividends, the pricing dynamics for an American put are examined.

> Unlike the call option, it is possible that a put option will be worth more "dead" than "alive." As a result, the American put can be potentially more valuable than a European put with the same maturity and striking price.

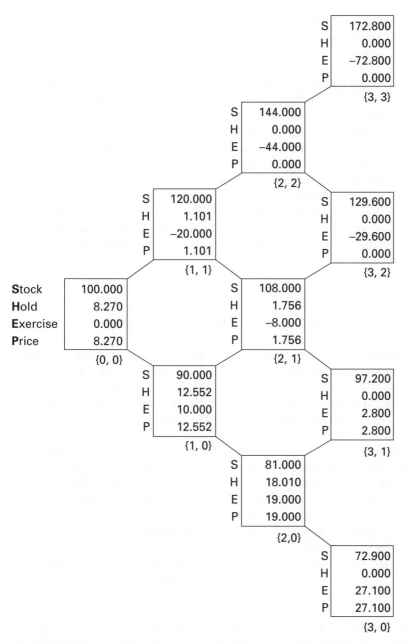

S	172.800
H	0.000
E	−72.800
P	0.000
	{3, 3}

S	144.000
H	0.000
E	−44.000
P	0.000
	{2, 2}

S	120.000
H	1.101
E	−20.000
P	1.101
	{1, 1}

S	129.600
H	0.000
E	−29.600
P	0.000
	{3, 2}

Stock	100.000
Hold	8.270
Exercise	0.000
Price	8.270
	{0, 0}

S	108.000
H	1.756
E	−8.000
P	1.756
	{2, 1}

S	90.000
H	12.552
E	10.000
P	12.552
	{1, 0}

S	97.200
H	0.000
E	2.800
P	2.800
	{3, 1}

S	81.000
H	18.010
E	19.000
P	19.000
	{2,0}

S	72.900
H	0.000
E	27.100
P	27.100
	{3, 0}

Figure 3.5   Pricing a three-period American put option with a $100 striking price. Riskless interest is 1 percent per binomial period

Figure 3.5 illustrates the pricing of an American put. Unlike the previous tables, values of Δ and B are omitted. In each state the stock price is shown along with the option's hold value, exercise value and final price.

Note that state $\{2,0\}$ is the only state in which premature exercise takes place. In this state, the value of holding the option for one more period is $18.01, but with the stock price at $81, the option can be exercised for $100 − $81 = $19. Thus, it would be irrational to hold onto the put, an action that carries an implicit value of $18.01, when approximately $1 of additional value can be obtained by exercising. For the purpose of valuing the option, I assume that all investors are rational and would exercise the option when it is optimal to do so. Thus, the option is assumed to take on a value of $19 in this state. The initial value of $8.27 reflects that the option will be exercised prematurely if state $\{2,0\}$ is reached. This is slightly higher than the $7.88 value for the European put option shown in figure 3.4.

3.3   Option Pricing with Dividend Payments

Continuing with the same examples, I now consider the effect of dividend payments in the pricing of put and call options. Generally, dividend payments will have the effect of reducing the value of the stock by the amount of the dividend payment on the date the stock goes ex-dividend. For the purposes of this analysis, I assume that the stock price decreases by the full amount of the dividend. However, due to the taxation of dividends, the stock price may actually fall by only a fraction of the dividend payment. But what is important in option pricing is not the dividend payment itself but the amount of expected decrease in stock value arising from the payment of a dividend. Thus, if a dividend of 2 percent were expected to result in a 1.5 percent decrease in the value of the stock on the ex-date, 1.5 percent should be used as the effective dividend amount for the purpose of pricing stock options.

Since the payment of dividends will cause an automatic decline in the value of the underlying stock, put options should be more valuable if the stock pays dividends, and call options should be less valuable. Moreover, if given the opportunity to exercise an American put just before or on the ex-dividend date, one should wait until the ex-date to take advantage of the decline in stock value. In contrast, if given the opportunity to exercise an American call option just before or just after the ex-date, one should exercise just prior to the stock going ex-dividend in order to receive the dividend as an owner of the underlying stock. This suggests that for

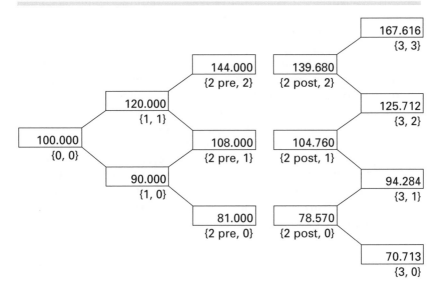

Figure 3.6 Binomial stock prices with $u = 1.2$, $d = 0.9$ and a 3 percent dividend at time 2

valuation purposes, the ex-date should be broken into pre-dividend and post-dividend segments.

Figure 3.6 shows the price path for the same underlying stock from previous examples, modified to reflect a 3 percent dividend payment at time 2. This dividend amount is higher than what one might typically observe in practice, but it allows the valuation effects of dividend payments to be seen more clearly.

Note that with a dividend payment of 3 percent at time 2, all of the post-dividend stock prices are $1 - 0.03 = 0.97$ times their corresponding pre-dividend values. Moreover, because of the commutative property of multiplication (the order in which you multiply numbers doesn't matter), the stock prices at time 3 are exactly 0.97 times what their values would be if no dividends were paid. Thus, if one were pricing a European option and were not concerned about the distribution of stock prices prior to maturity, one could simply take the original price tree from figure 3.1, which does not include dividends, and multiply each stock price at maturity by 0.97 to determine ex-dividend values for the stock, even though the dividend is actually paid prior to time 3. Similarly, if, in addition to the 3 percent dividend at time 2, a 2 percent dividend were paid at time 1, one could determine the relevant stock prices at maturity by taking the original stock values and multiplying by 0.98×0.97.

It is important to note that the stock price "tree" continues to recombine when the stock pays a dividend equal to a constant proportion of the stock price. In contrast, if the dividend is a fixed dollar amount, for example, $3, regardless of the price of the stock, the binomial tree will not recombine. Although, conceptually, there is no problem valuing options using binomial trees that do not recombine, using non-recombining trees can increase the number of calculations required to determine an option's price. In some cases, the calculations can become prohibitively time consuming, even on modern-day computers. Therefore, it is a good idea when formulating option pricing problems to maintain recombining trees, even if doing so causes a slight loss in accuracy and realism in the calculations.

Within this context, if a $3 dividend had been announced on a $100 stock, one might treat this as a 3 percent dividend for the purposes of pricing options using the binomial model, even though some accuracy would be lost in the calculation.

Pricing an American call when the stock pays a dividend

Figure 3.7 provides detailed calculations for the pricing of a three-period American call option with a striking price of $100 for the same stock and general setup used in the earlier examples but modified to reflect a 3 percent dividend. Compared with figure 3.3, which provides detail calculations for pricing the call without dividends, the maturity values of the call option are lower. This, in turn, results in lower hold values for the option at time 2.

Note that time 2 is broken into pre- and post-dividend components. For valuation purposes, if the option is held from the pre-dividend segment of time 2 into the post-dividend segment, the pre-dividend hold value should reflect the expectation of taking an optimal action with respect to holding or exercising during the post-dividend segment, or

$$P_{h,2\ pre,j} = P_{2\ post,j}.$$

In state $\{2, 2\}$, the option's hold value in both the pre- and post-dividend segments is $40.67, which reflects the value of maintaining a position in the option through its maturity date. But if the option is exercised during the pre-dividend segment when the stock is worth $144, $44 in value can be obtained by exercising which exceeds the hold value of $40.67. Thus, it would be optimal to exercise the option during the pre-dividend segment and receive the full $44. It should be noted that if the investor errs by

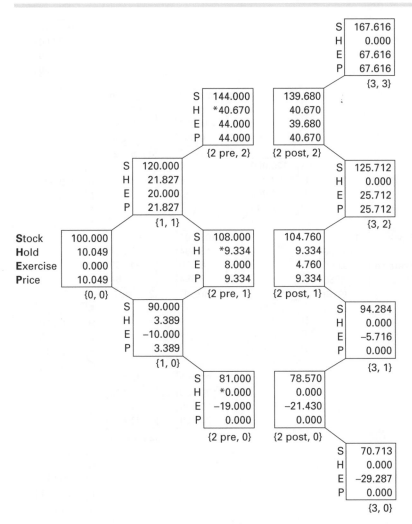

Figure 3.7 Pricing an American call option with a striking price of $100, with $u = 1.2$, $d = 0.9$ and a 3 percent dividend at time 2. *denotes value if held into post period

waiting until after the dividend payment to make the decision to exercise, it would be better to hold, since the post-dividend hold value is $40.67 which exceeds the corresponding exercise value of $139.68 − $100 = $39.68.

In this example, state {2, 2} is the only state affected by premature exercise. In the other two states at time 2 it is better not to exercise and simply hold onto the option through the pre-dividend segment and into the post-dividend segment.

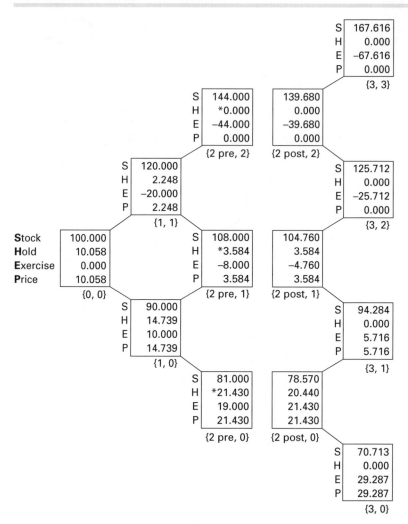

Figure 3.8 Pricing an American put option with a striking price of $100, with $u = 1.2$, $d = 0.9$ and a 3 percent dividend at time 2. *denotes value if held into post period

After going through the entire valuation procedure, the option's initial price is $10.05. Although detailed calculations are not provided, if the option were European, its value would be $9.61. Thus, the American option commands a $10.05 − $9.61 = $0.44 premium over its European counterpart due to the extra value obtained by exercising in state {2,2}.

Pricing an American put when the stock pays a dividend

Figure 3.8 provides detailed calculations for the pricing of an American put option with the same terms as the previous call option. As with the pricing of the call, if the option is held from the pre-dividend segment of time 2 into the post-dividend segment, the pre-dividend hold value of the put should reflect the expectation of taking an optimal action with respect to holding or exercising during the post-dividend segment, or

$$P_{h,2\ pre,j} = P_{2\ post,j}.$$

Note that it is optimal to exercise the put in state $\{2,0\}$ during the post-dividend time segment. At that time the exercise value of $100 − $78.57 = $21.43 exceeds the hold value of $20.44. If exercised during the pre-dividend segment, however, the option would bring only $100 − $81 = $19, which is less than the value of holding the put into the post-dividend segment. Thus, it is in the investor's best interest to wait until the post-dividend segment to consider exercising the option. This result generalizes for any put option on a dividend paying stock. It never pays to exercise immediately prior to the ex-date; it is always better to wait.

After completing the option pricing calculations, the initial price is $10.058. Although the calculations are not shown, if the same put option were European, its price would be $9.67. Thus, the American put option commands a price premium of $10.05 − $9.67 = $0.38 over the European put.

Recall from figures 3.4 and 3.5 that the prices of the same European and American puts are $7.88 and $8.27, respectively, if the stock pays no dividends. This results in a premium of $8.27 − $7.88 = $0.39, which is slightly higher than the premium with dividends. In general this relationship will always hold; dividends have the effect of reducing the premium associated with the American put price over the European price.

3.4 Summary

The binomial model provides an algebraic approach to option valuation. Although the model is a bit more mathematical than valuation methods presented in a typical introductory finance class, the mathematics are within the reach of most serious finance students and option investors.

In contrast to the binomial model, the Black–Scholes model is derived using stochastic calculus and relies on the solution to a differential equation from high-level physics. Despite these mathematical differences, I will show in the next chapter that the binomial model can be set up to give option values that approach those of the Black–Scholes model to any desired degree of accuracy. As such, any reader who understands the story behind the binomial model implicitly understands the story behind Black–Scholes.

Clearly, if we stopped here, the binomial model would not be of much practical use, since no rational investor would go about his business assuming simple two-state return outcomes over any significant period of time. Nevertheless, if the binomial time interval is very short, and the values of u and d are adjusted to reflect the shorter-term volatility characteristics of the underlying stock, the binomial model can be constructed to create very realistic return outcomes and, therefore, useful option prices. This process is explained in chapter 4.

Appendix: A CAPM-based Derivation of the Binomial Option Pricing Model

The following analysis employs the Sharpe (1964)–Lintner (1965) Mean-Variance Capital Asset Pricing Model (CAPM) to derive the binomial option pricing model and is developed in more detail in Rendleman (1999). Like the original derivation of the Black–Scholes model, the binomial model typically is developed within the context of riskless hedging or synthetic option replication using a dynamically revised portfolio of underlying stock and safe assets. However, both models can be shown to be consistent with pricing in a CAPM framework. In fact, the Black–Scholes model is derived using the CAPM in the original paper, but this derivation is rarely quoted or discussed.

The CAPM-based derivation of the binomial model illuminates the relationship between risk-neutral probabilities, true probabilities and investor preferences. As such, it is simple to show that the true probabilities and implied investor preferences do not just "fall out," but are actually embedded in the risk-neutral pricing weights.

Consider the standard statement of CAPM pricing:

$$E(r_i) = r + \beta_i(E[r_m] - r)$$

$$(A1)$$

In equation A1, $E(r_i)$ denotes the expected return of security i, $E(r_m)$ denotes the expected market return and, consistent with notation earlier in the chapter, r denotes the single-period riskless rate of interest. β_i is the beta coefficient of security i beta coefficient equal to $\text{cov}(r_i, r_m)/\text{var}(r_m) = \rho_{i,m}\sigma_i/\sigma_m$, where $\rho_{i,m}$ is the correlation coefficient between the returns of security i and the market. Let $\lambda_i = \rho_{i,m}(E[r_m] - r)/\sigma_m$, which can be interpreted as the market risk premium adjusted for the correlation between the returns of security i and the market. Then, the CAPM pricing equation can be rewritten as follows:

$$E(r_i) = r + \lambda_i \sigma_i$$

(A2)

or as

$$E(1 + r_i) = 1 + r + \lambda_i \sigma_i$$

(A3)

Assume asset i is an option written on a stock whose returns follow a binomial process. Let θ denote the true probability that an up state will occur from binomial time t to time $t + 1$. Then $E(1 + r_i) = (\theta P_{t+1,j+1} + (1 - \theta)P_{t+1,j})/P_{t,j}$. Similarly, $\sigma_i = ((P_{t+1,j} - P_{t+1,j+1})/P_{t,j})\sqrt{\theta(1 - \theta)}$. (This follows directly from standard binomial statistics.) Substituting for $E(1 + r_i)$ and σ_i in equation A3 and rearranging yields:

$$P_{t,j} = \frac{P_{t+1,j+1}\pi + P_{t+1,j}(1 - \pi)}{1 + r},$$

(A4)

where $\pi = \theta - \lambda_i\sqrt{\theta(1 - \theta)}$.

In this form one can see that the price of an option is a function of the true probabilities associated with the occurrence of the up and down states, θ and $1 - \theta$, and the correlation-adjusted market price of risk, λ_i. Together, these probabilities and the market price of risk determine the risk-neutral probabilities, π and $1 - \pi$.

To avoid riskless arbitrage opportunities among the underlying stock and any of its options, all must be priced with the same risk-neutral probabilities. Thus, each dollar invested in the underlying stock must be priced as follows:

$$1 = \frac{u\pi + d(1 - \pi)}{1 + r}$$

(A5)

Rearranging equation A5 and solving for π gives:

$$\pi = \frac{1 + r - d}{u - d},$$

(A6)

the risk-neutral probability of the binomial option pricing model.

An examination of equation A4 shows precisely why π should be interpreted as a risk-neutral probability. When $\lambda_i = 0, \pi$ will equal the true probability, θ. This will be the case if investors are truly risk-neutral, which implies there is no market risk premium ($E[r_m] - r = 0$) or if there is zero correlation between the returns of the underlying stock (and its options) and the return of the market (i.e., $\rho_{i,m} = 0$). In either case, the underlying stock and its options would be priced as if investors were risk-neutral.

When $\lambda_i > 0$, the stock and its options will be priced as if the up state, or favorable outcome, is less likely to occur than indicated by the true probability, and at the same time, priced as if the down state is more likely to occur. Thus, when pricing risky securities, risk averse investors can be viewed as adjusting the probability of the occurrence of the favorable outcome downward while adjusting the probability of the occurrence of the unfavorable outcome upward by the same amount to arrive at pricing weights.

REFERENCES

Ayres, H. F., "Risk Aversion in the Warrant Market." *Review Industrial Management* 5 (Fall 1963), 45–53.

Bachelier, L., "Théorie de la Spéculation." *Annales de l'Ecole Normale Superieur* 17, 1900, 21–86, translated into English by A. J. Boness in *The Random Character of Stock Market Prices*, P. H. Cootner, ed., MIT Press, Cambridge, Mass (1967), 17–78.

Black, F. and M. Scholes, "The Pricing of Options and Corporate Liabilities." *Journal of Political Economy* 81 (May/June 1973), 637–54.

Black, F., E. Derman, and W. Toy, "A One-Factor Model of Interest Rates and Its Application to Treasury Bond Options." *Financial Analysts Journal* 46 (January/February 1990), 33–9.

Boness, A. J., "Elements of a Theory of Stock Option Value." *Journal of Political Economy* 72 (April 1964), 163–75.

Cox, J. C., S. Ross, and M. Rubinstein, "Option Pricing: A Simplified Apporach." *Journal of Financial Economics* 7 (December, 1979), 229–64.

Heath, D., R. A. Jarrow, and A. Morton, "Bond Pricing and the Term Structure of Interest Rates: A New Methodology for Contingent Claims Valuation." *Econometrica* 60 (January 1992), 77–105.

Ho, T. S. Y. and S.-B. Lee, "Term Structure Movements and Pricing Interest Rate Contingent Claims." *Journal of Finance* 41 (December 1986), 1011–29.

Hull, J. and A. White, "Pricing Interest Rate Derivative Securities." *Review of Financial Studies* 3 (December 1990), 573–92.

Jeffrey, A. M., "Single Factor Heath-Jarrow-Morton Term Structure Models Based on Markov Spot Interest Rate Dynamics." *Journal of Financial and Quantitative Analysis* 30 (1995), 619–42.

Lintner, J., "The Valuation of Risk Assets and the Selection of Risky Investments in Stock Portfolios and Capital Budgets." *Review of Economics and Statistics* 47 (February 1965), 13–37.

Rendleman, R. J., Jr., "Option Investing from a Risk-Return Perspective." *The Journal of Portfolio Management* (May 1999), 109–21.

Rendleman, R. J., Jr. and B. J. Bartter, "Two-State Option Pricing." *Journal of Finance* 34 (December 1979), 1093–110.

Rendleman, R. J., Jr. and B. J. Bartter, "The Pricing of Options on Debt Securities." *Journal of Financial and Quantitative Analysis* (March 1980), 11–24.

Samuelson, P. A., "Rational Theory of Warrant Pricing." *Industrial Management Review* (Spring 1965), 13–31.

Sharpe, W. F., *Investments*. Prentice Hall, Englewood Cliffs, NJ (1978), chapter 14.

Sharpe, W. F., "Capital Asset Prices: A Theory of Market Equilibrium under Conditions of Risk." *Journal of Finance* 19, No. 3 (September 1964), 425–42.

Smith. C. W., "Option Pricing: A Review." *Journal of Financial Economics* 3 (1976), 3–54.

Sprenkle, C. M., "Warrant Prices as Indicators of Expectations and Preferences." *Yale Economic Essays* 1 (1961), 172–231.

QUESTIONS AND PROBLEMS

1. The current price of XYZ stock is $100 per share. After the end of one month, the price of XYZ can take on one of two values, $110 or $92. The risk free rate of interest is 1 percent per month and the stock pays no dividends. Determine the value of a one-month European call option on XYZ stock with an exercise price of $105. Verify that no-arbitrage-based valuation (calculating the option price by first calculating Δ and B) and risk-neutral valuation equation 3.3 give the same results.

2. Given the same set of circumstances as question 1, determine the value of a one-month European put option on XYZ stock with an exercise price of $105. Verify that no-arbitrage-based valuation (calculating option price by first calculating Δ and B) and risk-neutral valuation give the same results.

3. The current price of Internet.COM stock is $500 per share. After any one-month period, the price of the stock can either increase by 1.8 times its previous value or decrease to a value of 0.3 times its previous value. The risk-free rate of interest is one half of one per cent *per month* and the stock pays no dividends. What is the value of a two-month European call option on Internet.COM with a striking price of $600?

4. Assume the same set of circumstances as question 3. Using the most time-efficient method possible, determine the value of a two-month, $600 striking price European put option on Internet.COM stock.

5. Value the same put option in question 4 assuming it is American rather than European.

6. Assume the same set of circumstances as questions 3 to 5. Using the most time-efficient method possible, determine the value of a two-month, $600 striking price *American call* option on Internet.COM stock.

7. The current price of ABC stock is $100 per share. Over any three-month binomial period, the total return per dollar invested in ABC stock, including dividends, is 1.3 in the up state and 0.8 in the down state (i.e., $u = 1.3$ and $d = 0.8$). The risk-free rate of interest is 1 percent per three months.

    At the end of the first binomial period, ABC is expected to pay a dividend equal to 10 percent of the end-of-period stock price, and the price of the stock is expected to fall by the amount of the dividend payment. Determine the values of six-month *American* call and put options on ABC, assuming a striking price of $100 for each.

8. Assume the same set of circumstances as question 7 except that the dividend paid at the end of the first binomial period will be $6 in both the up and down states.

    Determine the values of six-month *American* call and put options on ABC, assuming a striking price of $100 for each.

9. Comparing your answers to questions 7 and 8, why do you think it is common practice in binomial-based option valuation to assume dividend payments equal a particular percentage of the stock price at the time of payment rather than assuming dividends equal to specific dollar amounts.

10. Extrapolating from your answer to question 7, should the payment of dividends have a greater effect on the pricing of European calls or on the pricing of American calls?

11. Extrapolating from your answer to question 7, should the payment of dividends have a greater effect on the pricing of European puts or on the pricing of American puts?

4

Advanced Binomial Option Pricing

4.1 Using the Binomial Model for Realistic Option Pricing

Throughout the previous chapter, the underlying stock is assumed to follow binomial price movements with up and down factors of 1.2 and 0.9, respectively. These values are arbitrary; they were not intended to represent realistic stock returns.

> This chapter will show how to determine values for u and d that result in a desired mean and variance of stock returns over the life of an option. When u and d are selected in this way, and the life of the option is broken into an infinite number of binomial periods, the price that results from the binomial model is identical to that of the classic Black and Scholes (1973) option pricing model.

In actual applications of the binomial model, values for u and d are determined in a way that will mimic or approximate those of a lognormal distribution of stock returns. A lognormal distribution is one for which the natural logarithm of the stock price (plus dividends) at the end of any period divided by the price at the beginning follows a normal distribution. If we were to allow the binomial process from previous examples to continue indefinitely, the resulting probability distribution of returns would converge to lognormality.

How to choose meaningful up and down factors

To begin understanding the connection between the binomial and Black–Scholes model, consider figure 4.1 which shows the distribution of stock

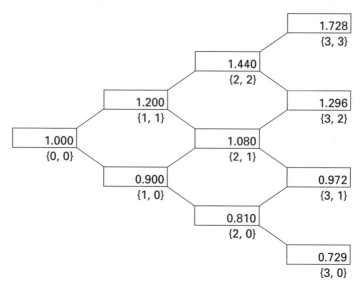

Figure 4.1 Binomial stock returns per dollar invested with $u = 1.2$ and $d = 0.9$

prices from the earlier example restated as returns per dollar invested. The entries in this figure are simply the stock prices from figure 3.1 divided by the initial stock price of $100. As such, they indicate the cumulative value of investing $1 in the stock, starting at time zero.

Figure 4.2 takes the entries in figure 4.1 and converts them to continuously compounded rates of return. One of the most important principles in the mathematics of finance is that the continuously compounded rate of return over any period of time is the natural logarithm of the return per dollar invested (one plus the rate of return) for the same period. Thus, the entries in figure 4.2 are simply the natural logarithms of the corresponding entries in figure 4.1. (Details on the mathematics of continuous compounding is provided in the appendix.)

Table 4.1 shows the mean, variance and standard deviation of the continuously compounded, or logarithmic, returns from figure 4.2 over one, two and three periods, assuming both 0.50 and 0.40 probabilities associated with up returns. Example calculations are provided in the table.

Note that both the mean and variance of the continuous return are directly proportional to time. For example, the mean continuous return for three periods is three times the mean return for one period. With a 0.5 probability associated with an up return, the three-period mean return of 0.11544 equals three times the one-period mean return of 0.03848. With a 0.4 probability, the three-period mean return of 0.02914 equals three times the one-period mean, 0.00971. Similarly, the variance of the

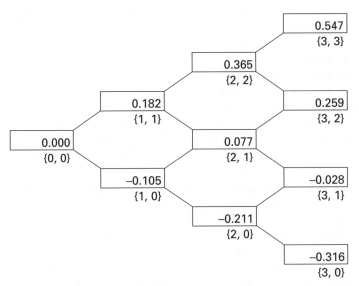

Figure 4.2 Continuously compounded rates of return per dollar invested

Table 4.1 Summary statistics associated with continuously compounded returns from figure 4.2

	t = 1	t = 2	t = 3
0.50 probability of up move			
Mean	0.03848	0.07696	0.11544
Variance	0.02069	0.04138	0.06207
Standard deviation	0.14384	0.20342	0.24914
0.40 probability of up move			
Mean	0.00971	0.01943	0.02914
Variance	0.01986	0.03973	0.05959
Standard deviation	0.14094	0.19931	0.24411

Example calculations:
The mean return for 3 periods, assuming a 0.4 probability associated with an up move is computed as follows:

$$0.4^3 \times 0.547 + 3(0.4^2 \times 0.6^1)(0.259) + 3(0.4^1 \times 0.6^2)(-0.0284)$$
$$+ 0.6^3 \times (-0.316) = 0.02914$$

The variance of any random variable, x, is given by $E(x^2) - E(x)^2$. The first part of this expression, $E(x^2)$, is computed as:

$$0.4^3 \times 0.547^2 + 3(0.4^2 \times 0.6^1)(0.259^2) + 3(0.4^1 \times 0.6^2)(-0.028^2)$$
$$+ 0.6^3 \times (-0.316^2) = 0.06044$$

Therefore, the variance is $0.06044 - 0.02914^2 = 0.05959$.

continuous return is directly proportional to time. With a 0.5 probability, the three-period variance of 0.06207 equals three times the one-period variance $(3 \times 0.02069 = 0.06207)$. With a 0.4 probability, the three-period variance of 0.05959 equals three times the one-period variance $(3 \times 0.01986 = 0.05959)$.

Since the variance is proportional to time, the standard deviation is proportional to the square root of time. For example, with an up probability of 0.5, the three-period standard deviation of 0.24914 equals the one-period standard deviation of 0.143841 times the square root of 3. This relationship also holds for an up probability of 0.4; $0.14095\sqrt{3} = 0.2441$.

> The fact that the mean and variance are proportional to time, and the standard deviation is proportional to the square root of time, is not unique to binomial outcomes. In fact, this property will hold for any probability distribution of returns, provided two conditions apply. First, returns from one period to the next must be independent. This means that the probability distribution of returns in one period is not a function of return outcomes in any prior period. Second, the mean and variance of one-period returns must be "stationary." As such, returns must be drawn from the same probability distribution in each period.

We are now equipped to determine appropriate values for u and d. Recall that the values of u and d underlying the entries in table 4.1 are 1.2 and 0.9, respectively. Assume that the true probability associated with an up movement in the stock price is 0.5. Table 4.1 shows that the three-period mean continuous return is 0.11544, and the three-period standard deviation is 0.24914.

To determine the values of u and d, we simply turn the numbers around. If we want to generate a distribution with a three-period mean continuous return of 0.11544 and standard deviation of 0.24914, we would have to set u and d to 1.2 and 0.9, respectively, assuming a 0.5 probability associated with an up move. This line of reasoning leads to the general conclusion that the values of u and d can be determined as functions of the mean and standard deviation of the continuous return and the probability associated with an increase in the stock price. Rendleman and Bartter (1979: 1098) have shown that these functions are as follows:

$$u = e^{\mu_a \tau / n + (\sigma_a \sqrt{\tau} / \sqrt{n})\sqrt{(1-\theta)/\theta}}$$

(4.1)

$$d = e^{\mu_a \tau / n - (\sigma_a \sqrt{\tau} / \sqrt{n})\sqrt{\theta/(1-\theta)}}$$

(4.2)

where μ_a is the annual mean continuous or logarithmic return, σ_a is the annual standard deviation of the continuous return, θ is the *true* probability associated with an increase in the stock price, τ is the number of years over the life of the option, n is the number of binomial periods over the option's life, and e is the mathematical constant $2.71828\ldots$.

Equations 4.1 and 4.2 can be checked using the numbers from the previous example. For the purposes of the check, assume that the life of the option, τ, is one year. Also, assume $\theta = 0.5, \mu_a = 0.11544, \sigma_a = 0.24914$ and $n = 3$. Substituting these values into equations 4.1 and 4.2 yields:

$$u = e^{0.11544(1)/3 + (0.24914\sqrt{1}/\sqrt{3})\sqrt{(1 - 0.5)/0.5}} = 1.2$$

$$d = e^{0.11544(1)/3 - (0.24914\sqrt{1}/\sqrt{3})\sqrt{0.5/(1 - 0.5)}} = 0.9$$

The equations can also be checked assuming $\theta = 0.4$. In this case, the mean and standard deviation are 0.02914 and 0.24111, respectively.

$$u = e^{0.02914(1)/3 + (0.24411\sqrt{1}/\sqrt{3})\sqrt{(1 - 0.4)/0.4}} = 1.2$$

$$d = e^{0.02914(1)/3 - (0.24411\sqrt{1}/\sqrt{3})\sqrt{0.4/(1 - 0.4)}} = 0.9$$

If u and d are computed using equations 4.1 and 4.2, both of which state the up and down factors as functions of the number of binomial periods over the option's life, the interest rate, or interest factor must also be adjusted for time. In the previous analysis, r, represents the riskless rate of interest over one binomial period. Therefore, $1 + r$, which appears in the binomial pricing equation 3.3, represents the return per dollar invested in a riskless asset for one binomial period.

Let r_a denote the continuously compounded annual rate of interest. Then, the return per dollar invested in the riskless asset over one binomial period of length τ/n years is given by:

$$1 + r = e^{r_a \tau/n}$$

$$(4.3)$$

Computing realistic option prices using a large number of binomial periods

In table 4.2 prices are shown for a one-year call option with a striking price of \$100 issued on a \$100 stock. All prices are computed assuming that the annual continuously compounded riskless rate of interest, r_a, equals 0.05 and σ_a, the annual standard deviation of the continuously compounded rate of return, equals 0.3. (A standard deviation, or "volatility," of 0.3 would be typical for a stock traded on the New York Stock Exchange.)

Table 4.2 Binomial prices as a function of the mean annual logarithmic return (μ_a), the number of binomial periods (n), and the true probability associated with an upward stock price movement (θ)

n	$\theta = 0.4$	$\theta = 0.5$	$\theta = 0.6$
$\mu_a = -0.10$			
10	14.733	14.399	14.074
25	14.412	14.279	13.993
50	14.356	14.219	14.063
75	14.371	14.194	14.133
100	14.347	14.241	14.141
500	14.280	14.233	14.188
∞	14.231	14.231	14.231
$\mu_a = 0.0$			
10	14.008	13.941	13.842
25	14.160	14.342	14.056
50	14.206	14.173	14.133
75	14.220	14.268	14.160
100	14.226	14.202	14.174
500	14.237	14.226	14.214
∞	14.231	14.231	14.231
$\mu_a = r_a - \frac{1}{2}\sigma_a^2 = 0.005$			
10	14.054	13.998	13.912
25	14.189	14.341	14.100
50	14.226	14.198	14.164
75	14.236	14.267	14.185
100	14.240	14.219	14.196
500	14.242	14.233	14.223
∞	14.231	14.231	14.231
$\mu_a = 0.10$			
10	14.335	14.488	14.656
25	14.138	14.306	14.346
50	14.153	14.234	14.299
75	14.204	14.205	14.323
100	14.201	14.250	14.305
500	14.213	14.234	14.259
∞	14.231	14.231	14.231

General parameters: stock price $= 100$; striking price $= 100$; $r_a = 0.05$; $\sigma_a = 0.3$; $\tau = 1$ year. Prices for $n = \infty$ computed using Black–Scholes model.

In table 4.2, n, the number of binomial periods, is varied between 10 and ∞. θ, the true probability associated with an up movement in the stock price, takes on values of 0.4, 0.5 and 0.6. μ_a, the annual mean continuously compounded stock return, takes on values of -0.10, 0, 0.005, and 0.10.

The mean values of -0.10, 0 and 0.10 are chosen arbitrarily. The value 0.005 is computed as $r_a - \frac{1}{2}\sigma_a^2 = 0.05 - \frac{1}{2}(0.3^2) = 0.005$ which, according to Rendleman and Bartter (p. 1101), causes the risk-neutral probabilities to converge in value to 0.5 at the fastest rate. This, in turn, will cause the binomial distribution to converge to a lognormal distribution at the fastest rate.

Consider the option prices in table 4.2 computed with the true probability of an up move, θ, equal to 0.5. Generally, regardless of the value of μ_a, the option values are almost identical for values of n ranging from 50 to ∞. Also, for each value of μ_a, the option price computed with $n = \infty$ is \$14.231. In fact, this is the case for all three values of θ; when $n = \infty$, the option price is \$14.231.

4.2 The Relationship Between the Binomial and Black–Scholes Models

In 1973 Fischer Black and Myron Scholes published their classic paper, "The Pricing of Options and Corporate Liabilities." Except for one important difference, the economic analysis in the Black–Scholes paper is identical to that which has been employed in developing the binomial model. The difference is that Black and Scholes assume that stock prices are lognormal, whereas in the binomial model, stock prices can take on only one of two values from one period to the next.[13]

Unfortunately, the Black–Scholes formula requires the use of stochastic calculus in its derivations – mathematics far beyond the grasp of most readers of this book. But there is a way to simplify the presentation of Black–Scholes by resorting to one of the most important theorems of statistics – the central limit theorem. This theorem states that a probability distribution representing the sum of many independently drawn random variables will converge in value to a normal distribution as the number of draws becomes infinite. Moreover, if the draws are from a binomial distribution, the convergence to normality will be rapid, but most rapid when the binomial probability is 0.5. This means that when an infinite number of binomially distributed logarithmic returns are added together, the resulting logarithmic returns will be normally distributed, and therefore, the overall distribution will be lognormal. As such, binomial option values computed with large values of n should converge to those computed via the Black–Scholes model.

This principle is evident in table 4.2. Regardless of the value of μ_a or θ, all binomial option values converge to \$14.231. This, in fact, is the

---

13. If a stock price is lognormally distributed, the stock's logarithmic, or continuously compounded rate of return, is normally distributed.

Black–Scholes price. Thus, we can think of the Black–Scholes price as the price which is obtained under the binomial model when $n \to \infty$, while u and d are chosen to hold the mean and variance of the stock's logarithmic return constant over the option's life and $1 + r$ is adjusted appropriately for time.

A quick glance at the entries in table 4.2 indicates that this convergence is the most rapid when $\theta = 0.5$. Although not quite as apparent, the convergence is also faster when $\mu_a = r_a - \frac{1}{2}\sigma_a^2$.

It can be shown that the binomial price for a European call option on stock which pays a continuous dividend at an annual rate of y_a will converge to the Black–Scholes formula as adjusted for dividends by Merton (1973).

$$call_E = Se^{-y_a\tau} N(d1) - Ke^{-r_a\tau} N(d2)$$

$$\tag{4.4}$$

$$d1 = \frac{\ln (S/K) + \left(r_a - y_a + \frac{1}{2}\sigma_a^2\right)\tau}{\sigma_a\sqrt{\tau}}$$

$$d2 = d1 - \sigma_a\sqrt{\tau}$$

In equation 4.4, $N(d1)$ is the area under a standard normal distribution (with a mean of zero and standard deviation of one) from $-\infty$ to $d1$ and $N(d2)$ is the area from $-\infty$ to $d2$.

The Black–Scholes value for a European put can be derived from equation 4.4 using put–call parity equation modified for the payment of a continuous divident at an annual rate of y_a:

$$put_E = call_E - Se^{-y_a\tau} + Ke^{-r_a\tau}$$

$$= Ke^{-r_a\tau} N(-d2) - Se^{-y_a\tau} N(-d1).$$

$$\tag{4.5}$$

Why should one go to the trouble to compute a binomial price as an approximation to a lognormal price when the Black–Scholes formulas, 4.4 and 4.5, can be used directly? Actually, it would be more efficient to use Black–Scholes model, and up to this point, all we gain by using the binomial model is the economic insight into Black–Scholes pricing without using high-powered mathematics. However, there are many examples of option pricing involving lognormal stock returns for which direct pricing formulas have not been derived. An example would be the pricing of American put options. However, the binomial model can be used to obtain good approximate values for an American put to any desired degree of accuracy. Similarly, the binomial model can be used to value corporate equity as a compound option to pay the firm's debt obligations. It can be used to value convertible debt, callable debt, and debt which is both callable and convertible. The list of potential applications goes on and on. Generally, the option pricing applications listed above require decisions to be made prior to the maturity of the instrument being valued and do not lend themselves to formula-type solutions. Accordingly, a numerical approximation procedure, such as the binomial model, must be used to obtain approximate security values.

4.3 Numerical Extensions

A short-cut method for computing u and d

Given that convergence to lognormality is fastest when $\theta = 0.5$, it is common practice to set $\theta = 0.5$ when computing u and d. It is also common practice to set μ_a to zero. Under these assumptions, the values for u and d simplify to:

$$u = e^{\sigma_a \sqrt{\tau}/\sqrt{n}}$$

(4.6)

$$d = e^{-\sigma_a \sqrt{\tau}/\sqrt{n}}$$

(4.7)

Comparing the binomial values in table 4.2 computed with $\mu_a = 0$ and $\mu_a = r_a - \frac{1}{2}\sigma_a^2 = 0.005$, there is very little difference in the option values. Nevertheless, it is possible that computing u and d using short-cut equations 4.6 and 4.7 could present computational problems if $e^{\sigma_a \sqrt{\tau}/\sqrt{n}} < e^{r_a \tau/n}$. In this case, both the "up" and "down" stock returns would be less than one could receive from a riskless asset, resulting in a riskless arbitrage opportunity and a computational mess. To avoid this problem, I recommend using the following values for u and d based on setting $\mu_a = r_a - \frac{1}{2}\sigma_a^2 \mu_a$:

$$u = e^{r_a \tau/n - \sigma_a^2 \tau/(2n) + \sigma_a \sqrt{\tau}/\sqrt{n}}$$

(4.8)

$$d = e^{r_a \tau/n - \sigma_a^2 \tau/(2n) - \sigma_a \sqrt{\tau}/\sqrt{n}}$$

(4.9)

Notes that as σ_a approaches zero in equations 4.8 and 4.9, both u and d approach $e^{r_a \tau/n}$, which is precisely how the returns should evolve for a riskless asset.

Pricing American puts and calls

Assume that we want to price an American put option on a stock whose price is lognormally distributed. Although equation 4.5 provides the Black–Scholes values of a European put, there is no corresponding formula for pricing an American put. Therefore, one must employ the binomial model or a similar numerical method to obtain an approximate option value.

Using the same $100 stock price, volatility, time and interest rate parameters as in table 4.2, table 4.3 provides an analysis of American put prices for striking prices of $90, $100 and $110. In an effort to obtain the "best" approximation, μ_a is set to $r_a - \frac{1}{2}\sigma_a^2 = 0.005$, and θ is set to 0.5.

Table 4.3 Binomial pricing of American put options on non-dividend paying stock

n	American price	European price	Difference	Black–Scholes+ difference
Striking price = 90				
10	5.773	5.536	0.237	5.545
25	5.628	5.394	0.234	5.542
50	5.577	5.337	0.239	5.547
75	5.542	5.296	0.247	5.555
100	5.559	5.310	0.249	5.557
500	5.551	5.307	0.244	5.552
∞	n/a	5.308	n/a	n/a
Striking price = 100				
10	9.727	9.121	0.606	9.961
25	9.971	9.464	0.507	9.861
50	9.849	9.321	0.529	9.883
75	9.904	9.390	0.514	9.869
100	9.864	9.342	0.521	9.875
500	9.871	9.355	0.516	9.871
∞	n/a	9.354	n/a	n/a
Striking price = 110				
10	15.836	14.929	0.907	15.562
25	15.685	14.704	0.981	15.636
50	15.611	14.618	0.992	15.647
75	15.625	14.663	0.962	15.618
100	15.641	14.683	0.958	15.613
500	15.622	14.659	0.962	15.618
∞	n/a	14.655	n/a	n/a

Stock price = 100; $r_a = 0.05$, $y_a = 0$, $\sigma_a = 0.3$, $\tau = 1$, $\theta = 0.5$, $\mu_a = r_a - \frac{1}{2}\sigma_a^2 = 0.005$. Prices for $n = \infty$ computed using Black–Scholes model.

For the purposes of this illustration, assume that the American put prices calculated using $n = 500$ binomial periods represents the "true" value of the American put, provided the returns of the underlying stock are lognormally distributed. For each of the three options, it appears that at least 100 binomial periods would be needed to obtain an American put price that is essentially identical to the "true" value. However, it is interesting to note that the difference between the binomial American and European prices, or premature exercise premium, is much less dependent on n. For example, with a striking price of 90, the difference between the American and European prices for $n = 25$ is $0.234 compared with $0.244 for $n = 500$, a mere $0.01 difference. For the same value of n, however, the total value of the American put calculated with $n = 25$ exceeds the "true" price ($n = 500$) by $5.628 − $5.551 = $0.077. It is also the case, however that the European price calculated with $n = 25$ exceeds the price with $n = 500$ by approximately the same amount; $5.394 − $5.307 = $0.087. Thus, although there is a reasonable amount of error in both price approximations when $n = 25$, there is much less error in the estimate of the premature exercise premium.

This suggests a more computationally efficient method, often called the "control variate" technique, for calculating the American option value. First, using a relatively small value n such as 25, calculate the price of both the American and European puts. Then take the difference in values as an approximation for the premature exercise premium. Finally, add this difference to the known Black–Scholes value for the European put.

As an example, for a $90 striking price, the estimate of the premature exercise premium would be $5.628 − $5.394 = $0.234. This difference, when added to the Black–Scholes European put value, provides an overall estimate of the value of the American put of $5.308 + $0.234 = $5.542 which is within $0.01 of the "true" value calculated via the binomial model with $n = 500$.

Computationally, the control variate method is quite fast. Generally, the number of calculations required when valuing one binomial option is $n(n + 1)/2$. For $n = 500$, the required number of calculations is 125,250, but with $n = 25$, the number of calculations is only 325. Thus, two binomial prices with $n = 25$ require only $2 \times 325 = 650$ calculations, and the time required using the control variate technique with $n = 25$ is roughly $650/125,250 = 0.005$ times that required to obtain a 500 period binomial price.

Table 4.4 Binomial pricing of American call options on stock paying a 6 percent continuous dividend

n	American price	European price	Difference	Black–Scholes + difference
Striking price = 90				
10	16.093	15.658	0.435	15.968
25	15.910	15.493	0.418	15.951
50	15.990	15.580	0.410	15.943
75	15.963	15.546	0.417	15.950
100	15.949	15.536	0.414	15.948
500	15.947	15.534	0.414	15.947
∞	n/a	15.534	n/a	n.a
Striking price = 100				
10	11.185	10.984	0.202	11.021
25	10.987	10.736	0.251	11.069
50	11.091	10.862	0.230	11.048
75	11.067	10.841	0.226	11.045
100	11.039	10.806	0.233	11.051
500	11.044	10.815	0.228	11.047
∞	n/a	10.819	n/a	n/a
Striking price = 110				
10	7.548	7.397	0.151	7.490
25	7.514	7.380	0.134	7.474
50	7.485	7.355	0.130	7.470
75	7.490	7.363	0.128	7.468
100	7.489	7.363	0.126	7.466
500	7.470	7.344	0.126	7.466
∞	n/a	7.340	n/a	n/a

Stock price = 100; $r_a = 0.05$, $y_a = 0.06$, $\sigma_a = 0.3$, $\tau = 1$, $\theta = 0.5$, $\mu_a = r_a - \frac{1}{2}\sigma_a^2 = 0.005$. Prices for $n = \infty$ computed using Black–Scholes model.

This method of computation can be applied to a wide range of problems. Often it is possible to obtain an analytical or very accurate estimate of the price of an option without including the feature that creates computational problems such as the possibility for premature exercise of an American put. The value of the additional feature can then be estimated using a relatively small value of n and added to the base option price to obtain an overall estimate of the option's value.

This principle is reinforced by the entries in table 4.4 which show prices of American call options under the same assumptions as in the previous table except that a continous dividend at an annual rate of 0.06 is assumed to be paid on the underlying stock. In this table there is very little difference in the premature exercise premiums (the "difference column") calculated for values of n ranging from 10 to 500. When the premium is added to the Black–Scholes price, one can have confidence that the resulting price represents a good approximation to that which would be computed if a Black–Scholes-type formula existed for the pricing of the American call.

The odd–even effect

As documented by Omberg (1987), there is a predictable relationship between the binomial prices calculated with odd and even values of n. Typically, if an option price calculated with a given value of n is over-priced relative to the true value of the option, the prices calculated with $n - 1$ and $n + 1$ binomial periods will be too low. The opposite relationship also tends to hold. As a result, one can use this relationship to obtain good option pricing approximations for relatively low values of n.

This principle is illustrated in table 4.5 in which the binomial and Black–Scholes prices are computed for European call options assuming the same general parameters as in the previous example except that dividend payments are zero. In table 4.5, n takes on values between 10 and 100 in increments of 10. For each value of n, a call price is calculated with $n - 1$, n and $n + 1$ binomial periods. A weighted average of these prices is computed with the binomial price calculated with n binomial periods getting twice as much weight as the prices calculated with $n - 1$ and $n + 1$ periods. This is equivalent to computing an average price using $n - 1$ and n binomial periods, computing a second average price using n and $n + 1$ periods, and then averaging the two averages. The Black–Scholes price is shown in the final column of the table.

The first row in table 4.5 shows that for $n = 10$, the binomial price exceeds the Black–Scholes price by $\$19.925 - \$19.697 = \$0.228$. The pricing error when $n = 9$ is $\$19.518 - \$19.697 = -\$0.179$ and for $n = 11$, $\$19.630 - \$19.697 = -\$0.067$. But when these prices are combined into a weighted average, the error reduces to $\$19.750 - \$19.697 = \$0.053$.

Glancing down the table, one can see that the weighted average prices are very close to the Black–Scholes prices, even for very low values of n. It appears that one could obtain a more accurate price using a weighted average centered around $n = 40$ rather than calculating a single binomial option price with $n = 100$. The weighted average would require $3 \times 40 \times 41/2 = 2,460$ binomial calculations compared with $100 \times 101/2 = 5,050$ calculations for $n = 100$.

Table 4.5 The odd–even effect in the binomial pricing of European calls

n	Binomial price $(n-1)$	Binomial price(n)	Binomial price $(n+1)$	Weighted average	Black–Scholes
Striking price $= 90$					
10	19.518	19.925	19.630	19.750	19.697
20	19.773	19.720	19.780	19.748	19.697
30	19.777	19.619	19.772	19.697	19.697
40	19.748	19.698	19.741	19.721	19.697
50	19.714	19.727	19.707	19.719	19.697
60	19.682	19.733	19.676	19.706	19.697
70	19.669	19.730	19.675	19.701	19.697
80	19.693	19.722	19.697	19.709	19.697
90	19.707	19.711	19.709	19.710	19.697
100	19.715	19.699	19.716	19.707	19.697
Striking price $= 100$					
10	14.541	13.998	14.484	14.255	14.231
20	14.377	14.125	14.363	14.247	14.231
30	14.326	14.166	14.320	14.245	14.231
40	14.301	14.186	14.297	14.243	14.231
50	14.286	14.198	14.284	14.241	14.321
60	14.277	14.205	14.275	14.241	14.231
70	14.270	14.210	14.269	14.240	14.231
80	14.265	14.214	14.264	14.239	14.231
90	14.261	14.217	14.260	14.239	14.231
100	14.258	14.219	14.257	14.238	14.231
Striking price $= 110$					
10	9.784	10.294	9.727	10.025	10.020
20	10.012	10.123	10.038	10.074	10.020
30	10.083	10.028	10.087	10.057	10.020
40	10.088	9.966	10.086	10.026	10.020
50	10.075	9.983	10.071	10.028	10.020
60	10.057	10.020	10.053	10.038	10.020
70	10.038	10.039	10.035	10.038	10.020
80	10.020	10.047	10.017	10.033	10.020
90	10.003	10.049	10.000	10.025	10.020
100	9.998	10.047	9.991	10.018	10.020

Stock price $= 100$; $r_a = 0.05$, $y_a = 0.0$, $\sigma_a = 0.3$, $\tau = 1$, $\theta = 0.5$, $\mu_a = r_a - \frac{1}{2}\sigma_a^2 = 0.005$.

4.4 Summary

In this chapter, the binomial up and down factors, u and d, are shown to be functions of the mean and standard deviation of the logarithmic return of the underlying stock and the length of the binomial time interval. Also, the binomial interest factor, $1+r$ is shown to be a function of the length of time represented by each binomial period. As the life of an option is broken into a large number of binomial time periods, and u, d and $1+r$ are computed to reflect the length of each period, binomial option values begin to converge to Black–Scholes values. Technically, as the life of an option is broken into an infinite number of infinitesimally short time intervals, binomial and Black–Scholes option price are the same. However, the convergence is so rapid that binomial option values closely approximate Black–Scholes values, even when the number of binomial time intervals is relatively small (for example, 100).

Because of the rapidity of convergence to Black–Scholes prices, the binomial model is often used as a numerical procedure for pricing Black–Scholes-type options when a closed-form formula-based solution cannot be derived. For example, there is no Black–Scholes formula for the price of an American put. However, the binomial model can be used to price an American put option under Black–Scholes assumptions to any desired degree of accuracy. Also, for many types of pricing problems, one can employ the control variate technique, or take advantage of the odd–even effect, to reduce the number of computations requried to obtain good binomial-based approximations.

Apart from the numerical properties of the binomial model, the fact that binomial values converge in value to those of Black and Scholes provides readers with the ability to understand the story, or economics, of the Black–Scholes model without getting bogged down in the details of stochastic calculus. Thus, if a reader understands the binomial model, and can visualize shrinking the length of the binomial time interval to zero while holding the mean and standard deviation of the stock's logarithmic return constant, then he has implicitly "derived" the Black–Scholes model using simple algebra and should understand the model as well as one who derives it directly using higher-order math.

Appendix: Continuous Compounding

In the analysis of options and other derivative securities, it is often convenient to employ continuous compounding of interest rather than annual compounding as would be used in an introductory finance course.

Annual compounding

Suppose you can earn 10 percent compounded annually. Then, for every dollar invested, you will earn a future value of 1.10 dollars after one year.

Semi-annual compounding

Suppose you can earn 10 percent per year compounded semi-annually. Then for every dollar invested, you will earn the following future value after one year:

$$\left(1 + \frac{0.10}{2}\right)^2 = 1.1025$$

Quarterly compounding

Suppose you can earn 10 percent per year compounded quarterly. Then for every dollar invested, you will earn the following future value after one year:

$$\left(1 + \frac{0.10}{4}\right)^4 = 1.1038129$$

Continuous compounding

This process could continue with monthly compounding which would yield 1.1047131, daily compounding which would yield 1.1051558, etc. In the limit as the number of compounding periods becomes infinite, we would have what is called continuous compounding. In this example, continuous compounding would produce $e^{0.10} = 1.1051709$, an amount which is not much more than the future value of a dollar with daily compounding.

To generalize this process, suppose you invest $1 and earn a return of r compounded x times a year for τ years. After τ years you will have a future value, FV, of:

$$FV = \left(1 + \frac{r}{x}\right)^{x\tau}$$

To facilitate the mathematics, let $z = x/r$. Then, future value can be rewritten as:

$$FV = \left(1 + \frac{1}{z}\right)^{rz\tau}, \quad \text{or}$$

$$FV = \left(\left[1 + \frac{1}{z}\right]^z\right)^{r\tau}$$

As the number of compounding periods, x, becomes infinite, $z = x/r$ also becomes infinite. As z becomes infinite, the term in brackets becomes the mathematical constant e, or 2.7182818... – In fact, this is how e is defined in high level mathematics. Thus, the future value of $1 earning an annual continuously compounded return of r_a for τ years is:

$$FV = e^{r_a \tau}.$$

Similarly, the present value of a dollar received in τ years using a rate of interest of r_a per year compounded continuously is:

$$PV = \frac{1}{FV} = e^{-r_a \tau}.$$

One of the nice things about continuous interest is that the overall continuous rate of interest earned, that is, $r_a \tau$, is linear in time. Also, the number of years for which interest is earned can be just as easily a fraction as an integer. For example, 10 percent compounded continuously for 9.367 years produces a future value per dollar invested of:

$$e^{0.10 \times 9.367} = 2.5515474$$

Finding the effective continuous rate of interest

Suppose you have an investment that is scheduled to pay 2.5515474 per dollar invested after 9.367 years. How could you compute the effective continuously compounded annual rate of interest?

Note that $e^{r_a \times 9.367} = 2.5515474$. To find r_a, take the natural log of both sides of the equation.

$$r_a \times 9.367 = \ln(2.5515474) = 0.9367.$$

Therefore, $r_a = 0.9367/9.367 = 0.10$. In general, $r_a = \ln(FV \text{ per dollar invested})/\text{number of years}$.

REFERENCES

Black, F. and M. Scholes, "The Pricing of Options and Corporate Liabilities." *Journal of Political Economy* 81 (May/June 1973), 637–54.

Merton, R. C., "Theory of Rational Option Pricing." *The Bell Journal of Economics and Management Science* (Spring 1973), 141–83.

Omberg, Edward, "A Note on the Convergence of Binomial-Pricing and Compound-Option Models." *The Journal of Finance* 42 (June 1987), 463–9.

Rendleman, R. J., Jr. and B. J. Bartter, "Two-State Option Pricing." *Journal of Finance* 34 (December 1979), 1093–110.

QUESTIONS AND PROBLEMS

1. Make the following assumptions for the purposes of computing option prices for XYZ stock.

   • The value of XYZ stock is $100 per share.
   • The standard deviation of XYZ's annual logarithmic return is 0.30.
   • The mean of XYZ's annual logarithmic return is 0.0.
   • The riskless rate of interest is 6 percent per year compounded continuously.
   • The true probability associated with an upward movement in the price of XYZ stock is 0.5.
   • All options expire in three months.
   • The life of the options will be broken into three binomial time periods.

   Compute the appropriate binomial-based up and down factors and interest factor $(1 + r)$ for options issued on XYZ stock.

2. So that you are not working with incorrect numbers, assume the following answers for question 1: $u = 1.10$; $d = 0.90$; $1 + r = 1.006$. (Note, these are *not* the correct answers to question 1.)

   Using these solution values and the most time-efficient method(s) of computation, determine binomial values for the following XYZ options:

   • A European call with a striking price of $110.
   • An American call with a striking price of $110.
   • A European put with a striking price of $110.
   • An American put with a striking price of $110.

3. Based on the assumptions from question 1, the Black–Scholes price for a European put with a striking price of $110 is $11.279. Combining this information with your answers to question 2, estimate what the price of an American put would be if the price of XYZ stock were lognormally distributed.

5

Practical Issues Associated with
Binomial and Black–Scholes-based
Option Replication

5.1 Introduction

As shown in chapter 3, an option replicating portfolio can be created
using stock and a safe asset, provided the portfolio is revised at the end
of each binomial period. In principle, a replicating portfolio should be
"self-financing." As such, whenever a portfolio revision must be made,
the proceeds from selling stock (or the safe asset) will produce exactly the
amount of funds needed to purchase additional amounts of the safe asset
(or stock). Thus, after the initial stock/safe asset position is taken, it is
not necessary for the investor to add or extract funds from the portfolio.
No matter what binomial-based path is taken by the underlying stock, the
replication of the option's final payoff is guaranteed.

This notion serves as the basis for much option-based arbitrage and
market-making activity. For example, suppose a floor trader on the Chicago
Board Options Exchange (CBOE) can buy or sell a call option on IBM for
$10 per underlying share of stock. At the same time, the trader determines
that an option-equivalent binomial-based stock/safe asset replicating portfolio can be purchased for $8. Assuming there are no transaction costs, and
the trader *knows* the stock's future price movements will be binomial (which
is not likely in the "real world"), the trader could guarantee an immediate
profit of $2 per share by purchasing the replicating portfolio for $8 and
selling the option in the market for $10. It must be remembered, however,
that the trader must also be prepared to make any necessary revisions in
the replicating portfolio over the life of the option. He can't just take the
initial position in the replicating portfolio and forget about it.

The theory of option replication is also used in market making activity
by both options exchange members, investment firms and financial institutions. For example, a customer of an investment firm bank might want
to purchase a sizable long-term put option on the Japanese Nikkei Index

to hedge against an adverse movement in the value of Japanese shares. Although exchange-traded options are available in the Nikkei Index, it is possible that no option with the particular striking price and maturity date desired by the investment firm's customer is available for purchase on an exchange. Therefore, the firm agrees to create an option and sell it to its customer. Assume that the aggregate purchase amount for the option is $100 million, but the investment firm believes the option is worth only $80 million.

After writing this option, the investment firm could take several courses of action. The simplest, but most unlikely course of action would be to do nothing other than write the option. By doing nothing, the firm would expect to profit by $20 million, the difference between the option's selling price and its intrinsic value. However, if the firm takes no further position in the option or its synthetic equivalent, it runs the risk that it may have a significant future liability to its customer in the event that the Nikkei Index takes a significant downturn in value. Thus, it is very unlikely that the investment firm or any other financial institution would write such an option without laying off or covering its risk.

The best way to neutralize the risk would be to find another customer who wants to write the same option (or an option that is substantially similar). Ideally, the investment firm would purchase the option from such a customer at a value lower than $100 million. For example, if the second customer were willing to write the option for $80 million, the investment firm could act as buyer to the second customer and writer to the first customer, pocketing a sure $100 million − $80 million = $20 million profit, provided the second party does not default on any future obligation as an option writer. In this instance, the investment firm would be acting as a dealer, buying the option wholesale for $80 million and selling it retail for $100 million, much the same way that a car dealer might buy a used car for $8,000 and sell it for $10,000.

Another way for the firm to lay off the risk would be to purchase the Nikkei put option synthetically. This would most likely be accomplished by taking positions in safe assets and Nikkei futures, rather than the index itself, making appropriate revisions until the maturity date of the option.[14] If a binomial-based replicating portfolio could be purchased for $80 million, the investment firm incurred no transaction costs in its portfolio revisions and the firm knew with certainty that the value of the Nikkei Index would

---

14. At this point we have not shown how one would use stock index futures, rather than stock itself, in the replicating portfolio. Nevertheless, it is a simple matter to replicate a long or short position in any index using futures and riskless securities. Thus, the futures–riskless securities position could substitute for the index position in the Nikkei put option replicating portfolio.

follow its projected binomial price movements, a $20 million profit could be guaranteed.

Obviously, there are some problems in implementing the binomial-based theory of option replication in practical applications such as the market making and arbitrage activity described above. The most significant of these problems are discussed below.

Transaction costs

Transaction costs may increase the cost of option replication and, thereby, reduce the profit from these arbitrage and market-making activities. For now, we will ignore this problem, saving it for Chapter 9 for a more in-depth analysis.

Security returns do not actually follow binomial distributions

In real financial markets, stock prices and stock index values do not follow binomial distributions. Clearly, over any period of time it is possible for stock prices and index values to take on far more than two values. As a result, if an investor sets up a replicating portfolio based on binomial outcomes for the underlying security, but the security's returns are more accurately described by a continuous lognormal distribution, error will be introduced into the replicating portfolio. This error will show up as over- or under-financing over the life of the replication program.

For example, assume a stock is currently worth $100. An options trader has estimated the volatility of the underlying stock, and based on this estimate, has priced the option and set up a replication program based on fifty binomial periods in which the stock price can go to either $101 or $99 at the end of the first binomial period. If the actual stock price ends up at exactly $101 or $99, the replicating portfolio will be self-financing. But if any other price occurs, the proceeds from selling stock or bonds will not match exactly what is needed to fund the position in the other security. It is possible that the proceeds will be too great, in which case money could be taken out of the program, thereby, reducing its cost. On the other hand, the proceeds may fall short of what is needed, causing the cost of replication to increase over the initial outlay.

It can be shown that these errors generally are not large, and that over the life of a replication program, the errors of over-financing tend to cancel out with the errors from under-financing. In the example in which the investment firm wrote a put option on the Nekkei Index, the binomial-based cost of option replication is $80 million. If the firm is correct in its volatility estimate of the Nikkei but errs in using a binomial distribution in replication rather than a continuous distribution, it could use a technique called Monte Carlo simulation to estimate the extent of potential error. Suppose these simulations indicate that there is a 95 percent chance that the actual cost of replicating the Nikkei put will fall between $77 million and $83 million. Then, in all likelihood, the investment firm would be willing to write the option for $100 million while simultaneously purchasing it synthetically at a cost, which with 95 percent certainty will fall between $77 million and $83 million.

Volatility misestimation

A third problem in using the theory of option replication as a basis for arbitrage and market making activities is that the investor or financial institution engaging in replicating activities may misestimate the volatility of the underlying security. This can lead to significant errors in estimating the cost of replication, and could easily eliminate a large profit that might have initially been anticipated. The next section provides an example that illustrates the nature of the problem.[15]

Model misspecification

Although the binomial and Black–Scholes (1973) models are used widely in option trading, these models may not capture how options should actually be priced. Therefore, error can be introduced in any replication program based on these models when a different model would do a better job capturing the pricing dynamics of the option. Although little work has been devoted to this particular issue, Green and Figlewski (1999) develop detailed simulation results to estimate the extent to which model misspecification could have affected return outcomes from call writing. They show that model misspecification can introduce significant error in "delta" hedging, discussed in chapter 6, but that the cost of such error can be substantially mitigated if an investor or financial institution can trade options at favorable prices in relation to model prices.

5.2   Volatility Misestimation: An Example

Assume an investor wishes to replicate the payoffs of a one-year call option on a $100 stock. The call has a striking price of $100. For the purposes of this example, the one-year life of the option is broken into four binomial periods, but in actual applications, a significantly larger number of periods

---

15.   The problem of volatility misestimation associated with synthetic portfolio insurance plans is also addressed in Rendleman and O'Brien (1990).

would be used. The risk-free rate of interest is 1 percent per binomial period.

The investor believes the standard deviation of logarithmic returns for the stock is 0.191 per year and uses equations 4.6 and 4.7 to compute the binomial up and down factors as follows:

$$u = e^{-(\sigma_a \sqrt{\tau})/\sqrt{n}} = e^{(0.191\sqrt{1})/\sqrt{4}} = 1.1$$

$$(4.6)$$

$$d = e^{-(\sigma_a \sqrt{\tau})/\sqrt{n}} = e^{-(0.191\sqrt{1})/\sqrt{4}} = \tfrac{1}{1.1} = 0.90909$$

$$(4.7)$$

These values of u and d along with a risk-free interest rate of 0.01 per binomial period imply the distribution of stock and option prices shown in figure 5.1.

Figure 5.1 indicates that the call option is worth $9.101 and that initially, the replicating portfolio consists of 0.613 shares of stock (actually 0.61264 shares) at $100 per share, or $61.264 in stock, and $52.163 of borrowing.

For the purposes of this example, assume that the volatility of the underlying stock is 0.3646 per year rather than the 0.191 value assumed by the investor. This higher volatility implies that actual binomial price movements will be based on up and down factors of 1.2 and 1/1.2 rather than 1.1 and 1/1.1. Unfortunately, the investor is not aware that his estimate of volatility is wrong. Moreover, for the purposes of the example, assume that the investor never learns that his replication program is based on the wrong volatility estimate. Thus, despite the fact that the underlying stock evolves with up and down factors of 1.2 and 1/1.2, the investor continues to assume that future price movements will be based on factors of 1.1 and 1/1.1.

If the world of stock returns were truly binomial, the investor would be incredibly stupid not to change his volatility estimate the moment he observes one return per dollar invested of 1.2 or 1/1.2 for the underlying stock. However, the real world of stock returns is not binomial. As a result, actual stock returns could be evolving based on a volatility of 0.3646, rather than 0.191, but before the investor had a chance to measure volatility and realize his estimate is wrong, it could be too late. Thus, I continue with the assumption that the investor does not change his volatility estimate. Therefore, the investor continues to estimate up and down factors of 1.1 and 1/1.1, even though actual binomial return factors turn out to be 1.2 and 1/1.2.

Consider what will happen to the replicating portfolio at the end of the first binomial period if the stock goes up, but goes to $120 rather than

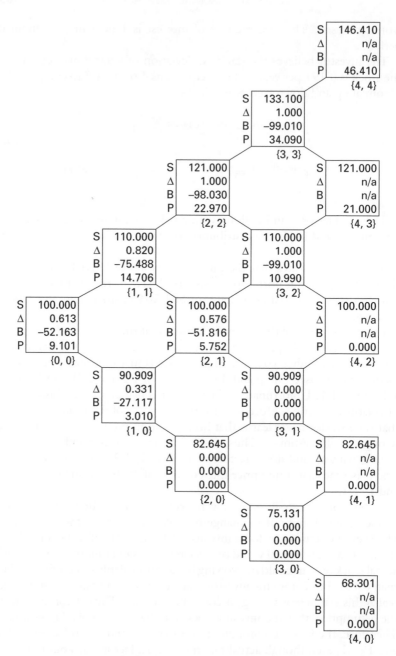

Figure 5.1 Binomial pricing dynamics with incorrect volatility estimate as viewed by investor at time 0. Riskless interest rate = 0.01 per binomial period

$110 as anticipated by the investor. In this situation, the replicating port-folio will consist of 0.61264 shares of stock at $120 per share, or $73.517 in stock, but will require $52.685 of borrowing to be repaid, including interest at 1 percent. Thus, the net value of the replicating portfolio will be $73.517 − $52.685 = $20.832 at the end of the first binomial period.

Recall that the option matures in four binomial periods. Therefore after the first binomial period, the option has three periods remaining until it matures. With the stock price at $120 and three binomial periods remaining, it can be shown that the call option should actually be worth $27.067 based on up and down factors of 1.2 and 1/1.2. Thus, the replicating portfolio, with a value of $20.832, has fallen far short of the true option value.

Despite the fact that the stock price has risen from $100 to $120, assume that the investor continues to believe the stock will evolve with returns based on up and down factors of 1.1 and 1/1.1. Figure 5.2 shows the price dynamics for the option and stock as viewed by the investor, starting with a $120 stock price at time 1. Using the values from this table, the investor determines that the replicating portfolio should consist of 0.906 shares of stock at $120 per share and $84.826 in borrowing, resulting in a net value of $23.942 that must be funded beyond the $84.826 in borrowings. Unfortunately, since the replicating portfolio is worth only $20.832, $23.942 − $20.832 = $3.11 must be borrowed to keep the replication program going.

It should be re-emphasized that if the investor had estimated volatility correctly, no additional borrowing would be required. The amount of funds needed to maintain the replicating portfolio could be funded directly from the positions carried forward. However, with an incorrect volatility estimate, the replication program will not finance itself.

It should also be pointed out that if the investor discovered that a sig-nificant amount of additional borrowing had to be done to maintain the replication program, this would be a good indication that true volatil-ity is higher than had originally been anticipated. On the other hand, if the positions in the replicating portfolio carried over from the prior period produced more money than needed, this is an indication that the investor has overestimated the stock's volatility. Thus, a smart investor might change his volatility estimate if he noticed that the replicating port-folio is not self-financing. Nevertheless, in this example, it is assumed that the investor does not recognize that the stock's volatility is different from his estimate.

For the remainder of the example, I assume that the stock price goes down at time 2, up at time 3 and up at time 4. Table 5.1 summarizes how the replicating portfolio will evolve through maturity and indicates

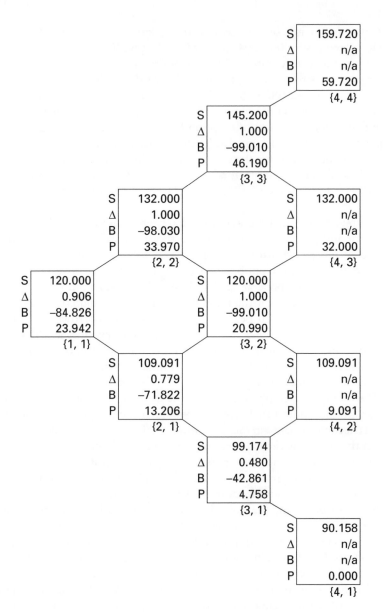

S	159.720	
Δ	n/a	
B	n/a	
P	59.720	
	{4, 4}	

S	145.200	
Δ	1.000	
B	–99.010	
P	46.190	
	{3, 3}	

S	132.000	
Δ	1.000	
B	–98.030	
P	33.970	
	{2, 2}	

S	132.000	
Δ	n/a	
B	n/a	
P	32.000	
	{4, 3}	

S	120.000	
Δ	0.906	
B	–84.826	
P	23.942	
	{1, 1}	

S	120.000	
Δ	1.000	
B	–99.010	
P	20.990	
	{3, 2}	

S	109.091	
Δ	0.779	
B	–71.822	
P	13.206	
	{2, 1}	

S	109.091	
Δ	n/a	
B	n/a	
P	9.091	
	{4, 2}	

S	99.174	
Δ	0.480	
B	–42.861	
P	4.758	
	{3, 1}	

S	90.158	
Δ	n/a	
B	n/a	
P	0.000	
	{4, 1}	

Figure 5.2 Binomial pricing dynamics with incorrect volatility as viewed by investor in state {1,1}. Riskless interest rate = 0.01 per binomial period

Table 5.1   Evolution of replicating portfolio with misestimated volatility assuming stock takes up, down, up, up path

(1)	(2)	(3)	(4)	(5)
Time	Stock price ($)	Portfolio value from positions carried forward ($)	Funds required to maintain portfolio ($)	Incremental borrowing requirement ($) (column 4 – column 3)
1	120.00	20.832	23.942	3.110
2	100.00	4.966	5.752	0.786
3	120.00	16.747	20.990	4.243
4	144.00	44.000	n/a	n/a

Initial stock price = $100; riskless interest rate = 0.01 per binomial period. Stock evolves with up and down factors of 1.2 and 1/1.2, but at the end of each period, positions in the replicating portfolio are based on the assumption that future stock price movements will be based on up and down factors of 1.1 and 1/1.1.
Cumulative borrowing with interest through time 4:

$$\$3.110 \times 1.01^3 + \$0.786 \times 1.01^2 + \$4.243 \times 1.01 = \$8.291$$

the extent to which additional funds must be borrowed to maintain the replication program.

Table 5.1 indicates that at time 4, with the stock price at $144, the value of the replicating portfolio will be $44, exactly the value of the call option with a $100 striking price that is being replicated. However, by using the incorrect volatility estimate, the investor has had to borrow to maintain the replicating portfolio, and an unforeseen debt of $8.291 has accumulated as of the option's maturity date. This debt must be paid back, leaving only $44.000 − $8.291 = $35.709 in the replicating portfolio. Thus, the replicating portfolio falls short of its anticipated value by an amount equal to the accumulated debt.

In the example, the stock is assumed to take a path of up, down, up, up. However, with four binomial periods, there are actually 16 possible paths that the stock can take. As in the previous example, there will always be a cumulative shortfall; the replication program will not be self-financing, and funds must be borrowed. However, the amount of cumulative borrowing will not necessarily be $8.291; the amount will depend upon the actual path taken by the price of the underlying stock. Table 5.2 summarizes the shortfall for all possible stock price paths.

The entries in table 5.2 show that the shortfall varies between $4.350 and $8.917. The average shortfall is $6.515.

Recall that the investor believes binomial price movements will be based on up and down factors of 1.1 and 1/1.1 when, in fact, the stock price evolves with factors of 1.2 and 1/1.2. It can be shown that the initial price of the option, based on factors of 1.2 and 1/1.2, is $15.363. Using up and

Table 5.2   Amount that replicating portfolio falls below the value of the call option being replicated

Stock path	Shortfall ($)
up, up, up, up	4.350
up, up, up, down	4.350
up, up, down, up	4.350
up, up, down, down	4.350
up, down, up, up	8.291
up, down, up, down	8.291
up, down, down, up	8.410
up, down, down, down	8.410
down, up, up, up	8.798
down, up, up, down	8.798
down, up, down, up	8.917
down, up, down, down	8.917
down, down, up, up	4.503
down, down, up, down	4.503
down, down, down, up	4.503
down, down, down, down	4.503

Initial stock price = $100; riskless interest rate = 0.01 per binomial period. Call option has a striking price of $100 and matures in four binomial periods.

Difference in theoretical prices using up and down factors of 1.2 and 1/1.2 and 1.1 and 1/1.1, respectively
$$= \$15.363 - \$9.101 = \$6.262.$$
$$\$6.262 \times 1.01^4 = \$6.516$$
Average shortfall assuming up and down returns are equally likely is $6.515.

down factors of 1.1 and 1/1.1, the investor believes the option is worth $9.101. Thus, his estimate of the option's value is too low by $15.363 − $9.101 = $6.262. If this amount is compounded forward to the option's maturity date using a 1 percent riskless interest rate per binomial period, the future value of the price difference is $6.262 × 1.01^4 = $6.516. Note the close correspondence between the future value of the price difference and the average shortfall, $6.516 vs. $6.515. Thus, in this example the average cost of the replication program is approximately the same as the true option value based on up and down factors of 1.2 and 1/1.2.

Table 5.3 shows the average shortfall from replication and the future value of the option values evaluated with the two sets of up and down factors for options with striking prices ranging from 80 to 120.

The entries in Table 5.3 indicate a very close correspondence between the average shortfall and the future value of the price differences based on the two sets of up and down factors for the at-the-money $100 striking

Table 5.3 Average shortfall from replication and future value of price difference between true call option price evaluated with up and down factors of 1.2 and 1/1.2 and price evaluated with misestimated up and down factors of 1.1 and 1/1.1

Striking price ($)	Average shortfall ($)	Future value of price difference ($)
120	6.2226	7.9323
110	5.5635	7.2243
100	6.5152	6.5164
90	4.2560	5.8229
80	3.0951	4.5436

Initial stock price = $100; riskless interest rate = 0.01 per binomial period. Call option matures in four binomial periods.

Table 5.4 Average shortfall from replication and future value of price difference between true call option price evaluated with up and down factors of 1.05 and 1/1.05 and price evaluated with misestimated up and down factors of 1.1 and 1/1.1

Striking price ($)	Average shortfall ($)	Future value of price difference ($)
120	−1.3988	−2.1518
110	−2.6915	−4.4191
100	−1.7397	−3.4003
90	−1.9448	−2.4832
80	−0.6242	−0.5778

Initial stock price = $100; riskless interest rate = 0.01 per binomial period. Call option matures in four binomial periods.

price call option. However, for options that are either in- or out-of the money, the average shortfall tends to be somewhat lower.

Table 5.4 repeats the analysis of table 5.3, assuming the true volatility is based on up and down factors of 1.05 and 1/1.05 rather than 1.2 and 1/1.2, while, at the same time, the investor believes the volatility is based on up and down factors of 1.1 and 1/1.1. Throughout the table the average shortfall is negative, implying that the replication program will generate additional cash that is not anticipated by the investor. Inasmuch as the average shortfall is negative, the cost of replication will be lower than anticipated. Generally, however, the average cost reduction is not as great as that which would have accrued to the investor had the up and down factors been estimated correctly from the outset. Moreover, unlike the entries in table 5.3, there is not a close correspondence between the average shortfall and future value of the price difference for the at-the-money option. Thus, the close correspondence between the two values shown in table 5.3 does not appear to generalize for all options.

> Summarizing the results of the above analysis, if volatility is underestimated, an investor engaged in option replication will be required to borrow additional funds to maintain the replication program over time. When the replication program is terminated, the value of the replicating portfolio will be reduced by the amount of borrowing that has accumulated. This, effectively, increases the cost of replication. If the volatility estimate is too high, cash will be generated by the replication program, and this will have the effect of decreasing the cost of replication.

Whether volatility is over or under-estimated, the ultimate cost of replication will be of the same order of magnitude as the replication cost associated with the true volatility estimate. However, the ultimate cost will depend upon the path taken by the underlying stock. Inasmuch as the cost will be path-dependent, a significant amount of uncertainty is introduced into the cost structure. This uncertainty can be mitigated by estimating volatility correctly. Even if volatility is estimated correctly, however, there will always be some error in replication which results from the continuous nature of stock returns and the inability to make continuous adjustments to the stock and bond positions in the replicating portfolio.

5.3 Black–Scholes-based Option Replication Using Actual Stock Prices

As shown in Chapter 4, the Black–Scholes model can be viewed as equivalent to the binomial model when the number of binomial periods over the life of the option is infinite. Therefore, option replication via the Black–Scholes model requires the investor to make an infinite number of portfolio revisions to maintain an option replicating portfolio. Since an infinite number of portfolio revisions would be impossible to achieve in practice, it is useful to consider how well Black–Scholes-based replication works when portfolio revisions are made less frequently.

For a call option on a non-dividend paying stock, it can be shown that the number of shares of stock and dollars invested in safe assets required to maintain a replicating portfolio with continuous revision, denoted as

Δ and B, respectively, are:

$$\Delta = N(d1); \quad d1 = \frac{\ln(S/K) + \left(r_a + 1/2\sigma_a^2\right)\tau}{\sigma_a\sqrt{\tau}}$$

(5.1)

$$B = -Ke^{-r_a\tau}N(d2); \quad d2 = d1 - \sigma_a\sqrt{\tau},$$

(5.2)

where all symbols are the same as defined in chapter 4.[16]

The analysis that follows shows how well the Black–Scholes model would have worked in replicating various hypothetical call options on Microsoft stock over the 1992–97 period using weekly portfolio revisions. For this period of time, split-adjusted weekly stock prices for Microsoft were obtained. At the beginning of each year, the following replicating programs were initiated:

1. Replication of a 51-week call option with a striking price equal to the beginning stock price.
2. Replication of a 51-week call option with a striking price equal to the beginning stock price times 1.10.
3. Replication of a 51-week call option with a striking price equal to the beginning stock price times 0.90.

In each case the annualized standard deviation of the weekly continuously compounded rate of return for the 51-week period was computed, and it was assumed that this standard deviation, or "volatility," was known in advance. Also, a risk-free rate of interest of 5.5 percent compounded continuously was assumed for each replication program. Microsoft stock has never paid a dividend. Therefore, it is reasonable to assume that an investor involved with option replication in Microsoft stock would not have anticipated a dividend payment over the 1992–97 period.

Table 5.5 summarizes the results of the three types of replication programs. Consider the figures for 1997 in the first panel of table 5.5 that summarizes the results of replicating at-the-money options. In this case, the split-adjusted stock price at the beginning of the 51-week period was $42.313 per share, and, therefore, the striking price of the call option being replicated is also assumed to be $42.313. The annualized standard deviation of the continuously compounded weekly stock return over the 51-week period was 0.286. In setting up the replicating program, it was

---

16. Δ is developed in more detail in chapter 6.

Table 5.5 Replicating a 51-week call option on Microsoft stock with weekly revisions

Year	Beginning stock price ($)	Ending stock price ($)	Volatility	Strike price ($)	Theoretical ending call value ($)	Replication error ($)
Strike price = beginning stock price						
1992	9.423	10.828	0.338	9.423	1.405	0.053
1993	10.891	10.079	0.277	10.891	0.000	0.016
1994	10.657	15.281	0.214	10.657	4.624	−0.037
1995	15.156	21.938	0.312	15.156	6.871	0.123
1996	21.594	42.125	0.252	21.594	20.531	−0.239
1997	42.313	60.375	0.286	42.313	18.063	−0.387
Strike price = beginning stock price × 1.10						
1992	9.423	10.828	0.338	10.365	0.463	0.145
1993	10.891	10.079	0.277	11.980	0.000	0.001
1994	10.657	15.281	0.214	11.723	3.558	0.053
1995	15.156	21.938	0.312	16.672	5.266	0.134
1996	21.594	42.125	0.252	23.753	18.372	−0.295
1997	42.313	60.375	0.286	46.544	13.831	−0.463
Strike price = beginning stock price × 0.90						
1992	9.423	10.828	0.338	8.481	2.347	0.011
1993	10.891	10.079	0.277	9.802	0.277	0.118
1994	10.657	15.281	0.214	9.592	5.690	−0.016
1995	15.156	21.938	0.312	13.640	8.297	0.096
1996	21.594	42.125	0.252	19.434	22.691	−0.152
1997	42.313	60.375	0.286	38.081	22.294	−0.254

Option replication is based on weekly revisions with perfect foresight of annualized volatility, σ_a, as measured over 51-week replication period. The annual continuously compounded riskless rate of interest is assumed to be 0.055 throughout.

assumed that the investor had perfect foresight regarding the volatility of Microsoft stock and, therefore, knew in advance that the annualized 51-week volatility would be 0.286. Thus, any error in replication must come from sources other than volatility misestimation.

Table 5.5 shows that the ending stock price in 1997 was $60.375. Therefore, a call option with a striking price of $42.313 should have been worth $60.375 − $42.313 = $18.063 after 51 weeks. However, in this particular case, the replicating program came up $0.387 short, producing $18.063 − $0.387 = $17.676 at the end of the 51-week period. Note that this is one of the largest replication errors in the entire table, with almost half of the errors being less than $0.10.

In table 5.5 there is a tendency for the error to be the highest in absolute magnitude in the middle panel where the options begin out-of-the money and lowest in the third panel where the options begin in-the-money. This is exactly what one should expect, since an in-the-money call option is similar to a pure leveraged position in the stock, and the option component of this implied leveraged position is less critical in both valuation and replication.

> Each error in table 5.5 results from several sources. The first, and most obvious, is that portfolio revisions are made once a week rather than continuously. A second source of error is non-constant volatility. In table 5.5 the volatility is not constant from year to year, and, therefore, should not be constant within each year. Even a continuously revised replication program would produce error if changes in volatility were not taken into account. A final source of error is model error, or the potential error associated with the assumption that stock returns are lognormal when, in fact, the actual statistical distribution of stock returns over the 51-week period may be different.

Despite the potential for error from these three sources, actual replication errors are not large and appear to be within the practical limits of a low-cost professional trader. For example, the initial theoretical value of the 51-week at-the-money call option for 1997 is $5.833 (not shown in the table). Suppose an investor could write this option for $8.000 per share while simultaneously purchasing the option synthetically for $5.833. Through this transaction, the investor would take in $8.000 − $5.833 = $2.167 up front, and at the end of the program would be subject to any replication error that might accrue. In this case, the investor would have to pay out $0.387 at the end of the program, but would still have made a nice profit. Although the investor would have had no advance knowledge of what the replication error would turn out to be, it is unlikely the error would have been so large that the entire $2.167 in profit would have been eliminated.

When transactions in a replication program are subject to commissions and other trading costs, the cost associated with replicating an option position can be much higher than the costs implied by the Black–Scholes and binomial models. This issue is addressed in chapter 9 along with the potential to reduce the cost of replication by including positions in other exchange-traded options.

5.4   Summary

Perhaps the single most important consideration in binomial and Black–Scholes-based option replication is properly estimating the volatility of the underlying stock. To the extent that volatility is underestimated when engaging in synthetic option replication, the initial outlay for the replication program will be too low. However, at maturity, the option replication program will come up short of the amount of funds expected, given the relationship between the ending stock price and the option's striking price. On average, the total cost of replication, including the initial cost and the eventual shortfall, will be approximately equal to what the cost would have been if the stock's volatility had been properly estimated. However, the actual total cost will depend upon the path taken by the price of the underlying stock in reaching its final value. The opposite will hold when volatility is over-estimated. Although the initial outlay for the replication program will be too high, the replication program will produce more funds at maturity than would otherwise be expected given the relationship between the ending stock price and the option's striking price.

Even if volatility is estimated correctly and the price of the underlying stock follows a true lognormal distribution, error can be introduced into an option replication program because of the inability to make continuous changes in the composition of the replication program. However, the analysis summarized in table 5.5 indicates that with weekly revisions, Black–Scholes-based option replication can still do a reasonably good job, and the risks associated with non-continuous trading do not appear to be large.

REFERENCES

Black, F. and M. Scholes, "The Pricing of Options and Corporate Liabilities." *Journal of Political Economy* 81 (May/June 1973), 637–54.

Green, T. F. and S. Figlewski, "Market Risk and Model Risk for a Financial Institution Writing Options." *Journal of Finance* 54 (August 1999).

Rendleman, R. J., Jr. and T. O'Brien, "Volatility Misestimation in Option Replication Portfolio Insurance." *Financial Analysts Journal* (May/June 1990).

RELATED WORK

Cox, J. C., S. Ross, and M. Rubinstein, "Option Pricing: A Simplified Approach." *Journal of Financial Economics* 7 (December 1979), 229–64.

QUESTIONS AND PROBLEMS

1. Assume a call option with a striking price of $100 issued on XYZ stock expires after one binomial time period. The current price of XYZ stock is $100 per share. You believe the appropriate up and down factors for pricing options on XYZ are 1.20 and 0.80, respectively. One

dollar invested in a safe asset will produce $1.05 as of the option's expiration date.

(a) Determine the initial composition of the stock-safe asset replicating portfolio for the call option.

(b) Verify that the replicating portfolio will produce $20 in the up state and $0 in the down state.

(c) Although you assumed up and down factors of 1.20 and 0.80 when setting up the replicating portfolio, you were wrong. The up and down factors are actually 1.30 and 0.70. How will your ending portfolio values compare to those that would have obtained if you had estimated the up and down factors correctly?

(d) Repeat part (c) assuming the up and down factors are actually 1.10 and 0.90. How will your ending portfolio values compare to those that would have obtained if you had estimated the up and down factors correctly?

(e) Based on the results of this exercise, what, if anything can you say about the relationship between ending option replication-based portfolio values and the extent to which the volatility of the underlying stock is misestimated?

(f) In this exercise, the initial cost of the replicating portfolio is $11.905. If the up and down factors for the stock are actually 1.3 and 0.7, rather than 1.2 and 0.8, as originally anticipated, the replicating portfolio should have cost $16.667. How does the difference between the actual up-front cost and the cost that should have been incurred compare with the cost at the end of coming up short?

2. (Project) Obtain the Excel files Microsoft 1997.xls and Black_Scholes. xls from the website http://www.rendleman.com/book. Microsoft 1997.xls contains end-of-week stock prices for Microsoft Corporation for the entire calendar year 1997. Black_Scholes.xls contains a function written in Visual Basic that computes the Black–Scholes price for a call or put option. Examine the cells in the Black–Scholes file that compute the option price and delta to determine how these functions are accessed within the worksheet.

Create a new worksheet within the Black–Scholes file and paste the Microsoft weekly price data into this worksheet. This will enable you to have access to the Black–Scholes functions while processing the Microsoft price data.

During the 1997 calendar year the annualized standard deviation of the logarithmic return for Microsoft stock was 0.286. Assume the risk-free rate of interest was 5.5 percent per year compounded continuously and that at the beginning of the year you knew that the standard deviation of the logarithmic return for Microsoft would be 0.286.

(a) Assume that on 1/3/97 you set up a Black–Scholes-based option replication program to replicate the payoff for a call option with a striking price of $50 that matures on 12/26/97. At the end of each week you revise the portfolio and re-establish a new option replication position based on the new stock price and the amount of time that remains on the option. Since the actual stock price on 12/26/97 was $60.375, your option replication program should produce an ending portfolio close to $60.375 − $50 = $10.375. Determine how well the replication program with weekly revisions would have actually worked out. Hint: To check your work, you can change the striking price to $46.544 to determine whether your final portfolio value corresponds to that shown in the middle panel of table 5.5. Don't worry if there appears to be a little rounding error.

(b) Repeat the analysis of part (a) assuming standard deviations of 0.50 and 0.15. What, if anything, does this exercise suggest about the relationship between the ending portfolio value and the extent to which volatility is misestimated?

The Black–Scholes Model: Using and Interpreting the "Greeks"

6.1 Introduction

In the *binomial* model, if the up and down factors are chosen to be consistent with a given volatility estimate over the option's life, and the interest rate per binomial period is selected consistently with the rate of interest to be earned over the life of the option, the binomial option price will converge in value to the Black–Scholes (1973) price as the number of binomial time periods becomes infinite. With Merton's (1973) modification to reflect the payment of a continuous dividend, the model becomes:

$$call_E = Se^{-y_a \tau} N(d1) - Ke^{-r_a \tau} N(d2)$$

$$put_E = Ke^{-r_a \tau} N(-d2) - Se^{-y_a \tau} N(-d1)$$

$$d1 = \frac{\ln(S/K) + \left(r_a - y_a + \frac{1}{2}\sigma_a^2\right)\tau}{\sigma_a \sqrt{\tau}}$$

$$d2 = d1 - \sigma_a \sqrt{\tau}$$

(6.1)

Symbols used in equation 6.1 are defined as follows:

S = the price of the underlying stock;
K = the option's striking price;
r_a = the annual continuously compounded risk-free rate of interest;
σ_a = the annual standard deviation of the underlying stock's continuously compounded return;
τ = the number of years remaining until the option matures;
y_a = the annual rate of continuous dividend payment.

To make the presentation of the model as simple as possible, this book presents the binomial model first and then develops Black–Scholes as its limiting case without developing the mathematics of the Black–Scholes model. Those who are interested in more mathematical detail should look to Hull (2000) which presents the mathematics of Black–Scholes in a way accessible to readers who are well-schooled in basic calculus but do not have a background in higher-level stochastic calculus.

This book uses calculus in developing certain risk measures from the Black–Scholes model. These risk measures are useful in practical applications of options-based arbitrage, hedging and in understanding the risk-return principle as it applies to options. But don't panic. The level of calculus training required to understand these applications does not go beyond what one would learn in one or two semesters of ordinary college calculus. But even if you haven't had calculus, the material on calculus-based risk measures will be presented in a way that will allow you to become a well-informed user of this information. There are thousands of successful options investors who could never take a calculus-based derivative, but, nevertheless, use the calculus of Black–Scholes daily. The mathematics itself is not important. But knowing how to use the mathematics is very important.

6.2   A Little Calculus Background

Consider the simple linear function $y = 2x + 1$. Suppose we want to know how the value of y changes with x. An inspection of the equation indicates that if x is changed by one unit, y will change by exactly two times the change in x. For example, if $x = 100$, $y = 2(100) + 1 = 201$. If x is then changed to 101, $y = 2(101) + 1 = 203$, and the change in y is two times the change in x. Similarly, if x is changed from 20 to 21, y will change from 41 to 43, again, a net change of 2 times the change in x. In this example, if x is changed by one unit, y will change by exactly 2 units. Moreover, y will change by exactly two times the change in x, no matter what value of x we start with or how much we change x.

Now consider the slightly more complex mathematical function, $y = x^2 + 3$. With this function, it is a little more difficult to inspect the equation and determine how just much y will change if x changes. But we can plug some numbers into the equation to evaluate the change in y in relation to the change in x. For example, if x is changed from 100 to 101, y will change from 10,003 to 10,204, or 201 units. Similarly, if x is changed from 20 to 21, y will change from 403 to 444, or 41 units.

In this example, the amount that y changes in relation to a change in x depends upon the starting value of x. If the starting value of x is 100, the change in y per unit change in x is 201. If the starting value of x is 20, the change in y per unit change in x is only 41.

Using the second function, consider what happens to y when x is changed from 20 to 21 and then changed again from 21 to 22. As x changes from 20 to 21, y changes by 41 units. But as x changes from 21 to 22, x changes by 43 units. Thus, as x changes, the amount by which y changes in relation to a change in x also changes, a property that will hold for any non-linear function.

Knowing how an option's price should change in relation to a change in one of its underlying determinants is a particularly important concept in options trading. Normally, to determine how the value of a mathematical function should change in relation to a change in an underlying variable, we take derivatives of the function, rather than plugging in specific numerical values as has been done above.

Using the Black–Scholes model, suppose an options trader determines that the price of a call option will increase or decrease by approximately $0.50 if the price of the underlying stock moves up or down by $1. With this information, the trader hedges a position in stock by writing options on two shares for every share of stock that he holds. But if he is a good trader, he should know that the rate of change in the option price relative to the stock price will change as the stock price changes, and he will adjust his hedge through time to reflect these changes – just as with the binomial model.

Derivatives from calculus, when applied to option markets, help investors understand how the price of an option should change in relation to a change in the stock price or in relation to changes in the values of other variables that influence the option's price. Second derivatives from calculus help investors understand how the derivatives change, and, therefore, indicate how much *more* change can be expected in an option's price when the stock price or the value of another variable changes by a large amount. From the earlier examples based on the mathematical function $y = x^2 + 3$, y changes by *approximately* $2x$ times the change in x. For example if x changes from 20 to 21, y changes from 403 to 444, a net change of 41 units, which is *approximately* equal to $2x$, or $2(20) = 40$. If x changes from 21 to 22, y will change by 43 units, again a change *approximately* equal to $2x$, or $2(21) = 42$.

From calculus, the derivative of y with respect to x, also called the first derivative, indicates *approximately* how much y will change in relation to a change in x. For the function $y = x^2 + 3$, the derivative of y with respect to x, denoted dy/dx, is $2x$. With a linear function, dy/dx indicates *exactly* how much the value of y will change for a given change in x. But for a non-linear function dy/dx works best in predicting how the value y will change in relation to a change in x when the change in x is small. Moreover, the relationship is exact only for infinitesimally small changes in x. For example, for the function $y = x^2 + 3$, if x changes from 20 to 20.01, y will change from 403 to 403.4001 = 0.4001. In this case, the derivative-based estimate that the change in y will equal $2x$ times the change in x provides a much more accurate estimate of the change in y than when x changes by a full unit from 20 to 21. In this example, with $x = 20, 2x = 2(20) = 40$. 40 times the change in x of 0.01 equals 0.4000, which is very close to 0.4001.

> When using derivative-based risk measures in options-based arbitrage and hedging, it is especially important to remember that calculus derivatives are only exact for infinitesimally small changes in the variables that effect option prices and only serve as approximations when such variables are changed by larger amounts.

Second derivatives from calculus are derivatives of derivatives. As such, they provide an estimate of how much a derivative should change per unit change in an underlying parameter. For the function $y = x^2 + 3$, the second derivative, denoted d^2y/dx^2, is equal to 2. This means that for every unit change in x, the derivative of y with respect to x should change by *approximately* 2 units. In fact, for this particular function, the second derivative is exact, but for most functions, the second derivative, like the first derivative, will be an approximation. For example, when x equals 20, $dy/dx = 40$. When x equals 21, $dy/dx = 42$. Thus, when x changes from 20 to 21, the derivative of y with respect to x changes by 2 units, exactly the amount predicted by the second derivative.

One final note an derivatives from calculus. When a mathematical function has more than one right-hand side variable, such as $y = x^2 + 6z^3$, any derivative that computes the change in y in relation to a change in only one of the right-hand side variables, *while the others are held constant*, is called a partial derivative. The notation for partial derivatives is a little different from that of ordinary derivatives. The partial derivative of y with respect to x is denoted $\partial y/\partial x$, rather than dy/dx, and the second partial derivative is denoted as $\partial^2 y/\partial x^2$, rather than d^2y/dx^2. Derivatives of the Black–Scholes price are partial derivatives, since there is more than one variable in the Black–Scholes pricing function that can influence the option's price.

For some of the Black–Scholes derivatives, it is important to remember that the derivative is a partial derivative rather than a total derivative. For example, using calculus, we could determine the partial derivative of an option's price with respect to the annual volatility of underlying stock returns. (This derivative is often called vega.) Suppose this derivative turns out to be 38. This means that for this particular option, the option price should change by approximately 38 times the change in the standard deviation of stock returns, measured as a decimal fraction. Therefore, if the annual standard deviation increases from 0.2 to 0.3, the option price should increase by approximately $38 \times (0.3 - 0.2) = \$3.80$. The partial derivative does not reflect that if the stock is suddenly perceived as being more volatile, investors might not value it as highly, and the stock price could fall. Thus, knowing that vega equals 38 would help an options trader know that an option with a given set of terms on a $100 stock with 0.3 volatility should be worth approximately $3.80 more than an otherwise identical option on a different stock which also happens to have a $100 stock price but a volatility of 0.2. Since the partial derivative ignores any effect of a change in volatility on the stock price itself, it doesn't necessarily indicate that if the volatility of a stock suddenly increases from 0.2 to 0.3, the option price will increase by approximately $3.80.

> Being aware of the subtle difference between partial and total derivatives can make the difference between being a successful options trader and going bankrupt!

The next section develops some of the most widely used first and second partial derivatives of the Black–Scholes option pricing model. There is no need to know how to take these derivatives. But knowing how to *use* them intelligently provides the key to effective hedging and arbitrage activities in the options market and, also, for understanding the risk-return principle as it applies to options.

6.3 The Important Partial Derivatives from Black–Scholes

This section will focus on five important partial derivatives of the Black–Scholes model, known by professional options traders as *delta, gamma, theta, vega,* and *rho*. *Delta* is the partial derivative of the option price with respect to the stock price. *Gamma* is the second partial with respect to the stoke price. *Theta* is the partial derivative with respect to time, *vega* is the partial with respect to volatility, and *rho* is the partial with respect to the riskless interest rate.

I will also develop a sixth risk measure, *elasticity*, which measures the extent to which returns in the option can be expected to change relative to those for the underlying stock. This *elasticity* measure, when multiplied by the "beta" of the stock,[17] provides an estimate of the option's beta, or its sensitivity of the option's returns to returns in the overall stock market.

---

17. A stock's beta is defined as $\text{cov}\,(r_s, r_m)/\text{var}\,(r_m)$, where r_s is the return for the stock, r_m is the return on the market portfolio, and $\text{cov}(\cdot, \cdot)$ and $\text{var}(\cdot)$ denote

Table 6.1 Black–Scholes pricing data for options on hypothetical non-dividend paying stock (Stock price = $100)

Option	Striking price ($)	Type	Black–Scholes price ($)	Delta	Gamma	Theta	Vega	Rho	Elasticity
A	110	Call	10.0201	0.4996	0.0133	−7.9811	39.8942	39.9387	4.9859
B	100	Call	14.2312	0.6243	0.0126	−8.1012	37.9433	48.1939	4.3865
C	90	Call	19.6975	0.7479	0.0106	−7.5425	31.9192	55.0917	3.7969
D	110	Put	14.6553	−0.5004	0.0133	−2.7493	39.8942	−64.6966	−3.4145
E	100	Put	9.3542	−0.3757	0.0126	−3.3450	37.9433	−46.9290	−4.0169
F	90	Put	5.3081	−0.2521	0.0106	−3.2619	31.9192	−30.5190	−4.7495

Annual volatility = 0.3; annual continuously compounded risk-free interest rate = 0.05; time to maturity = 1 year.

As many readers should know, the Capital Asset Pricing Model, which, typically, is applied to stocks and equity-like securities, provides a theoretical framework for estimating a security's expected return as a function of its beta risk. This same model can also be used to again insight into the returns which one can expect from holding options and portfolios which combine options with positions in other securities such as stock and safe assets. Chapter 8 is devoted to applying the Capital Asset Pricing Model to option markets to gain a better understanding of both the risks and expected returns from common option positions.

The five partial derivatives, delta, gamma, theta, vega and rho, along with *elasticity*, are illustrated using the pricing data for a hypothetical stock shown in table 6.1.

Delta

In chapter 3, $\Delta_{t,j}$ is used in the binomial model to denote the number of shares of stock to hold in state $\{t, j\}$ in a stock/safe asset option replicating portfolio. Suppose $\Delta_{0,0}$ equals 0.6. Then, an investor must hold 0.6 shares of stock, along with a certain quantity of safe assets, to replicate the initial end-of-period value of an option issued on one share of stock.

Another way to think about this quantity is in terms of price action. If the option price should move by approximately $0.60 when the stock price moves by $1.00, then an option position provides the same immediate price action as 0.6 shares of stock. In other words, if an investor held 0.6 shares stock, and the stock price were to move by $1.00, he should also gain or lose $0.60. Therefore, to replicate the price action in the option using stock and safe assets, an investor must hold 0.6 shares of stock.

This line of reasoning leads to the conclusion that there is a very close parallel between what we called $\Delta_{t,j}$ in chapter 3 and the partial derivative of the option price with respect to the stock price. Because of this parallel, this partial derivative will be denoted as Δ, without using subscripts. Moreover, this terminology is consistent with "street language" in the options market. Almost any professional options trader can tell you that delta indicates approximately how much the option price should change per dollar change in the price of the underlying stock. But many of those who use delta regularly may not know that delta is a derivative from calculus, and most who do know have no desire to take the derivative.

covariance, respectively. Beta can also be viewed as the expected slope coefficient from a regression equation in which the returns of the stock are regressed against those of the market portfolio. As such, beta provides an estimate of the extent to which the stock's returns should vary with those of the market.

Deltas for individual options

For options with a current price of P on a non-dividend paying stock currently worth S, the Black–Scholes delta, $\partial P/\partial S$, denoted as Δ, is given by:

$$\Delta = \frac{\partial P}{\partial S} = N(d1) \text{ for a call,}$$

$$= \frac{\partial P}{\partial S} = N(d1) - 1 \text{ for a put.}$$

(6.2)

Deltas for call options must fall between the range of 0 to 1. Calls that are way in-the-money have deltas close to one, and those that are way out-of-the money have deltas close to zero. Near-the-money calls have deltas that are around 0.5 or slightly higher. Finally, a long position in the stock itself, which some option traders like to think of as a call option with a zero striking price, has a delta of 1.

Deltas for put options must fall between -1 and 0. Way in-the-money puts have deltas that approach -1, and way out-of-the money puts have deltas that approach 0. A short position in the stock, equivalent to a put option with an infinite striking price, has a delta of -1.

An inspection of equation 6.2 indicates that the sum of the absolute values of deltas for a call and put option with the same striking price and maturity equals 1. This is the case only if the underlying stock pays no dividends and both options are European. If the options are American, the sum of the absolute values of the deltas can exceed 1.0 by a very small amount.

Consider option B from table 6.1, a one-year call with a $100 striking price on a $100 stock. The annual volatility of returns for the underlying stock is assumed to equal 0.30, and the annual continuously compounded riskless rate of interest is 0.05.

In this example, the delta for the call option is 0.6243. Therefore, the change in the option price per unit change in the price of the underlying stock evaluated over an infinitesimally small change in the stock price is 0.6243. For a larger change in the stock price, the price of the call option should change by *approximately* $0.6243 times the change in the stock price. For example, if the stock price is changed from $100 per share to $101 per share, holding all other parameters of the model constant, it can be shown that the Black–Scholes call price increases from $14.2312 to $14.8618. This difference of $14.8618 − $14.2312 = $0.6306 is approximately the amount of change predicted by the delta of 0.6243, but since the change in the stock price is not infinitesimally small, the predicted change is not exact.

Consider a much smaller change in the stock price, from $100 to $100.10. In this case the option price should change from $14.2312 to $14.2937, a change of 0.0625, which is almost exactly what would be predicted from delta, given a $0.10 change in the price of the underlying stock.

Now consider a large change in the stock price from $100 to $110. In this case, delta would predict a $0.6243 \times \$10 = \$6.24$ change in the option price. The actual price change, however, is $21.0610 − $14.2312 = $6.83. Thus, we see that delta does not do as well predicting the change in the option price per unit change in the price of the underlying stock when the change in the stock price is large.

Portfolio deltas

Often options traders are concerned about the deltas of portfolios rather than the deltas of specific options.

> The delta of a portfolio of options on the same underlying stock is simply the sum of the deltas of each component option multiplied by the number of options held. For computational purposes, if the portfolio involves a short or writing position in an option, the quantity held is considered to be negative.

Consider the options, a subset of those from table 6.1, which comprise the portfolio summarized in table 6.2. This portfolio consists of 20 units of option A held long, a writing or short position in 10 units of option C, and 30 units of option D held long. As shown at the bottom of table 6.2, the overall portfolio delta is −11.263. Therefore, if the price of the underlying stock moves up (or down) by $1, the portfolio can expect to lose (or gain) approximately $11.263 in value per share of underlying stock on which the options are written. If the portfolio consists of typical exchange-traded options written on 100 shares of stock, the portfolio should lose (or gain) approximately $11.263 \times 100 = \$1,126$ from a $1 per share increase (or decrease) in the stock price. Inasmuch as one would lose (or gain) $1,126 from a $1 increase (or decrease) in the stock price by shorting 1,126 shares of stock, this portfolio would be considered equivalent in risk to 1,126 shares of stock sold short.

Table 6.2 Delta calculation for hypothetical option portfolio

Option	Type	Quantity held*	Delta
A	Call	20	0.4996
B	Call	−10	0.6243
D	Put	30	−0.5004

*A negative quantity indicates a writing (short) position.

portfolio delta $= 20 \times 0.4996 + (-10) \times 0.6243$
$\qquad\qquad +30 \times (-0.5004) = -11.263$

> A common practice among options traders is to hold "delta-neutral" portfolios, portfolios whose value should be unaffected by relatively small changes in the price of the underlying stock.

Suppose in the example above that option A is under-priced relative to the theoretical Black–Scholes value, and the position in 20 long A options is being held to take advantage of the mispricing. Similarly, option B may be over-priced, and, therefore, a short position is taken to exploit the mispricing in option B. Finally, 30 units of option C are being held, presumably to take advantage of underpricing. Hopefully, in a short period of time, the price of each option will converge to its theoretical value, and the portfolio will earn a profit equal to the aggregate amount of mispricing.

Unfortunately, this particular portfolio, equivalent in risk to shorting 1,126 shares of stock, could lose a significant amount of its value if the stock price moves up before the three option prices converge to their theoretical values. To avoid taking this type of risk, a portfolio manager seeking to profit from price discrepancies in the options market, would attempt to form a delta-neutral portfolio, one whose value should be relatively unaffected by a small change in the price of the underlying stock.

Ideally, the portfolio manager would purchase additional under-priced calls and/or sell over-priced puts in a sufficient quantity to bring the portfolio's delta to zero. But it is possible that no such opportunities exist and that the only call options available for purchase are over-priced and the only puts available to write are under-priced. To avoid having to reduce the potential profit in the portfolio by buying over-priced calls or writing under-priced puts, one could purchase 1,126 shares of stock. As such, the overall portfolio, equivalent in risk to 1,126 shares of stock sold short plus 1,126 shares held long, would be equivalent in risk to zero shares of stock. Therefore, there would be very little risk that the portfolio's value could be adversely affected by a small change in the stock price.

Gamma

Gamma is the second partial derivative of the option price with respect to the stock price. Gamma can also be viewed as the partial derivative of delta with respect to the stock price. Thus, gamma tells us how much delta should change per unit of infinitesimally small change in the price of the underlying stock.

Gammas for individual options

Gammas for European calls and puts are the same. Mathematically, the Black–Scholes-based gamma for both types of options is given as follows:

$$\Gamma = \frac{\partial^2 P}{\partial S^2} = \frac{N'(d1)}{S\sigma_a \sqrt{\tau}}$$

$$N'(d1) = \frac{1}{\sqrt{2\pi}\sigma_a} e^{-(d1-u_a)^2/(2\sigma_a^2)}$$

(6.3)

In equation 6.3, the symbol π is the mathematical constant, $3.141559\ldots$. $N'(d1)$ is the ordinate or actual value of the standard normal distribution function evaluated at $d1$. In contrast, $N(d1)$, without the prime, is the area under a standard normal distribution function from $-\infty$ to $d1$. Most computer routines that evaluate $N(d1)$ will also return a value of $N'(d1)$.

> Since the delta for a long position in stock is 1, regardless of the level of the stock price, the gamma for a stock position is zero. Stated differently, since the delta for a stock is always 1 and, therefore, cannot change, the partial derivative of the stock's delta with respect to the stock price must be zero.

Even though stock can be used to manage the delta risk in an options portfolio, it cannot be used to manage gamma, since a stock's gamma is always zero. Therefore, additional options must be purchased or sold to bring the gamma of an options portfolio to a desired level. Sometimes, positions in options must be taken on the wrong side of the market, that is, one may be forced to purchase over-priced options or sell under-priced options. In such instances, the potential profit in the portfolio could be reduced significantly in an attempt to bring the portfolio's gamma to an acceptable level.

Re-consider option B from table 6.1. The gamma for option B is 0.0126. This indicates that the delta for option B, initially 0.6243, should change by approximately 0.0126 per unit change in the price of the underlying stock. If the stock price is increased by $1 from $100 to $101, the option's delta will increase to 0.6368, a net change of 0.0125, which is almost identical to the initial gamma value of 0.0126.

Note that delta and gamma can be used in combination to get a better prediction of how much an option's price should change in conjunction with a large change in the stock price. As noted previously, if the stock price is increased from $100 to $110, the price of the call option will increase from $14.23 to $21.06, a change of $6.83. With the stock price at $100, the delta and gamma are 0.6243 and 0.0126, respectively. Using the gamma value of 0.0126, if the stock price increases by $10, the option's delta should increase to approximately $0.6243 + 10 \times 0.0126 = 0.7503$. On average, over this range, the delta should be approximately $(0.6243 + 0.7503)/2 = 0.6873$. Thus, with an (approximate) average delta of 0.6873, one would expect a change in the option price of $10 \times 0.6873 = \$6.87$, given a change in the stock price from $100 to $110. This compares very favorably with the actual price change of $6.83.

Portfolio gammas

> The gamma of a portfolio is the sum of the gammas of its component securities multiplied by the number of units of each security held in the portfolio.

Table 6.3 below computes the gamma of the same portfolio consisting of 20 units of option A held long, 10 units of option B sold short (written), and 30 long units of option D.

According to table 6.3, the gamma of the portfolio is 0.5390. This indicates that the portfolio's delta, originally −11.263, will increase by approximately $0.5390 per dollar increase in the price of the underlying stock and, conversely, will become even more negative by an amount of 0.5390 per unit decrease in the price of the underlying stock. Assuming each option in the portfolio is an exchange-traded option issued against 100 shares of stock, the portfolio's immediate risk is equivalent to 1,126

Table 6.3   Gamma calculation for hypothetical option portfolio

Option	Type	Quantity held*	Gamma
A	Call	20	0.0133
B	Call	−10	0.0126
D	Put	30	0.0133

*A negative quantity indicates a writing (short) position.

$$portfolio\ gamma = 20 \times 0.0133 + (-10) \times 0.0126$$
$$+30 \times 0.0133 = 0.5390$$

portfolio delta (from table 6.2) $= -11.263$

shares of stock sold short. A positive gamma of 0.5390, or 53.90 in share-equivalence on options issued against 100 shares of stock, indicates that if the stock price increases, the option portfolio should become less risk-equivalently short by an amount equal to approximately 53.90 shares per dollar increase in the stock price. If the stock price declines, the portfolio should become more risk-equivalently short by the same amount.

Suppose this same option portfolio is made delta-neutral by purchasing 1,126 shares of stock. Since stock has zero gamma, the neutralization of delta risk in this fashion has no effect on the portfolio's gamma risk. Thus, even though such a portfolio is, initially, equivalent in risk to zero shares of stock, as the stock price increases, the portfolio will become risk-equivalently long in stock by an amount of approximately 53.90 shares per dollar increase in the stock price and risk-equivalently short in stock by approximately 53.90 shares per unit decrease in the stock price.

Some option portfolio managers, wishing to take advantage of price discrepancies in the options market by forming a portfolio of options A, B and D along with a delta-neutralizing stock position may find this level of risk tolerable and not seek to bring the gamma risk to zero. However, if it were necessary also to neutralize the portfolio's gamma, it is likely that some of the potential profit in the portfolio would have to be sacrificed. Chapter 10 addresses the issue of determining the optimal mix of securities in an options portfolio subject to multiple risk objectives.

Delta and gamma via the binomial model

As was emphasized in chapter 4, the Black–Scholes model can be viewed as the limiting case of the binomial model as the number of binomial time intervals over the life of the option becomes infinitely large. Given the close correspondence between the two models, there must be an equivalent binomial counterpart to delta and gamma neutrality.

In the binomial model, a portfolio that is delta-neutral will have the same value in both the up and down states at the end of the first binomial period. Just as with the Black–Scholes model, the value of such a portfolio will be unaffected by a small change in the price of the underlying stock as represented by the first binomial outcome. However, a portfolio that is structured to give the same value in the initial up and down states is more likely than not to give different values in subsequent states.

> The binomial-equivalent of a portfolio that is both gamma and delta neutral is one that gives the same value in all three binomial states at the end of the second binomial period.[18] According to binomial pricing theory, it takes two securities to obtain a desired set of portfolio payoffs in the two states that can occur at the end of any binomial period. Similarly, if an investor wants to create a specific payoff pattern over the three states that can occur at the end of the second binomial period, positions in three securities will be needed.[19] Thus, in the binomial model, it is necessary to take positions in at least three securities to achieve delta and gamma neutrality simultaneously. Likewise, with Black–Scholes pricing, a minimum of three securities are needed to achieve simultaneous delta and gamma neutrality.

Theta

Theta is the partial derivative of the option's price with respect to time (or the negative of the partial derivative with respect to τ, since τ decrease in value as we move forward in time). Black–Scholes thetas for European call

---

18. Both delta and gamma, when used within the context of the Black–Scholes model, are partial derivatives, rather than total derivatives, which means that everything else in the equation is being held constant. However, in the binomial model, time must pass before any price change can occur. Thus, gamma-neutrality, as defined here, is not precisely the same as that Black–Scholes-based gamma-neutrality. Nevertheless, visualizing gamma-neutrality in terms of the binomial model still provides insight into the type of risk reduction that occurs when a portfolio is gamma-neutral.
19. The payoffs of the three securities must be "linearly independent" which means that the payoffs to any one security cannot be expressed as a linear function of the payoffs to any of the other securities.

and put options on non-dividend paying stocks are shown in equation 6.4.

$$\Theta = -\frac{\partial P}{\partial \tau} = -\frac{SN'(d1)\sigma_a}{2\sqrt{\tau}} - r_a K e^{-r_a \tau} N(d2) \quad \text{for a call,}$$

$$(6.4)$$

$$\Theta = -\frac{\partial P}{\partial \tau} = -\frac{SN'(d1)\sigma_a}{2\sqrt{\tau}} + r_a K e^{-r_a \tau} N(-d2) \quad \text{for a put.}$$

Thetas for call options are always negative. Thus, over time, there is a natural decay in the price of any call option. Although one might think there should be a corresponding natural decay in the price of a European put, this is not necessarily the case for all puts. For example, consider a put that is so far in-the-money, that there is almost no chance whatsoever that the put could end up out-of-the-money before maturity. In this case, the put's value would be given by:[20]

$$P \approx K e^{-r_a \tau} - S.$$

For example, with a striking price of 100, a stock price 50 and $r_a \tau = 0.03$, the put's price would equal $100 \times 0.9704 - \$50 = \$47.04$. If the stock's price did not change by maturity, the option's price would eventually increase to $50. Thus, in this case, there would be a natural *increase* in the put's price over time due to the fact that the almost certain proceeds from the exercise of the option are worth less today than at maturity. If the put is closer to-the-money, this natural increase in value could be partially or even totally offset by the decrease in value which results from the erosion over time in potential volatility in the stock over the remaining life of the option.

Portfolio thetas

> The theta of a portfolio is the sum of the thetas of its component securities weighted by the number of each security held in the portfolio.

Consider the same portfolio consisting of options A, B and D used in previous examples. As shown in table 6.3, this portfolio has a delta of -11.263 and a gamma of 0.5390. Assume that the portfolio is made delta-neutral by purchasing 11.263 shares of stock (or 1,126 shares if each option

---

20. This follows from pricing relationship 2.13 from chapter 2, $put_E \geq PV(K) - S$, which gives the minimum value of a Euopean put option as an extension of the put–call parity equation.

is written on 100 shares). Since stock has a gamma of zero, the portfolio's gamma will remain at 0.5390. Thus, this portfolio is delta-neutral and gamma-positive.

With positive gamma, the portfolio's delta will go from its initial value of zero to a more positive amount if the stock goes up, and the delta will become negative if the stock goes down. Thus, it would appear that there is no way to lose money by holding this portfolio; at worst the stock will do nothing and the portfolio will break even. If the stock goes up, the portfolio will become risk-equivalently longer in the stock and make money, and if the stock goes down, the portfolio will become risk-equivalently shorter, also making money.

But there is a problem in this logic. Recall that delta and gamma are partial derivatives. As such, they indicate rates of change in the option's price and its delta, while all the other factors which influence the option's price are held constant. But in order to even get a change in the stock price, some time must pass. Therefore, it is inappropriate to ignore the passage of time when analyzing the effects of positive and negative stock price changes on the portfolio's value. The portfolio's theta, calculated in table 6.4, indicates how the portfolio's value will be affected by the passage of time.

Table 6.4 shows that the portfolio's theta is -161.1. Inasmuch as the version of the Black–Scholes model presented in this book is set up so that time is measured in years, the portfolio should lose value with the passage of time at a rate of $161.1 per year. This amounts to a rate of $161.1/365 = $0.4413 per day, or $44.13 per day for a portfolio of options written on 100 shares of stock. Thus, any increase in portfolio value that results from a large increase or decrease in the stock price must first offset approximately $44.13 of natural loss per day, due to the passage of time, before the portfolio can become profitable.

Table 6.4   Theta calculation for hypothetical option portfolio

Option	Type	Quantity held*	Theta
A	Call	20	−7.9811
B	Call	−10	−8.1012
D	Put	30	−2.7493
Stock	Stock	11.263	0.0000

*A negative quantity indicates a writing (short) position.

portfolio theta $= 20 \times (-7.9811) + (-10) \times (-8.1012)$
$\qquad\qquad + 30(-2.7493) + 11.263 \times 0 = -161.1$

portfolio gamma $= 0.5390$
portfolio delta $= 0$

Vega and rho

Vega and *rho*, given in equations 6.5 and 6.6 for European options on a non-dividend paying stock, are the partial derivatives of the option price with respect to volatility and the riskless interest rate, respectively.[21]

$$vega = \frac{\partial P}{\partial \sigma_a} = S\sqrt{\tau}N'(d1) \quad \text{for calls and puts,}$$

(6.5)

$$rho = \frac{\partial P}{\partial r_a} = \tau e^{-r_a \tau} KN(d2) \quad \text{for a call,}$$

(6.6)

$$rho = \frac{\partial P}{\partial r_a} = -\tau e^{-r_a \tau} KN(-d2) \quad \text{for a put.}$$

Unlike the use of delta, gamma and theta as direct measures of risk in an options portfolio, one should use caution in employing vega and rho as measures of risk. The reason for this caution is that both are partial derivatives, meaning that all other variables which could potentially affect an option's price are held constant. But it is difficult to believe that stock prices themselves are not influenced by interest rates and investors' perceptions of volatility. Generally, when interest rates go up, stock prices go down, and when investors suddenly believe a company and its stock will be riskier or more volatile, the stock will become less valuable. Both rho and vega ignore these effects and, therefore, are very limited in their effectiveness in option's portfolio management. Moreover, the Black–Scholes model does not provide a mathematical link between interest rates and stock prices or volatility and stock prices so that one could actually estimate the *total* change in an option's price that should come about due to a change in interest rates or volatility.

> As with the other partial derivatives, portfolio vegas and rhos are simply the sums of vegas and rhos of the portfolio's component securities, with each vega or rho weighted by the number of securities held.

Table 6.5 computes the vega and rho for the same portfolio of options from the previous examples.

---

21. Note, there is no Greek symbol vega. Therefore, for notational purposes, the word "vega" is written out in equation 6.4. Sometimes, however, the upper case of the Greek symbol lambda, Λ, is used to denote vega. Occassionally, vega is referred to as lambda. Although ρ is the Greek symbol for rho, I have chosen to write out the word "rho," to avoid confusion with the earlier use of the symbol ρ as a correlation coefficient.

Table 6.5   Vega and rho calculations for hypothetical
option portfolio

Option	Type	Quantity held*	Vega	Rho
A	Call	20	39.8942	39.9387
B	Call	−10	37.9433	48.1939
D	Put	30	39.8942	−64.6966

*A negative quantity indicates a writing (short) position.

portfolio vega = 20×39.8942 + (− 10) × 37.9433 + 30
×39.8942 = 1,615

portfolio rho = 20×39.9387 + (− 10) × 48.1939 + 30
× (− 64.6966) = −1,624

With a vega of 1,615 or 161,500 for a portfolio written on options issued against 100 shares of stock, the portfolio should gain approximately $161,500 for every unit change in volatility, provided volatility is measured as a decimal fraction rather than as a percentage. For example, if volatility increases from 0.30 to 0.31, the portfolio should increase in value by approximately $(0.31 − 0.30)($161,500) = $1,615$. This, of course, ignores the possibility of a decrease in the stock price due to an increase in volatility.

With a rho of −1,624, or −162,400 for a portfolio of options on 100 shares of stock, the portfolio should lose approximately −$162,400 per unit increase in the riskless rate of interest. Again, as with volatility, we must remember that the riskless interest rate is measured as a decimal fraction, not as a percentage. Thus, if interest rates increase from 5 percent to 6 percent, the portfolio should decrease in value by approximately $(0.06 − 0.05)($162,400) = $1,624$, provided the stock price itself does not change along with the increase in the interest rate.

Elasticity and Beta

Elasticity is the proportional change in an option's price per unit of proportional change in the stock price. An *elasticity* of 5 would indicate that an option should earn an unexpected return of approximately 0.05, or 5 percent, if the stock earns an unexpected return of 0.01, or 1 percent.

Recall that delta is the dollar change in the option price per dollar change in the price of the underlying stock. If dollar changes in the price of each security are divided by the price of the security, they become proportional changes. Thus, the *elasticity* of the option price with respect to the stock price, denoted $\beta_{P,S}$, is given by

$$\beta_{P,S} = \Delta \frac{S}{P}$$

(6.7)

Consider the *elasticities* of the call options in table 6.1, labeled A through C, and the put options, labeled D through F. The call options in this table have *elasticities* of the order of 4 while the puts have *elasticities* of the order of −4. Note that the *elasticities* of the calls become greater as the options becomes more out-of-the-money, and the *elasticities* for the puts become more negative as the puts become more out-of-the money. Generally, very out-of-the-money calls should have very high *elasticities* and very out-of-the-money puts should have very negative *elasticities*. Call *elasticities* are always greater than 1, but approach 1 from above as the stock price becomes infinite. Put *elasticities* are always less than −1, but approach −1 from below as the stock price approaches zero.

Suppose the hypothetical stock on which these options are written has a beta of 1.0. This means that if the market earns an unexpected return of 1 percent, the stock should also earn an unexpected return of 1 percent plus or minus some error, with the magnitude of the error depending upon the strength of the statistical relationship between the two returns. Consider option A with an *elasticity* of 4.99. For this option, if the market earns an unexpected 1 percent return, the stock can be expected to earn a return of 1 percent and the option a return of 4.99 percent, implying a beta for the option of 4.99.

Suppose the hypothetical stock has a beta of 2. Then, an unexpected market return of 1 percent should be associated with an unexpected stock return of 2 percent and an unexpected option return of 2 × 4.99 = 9.88 percent. Thus, the option would have a beta relative to the market of 9.98, or in general, a beta relative to the market, denoted $\beta_{P,M}$ of:

$$\beta_{P,M} = \beta_{P,S}\beta_{S,M} = \left(\Delta \frac{S}{P}\right)\beta_{S,M},$$

(6.8)

where $\beta_{S,M}$ is the beta of the stock relative to the market.

Why should we be interested in option *elasticities* and betas? The primary reason is that these risk measures, when used in conjunction with standard risk–return theory, can provide insight into the returns that can be expected from various option positions and option strategies. Chapter 8 addresses this issue by using the betas of option portfolios as inputs to the Capital Asset Pricing Model, the traditional model for estimating expected security and portfolio returns as a function of risk.

REFERENCES

Black, F. and M. Scholes, "The Pricing of Options and Corporate Liabilities." *Journal of Political Economy* 81 (May/June 1973), 637–54.
Hull, J. C., *Options, Futures and Other Derivatives.* 4th edn, Prentice Hall, Upper Saddle River, NJ, 2000.
Merton, R. C., "Theory of Rational Option Pricing." *The Bell Journal of Economics and Management Science* (Spring 1973), 141–83.

QUESTIONS AND PROBLEMS

These problems require that you use the Excel program Black_Scholes.xls which can be obtained from the website http://www.rendleman.com/book.

Assume the volatility for XYZ stock is 0.3 per year, the price of XYZ stock is $100 per share, and the annual riskless rate of interest is 0.05 per year compounded continuously. You hold the following portfolio of options on XYZ:

Type	Strike	Days till maturity	Quantity
Call	100	300	10
Call	110	210	−30

1. What is the delta of your portfolio?
2. What is the gamma of your portfolio?
3. Assuming each option is written on 100 shares of stock, what stock position would be required to bring the portfolio's delta to zero.
4. Instead of using stock to control the portfolio's delta, assume you can buy or sell a put with a $95 striking price that matures in 120 days. Again, assuming each option is written on 100 shares of stock, what position involving the put would be required to bring the portfolio's delta to zero?
5. After adjusting the portfolio's delta to zero with the put, what is the portfolio's gamma?
6. If the stock price makes a significant downward change in value, should your delta-neutral portfolio from problems 4 and 5 gain or lose value?
7. Assume you have formed a portfolio of options that is rho-neutral. Stated differently, the partial derivative of the portfolio's value with respect to a change in the risk-free interest rate is zero. Should this portfolio be immunized against an adverse change in the risk-free rate of interest? Why or why not? Discuss.

8. Assume you have developed the modern-day successor to the Black–Scholes model. According to your model, the prices of European put and call options are both functions of the outdoor temperature in the city of Chicago. You have developed a new "Greek" for your model called "zeta," the partial derivative of the option's price with respect to the outdoor temperature.

   According to your model, the price of a one-year call option on a $100 stock with a striking price of $100 is $10 and the same call has a zeta of 3. Assuming an interest rate of 0.05 per year compounded continuously, a volatility of 0.30 per year and no dividends, what is the zeta of the one-year European put with a $100 striking price?

7

Options Arbitrage

7.1   Implied Volatility

The Black–Scholes (1973) model, modified for dividends,[22] determines the price of an option as a function of six different parameters: the price of the underlying stock, the option's striking price, the time remaining until the option matures, the riskless interest rate, the dividend yield of the underlying stock, and the volatility of returns for the underlying stock. The first five of these parameters are directly observable or easily estimated. But estimating the volatility, or annual standard deviation of the underlying stock's logarithmic return, can be more difficult.

According to the standard version of Black–Scholes, all options on the same stock, regardless of their striking price or maturity, should be priced using the same annualized volatility estimate. One way to test the model is to compute what is called an "implied volatility" for each option (see Latané and Rendleman [1976]).

> An option's implied volatility is the annualized volatility, which when input into the Black–Scholes model, produces a model price which coincides with the option's observed market price.

But even if the Black–Scholes model is perfect, there could still be some differences in implied volatilities for options on the same underlying stock. Some large differences in implied volatilities could indicate potentially profitable pricing inconsistencies. However, differences in implied volatilities also can occur, even if options on the same stock are generally priced consistently with one another. Such differences could occur for the following reasons.

---

22.   Merton (1973).

First, market prices of options are quoted in 1/16ths of a point for prices under $3 and in 8ths for prices of $3 and over. Thus, if the Black–Scholes price for a given option is, for example, $4.44, the market price would most likely be $4⅜ or $4½, and neither of these prices would produce an implied volatility exactly the same as that associated with the theoretical price of $4.44.

Second, if implied volatilities are computed from option prices associated with the most recent trades, some trades could be "stale." For example, suppose a particular call option trades at a price of $5 at 1:00 pm with the stock also trading at $50 per share. At the time of the trade, the $5 option price coincides exactly with the Black–Scholes price. Assume further that the stock price moves from $50 to $51 at the close of trading, but the option does not trade again during the same day. In this case, an investor, looking at closing option and stock price data, will observe that the closing call option and stock prices are $5 and $51, respectively. With the stock at $51, the call option price of $5 would appear to be too low, and hence, the implied volatility associated with this option price would also be too low. This is a well-recognized problem, and as a result, professional option traders are very unlikely to use closing prices as the basis for identifying over and under-priced options. Instead, professionals, with access to real-time computerized quotation systems, will base their trading on the latest bid and offer prices for both options and stock. Compared with transaction prices, these quotations should provide a much more accurate reflection of the state of the market at any point in time.

As a third source of difference in implied volatilities, at any moment during the trading day, market makers, specialists and other floor traders should be actively quoting bid and offer prices for each option and for the underlying stock, even if no trading actually takes place. When transaction prices are observed, there is no indication of whether the trade took place at the market's bid or offer or, perhaps, somewhere in between. Nevertheless, if one observes an option transaction price that appears to be too high in relation to prices of other options on the same stock, there is a good chance that the transaction took place at the market's asking or offer price. Conversely, if the transaction price seems too low, the trade, in all likelihood, took place at the bid.

For a brief period in the late 1970s I traded options on the floor of the Chicago Board Options Exchange. Each morning on the 45-minute train ride into Chicago, I would take prices from the *Wall Street Journal* and compute implied volatilities for the options in which I traded. I would then base my initial trading strategy for the day on this analysis.

Box cont'd

As was almost always the case, I was unable to trade the most mispriced options at the prices shown in the newspaper. These options were often the most inactive, and hence, the most likely to be subject to stale price data. Even with actively traded options, I would find that the options that looked most attractive to buy were showing last trades based on bids, and if I wanted to guarantee the immediate purchase of such options, I would have to pay the higher ask price. Similarly, if I wanted to sell over-priced options, I would typically have to do so at bid prices below the previous day's close.

After a while I learned the importance of using current bid and offer (or ask) prices for the options and underlying stock, taking long positions only when ask prices seemed too low and short positions only when bid prices seemed too high. I also learned to use caution and trade very carefully when prices in one or more options seemed to suddenly get out of line with others in the same stock. In these situations, I learned there is a good chance that someone on the other side of the transaction may have information concerning the future direction of the stock price that could justify paying a premium for the purchase of options or taking a hit in their sale. It is a terrible feeling, indeed, to sell what appears to be a very over-priced call option only to find out within a few minutes that the company on whose stock the option is issued is making an announcement that has a very positive effect on the stock price. These observations are consistent with the empirical findings of Manaster and Rendleman (1982) who show that option prices can reflect information about the fundamental value of the underlying stock that is not immediately reflected in the price of the stock itself and that actual stock prices tend to move in the direction of those implied by option prices.

Some option prices are so insensitive to the volatility parameter that there is little, if any, informational value associated with the implied volatility for such options. For example, a call option that is way in-the-money with just a few days remaining will have a price approximately equal to the difference between the stock price and striking price, regardless of the volatility estimate. Thus, observing that the implied volatility of such an option is out of line with those of other options on the same stock is of little consequence.

Implied volatilities can be time-dependent

In an analysis that will be developed more fully later in this chapter, we will see options with different maturities can be priced with different implied volatilities. When this happens, it does not mean that the market is inefficient. It simply means that the market is forecasting a change in the underlying stock's volatility over time.

On April 5, 2000, I downloaded bid and ask option and stock prices for Microsoft from the CBOE's website. All option and stock prices were taken as of 10:03 am of that day. Readers may remember that the previous day was one of the most volatile in the history of Wall Street. Both the Dow Jones Industrial Average and the NASDAQ Index lost over 500 points during the day, but recovered most of their losses by the end of trading. Much of the volatility was attributed to uncertainty in technology stocks following the announcement earlier in the week that settlement talks in the US government's antitrust suit against Microsoft had broken down. Omitting the details of the analysis, options in Microsoft were priced with the volatilities as shown in table 7.1.

Table 7.1   Implied volatilities for Microsoft options as of 10:03 am, April 5, 2000

Maturity	Implied volatility
April	0.59958
May	0.55086
July	0.50265
October	0.46583
	Incremental volatility*
April	0.59958
April to May	0.53324
May to July	0.48143
July to October	0.44465

*Let σ_1^2 denote the annualized variance of the log return over the first period of length t_1, σ_2^2 denote the variance of the log return over the second period of length t_2, and $\sigma_{1,2}^2$ denote the variance of the log return over the entire period of length $t_1 + t_2$. Since the variance of the log return is proportional to time, the variance over the time period of length $t_1 + t_2$ will be a time-weighted average of the variances over the two component periods. This implies that $\sigma_2^2 = \sigma_{1,2}^2((t_1 + t_2)/t_2) - \sigma_1^2(t_1/t_2)$ and $\sigma_2 = \sqrt{\sigma_{1,2}^2(t_1 + t_2)/t_2 - \sigma_1^2(t_1/t_2)}$.

As is evident from the entries in table 7.1, Microsoft options were being priced as if the market expected a significant amount of uncertainty in the price of the stock over the short-run while expecting the volatility over the summer and into the fall to be somewhat lower. The incremental volatilities indicate that the implied market forecast of annualized volatility was 0.59958 between April 7 and April 20, the maturity date of the April options, 0.53787 between April 20 and the May 19 maturity, 0.48862 between May 19 and the July 21 maturity, and 0.44465 between July 21 and the final maturity date, October 20. The fact that the volatility forecasts are different does not imply that the market is inefficient. It simply reflects the extreme uncertainty in the future of Microsoft in early April, 2000.

How well does the Black–Scholes model work?

Before we can use any model to identify over and under-priced options, we must have confidence that it does a good job of describing option prices. After all, if we observe that some option prices differ significantly from model prices, perhaps we should conclude that the model is not very good rather than conclude that the market has somehow mispriced the options. Although there are a number of empirical studies which have shown that Black–Scholes-type models do a reasonably good job describing option prices, the analysis below presents a simple "quick and dirty" test of the model in the recent pricing of call and put options on a single stock, Microsoft Corporation, on October 1, 1996.

The analysis of Microsoft options is based on closing option and stock price data as reported in the *Wall Street Journal* on October 1, 1996. Basic pricing information for these options is presented in table 7.2. Because of the aforementioned problems in using individual implied volatilities for assessing the degree of mispricing in options on the same underlying stock, this analysis takes a slightly different approach. It searches for a *single* annualized volatility estimate, which when used to price each Microsoft

Table 7.2   Data for 10/01/96 Microsoft example

	October 96	November 96	January 97
Maturity date	10/18/96	11/15/96	01/17/97
Annual t-bill rate (%):			
Annualized ask yield	4.84	4.96	5.12
Continuous equivalent	4.73	4.84	4.99

Stock price = 132.125; The stock pays no dividends.

option, minimizes the sum of squared differences between market and model prices.[23] This approach is much like a regression analysis that finds the intercept and slope coefficients of a linear equation while minimizing the sum of squared deviations between observed outcomes and predicted outcomes. For the Microsoft options whose prices are shown in table 7.3, 0.318 is the annualized volatility estimate that minimizes the sum of the squared pricing errors.[24]

Note the fourth column of table 7.3 marked "Model − Market," which denotes the difference between the model and market price when model prices are evaluated with an annualized volatility estimate of 0.318. Although, by construction, there should be minimum pricing error with the 0.318 volatility estimate, it is striking that any one estimate of volatility could be chosen that would produce such a small amount of pricing error. Five of sixteen market prices are within one trading tick of the model price and twelve are within two ticks.

Note that the three options with the most trading volume, the October 130 puts, October 130 calls, and October 135 calls, are the most accurately priced. Given the high volume in these options, it is quite unlikely that their closing prices are stale. Therefore, any error in their pricing is probably due to minimum trading ticks and bid–asked spreads.

It is interesting that the fourth most actively traded option, the October 135 put, is relatively mispriced. If I were a professional trader, this option might get my attention, especially if I could purchase it at the closing price of \$4.75 or an eighth of a point higher. In all likelihood, however, the \$4.75 price is a stale quote and/or there is a $\frac{1}{4}$ to $\frac{3}{8}$ of a point bid–ask spread in this option, with the closing price taking place at the bid. Nevertheless, it would be worthwhile taking a

---

23. Manaster and Rendleman (1982) were the first to use this approach, but instead of solving for just the best volatility estimate, they also solved for the best implied stock price and attempted to determine whether there was informational value in implied stock prices that was not contained in observed prices. The maturity-specific implied volatilites summarized in table 7.1 were also calculated using this procedure.

24. The closing price for Microsoft stock on 10/01/96 was \$132$\frac{1}{8}$. The analysis is limited to call and put options with striking prices at two levels above \$132$\frac{1}{8}$, \$135 and \$140 and two levels below, \$130 and \$125. Generally, the most trading activity, and hence, the least amount of potential pricing error, is in the options with striking prices close to the current stock price.

Inasmuch as Microsoft stock pays no dividends, the European-based Black–Scholes model can be used to price American call options, since both American and European options on the same stock should have the same value. However, given the possibility of premature exercise for puts, the Black–Scholes model is not employed. Instead, a 100-period binomial-based American put pricing model with the same parameters as Black–Scholes is used.

Table 7.3 Option pricing information for Microsoft stock price = 132.125; volatility = 0.318

Strike	Model price	Market price	Model– market	(Model– market)/Δ	Delta	Gamma	Vega	Volume
October calls								
125	8.383	8.500	−0.117*	−0.144	0.8092	0.03004	7.757	51
130	4.913	5.000	−0.087*	−0.140	0.6190	0.04207	10.865	691
135	2.502	2.500	0.002*	0.006	0.4022	0.04272	11.032	768
140	1.095	0.938	0.157	0.720	0.2182	0.03254	8.404	416
November calls								
125	10.476	10.875	−0.399	−0.548	0.7279	0.02253	15.400	134
130	7.375	7.625	−0.250**	−0.417	0.6005	0.02621	17.917	53
135	4.943	4.750	0.193**	0.413	0.4666	0.02698	18.443	62
January calls								
130	11.116	11.250	−0.134**	−0.222	0.6048	0.01687	27.677	56
October puts								
125	0.981	1.125	−0.144**	0.753	−0.1908	0.03034	7.757	151
130	2.515	2.500	0.015*	−0.040	−0.3833	0.04268	10.865	2877
135	5.119	4.750	0.369	−0.613	−0.6029	0.04352	11.032	672
140	8.730	8.500	−0.230**	−0.290	−0.7913	0.03366	8.404	12
November puts								
125	2.641	2.813	−0.172**	0.623	−0.2752	0.02294	15.400	133
130	4.530	4.625	−0.095*	0.235	−0.4048	0.02685	17.917	45
135	7.085	7.250	−0.165**	0.305	−0.5424	0.02796	18.443	60
January puts								
130	7.242	6.750	0.492	−1.213	−0.4058	0.01765	27.677	25

Model prices are based on an annualized volatility of 0.318. This volatility minimizes the sum of squared differences between model and market prices. Pricing based on annual volatility of 0.318. Put prices evaluated with binomial model taking premature exercise into account using 100 binomial time periods.
*Indicates pricing error is within one tick ($\frac{1}{16}$ for prices less than $3 and $\frac{1}{8}$ for prices over $3).
**Indicates pricing error is within two ticks.

closer look at this option to see if its price is really out of line with the others.

The option with the most pricing error, the January 130 puts, shows a trading volume of only 25 contracts. With this low amount of volume, it is quite possible that the closing price of $6.75 occurred several hours before the close of trading at a time when the stock price was a point or more lower.

Overall, the model, evaluated with a 0.318 volatility estimate, appears to do an excellent job describing option prices in Microsoft on 10/1/96. Despite some pricing error in these options, I am certain I could make more money as a finance professor than as a trader trying to exploit these small price differences.

The volatility smile

Although not evident in the analysis above, it has been documented (MacBeth and Merville [1979] and Rubinstein [1985]) that for some stocks and indices, implied volatility can be systematically related to the striking prices of their listed options. When plotted against the striking prices of available options, implied volatilities can sometimes exhibit the form of a smile or sneer shape. This suggests that one or more of the assumptions of the Black–Scholes model may be violated in the pricing of actual exchange-traded options.

Rubinstein (1994) and Derman and Kanai (1994) suggest that the volatility smile can occur if the volatility of an underlying stock or index is expected to be a function of both time and the level of future stock prices, although empirical tests by Dumas et al. (1998) cast doubt on this explanation. Hull and White (1987) and Heston (1993) suggest that the volatility smile can be explained by the expectation of stochastic (random) volatility, especially if there is a negative correlation between volatility and the level of future stock prices. Through simulation, Dennis (1996) shows that the volatility smile can occur under standard Black–Scholes assumptions in the presence of transaction costs (see chapter 9).

The importance of volatility estimation in option trading

We can use the Microsoft example to conclude two things. First, the Black–Scholes model appears to be working. Second, the market, in its apparent use of the model, is telling the world that the annualized volatility of Microsoft is approximately 0.318 or 31.8 percent. Inasmuch as volatility is the only parameter of the model which is in any way up for grabs, the key to exploiting mispricing of Microsoft options is knowing whether the 31.8 percent volatility estimate accurately reflects the future volatility characteristics of Microsoft stock. If 31.8 percent does not reflect the future volatility characteristics of Microsoft, there can be a significant amount of money to be made by coming up with a better estimate.

For example, assume that as a professional options trader, you are in better position to estimate volatility than the marginal investor in the options market. You are equipped with a substantial amount of historical stock price data for Microsoft and other stock issues, you have a staff of PhDs with

Table 7.4 Option pricing for Microsoft with volatilities of 0.27 and 0.32

	Volatility = 0.270			Volatility = 0.370		
Strike	Model price	Market price	Model−market	Model price	Market price	Model−market
October calls						
125	8.036	8.500	−0.464	8.811	8.500	0.311
130	4.399	5.000	−0.601	5.485	5.000	0.485
135	1.981	2.500	−0.519	3.084	2.500	0.584
140	0.717	0.938	−0.221	1.556	0.938	0.618
November calls						
125	9.762	10.875	−1.113	11.300	10.875	0.425
130	6.524	7.625	−1.101	8.316	7.625	0.691
135	4.066	4.750	−0.684	5.910	4.750	1.160
January calls						
130	9.801	11.250	−1.449	12.568	11.250	1.318
October puts						
125	0.639	1.125	−0.486	1.422	1.125	0.297
130	2.006	2.500	−0.494	3.081	2.500	0.581
135	4.595	4.750	−0.155	5.699	4.750	0.949
140	8.364	8.500	−0.136	9.183	8.500	0.683
November puts						
125	1.903	2.813	−0.909	3.446	2.813	0.634
130	3.665	4.625	−0.960	5.479	4.625	0.854
135	6.220	7.250	−1.030	8.050	7.250	0.800
January puts						
130	5.919	6.750	−0.831	8.689	6.750	1.939

Put prices evaluated with binomial model taking premature exercise into account using 100 binomial time periods.

degrees in financial economics, statistics and physics, and an MBA staff member whose only job is to stay abreast of changes in the fundamentals of Microsoft and the computer software industry. With these resources at your disposal, you estimate that the volatility of Microsoft stock will be 0.27 rather than 0.318. Table 7.4, shows the extent of mispricing in Microsoft options under the 0.27 volatility scenario along with a summary of mispricing using a 0.37 volatility estimate.

The entries in table 7.4 indicate that all the Microsoft options are over-priced if the true volatility is 0.27 and that all are under-priced if the true volatility is 0.37. Assuming your estimate is 0.27, either you know more about the volatility characteristics of Microsoft than the great majority of other market participants, or they know more than you. Moreover, when the pricing discrepancies in table 7.4 are compared with those in table 7.3, it is clear that there is much money to be made by coming up with better estimates of volatility than those which are impounded in the market prices of options.

If, indeed, you are equipped with the resources described above, then, perhaps, it is reasonable to assume that your 0.27 volatility estimate is better than the market's and that you can make money by taking advantage of your superior knowledge. However, . . .

> if you are just an ordinary investor, who happens to know something about the Black–Scholes model because you took a course in option markets at business school, and using your business school knowledge and an Excel spreadsheet you worked up the analysis in table 7.4 based on the 0.27 estimate, you can rest assured that over the long run you will lose money betting against the market's volatility estimate.

As a trader, one should recognize that a large proportion of option trading is conducted by firms with resources such as those described above, and the prices of options observed in the market will, to a large extent, reflect the information from these resources. Thus, any ordinary investor is at a distinct disadvantage when betting against the market and its implied estimate of volatility. Nevertheless, many individuals and professional investors who are not equipped to play with the "big boys" continue to try to outguess the market, either explicitly or implicitly in their trading methods, thereby providing money to fund the profits of professionals in what is inherently a zero-sum game.

Picking the best options to buy and sell in "riskless" arbitrage

Investors are motivated to trade options for many reasons. Some may use options purely as a tool for risk management. For example, it is common practice to purchase put options as a means to insure the downside risk of holding a stock or stock portfolio. Another common risk reducing technique is selling call options against individual stocks held in a portfolio. Although the primary motivation in each of these strategies is risk reduction rather than immediate profit, it is nevertheless the case that investors wishing to control risks will be better off purchasing under-priced options and selling options that are over-priced.

In options arbitrage, the sole purpose is to make money without incurring substantial risks. Clearly, in this activity, identifying over- and under-priced options is critical, since the arbitrageur profits by purchasing options whose prices are too low and selling options whose prices are too high. Although arbitrage is a sophisticated activity, pursued primarily by professional investors, it is instructive for non-professionals to examine the economics of arbitrage, since many of the trading principles associated with this activity also apply to less sophisticated forms of option investing.

To illustrate the economics of arbitrage, I will continue with the Microsoft example and assume that the arbitrageur takes the market's implied volatility estimate as the best estimate of the stock's future volatility characteristics. Thus, the pricing analysis of table 7.3, based on an implied volatility estimate of 0.318, will serve as the basis for the arbitrageur's trading strategy. For the purposes of illustrating arbitrage in option markets, I will assume that the closing option and stock prices shown in table 7.3 reflect the current state of the market and are not subject to bid–ask spread problems. Thus, the investor can buy or sell any quantity of options and stock at the market prices shown in the table. Obviously, this is an oversimplification and will cause the potential profit from arbitrage to be overstated. Transaction costs and taxes are also ignored.

Delta-neutral portfolios

One of the simplest forms of "riskless" arbitrage is combining over- and under-priced options into a delta-neutral portofolio. The "model – market" column of table 7.3 shows the extent of mispricing in each Microsoft option and indicates that some options are over-priced while others are under-priced. But which of the under-and over-priced options would be the best to buy and sell in a delta-neutral portfolio?

On the surface it might appear that the best option to buy would be that which has the largest difference between the model and market price, and the best option to sell would be the option with the most negative difference. But there are two problems with this logic.

First, if the most under-priced option is a call and the most over-priced is a put, a portfolio that consists of some quantity of long calls and short puts would not be delta-neutral. Both positions should gain value as the stock price increases and lose value as the stock price decreases, and, therefore, the risks would not be offsetting. Thus, an investor attempting to identify an under-priced call as the best option to buy must seek either another over-priced call to sell or an under-priced put to purchase.

Second, the price discrepancies shown in the "model – market" column are all associated with different levels of delta or stock-equivalent risk, and are, therefore, not directly comparable. To make the price discrepancies comparable, they should all be measured relative to the same amount of stock-equivalent risk. This is accomplished by dividing each "model – market" figure by delta. The net effect is to compute the amount of price discrepancy per share of stock-equivalent risk. This is the relevant figure for choosing the best option positions in a delta-neutral portfolio, since the amount of long stock-equivalent risk in the portfolio must equal the amount of short stock-equivalent risk.

The above analysis suggests that the investor should combine the most profitable stock-equivalent long position per unit of delta with the most profitable stock-equivalent short position per unit of delta to form the best delta-neutral portfolio. Stock-equivalent long positions can involve either the purchase of calls or the sale of puts. Thus, ...

> to identify the best stock-equivalent long position, one must find the call that is most under-priced per unit of delta and the put that is the most over-priced per unit of (negative) delta by taking a position in the option for which the quantity ($model - market)/delta$ is the highest.

In table 7.3, the call option with the largest profit per unit of delta is the October 140 call with a value of (model − market)/delta = \$0.720. Thus, for every share of long stock-equivalent risk that is taken, a long position in $1/delta = 1/0.2182 = 4.583$ units of this option should provide \$0.72 in potential profit if the market price of the option converges to the model price. (Readers should not be concerned about fractional units of options since, positions can always be scaled up.) The put option with the largest value of (model − market)/delta is the October 125 put with a profit per unit of delta of \$0.753. The \$0.753 in potential profit would be obtained by writing $1/|delta| = 1/|-0.1908| = 5.241$ units of the put. Since writing 5.241 puts or buying 4.538 calls provides the same amount of stock-equivalent delta risk, but the put position provides \$0.753 in potential profit, compared with \$0.720 for the call position, the best stock-equivalent long position would be to sell 5.241 puts per share of long stock-equivalent risk.

This analysis leads to the conclusion that the best stock-equivalent long position should be taken in the call or put with the largest value of (model−market)/delta, regardless of option type. Thus, it is really not necessary to select the best call to buy and best put to sell and take the better of the two. Instead, we simply take an appropriate stock-equivalent long position in the put or call option for which the value of (model − market)/delta is the highest.

Similarly, . . .

> the best stock-equivalent short position should be taken in the option for which the value of (*model − market*)/*delta* is the smallest, or in this case, the most negative.

With a (model − market)/delta value of −1.213, the January 130 puts are the best candidates for creating a stock-equivalent short position. In this case, one would purchase 1/|delta| = 1/|−0.4058| = 2.464 puts to create the stock-equivalent of one share of stock sold short.

Combining the two positions, the most profitable delta-neutral portfolio consists of buying 2.464 January 130 puts and selling 5.241 October 125 puts for every share of long and short stock-equivalent risk. Stated differently, for every 2.464 January 130 puts that are purchased, 5.241/2.464 = 2.127 October 125 puts should be sold.

In actual applications, option traders would take much larger positions. Suppose, for example, that an arbitrageur took a position that was equivalent in risk, on both the long and short sides, to 10,000 shares of stock. In this situation, the trader would buy January 130 puts on 24,640 shares and sell October 125 puts on 52,410 shares, or approximately 246 exchange-traded January 130's and 524 October 125's. Since the short position in October 125 puts provides $0.753 in potential profit per share of long stock-equivalent risk, and the long position in January 130 puts provides $1.213 in potential profit per share of short stock-equivalent risk, the total profit potential in the portfolio is 10,000 × $0.753 + 10,000 × $1.213 = $19,660. By taking this position the arbitrageur hopes to profit by $19,660 while maintaining a portfolio whose value should not be affected to any significant extent by adverse stock price movements. Although the stock price may change before the options converge in value to the values predicted by the Black–Scholes model, there should be little risk in the portfolio, since any loss in one option position should be offset, approximately, by an equivalent gain in the other. However, as noted earlier in this chapter, option deltas are subject to change. As the stock price changes, the deltas of both options should change, but not necessarily by the same amount. Therefore, if the stock price changes by a significant amount before the option prices converge to model values, the portfolio may lose its delta-neutral characteristics, and, therefore, may subject the investor to risks associated with adverse stock price movements. To mitigate this type of risk, option traders often form portfolios that are both delta-neutral and gamma-neutral.

Delta- and gamma-neutral portfolios

The best delta-neutral portfolio in Microsoft options, consisting of a long position in 2.464 January 130 puts and a short position in 5.241 October 125 puts for every unit of stock-equivalent risk, has a gamma of $2.464(0.01765) + (-5.241)(0.03034) = -0.1155$. This implies that if the stock price changes immediately from 132.125 to 133.125, the portfolio's delta should decrease from zero to approximately -0.1155. Similarly, if the stock price falls by \$1 per share, the portfolio's delta should increase approximately to 0.1155. For a portfolio of long January 130 puts on 24,640 shares and short October 125 puts on 52,410 shares, equivalent in risk to a position in 10,000 short shares of stock netted against 10,000 long shares, the gamma is $10,000 \times (-0.1155) = -1,155$. Thus, even though this large position starts out being delta-neutral, an increase (or decrease) in the stock price of only \$1 per share will decrease (increase) the portfolio's delta by approximately 1,155 share-equivalent units.

The original portfolio could be made both gamma- and delta-neutral by combining it with another delta-neutral portfolio in such as way that the gammas offset. For example, consider a hypothetical delta-neutral portfolio consisting of options A and B. Assume this portfolio has a gamma of 0.1. Also, assume that a delta-neutral portfolio consisting of options C and D has a gamma of 0.2. In this situation, delta- and gamma-neutrality can be achieved simultaneously by selling two units of portfolio A–B for every long unit of portfolio C–D, or vice versa. But even if a short position in portfolio A–B is the best delta-neutral portfolio, and a long position in portfolio C–D is the next-best delta-neutral portfolio, the combined position will not represent the best portfolio that is simultaneously delta- and gamma-neutral. For example, there may be a way of combining three of the options such that the resulting position is both delta- and gamma-neutral and still more profitable, per unit of stock-equivalent long or short risk, than the gamma-neutral combination of portfolio A–B with C–D. As demonstrated in the next section, the most profitable portfolio that is simultaneously delta- and gamma-neutral can be determined using linear programming.

7.2 The Use of Linear Programming in Option Portfolio Selection

Linear programming (LP) is used to determine the optimal combination of various decision variables subject to a number of constraints, when both the objective function and constraints are linear. A classic example of linear programming is determining the lowest-cost diet that will meet or exceed daily minimum nutritional requirements.

In determining the most profitable options portfolio that is both delta- and gamma-neutral, the linear program takes the following form:

Maximize: Profit from all option positions.

Subject to:

Scale constraint: The total delta of stock-equivalently long (or short) or short positions in the portfolio must not exceed a pre-specified number of stock-equivalent shares. Stock-equivalently long positions include long stock, long calls and short puts. Stock-equivalently short positions include short stock, short calls and long puts.

Delta constraint: The portfolio's delta must equal zero.

Gamma constraint: The portfolio's gamma must equal zero.

Readers who are interested in the mathematical details of LP-based option portfolio selection should refer to Rendleman (1995). However, a few of the details need to be mentioned here.

First, the amount of stock-equivalent long or short risk specified in the scale constraint can be any convenient amount. To maintain consistency with the preceding analysis, the examples that follow impose a constraint of 10,000 stock-equivalent shares. However, we could take portfolio solution values for an LP formulated with a scale constraint of one stock-equivalent share and multiply these values by 10,000 to obtain the optimal solution for an LP scaled to 10,000 shares. Thus, the amount of stock-equivalent risk specified in the scale constraint is not important. However, the constraint is necessary to prevent the LP model from finding positively and/or negatively infinite solution values for the components of the portfolio.

Second, in formulating the LP it is important to include the underlying stock as a security that can be bought or sold. One should assume that there is no mispricing in the stock, that its delta is 1.0 and its gamma is zero. In applications involving other option risk measures, such as vega and rho, these risk measures should also be assumed to be zero for the underlying stock. Although there is no potential to profit from mispricing in the stock, in some situations, taking a position in stock, along with positions in options, may be the most cost-effective way to achieve delta- and gamma-neutrality, since it prevents having to buy an over-priced option or sell an under-priced option to meet the portfolio's objectives.

In the remainder of this section two LP portfolio selection models are presented. The first, based on the October 1, 1996 Microsoft data summarized in tables 7.2 through 7.4, ignores transaction costs and assumes that a single volatility estimate applies to the pricing of options of all maturities. The second model, based on the April 5, 2000 Microsoft data that underlies table 7.1, takes the cost of the bid–asked spread into account when trading options and stock and also allows the investor's estimate of underlying stock volatility to depend upon the maturity of each option.

No transaction costs analysis using October 1, 1996 Microsoft data

The first panel of table 7.5 presents solution values for the LP model formulated to find the most profitable portfolio of Microsoft options and stock, as of October 1, 1996, which is delta-neutral, and the second panel provides solution values for the optimal portfolio which is both delta- and gamma-neutral. In both cases, solution values are scaled so that the portfolio has no more than 10,000 shares of stock-equivalent long or short risk.

Table 7.5 Solution values for optimal LP portfolios using October 1, 1996 Microsoft data

Constraint: portfolio delta = 0
  Long 24,644 January 130 puts*
  Short 52,403 October 125 puts
  Value of objective function = $19,660

Constraints: portfolio delta = 0; portfolio gamma = 0
  Long 17,178 October 140 calls
  Long 24,644 January 130 puts
  Short 32,760 October 125 puts
  Value of objective function = $19,537

Constraints: portfolio delta = 0; portfolio gamma = 0; portfolio vega = 0
  Long 5,241 October 140 calls
  Long 7,665 October 135 puts
  Long 13,256 January 130 puts
  Short 32,176 November 125 puts
  Value of objective function = $15,699

Each portfolio takes as its objective function maximizing the total profit from the mispricing of securities in the portfolio. Each portfolio is also selected subject to a scale constraint in which the total portfolio delta associated with stock-equivalently long (or short) positions must equal 10,000.

*Each option is assumed to be issued on one share of stock. Thus a long position in 24,640 puts would be equivalent to 246 exchange-traded puts issued on 100 shares of stock. The optimal LP solution differs slightly from the solution developed earlier in the text due to rounding error in the text solution.

Note that the portfolio that is both delta- and gamma-neutral consists of three security positions, while the delta-neutral portfolio consists of only two securities. This is a common property of optimal portfolios based on LP. Generally, the number of securities in the portfolio will equal the number of binding constraints, inclusive of the scale constraint.

The composition of the gamma- and delta-neutral portfolio is similar to that of the delta-neutral portfolio. Both consist of a long position in January puts on 24,644 shares of stock and a short position in October 125 puts. However, to achieve simultaneous delta- and gamma-neutrality, a long position in October 140 calls on 17,178 shares is substituted for a portion of the short position in October 125 puts. In this particular case, making this substitution has little effect on the profitability of the portfolio; without the gamma constraint, the optimal portfolio has an expected profit of $19,660; with the gamma constraint, the expected profit is $19,537. Thus, in this particular example, going from delta-neutrality to both delta- and gamma-neutrality is almost costless. However, this is an unusual example. Often, adding a requirement of gamma-neutrality on top of a requirement of delta-neutrality can be very costly. In some cases, to achieve neutrality on both dimensions, one may be forced to buy an over-priced option or sell an under-priced option. In such cases, one would want to weigh the benefits from fine-tuning the portfolio's risks against the costs necessary to achieve such fine-tuning before committing to the portfolio.

> LP can be formulated to handle additional constraints including risk constraints, constraints on absolute position sizes and con-straints on relative position sizes. For example, an arbitrageur may want to ensure that the number of shares on which calls are writ-ten does not exceed some multiple of the number of shares held long or the number of options that can be converted to long stock positions through exercise.

The third panel of table 7.5 adds a constraint of vega-neutrality to the delta- and gamma-neutrality constraints. Recall that all model prices are determined using a common implied annual volatility of 0.318. It is possible that all option positions will converge to their theoretical Black–Scholes values, but when convergence takes place, the market's assessment of volatility may be different from 0.318. Imposing a constraint of vega neutrality ensures that there will not be significant adverse changes in the value of the portfolio if the market's assessment of volatility changes while the portfolio is being held.[25]

---

25. The vega neutrality constraint will only provide effective immunization against a change in the market's assessment of volatility if the reassessment does not also

Table 7.5 indicates that the optimal portfolio which is simultaneously vega, gamma- and delta-neutral has a expected profit of $15,699. Thus, imposing the vega constraint reduces portfolio profit by approximately $4,000. The composition of this portfolio is quite a bit different from that which is only delta- and gamma-neutral. Both portfolios include long positions in October 140 calls and January 130 puts, although the position sizes are substantially different in the two portfolios. However, each portfolio includes positions in options that are not included in the other portfolio.

> The forgoing analysis indicates that it is possible to use linear programming to determine the optimal combination of options to achieve a set of risk objectives. Given the linear nature of the objective function, the linear programming model guarantees an optimal solution and should be superior to any "rule-of-thumb" that might be employed by option market practitioners. With linear programming, one can not only determine optimal portfolio composition, but also determine the extent to which imposing additional constraints in portfolio selection reduces potential profit. This information can then be used to make a subjective judgment as to whether the cost associated with the reduction in profit outweighs the benefit of imposing the constraints.

Analysis with bid–asked transaction costs using April 5, 2000 Microsoft data

The following analysis employs bid and asked option and stock prices for Microsoft as of 10:03 am on April 5, 2000 taken from the CBOE's web site, www.cboe.com. Throughout, the risk-free rate of interest is assumed to be 6 percent per year compounded continuously. Tables 7.6 and 7.7 summarize the bid and ask pricing data and provide theoretical prices for each option based the maturity-specific implied volatility that minimizes the sum of squared differences between theoretical and market (average of bid and ask) prices using call and put prices simultaneously.[26]

---

cause the stock price to change. Standard risk-return theory suggests that a change in a stock's systematic or beta risk should be accompanied by a stock price change. A change in beta, in turn, has the potential to change the standard deviation of the stock's return.

26. Theoretical prices are based on the Black–Scholes model for calls and a 100-period binomial model with premature exercise for puts.

Table 7.6 CBOE quotes for Microsoft stock and calls 10:03 am April 5, 2000, and theoretical prices using maturity-specific implied volatilities

Security		Strike	Days	Bid	Ask	B/S price	Long profit	Short profit	Delta	Gamma	Vega
Stock		n/a	n/a	86.9375	87.0000	86.9688	−0.031	−0.031	1.0000	0.0000	0.0000
APR	Call	75	15	13.0000	13.5000	12.6609	−0.839	0.339	0.9031	0.0162	3.0245
APR	Call	80	15	8.7500	9.1250	8.5929	−0.532	0.157	0.7788	0.0281	5.2363
APR	Call	85	15	5.3750	5.7500	5.3410	−0.409	0.034	0.6062	0.0364	6.7828
APR	Call	90	15	3.0000	3.2500	3.0234	−0.227	−0.023	0.4204	0.0370	6.8931
APR	Call	95	15	1.6875	1.7500	1.5580	−0.192	0.130	0.2593	0.0306	5.7103
APR	Call	100	15	0.8750	1.0000	0.7333	−0.267	0.142	0.1428	0.0213	3.9780
APR	Call	105	15	0.5000	0.6875	0.3171	−0.370	0.183	0.0709	0.0128	2.3909
MAY	Call	75	44	14.5000	15.0000	14.3158	−0.684	0.184	0.8024	0.0154	8.3935
MAY	Call	80	44	10.8750	11.3750	10.8087	−0.566	0.066	0.7054	0.0190	10.4117
MAY	Call	85	44	8.0000	8.3750	7.8986	−0.476	0.101	0.5983	0.0214	11.6791
MAY	Call	90	44	5.5000	5.8750	5.5919	−0.283	−0.092	0.4897	0.0220	12.0423
MAY	Call	95	44	3.7500	4.0000	3.8416	−0.158	−0.092	0.3876	0.0212	11.5653
MAY	Call	100	44	2.5625	2.8125	2.5664	−0.246	−0.004	0.2924	0.0191	10.4575
MAY	Call	105	44	1.6250	1.8750	1.6710	−0.204	−0.046	0.2218	0.0164	8.9818

JUL	Call	75	107	17.2500	17.7500	16.8818	-0.868	0.368	0.7494	0.0113	14.9827
JUL	Call	80	107	14.0000	14.5000	13.7496	-0.750	0.250	0.6822	0.0126	16.7910
JUL	Call	85	107	11.2500	11.7500	11.0533	-0.697	0.197	0.6130	0.0136	18.0272
JUL	Call	90	107	9.0000	9.3750	8.7793	-0.596	0.221	0.5442	0.0140	18.6700
JUL	Call	95	107	6.8750	7.2500	6.8966	-0.353	-0.022	0.4778	0.0141	18.7563
JUL	Call	100	107	5.2500	5.6250	5.3641	-0.261	-0.114	0.4154	0.0138	18.3617
JUL	Call	105	107	4.1250	4.5000	4.1350	-0.365	-0.010	0.3580	0.0132	17.5819
OCT	Call	75	198	19.7500	20.2500	20.1950	-0.055	-0.445	0.7500	0.0099	20.3540
OCT	Call	80	198	17.1250	17.2500	17.3585	0.108	-0.233	0.6912	0.0110	22.5591
OCT	Call	85	198	14.1250	14.6250	14.8462	0.221	-0.721	0.6311	0.0118	24.1621
OCT	Call	90	198	11.7500	12.2500	12.6417	0.392	-0.892	0.5712	0.0123	25.1457
OCT	Call	95	198	9.8750	10.2500	10.7230	0.473	-0.848	0.5130	0.0124	25.5404
OCT	Call	100	198	8.3750	8.6250	9.0651	0.440	-0.690	0.4575	0.0124	25.4092
OCT	Call	105	198	6.7500	7.1250	7.6414	0.516	-0.891	0.4055	0.0121	24.8339

All call options are priced using the Black–Scholes option pricing model, assuming $r_a = 0.06$. The volatility used for the pricing of each option is maturity-specific and represents the volatility that minimizes the sum of the squared differences between market (average of bid and ask) and model prices. Volatility (σ_a) solution values APR = 0.59958, MAY = 0.55086, JUL = 0.50265, and OCT = 0.46583. The Black–Scholes stock price is the average of the bid and the offer. Long profit is the profit if the option or stock is purchased at the ask price and sold at the Black–Scholes price. Short profit is the profit if the option or stock is sold at the bid price and purchased at the Black–Scholes price.

Table 7.7 CBOE quotes for Microsoft puts 10:03 am April 5, 2000, and theoretical prices using maturity-specific implied volatilities

Security		Strike	Days	Bid	Ask	Binomial price	Long profit	Short profit	Delta	Gamma	Vega
APR	Put	75	15	0.4375	0.5625	0.5115	−0.051	−0.074	−0.0969	0.0162	3.0245
APR	Put	80	15	1.3125	1.3750	1.4270	0.052	−0.114	−0.2212	0.0281	5.2363
APR	Put	85	15	2.8750	3.0000	3.1821	0.182	−0.307	−0.3938	0.0364	6.7828
APR	Put	90	15	5.3750	5.7500	5.8494	0.099	−0.474	−0.5796	0.0370	6.8931
APR	Put	95	15	8.7500	9.2500	9.3936	0.144	−0.644	−0.7407	0.0306	5.7103
APR	Put	100	15	13.0000	13.5000	13.5884	0.088	−0.588	−0.8572	0.0213	3.9780
APR	Put	105	15	17.8750	18.1250	18.2009	0.076	−0.326	−0.9291	0.0128	2.3909
MAY	Put	75	44	1.8125	2.0625	1.8119	−0.251	−0.001	−0.1976	0.0154	8.3935
MAY	Put	80	44	3.1250	3.3750	3.2958	−0.079	−0.171	−0.2946	0.0190	10.4117
May	Put	85	44	5.0000	5.2500	5.3568	0.107	−0.357	−0.4017	0.0214	11.6791
MAY	Put	90	44	7.6250	8.0000	8.0480	0.048	−0.423	−0.5103	0.0220	12.0423
MAY	Put	95	44	10.7500	11.2500	11.2801	0.030	−0.530	−0.6124	0.0212	11.5653
MAY	Put	100	44	14.5000	15.0000	15.0348	0.035	−0.535	−0.7026	0.0191	10.4575
MAY	Put	105	44	18.6250	19.1250	19.1630	0.038	−0.538	−0.7782	0.0164	8.9818

JUL	Put	75	107	3.5000	3.7500	3.6617	-0.088	-0.162	-0.2506	0.0113	14.9827
JUL	Put	80	107	5.1250	5.2500	5.4764	0.226	-0.351	-0.3178	0.0126	16.7910
JUL	Put	85	107	7.1250	7.5000	7.7305	0.231	-0.606	-0.3870	0.0136	18.0272
JUL	Put	90	107	9.7500	10.1250	10.4199	0.295	-0.670	-0.4558	0.0140	18.6700
JUL	Put	95	107	13.0000	13.5000	13.5191	0.019	-0.519	-0.5222	0.0141	18.7563
JUL	Put	100	107	16.3750	16.8750	16.9882	0.113	-0.613	-0.5846	0.0138	18.3617
JUL	Put	105	107	20.1250	20.6250	20.7802	0.155	-0.655	-0.6420	0.0132	17.5819
OCT	Put	75	198	5.1250	5.5000	5.2384	-0.262	-0.113	-0.2644	0.0085	20.9572
OCT	Put	80	198	7.0000	7.1250	7.2076	0.083	-0.208	-0.3143	0.0092	22.7335
OCT	Put	85	198	9.2500	9.5000	9.5563	0.056	-0.306	-0.3645	0.0098	24.0663
OCT	Put	90	198	11.5000	12.0000	12.2703	0.270	-0.770	-0.4141	0.0101	24.9598
OCT	Put	95	198	14.6250	15.1250	15.3061	0.181	-0.681	-0.4624	0.0103	25.4402
OCT	Put	100	198	17.8750	18.3750	18.6256	0.251	-0.751	-0.5086	0.0104	25.5480
OCT	Put	105	198	21.5000	22.0000	22.1973	0.197	-0.697	-0.5526	0.0103	25.3319

All put options are priced using a 100-period binomial American put pricing model assuming $r_a = 0.06$. The volatility used for the pricing of each option is maturity-specific and represents the volatility that minimizes the sum of the squared differences between market (average of bid and ask) and model prices. Volatility (σ_a) solution values are APR = 0.59958, MAY = 0.55086, JUL = 0.50265, and OCT = 0.46583. Long profit is the profit if the option is purchased at the ask price and sold at the binomial price. Short profit is the profit if the option is sold at the bid price and purchased at the binomial price.

With just a few exceptions, the entries in tables 7.6 and 7.7 show that very little profit could be made by purchasing options at ask prices and subsequently selling at theoretical prices, assuming the market corrects to theoretical prices based on each maturity-specific volatility estimate. Similarly, little profit could be made by selling calls or puts at bid prices and subsequently reversing positions by purchasing the same options at the theoretical price after a market correction. Therefore, in order to profit by purchasing or selling mispriced options, one must be able to forecast volatility more accurately that the volatility forecasts implied in the market prices of the call and put options.

Assume that you believe the market has overreacted to events in Microsoft. Despite recent events, you expect that the volatility of Microsoft stock will be a constant 50 percent per year through each option maturity date. Tables 7.8 and 7.9 summarize the pricing of Microsoft options and the potential profit from trading off pricing errors based on the 50 percent volatility estimate.

With the 50 percent volatility estimate, tables 7.8 and 7.9 show that the April and May options are somewhat over-priced while the July and October options are somewhat under-priced. Although the price discrepancies are not huge, it does appear that a trader could take advantage of the mispricing even after buying options at ask prices and writing options at bids.

Table 7.10 presents LP solution values assuming that the total delta of stock-equivalently long (or short) positions equals 10,000. As in Table 7.5, the first panel provides solution values for a portfolio constrained to be delta-neutral, the second panel provides solution values for a portfolio constrained to be both delta- and gamma-neutral, and the third panel adds a vega-neutrality constraint.

Note how the imposition of constraints reduces the potential profitability of the optimal portfolio. If the only constraint is a delta-neutrality constraint, the portfolio's expected profit is $131,100. However, if a gamma-neutrality constraint is added, the expected profit falls to $58,067. Similarly, if a vega-neutraility constraint is included, along with a delta- and gamma-neutrality requirement, the portfolio's expected profit falls to $37,881. Unlike the previous LP example using October 1, 1996 data, adding risk constraints beyond the delta-neutrality constraint significantly reduces the portfolio's profit potential. Therefore, an options investor, knowing the potential reduction in profit associated with each additional constraint, might want to evaluate whether imposing the additional constraints is cost-effective. Although each additional constraint reduces portfolio risk, the risk–reward tradeoff may not work in the investor's favor in this particular example.

As an aside, generally one would expect four securities to enter the optimal portfolio in the third panel of table 7.10. However, only three securities enter the optimal solution in the third panel. The reason is rather subtle.

An examination of the mathematical expressions for gamma and vega from chapter 6 reveals that vega is directly proportional to gamma, and that a portfolio of options *of the same maturity* that has a gamma of zero will also have a vega of zero.

$$\Gamma = \frac{\partial^2 P}{\partial S^2} = \frac{N'(d1)}{S\sigma_a\sqrt{\tau}} \quad \text{for calls and puts}$$

$$(6.3)$$

$$vega = \frac{\partial P}{\partial \sigma_a} = S\sqrt{\tau}N'(d1) \quad \text{for calls and puts}$$

$$= \Gamma S^2 \sigma_a \tau$$

$$(6.5)$$

Therefore, when all options in the optimal portfolio *have the same maturity*, the constraints setting vega and gamma to zero are redundant, and one fewer security than normal is needed to simultaneously satisfy the constraints of the LP.

7.3   Summary

The key to using the Black–Scholes model in the valuation of stock options is making an accurate estimate of the volatility of the underlying stock. The volatility estimate that causes the theoretical price of an option to equal its observed market price is called the option's implied volatility. In principle, if the Black–Scholes and related models accurately describe the pricing of exchange traded options, all options issued on the same underlying stock should have roughly the same implied volatility. Moreover, it is possible to find a single volatility estimate that does the best job fitting observed market prices of options to their corresponding theoretical values.

To the extent that an investor can predict volatility more accurately than implied estimates, there is money to be made by trading off significant discrepancies in the pricing of options. Often professional traders engaged in options arbitrage are confident that they can identify over and under-priced options but do not want to take positions in options that risk loss from an adverse movement in the price of the underlying stock. To guard against such risk, options arbitrageurs often set up "delta-neutral" portfolios that,

Table 7.8   CBOE quotes for Microsoft stock and calls 10:03 am April 5, 2000, using a volatility estimate of 0.50

Security		Strike	Days	Bid	Ask	B/S price	Long profit	Short profit	Delta	Gamma	Vega
Stock		n/a	n/a	86.9375	87.0000	86.9688	-0.031	-0.031	1.0000	0.0000	0.0000
APR	Call	75	15	13.0000	13.5000	12.4011	-1.099	0.599	0.9377	0.0139	2.1629
APR	Call	80	15	8.7500	9.1250	8.0965	-1.029	0.654	0.8157	0.0302	4.6953
APR	Call	85	15	5.3750	5.7500	4.6683	-1.082	0.707	0.6183	0.0433	6.7222
APR	Call	90	15	3.0000	3.2500	2.3414	-0.909	0.659	0.3963	0.0437	6.7944
APR	Call	95	15	1.6875	1.7500	1.0165	-0.734	0.671	0.2129	0.0330	5.1220
APR	Call	100	15	0.8750	1.0000	0.3831	-0.617	0.492	0.0964	0.0194	3.0116
APR	Call	105	15	0.5000	0.6875	0.1264	-0.561	0.374	0.0372	0.0092	1.4329
MAY	Call	75	44	14.5000	15.0000	13.9231	-1.077	0.577	0.8368	0.0163	7.4427
MAY	Call	80	44	10.8750	11.3750	10.2936	-1.081	0.581	0.7289	0.0219	10.0038
MAY	Call	85	44	8.0000	8.3750	7.3058	-1.069	0.694	0.6027	0.0255	11.6448
MAY	Call	90	44	5.5000	5.8750	4.9802	-0.895	0.520	0.4725	0.0264	12.0177
MAY	Call	95	44	3.7500	4.0000	3.2661	-0.734	0.484	0.3518	0.0246	11.2058
MAY	Call	100	44	2.5625	2.8125	2.0656	-0.747	0.497	0.2496	0.0210	9.5869
MAY	Call	105	44	1.6250	1.8750	1.2633	-0.612	0.362	0.1693	0.0167	7.6215

JUL	Call	75	107	17.2500	17.7500	16.8440	-0.906	0.406	0.7725	0.0128	14.2091
JUL	Call	80	107	14.0000	14.5000	13.7058	-0.794	0.294	0.6946	0.0149	16.5041
JUL	Call	85	107	11.2500	11.7500	11.0055	-0.745	0.245	0.6121	0.0163	18.0381
JUL	Call	90	107	9.0000	9.3750	8.7296	-0.645	0.270	0.5294	0.0169	18.7343
JUL	Call	95	107	6.8750	7.2500	6.8471	-0.403	0.028	0.4499	0.0168	18.6369
JUL	Call	100	107	5.2500	5.6250	5.3166	-0.308	0.067	0.3762	0.0161	17.8737
JUL	Call	105	107	4.1250	4.5000	4.0908	-0.409	-0.034	0.3101	0.0150	16.6140
OCT	Call	75	198	19.7500	20.2500	20.1950	-0.055	-0.445	0.7500	0.0099	20.3540
OCT	Call	80	198	17.1250	17.2500	17.3585	-0.108	-0.233	0.6912	0.0110	22.5591
OCT	Call	85	198	14.1250	14.6250	14.8462	0.221	-0.721	0.6311	0.0118	24.1621
OCT	Call	90	198	11.7500	12.2500	12.6417	0.392	-0.892	0.5712	0.0123	25.1457
OCT	Call	95	198	9.8750	10.2500	10.7230	0.473	-0.848	0.5130	0.0124	25.5404
OCT	Call	100	198	8.3750	8.6250	9.0651	0.440	-0.690	0.4575	0.0124	25.4092
OCT	Call	105	198	6.7500	7.1250	7.6414	0.516	-0.891	0.4055	0.0121	24.8339

The Black–Sholes stock price is the average of the bid and the offer. Long profit is the profit if the option or stock is purchased at the ask price and sold at the Black–Scholes price. Short profit is the profit if the option or stock is sold at the bid price and purchased at the Black–Sholes price. All options priced with $\sigma_a = 0.5$.

Table 7.9 CBOE quotes for Microsoft puts 10:03 am. April 5, 2000, using a volatility estimate of 0.50

Security		Strike	Days	Bid	Ask	Binomial price	Long profit	Short profit	Delta	Gamma	Vega
APR	Put	75	15	0.4375	0.5625	0.2459	−0.317	0.192	−0.0623	0.0139	2.1629
APR	Put	80	15	1.3125	1.3750	0.9363	−0.439	0.376	−0.1843	0.0302	4.6953
APR	Put	85	15	2.8750	3.0000	2.5040	−0.496	0.371	−0.3817	0.0433	6.7222
APR	Put	90	15	5.3750	5.7500	5.1706	−0.579	0.204	−0.6037	0.0437	6.7944
APR	Put	95	15	8.7500	9.2500	8.8650	−0.385	−0.115	−0.7871	0.0330	5.1220
APR	Put	100	15	13.0000	13.5000	13.2609	−0.239	−0.261	−0.9036	0.0194	3.0116
APR	Put	105	15	17.8750	18.1250	18.0548	−0.070	−0.180	−0.9628	0.0092	1.4329
MAY	Put	75	44	1.8125	2.0625	1.4138	−0.649	0.399	−0.1632	0.0163	7.4427
MAY	Put	80	44	3.1250	3.3750	2.7484	−0.627	0.377	−0.2711	0.0219	10.0038
MAY	Put	85	44	5.0000	5.2500	4.7244	−0.526	0.276	−0.3973	0.0255	11.6448
MAY	Put	90	44	7.6250	8.0000	7.3629	−0.637	0.262	−0.5275	0.0264	12.0177
MAY	Put	95	44	10.7500	11.2500	10.6127	−0.637	0.137	−0.6482	0.0246	11.2058
MAY	Put	100	44	14.5000	15.0000	14.3762	−0.624	0.124	−0.7504	0.0210	9.5869
MAY	Put	105	44	18.6250	19.1250	18.5379	−0.587	0.087	−0.8307	0.0167	7.6215

JUL	Put	75	107	3.5000	3.7500	3.5676	−0.182	−0.068	−0.2275	0.0128	14.2091
JUL	Put	80	107	5.1250	5.2500	5.3422	0.092	−0.217	−0.3054	0.0149	16.5041
JUL	Put	85	107	7.1250	7.5000	7.5547	0.055	−0.430	−0.3879	0.0163	18.0381
JUL	Put	90	107	9.7500	10.1250	10.1916	0.067	−0.442	−0.4706	0.0169	18.7343
JUL	Put	95	107	13.0000	13.5000	13.2220	−0.278	−0.222	−0.5501	0.0168	18.6369
JUL	Put	100	107	16.3750	16.8750	16.6043	−0.271	−0.229	−0.6238	0.0161	17.8737
JUL	Put	105	107	20.1250	20.6250	20.2914	−0.334	−0.166	−0.6899	0.0150	16.6140
OCT	Put	75	198	5.1250	5.5000	5.8245	0.324	−0.699	−0.2500	0.0099	20.3540
OCT	Put	80	198	7.0000	7.1250	7.8278	0.703	−0.828	−0.3088	0.0110	22.5591
OCT	Put	85	198	9.2500	9.5000	10.1554	0.655	−0.905	−0.3689	0.0118	24.1621
OCT	Put	90	198	11.5000	12.0000	12.7908	0.791	−1.291	−0.4288	0.0123	25.1457
OCT	Put	95	198	14.6250	15.1250	15.7120	0.587	−1.087	−0.4870	0.0124	25.5404
OCT	Put	100	198	17.8750	18.3750	18.8940	0.519	−1.019	−0.5425	0.0124	25.4092
OCT	Put	105	198	21.5000	22.0000	22.3102	0.310	−0.810	−0.5945	0.0121	24.8339

Long profit is the profit if the option is purchased at the ask price and sold at the binomial price. Short profit is the profit if the option is sold at the bid price and purchased at the binomial price. All options priced with $\sigma_a = 0.5$.

Table 7.10   Solution values for optimal LP portfolios using April 5, 2000 Microsoft data

---

Constraint: portfolio delta = 0
   Short 268,625 April 105 calls*
   Short 160,511 April 75 puts
   Value of objective function = $131,100

Constraints: portfolio delta = 0; portfolio gamma = 0
   Short 62,079 April 105 calls
   Long 24,660 October 105 puts
   Long 24,901 October 80 puts
   Value of objective function = $58,067

Constraints: portfolio delta = 0; portfolio gamma = 0; portfolio vega = 0
   Long 46.992 April 95 calls
   Short 208,017 April 105 calls
   Long 12,241 April 80 puts
   Value of objective function = $37,881

Each portfolio takes as its objective function maximizing the total profit from the mispricing of securities in the portfolio, assuming all options are purchased at ask prices and sold at bid prices. Each portfolio is also selected subject to a scale constraint in which the total portfolio delta associated with stock-equivalently long (or short) positions must equal 10,000.

*Each option is assumed to be issued on one share of stock. Thus a long position in 268,625 calls would be equivalent to 2,686 exchange-traded calls issued on 100 shares of stock.

theoretically, are immunized against an adverse regular price movement in the underlying stock. Arbitrageurs can also impose risk constraints that immunize the option portfolio against large stock price changes and/or changes in the market's estimate of volatility. Linear programming can be used to determine the optimal composition of an options portfolio that is subject to various risk constraints. By solving the LP problem for various combinations of constraints, the investor can determine the extent to which a given constraint reduces the portfolio's potential profitability and then determine whether the imposition of the constraint is cost effective.

REFERENCES

Black, F. and M. Scholes, "The Pricing of Options and Corporate Liabilities." *The Journal of Political Economy* 81 (May/June 1973), 637–59.

Dennis, P. J., "Optimal No-Arbitrage Bounds on S&P500 Index Options and the Volatility Smile." Working paper, McIntire School of Commerce, The University of Virginia (September 4, 1996).

Derman, E. and I. Kanai, "Riding on a Smile." *Risk* 7 (February 1994), 32–9.

Dumas, B., J. Fleming and R. E. Whaley, "Implied Volatility Functions: Empirical Tests." *Journal of Finance* 53 (December 1998), 2059–106.

Heston, S., "A Closed-Form Solution for Options with Stochastic Volatility with Applications to Bond and Currency Options." *Review of Financial Studies* 6 (No. 2, 1993), 327–44.

Hull., J. C. and A. White, "The Pricing of Options on Assets with Stochastic Volatilities." *Journal of Finance* 42 (June 1987), 281–300.

Latané, H. A. and R. J. Rendleman, Jr., "Standard Deviations of Stock Price Ratios Implied in Option Prices." *Journal of Finance* 31 (May 1976), 369–81.

MacBeth, J. D. and L. J. Merville, "An Empirical Examination of the Black–Scholes Option Pricing Model." *Journal of Finance* 34 (December 1979), 1173–86.

Manaster, S. and R. J. Rendleman, Jr., "Option Prices as Predictors of Equilibrium Stock Prices." *Journal of Finance* 37 (September 1982), 1043–57.

Merton, R. C., "Theory of Rational Option Pricing." *The Bell Journal of Economics and Management Science* (Spring, 1973), 141–83.

Rendleman, R. J., Jr., "An LP Approach to Option Portfolio Selection." *Advances in Futures and Options Research* 8 (1995), 31–52.

Rubinstein, M., "Nonparametric Tests of Alternative Option Pricing Models Using All Reported Trades and Quotes on the 30 Most Active CBOE Option Classes from August 23, 1976 through August 31, 1978." *Journal of Finance* 40 (June 1985), 455–80.

Rubinstein, M., "Implied Binomial Trees." *Journal of Finance* 49 (July 1994), 771–818.

RELATED WORK

Chiras, D. and S. Manaster, "The Information Content of Option Prices and a Test of Market Efficiency." *Journal of Financial Economics* 6 (June/September 1978), 213–34.

QUESTIONS AND PROBLEMS

1. You observe a market price of \$6$\frac{5}{8}$ for a call option with a striking price of \$50. The option has exactly 0.5 years until it matures. The price of the underlying stock is \$53, the stock pays no dividend, and the risk-free rate of interest is 0.06 per year compounded continuously.

    Using the Excel program Black_Scholes.xls from the website-http://www.rendleman.com/book, estimate the option's implied volatility.

2. Consider the following table of option values and implied volatilities for calls listed on ABC stock. Presently, the price of ABC stock is $100 per share and the risk-free rate of interest is 5 percent per year compounded continuously. Each call option expires in 73 days. Assume that all options can be bought or sold at the prices shown in the table.

	Call options on ABC stock	
Market price	Striking price	Implied volatility
40.65	60	0.50
20.99	80	0.30
5.83	100	0.30
0.69	120	0.30

Note that the first call option is priced with an implied volatility of 0.50 whereas all the other options are priced with a 0.30 implied volatility. Based on these prices and implied volatilities, one can reasonably infer that the market is pricing ABC options as if the volatility of returns for XYZ is 0.30 per year. Therefore, is it necessarily the case that the first option listed is a good candidate to sell against a long position in one of the others? Briefly discuss.

3. The following information applies to pricing of call and put options on Microsoft stock as of September 13, 1999. At that time, the price of Microsoft stock was $94. All the options in the table are priced as if the risk-free interest rate is 0.05 per year compounded continuously and the standard deviation of the logarithmic return of the underlying stock is 0.35.

Maturity	Strike	Type	Years	Market price	Model price	Delta
10/15/99	92.5	Call	0.0877	5.0000	4.8722	0.5985
10/15/99	92.5	Call	0.0877	3.7500	3.6113	0.4968
10/15/99	100.0	Call	0.0877	1.8750	1.8176	0.3075
10/15/99	92.5	Put	0.0877	3.2500	2.9676	−0.4015
10/15/99	95.0	Put	0.0877	4.3750	4.1958	−0.5032
10/15/99	100.0	Put	0.0877	7.5000	7.3802	−0.6925
1/21/00	95.0	Call	0.3562	8.500	8.1338	0.5553
1/21/00	95.0	Put	0.3562	7.750	7.4570	−0.4447

Using the data above, determine the most profitable delta-neutral portfolio in Microsoft options subject to the constraint that the stock-equivalently long side of the portfolio cannot exceed 1,000 shares of stock-equivalent risk. In your answer make sure that you properly identify each option in the portfolio, that you indicate the quantity of each option that enters the portfolio and that you indicate for each option in the portfolio whether you are long or short. Assume each option is issued on one share of stock.

4. On the website http://www.rendleman.com/book, you will find an Excel file called Msft_Project.xls. This file contains the April 5, 2000 data and programs used to produce tables 7.6 through 7.10 but does not contain the LP formulation.

Note that in this file, the user (you) is estimating volatility to be 0.55 for April options, 0.50 for May options, 0.45 for July options and 0.43 for October options. Based on these estimates, theoretical prices based on the Black–Scholes model (for calls) and the binomial model (for puts) have been calculated and appear in the column labeled "Theoretical Price."

The objective of this exercise is to solve the same type of linear programming problem, whose solution is summarized in table 7.10, using the modified volatility estimates. You will need to use Excel's Solver program, accessed in the tools menu of Excel, to solve this problem. Solver has already been set up within the Excel worksheet to solve a general linear programming problem using decision variables (quantities of each option to buy or sell) constrained to equal or exceed zero. However, you must formulate the linear programming problem within the worksheet, and then provide an objective function for Solver along with appropriate delta, gamma and vega and scale constraints.

To set up the LP, you must create two additional columns within the worksheet. The first defines the quantity that you will be long for each option and the second the quantity you will be short. Within Solver, these are the decision variables that must be changed in order to find an optimal solution.

Your job is to do whatever is necessary within the worksheet and within solver to solve the following LP problems:

Problem 1

Maximize portfolio profit

Subject to:

Total delta of stock-equivalently long positions equals 100*

Portfolio delta = 0.

Problem 2

Maximize portfolio profit

Subject to:

Total delta of stock-equivalently long positions equals 100
Portfolio delta = 0
Portfolio gamma = 0

Problem 3

Maximize portfolio profit

Subject to:

Total delta of stock-equivalently long positions equals 100
Portfolio delta = 0
Portfolio gamma = 0
Portfolio vega = 0

*Total delta of long stock, long calls and short puts.

You can check the accuracy of your analysis by using a volatility estimate of 0.5 for all option maturities, the same estimate used to produce table 7.10. Your optimal position sizes and resulting portfolio profit should be 1/100 of those shown in table 7.10, since your portfolio is constrained to have a total delta for stock-equivalently long positions equal to 100, compared with 10,000 in table 7.10.

8

Option Investing from a Risk–Return Perspective[27]

8.1 Introduction

Typically, the binomial and Black–Scholes option pricing models are derived using no-arbitrage arguments based on the theory of option replication. However, it is also possible to derive both models using the risk–return theory of the Sharpe (1964)–Lintner (1965) Capital Asset Pricing Model (CAPM). The appendix to chapter 3 shows how the binomial model can be derived using the CAPM as the starting point. And although rarely cited, Black and Scholes also provide a CAPM-based derivation of their option pricing model in their original (1973) paper.

Both CAPM-based derivations are built upon the idea that an option's instantaneous expected return should be the same as that which is implied by the CAPM. According to the Black–Scholes derivation, an option's instantaneous beta is given by $\beta_{option} = \beta_{stock}(\partial P/\partial S) \cdot S/P$, where P is the option's price and S is the price of the underlying stock. Although this beta should change continuously with the passage of time and as the price of the underlying stock changes, at any moment, an option's immediate expected return should be equal to that which is predicted by the CAPM. Omitting the mathematical details, this line of reasoning leads to the Black–Scholes partial differential equation and, ultimately, to the same pricing equation derived via the no-arbitrage approach.

> Although the relationship between option pricing theory and the CAPM should be obvious to those who understand both, it is my firm belief that the principle of risk and return as it applies to

---

27. Much of the material in this chapter is taken directly from Rendleman (1999) with permission from the publisher.

Box cont'd

option pricing is not well understood.[28] Once understood, some conventional notions about the return prospects of some common option-based investment strategies must be drastically revised. In essence, when viewed in a risk–return context, there should be no investment strategy involving options that should decrease risk and simultaneously increase expected return (e.g., covered call writing as viewed by some investors). Efficient capital markets just don't work that way. There should be no "free lunch" in the stock market, bond market, option market, or any other market in which pricing is efficient.

8.2   Examples of the Risk–return Principle Applied to Common Option Investments

In this section, a set of examples is presented to illustrate the risk–return principle as applied to binomial option pricing. All examples are based on a common set of pricing parameters summarized in table 8.1.

Expected returns from buying and writing calls

Figure 8.1 shows the evolution of the binomial price for a three-period call with a striking price of $100 issued on a stock, initially worth $100 per share, and the expected return from holding the call over each binomial period. In each period the probability associated with an up movement in the underlying stock is 0.50, and the up and down returns per dollar invested for the stock are $u = 1.3$ and $d = 0.8$, respectively, implying an expected stock return of $0.5(1.3) + 0.5(0.8) - 1 = 0.05$ per binomial period. The riskless interest rate is 0.02 per period.

The entries in figure 8.1 show that the expected return of the call option is higher than that of the stock in each binomial state. At any point in time, the expected return of the call is lower in the states for which the option is more in-the-money. Stated differently, the option's expected return will approach that of the underlying stock as the option becomes more stock-like. Therefore, in the states for which the stock price is the highest, in

---

28. Cox and Rubinstein (1985), pages 185–96, show that the expected return of an option that is priced according to the binomial model is also consistent with CAPM pricing but do not derive the binomial model using the CAPM. They also point out that the standard arbitrage-based derivation of the binomial model does not require the underlying stock to be priced according to the CAPM.

Table 8.1 Parameters for binomial pricing examples

Initial stock price	$100
Up factor (u)	1.3
Down factor (d)	0.8
True probability associated with up return (θ)	0.5
Stock's beta	1.0
Riskless interest rate per period (r)	0.02
Option maturity	3 binomial periods
Option strike price	$100

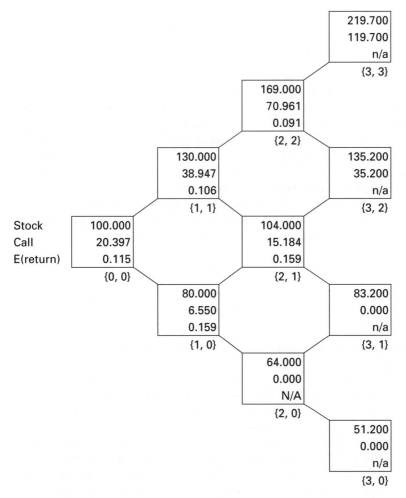

Figure 8.1 Expected returns from a long call option ($100 striking price)

which it is less likely that the call will end up out-of-the-money, expected returns are the lowest. Also, the option's expected return tends to increase as its maturity gets closer, thereby decreasing the probability that an out-of-the money call will end up in-the-money.

The expected returns shown in figure 8.1 depend only on the assumption that the stock's up and down returns are equally likely to occur. However, the expected returns could also be calculated in each state using the CAPM. Consider, for example, the initial state $\{0, 0\}$. To compute the option's CAPM-based expected return, the option's beta must first be computed. According to Black and Scholes, an option's beta is given by:

$$\beta_{option} = \beta_{stock} \frac{\partial P}{\partial S} \cdot \frac{S}{P}$$

(8.1)

where P is the option's price and S is the price of the underlying stock. The binomial equivalent to $\partial P / \partial S$, also known as *delta*, is $\Delta_{t,j} = (P_{t+1,j+1} - P_{t+1,j})/(S_{t+1,j+1} - S_{t+1,j})$. Therefore, the binomial-based beta for the call option in state $\{t, j\}$ is $\beta_{option} = \beta_{stock}((P_{t+1,j+1} - P_{t+1,j})/(S_{t+1,j+1} - S_{t+1,j})) \cdot (S_{t,j}/P_{t,j})$. Assuming the beta for the underlying stock in the binomial pricing examples is 1.0, the option's beta in the initial state is $\beta_{call} = 1.0((38.947 - 6.550)/(130 - 80)) \cdot (100/20.397) = 3.1766$. Using the option's beta of 3.1766 in connection with the CAPM, along with a risk-free rate of 0.02 and an expected market return of 0.05 (with a beta of 1, the stock and market should have the same expected return), the CAPM-based expected return for the call option is:

$$E(r_{call}) = r + \beta_{call}(E[r_m] - r)$$
$$= 0.02 + 3.1766(0.05 - 0.02)$$
$$= 0.1153,$$

the same value calculated using the option values in figure 8.1

Generalizing from this example, it can be shown that any call option should have a beta that is greater, in absolute value, than that of its underlying stock. Depending on the terms of the option, the option's beta can be very high in relation to that of the stock. Assuming the beta for the underlying stock is positive, the expected return from a long call option position should be much higher than that of its underlying stock. But the high expected return simply reflects that a long position in a call option exposes

Box cont'd

an investor to much higher-than-average systematic or market risk. If a call option is held as part of a larger stock portfolio, its inclusion in the portfolio would exacerbate the non-diversifiable risks from holding stock, and risk-averse investors should require a high expected return to bear this increased risk. Thus, there is no bargain here, just more risk.

It should be noted that an option's beta will change in each binomial state, or more generally, the beta of an option will change with the passage of time and as the price of the underlying stock changes. At any point in time, however, the option's immediate, or instantaneous, expected return should be consistent with that predicted by the CAPM. In the context of the binomial model, "immediate" or "instantaneous" means the next binomial period. But even if the stock itself is not priced in accordance with the CAPM, the mathematics of leverage imply the following CAPM-type expected return relationship between the option and its underlying stock:[29]

$$E(r_{option}) = r + \beta_{P,S}(E[r_{stock}] - r),$$

where $\beta_{P,S} = (\partial P / \partial S) \cdot S / P$ for Black–Scholes, and

$$\beta_{P,S} = \left(\frac{P_{t+1,j+1} - P_{t+1,j}}{S_{t+1,j+1} - S_{t+1,j}} \right) \cdot \frac{S}{P} \text{ for the binomial model.}$$

Getting back to the example, suppose one were to write the same call option. Since the expected return from buying the call is very positive, the expected profit from writing the call must be very negative. Inasmuch as call writing involves a negative investment, it is impossible to compute an expected return from a pure call writing position. Nevertheless, given the zero-sum nature of option contracting, it is clear that, on average, one should expect to lose when writing calls.

---

29. Beginning with Fama and French (1992), there is a significant amount of empirical evidence indicating that the CAPM does a poor job in capturing the risk–return relationship in stock market returns and that other proxies for risk such as size and book-to-market ratios seem to correlate more highly with actual stock market returns. Nevertheless, the mathematics of leverage, upon which the binomial and Black–Scholes models are based, imply a CAPM-like pricing relationship between the stock and its options, even though the CAPM may not capture the pricing of the underlying stock in relation to the market.

If call writing produces losses, why should anyone bother to engage in call writing? The answer is very simple. When calls are written in connection with a larger portfolio of stocks, the inclusion of the call writing position should reduce the portfolio's overall systematic risk. As such, risk-averse investors should be willing to pay for this type of risk reduction by accepting an expected loss when writing calls. Therefore, the potential for this type of risk reduction causes the average profit from writing a call to be negative.

Expected returns from covered call writing

Figure 8.2 illustrates the risk-reduction principle in connection with covered call writing. It shows that the expected return from covered call writing is less than that of the stock in all states in which the call has positive value. Essentially, writing the call reduces the risk of holding the stock and, therefore, should reduce the expected return.

The expected return from covered call writing can also be computed *vis-à-vis* the CAPM. Recall that the beta of the call option is 3.1766 in the initial state. The total investment required for covered call writing is the stock price of $100 less the option price of $20.397, or $79.603. With covered call writing, the proportion $100/$79.603 = 1.2562 is invested in the stock and the proportion $-$20.397/$79.603 = -0.2562$ is invested in the call option. The portfolio's beta is the sum of the betas of each of its components weighted by the respective portfolio proportions, or $1.0(1.2562) + 3.1766(-0.2562) = 0.4424$. Therefore, the portfolio's CAPM-based expected return in the initial state is:

$$E(r_{port}) = r + \beta_{port}(E[r_m] - r)$$
$$= 0.02 + 0.4424(0.05 - 0.02)$$
$$= 0.0333$$

the same value shown in figure 8.2.

I continue to be amazed by professional investors and sales people who do not understand that covered call writing is a risk-reducing strategy and, therefore, should decrease the expected return from holding stock. A standard argument in favor of fully-covered call writing is that the proceeds from writing the call produce additional income which can increase the return from holding stock. Alternatively, if an investor has decided to sell the stock, some investors feel that writing the call can only enhance the overall return. But these arguments ignore the risk-reducing aspect of

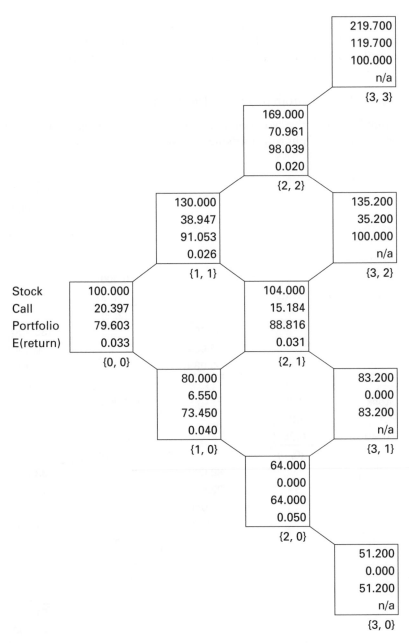

Figure 8.2 Expected returns from covered call writing ($100 striking price)

covered call writing which should cause the overall expected return from covered call writing to be lower than that of an unhedged stock position, regardless of one's motivation for writing calls in the first place.

Expected returns from buying and writing puts

Figure 8.3 shows the evolution of the binomial price and expected return for a three-period put with a striking price of $100 issued on the same stock

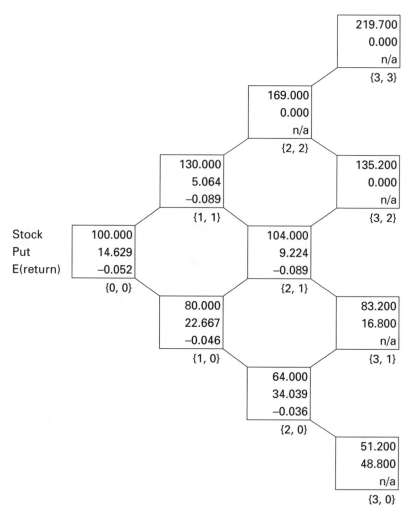

Figure 8.3   Expected returns from a long put option ($100 striking price)

as the previous examples. Note that the put's expected return is negative in all states, and becomes more negative as the put gets out-of-the-money and closer to maturity.

Drawing on CAPM-based pricing theory, if the underlying stock has a positive beta, a put should have a negative beta, and, therefore, an expected return less than the risk-free rate of interest. Although in some limited cases a put's expected return could turn out to be positive (but less than the risk-free rate), for most puts, the expected return will be negative, as is the case throughout figure 8.3.

In the initial binomial state of figure 8.3, the put's beta is:

$$\beta_{put} = \beta_{stock} \left(\frac{P_{t+1,j+1} - P_{t+1,j}}{S_{t+1,j+1} - S_{t+1,j}} \right) \cdot \frac{S}{P}$$

$$= 1.0 \left(\frac{5.064 - 22.667}{130 - 80} \right) \left(\frac{100}{14.629} \right)$$

$$= -2.4066$$

Substituting this beta into the CAPM yields the following expected return for the put option in the initial state:

$$E(r_{put}) = r + \beta_{put}(E[r_m] - r)$$

$$= 0.02 - 2.4066(0.05 - 0.02)$$

$$= -0.0522,$$

the same value shown in figure 8.3.

How could a rational investor purchase a put option knowing that, on average, it should be a losing proposition? To shed light on this issue, I will pose some additional questions. What returns does one generally expect from purchasing life insurance, automobile liability insurance and homeowners policies? And what do these forms of insurance have in common?

First, these forms of insurance protect against large non-diversifiable losses which most people, either by law or willingly, wish to avoid. Generally, people in good heath who purchase term life insurance do not expect to make money off the insurance company. Most conscientious drivers don't expect to earn a profit from purchasing automobile liability and collision insurance policies, and most homeowners don't expect to profit from insurance claims against their homeowners policies. If they do expect to profit, they might believe that the risks being insured are greater than those expected by the insurance companies. However, it is more likely that they have performed a faulty analysis and never stopped to consider how the insurance companies could possibly stay in business, covering both the risks of writing insurance and significant overhead costs, if the buyers of insurance, on average, came out ahead. Thus, from casual observation of insurance practice, we can conclude that rational people enter into insurance contracts, expecting to lose, because they can sleep better at night knowing that they will never have to face catastrophic financial losses. Economists would say that insurance increases "expected utility" and is, therefore, worth the price of an expected loss. Readers of this chapter can think of the same concept in terms of sleep. If insurance makes you sleep better, then it could be rational to pay a premium to rest well.

> Put options are pure forms of stock insurance but without the significant overhead costs associated with commercial insurance products. Rational investors should be willing to pay a premium for this type of insurance just as they pay for other forms of insurance.

Since, on average, buying puts should produce large losses, writing puts should produce large gains. Therefore, should investors make a practice of writing puts to produce high returns? Probably not. Would you make a side bet with your neighbor in which the neighbor paid you a sum of money up front, and then if *your* house burned down, you would pay the neighbor the value of your house?

It's hard to imagine that anyone would find it to their advantage to make such a bet, causing the catastrophic loss of a home to be exacerbated even further. The same principle applies to writing puts. The financial losses from a significant decline in the stock market could be multiplied many times over for an investor who was unfortunate enough to have been writing put options. Many investors who wrote naked puts going into the 1987 stock market crash and during the late summer and early fall of 1998 learned this lesson the hard way.

Expected returns from stock insured with the purchase of a put

Another common risk reducing strategy involving options is portfolio insurance, that is, buying a protective put to place a floor on the value of an underlying stock or stock portfolio. Figure 8.4 shows the expected returns for a strategy in which the underlying stock from the previous examples is purchased along with the same put option. The entries in figure 8.4 show that in all states for which the put has positive value, the expected return from the insurance strategy is less than that of the stock. Since the put reduces the risk of holding the stock, this is exactly what one should expect.

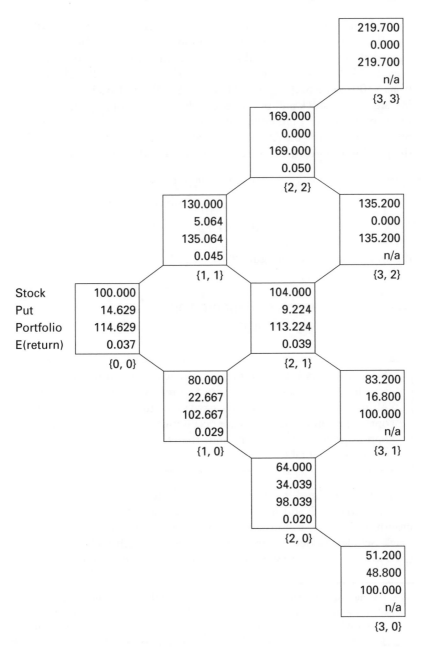

Figure 8.4 Expected returns from buying stock and put ($100 striking price)

The expected returns in figure 8.4 are also consistent with CAPM pricing. Recall that the beta of the put option is −2.4066 in the initial state. The total investment required for the insured stock portfolio is the stock price of $100 plus the put price of $14.629, or $114.629. The proportions $100/$114.629 = $0.8724 and $14.629/$114.629 = $0.1276 are invested in the stock and put, respectively. The portfolio's beta is the sum of the betas of each of its components weighted by the respective portfolio proportions, or $1.0(0.8724) + (−2.4066)(0.1276) = 0.5653$. Therefore, the portfolio's CAPM-based expected return in the initial state is

$$E(r_{port}) = r + \beta_{port}(E[r_m] - r)$$
$$= 0.02 + 0.5653(0.05 - 0.02)$$
$$= 0.0370,$$

the same value shown in figure 8.4.

8.3 A Comparison of Expected and Most Likely Returns

> Many investors appear to confuse average returns with most likely returns when assessing the return potential of option writing. Although it is true that the passage of time causes a natural decay in option premiums, this does not necessarily imply that, on average, option premiums go down, and, therefore, that option writing should be profitable.[30]

To illustrate the difference between expected and most likely option payoffs, tables 8.3 and 8.4 summarize the risk–return profiles for one-month and one-year European calls and puts priced according to the Black–Scholes model. Assumptions common to both tables are summarized in table 8.2. The riskless rate of interest is assumed to be zero so that

---

30. Technically, the partial derivative with respect to time for a European put can be either positive or negative. However, for the partial derivative to be positive, the put must be way-in-the-money and/or have a very long-term maturity. Consider, for example, a 50-year put with a $100 striking price on a stock whose price has reached zero. In this case, the put is, essentially, a $100 par 50-year zero-coupon bond, and its value should get higher over time. The rate of price increase would be a positive function of the interest rate but would be zero if the interest rate were zero.

Table 8.2 Parameters for Black–Scholes risk–return profiles

Assumed values	
Initial stock price	$100
Stock's beta	1.0
Annual continuously compounded riskless rate of interest (r_a)	0
Annual variance of logarithmic stock returns (σ^2)	0.08
Annual mean logarithmic stock return (μ)	0.03
Calculated values	
Annual standard deviation of logarithmic stock returns (σ)	0.2828
Expected annualized instantaneous stock return ($\mu + 0.5\sigma^2$)*	0.07
Expected stock price in one month*	$100e^{0.07/12} = 100.585$
Expected stock price in one year*	$100e^{0.07} = 107.251$

*Based on lognormal math. For lognormal stock returns, the expected return per dollar invested after τ years is $e^{(\mu_a + (1/2)\sigma_a^2)\tau}$. The expected annualized instantaneous return is the natural log of the expected return per dollar invested divided by τ, which works out to $\mu_a + \frac{1}{2}\sigma_a^2$.

the partial derivative of price with respect to time will be unambiguously negative for both the call and put option. (See footnote 30.)

In tables 8.3 and 8.4, options are evaluated with striking prices ranging from $70 to $130 shown in the first column. The second column shows Black–Scholes prices using the parameters of table 8.2. The third column shows the options' expected maturity values using Sprenkle's (1961) formula, below:

$$E(call) = Se^{(\mu_a + \sigma_a^2/2)\tau} N(b1) - KN(b2)$$

$$E(put) = E(call) + K - Se^{(\mu_a + \sigma_a^2/2)\tau}$$

$$b1 = \frac{\ln(S/K) + (\mu_a + \sigma_a^2)\tau}{\sigma_a\sqrt{\tau}} \qquad (8.2)$$

$$b2 = b1 - \sigma_a\sqrt{\tau}$$

where S is the stock price, K is the striking price, τ is the time remaining until the option matures (in years) and all other symbols are as defined in table 8.2.

The fourth column shows the options' instantaneous elasticities with respect to the stock, which are also equal to the options' beta, assuming the beta for the stock is 1.0. The fifth column shows the natural log of the ratio of the option's expected maturity value to the initial Black–Scholes value for each option, all divided by the life of the option in years (τ). This

Table 8.3 Risk–return profiles for 1-month options

Strike	B–S value	Expected maturity value	Beta	Lifetime expected return	CAPM expected return	Probability in-the-money	Probability profitable
Calls							
70	30.000	30.585	3.333	0.232	0.233	1.000	0.512
80	20.007	20.591	4.984	0.345	0.349	0.997	0.512
90	10.360	10.895	8.769	0.604	0.614	0.907	0.495
100	3.256	3.567	15.854	1.092	1.110	0.512	0.359
110	0.513	0.594	25.324	1.750	1.773	0.128	0.116
120	0.040	0.049	35.688	2.473	2.498	0.014	0.014
130	0.002	0.002	46.260	3.240	3.238	0.001	0.001
Puts							
70	0.000	0.000	−45.313	−3.184	−3.172	0.000	0.000
80	0.007	0.005	−39.929	−2.818	−2.795	0.003	0.003
90	0.360	0.309	−25.453	−1.805	−1.782	0.093	0.085
100	3.256	2.982	−14.854	−1.058	−1.042	0.488	0.331
110	10.513	10.009	−8.275	−0.590	−0.579	0.872	0.463
120	20.040	19.464	−4.919	−0.350	−0.344	0.986	0.486
130	30.002	29.417	−3.331	−0.236	−0.233	0.999	0.488

Pricing parameters: $S = 100$; $r_a = 0$; $\sigma_a^2 = 0.08$; $\mu_a = 0.03$; $\tau = \frac{1}{12}$.
Other:
B–S value = Black–Scholes value.
Lifetime expected return is ln(exp. maturity value/Black–Scholes value)/τ.
CAPM expected return is $r_a + \beta_{option}(\mu_a + \frac{1}{2}\sigma_a^2)$.
Both expected returns are annualized instantaneous rates of return expressed as proportional rates rather than as percentage rates.

quantity, referred to as the lifetime expected return, can be interpreted as the continuously compounded annualized expected return from holding the option until it matures.[31] The sixth column shows continuously compounded annualized expected returns computed from the CAPM using each option's initial beta and an annualized expected market (and stock) return of $\mu_a + \frac{1}{2}\sigma_a^2 = 0.03 + \frac{1}{2}(0.08) = 0.07$ and an annualized continuously compounded riskless interest rate of zero. This return should *not* be interpreted as the annualized expected return over the life of the option but rather the annualized expected return taken over the next instantaneous moment before the option's beta has a chance to change. If viewed in the context of the binomial model, this is the equivalent to computing the

---

31. The expected rate of return for an option can actually be computed over any fraction of its life, taking into account potential mispricing of the option, using the formula developed by Rubinstein (1984).

Table 8.4 Risk–return profiles for 1-year options

Strike	B–S value	Expected maturity value	Beta	Lifetime expected return	CAPM expected return	Probability in-the-money	Probability profitable
Calls							
70	31.162	37.950	2.951	0.197	0.207	0.914	0.526
80	23.083	29.273	3.569	0.238	0.250	0.815	0.499
90	16.411	21.763	4.243	0.282	0.297	0.684	0.455
100	11.246	15.632	4.946	0.329	0.346	0.542	0.393
110	7.468	10.890	5.657	0.377	0.396	0.409	0.322
120	4.831	7.391	6.364	0.425	0.445	0.295	0.249
130	3.059	4.907	7.057	0.473	0.494	0.206	0.183
Puts							
70	1.162	0.699	−6.919	−0.508	−0.484	0.086	0.077
80	3.083	2.023	−5.712	−0.421	−0.400	0.185	0.151
90	6.411	4.512	−4.736	−0.351	−0.332	0.316	0.230
100	11.246	8.381	−3.946	−0.294	−0.276	0.458	0.299
110	17.468	13.640	−3.306	−0.247	−0.231	0.591	0.352
120	24.831	20.140	−2.789	−0.209	−0.195	0.705	0.389
130	33.059	27.656	−2.372	−0.178	−0.166	0.794	0.415

Princing parameters: $S = 100; r = 0; \sigma_a^2 = 0.08; \mu_a = 0.03; \tau = 1$.
Other:
B–S value = Black–Scholes value.
Lifetime expected return is ln (exp. maturity value/Black–Scholes value)/τ.
CAPM expected return is $r_a + \beta_{option}(\mu_a + \frac{1}{2}\sigma_a^2)$.
Both expected returns are annualized instantaneous rates of return expressed as proportional rates rather than as percentage rates.

option's expected return in the initial binomial state and then annualizing the result.

The seventh column shows the probabilities that the options will end up in-the-money. For a call option, this probability is simply $N(b2)$ from equation set 8.2 above and $1 - N(b2)$ for a put. The final column shows the probabilities that the options will be profitable. For a call option, this value is calculated as $N(b2)$, after substituting the strike price *plus* the Black–Scholes call price for the strike price in the $b2$ term of equation set 8.2. For a put option, the probability is computed as $1 - N(b2)$, after substituting the strike price *minus* the Black–Scholes put price in the $b2$ term.

Risk–return profiles for calls

Consistent with the previous binomial-based analysis, the annualized expected returns from calls are very high and those for puts are very negative. Generally, the annualized expected returns are much higher in absolute magnitude for the one-month options compared with the one-year options. Also, the lifetime and CAPM-based expected returns are almost identical for the one-month options. Thus, it appears that little damage is done by extrapolating a CAPM-based instantaneous expected return calculation over the entire monthly holding period, even though the option's beta and its expected return will be changing.[32] Moreover, even though the difference between the lifetime and CAPM-based annualized expected returns is larger for one-year options than for one-month options, these differences are still not significant. Therefore, it appears that a CAPM-based expected return calculation can provide a good approximation to the annualized expected return over an option's life.

The most significant sections of tables 8.3 and 8.4 are the probability values shown in the final two columns. Note that for calls, there is a strong inverse relationship between an option's expected return and the likelihood that it will be in-the-money at maturity or be profitable. Table 8.3 indicates less than a 12 percent chance that the out-of-the-money 110 call will be profitable, despite the fact that its projected annualized lifetime expected return is 175 percent. The 130 call has a chance of one in one thousand of being profitable, yet its expected return is 324 percent.

Turning these numbers around, the likelihood of making money by writing naked calls is very high, although the profit, on average should be negative. Using the one-month 120 calls, an investor could write this call, or one like it, and expect to lose only 14 out of 1000 times. That being the case, it is easy to see why so many investors believe call writing is a profitable strategy. It is possible that one could follow a strategy of writing way out-of-the money calls for years and never sustain a single loss from option writing. Under such circumstances, it's no wonder investors may not understand the expected returns from call writing.

Risk–return profiles for puts

Tables 8.3 and 8.4 indicate that the annualized expected returns for all one-month and one-year puts are negative, with the most negative expected returns being associated with the puts that are out-of-the-money and/or close to maturity. As with calls, the lifetime and CAPM-based annualized expected returns are almost identical for one-month puts and within two percentage points for one-year puts. Since the expected returns of all puts are negative, the expected profit from writing each of the puts must be positive.

---

32. This same type of relationship is evident in Rubinstein (1984, p. 1506) for call options with maturities of one, four and seven months.

Tables 8.3 and 8.4 also show less than a 50 percent chance that any long put position will be profitable. This, in turn, implies there is greater than 50 percent chance that the writing of any of the puts should be profitable. Thus, unlike call writing, where the expected and most likely profits are of opposite sign, when writing puts, both the expected and most likely profits are positive. Thus, if one were inclined to use the options market as a gambling device, with no concern for the general portfolio implications of gambling outcomes, writing puts would appear to be the best strategy, since both the expected and most likely outcomes are positive. In contrast, from a pure gambling perspective, the most likely profit from writing calls is positive, but the average profit is negative.

Of course, portfolio theory tells us that we should not evaluate an investment in terms of its own risk–return profile without also considering how the outcomes of the investment affect the overall returns of a well-diversified portfolio. Viewed in this context, . . .

> if options are properly priced, there should be no strategy involving the purchase or sale of options that is dominant in a risk–return sense.

Option strategies that increase non-diversifiable risks (buying calls and writing puts) should increase expected return and those which decrease non-diversifiable risks (writing calls and buying puts) should decrease expected returns. Nevertheless, if options are priced to provide no risk–return advantage for an investor who holds a well-diversified portfolio, certain option investment strategies could dominate others for an investor who is unconcerned about overall portfolio risks.

8.4 Summary

If standard notions of risk and return are applied to options, call options issued on positive beta stocks should have very positive betas, and therefore, very high expected returns. Put options, on the other hand, should have very negative betas and expected returns significantly less than the risk-free rate of interest and generally negative. As a result, risk-reducing strategies such as covered call writing and portfolio insurance should have expected returns less than that of the underlying stock.

Some strategies involving options, such as writing uncovered calls, have expected returns that are very negative but most likely returns that are very positive. Therefore, it is easy to extrapolate from a prior history of favorable returns and conclude that the average returns from such strategies are positive. Even though history may repeat itself to a large degree, when it does not repeat, losses can be so large that expected returns can be very negative. Therefore, it is very important for option traders not to get most likely and average returns confused. It is also important for all option investors to understand that there can be no special strategies involving options that consistently reduce risk and increase return, unless options are significantly mispriced. Unless one is in a position to identify mispriced options on a consistent basis, there should be no inherent risk–return advantage to investing in options over any other security.

REFERENCES

Black, F. and M. Scholes, "The Pricing of Options and Corporate Liabilities." *The Journal of Political Economy* 81 (May/June 1973), 637–59.

Cox, J. C., S. Ross, and M. Rubinstein, "Option Pricing: A Simplified Approach." *Journal of Financial Economics* 7 (December, 1979), 229–64.

Cox, John C. and Mark Rubinstein, *Options Markets*, Prentice Hall, Englewood Cliffs, NJ, (1985).

Fama, E. F. and K. R. French, "The Cross Section of Expected Stock Returns." *Journal of Finance* 47 (June 1992), 427–65.

Lintner, J., "The Valuation of Risk Assets and the Selection of Risky Investments in Stock Portfolios and Captial Budgets." *The Review of Economic and Statistics* 47 (February 1965), 13–37.

Rendleman, R. J., Jr., "Option Investing from a Risk-Return Perspective." *The Journal of Portfolio Management* (May 1999), 109–21.

Rendleman, R. J., Jr. and B. J. Bartter, "Two-State Option Pricing." *Journal of Finance* 34 (December 1999), 1093–110.

Rubinstein, M., "A Simple Formula for the Expected Rate of Return of an Option over a Finite Holding Period." *Journal of Finance* 39 (December 1984), 1503–9.

Sharpe, William F., "Capital Asset Prices: A Theory of Market Equilibrium under Conditions of Risk." *Journal of Finance* 19 (September 1964), 425–42.

Sprenkle, C. M., "Warrant Prices as Indicators of Expectations and Preferences." *Yale Economic Essays* 1, No. 2 (1961), 172–231.

RELATED WORK

Coval, J. D. and T. Shumway, "Expected Option Returns." *Journal of Finance* 56 (June 2001), 983–1009.

Merton, Robert C., "An Intertemporal Capital Asset Pricing Model." *Econometricia* 41 (September 1973), 867–87.

QUESTIONS AND PROBLEMS

1. Consider a stock for which listed call and put options are traded. The stock is currently worth $100 per share. The risk-free rate of interest is 5 percent per year compounded continuously, and the standard deviation of the stock's logarithmic return is 0.30 per year. Finally assume the CAPM-based market risk premium is 6 percent per year compounded continuously and that the stock's beta is 1.0.

    Using the Excel program Black_Scholes.xls found on the website http://www.rendleman.com/book, complete the entries in the following two tables.

CAPM-based annualized expected returns for call options

Striking price	Maturity = 0.10 years	Maturity = 0.5 years	Maturity = 1 year
80	Option beta=4.86 Option expected return=34.2%	Option beta= Option expected return=	Option beta= Option expected return=
100	Option beta= Option expected return=	Option beta= Option expected return=	Option beta= Option expected return=
120	Option beta= Option expected return=	Option beta= Option expected return=	Option beta= Option expected return=

CAPM-based annualized expected returns for put options

Striking price	Maturity = 0.10 years	Maturity = 0.5 years	Maturity = 1 year
80	Option beta= Option expected return=	Option beta= Option expected return=	Option beta= Option expected return=
100	Option beta= Option expected return=	Option beta= Option expected return=	Option beta= Option expected return=
120	Option beta= Option expected return=	Option beta= Option expected return=	Option beta= Option expected return=

2.   Based on the entries in the tables you completed in problem 1, what general inferences can you draw about the relationship between an option's. CAPM-based expected return, its maturity and the extent to which the option is in- or out-of- the money.

3.   Consider the following binomial pricing situation. Assume a stock price of $100, $u = 1.3$, $d = 0.8$ and a risk-free rate of 0.01 per binomial period.

   a.   Using the binomial model, compute the price for a call and put option, both of which have a striking price of $100 and mature after one binomial period.

   b.   Assume that the true probability that the stock will increase in value is 0.5. With this assumption, the stock's expected return over the single binomial period is 5 percent. Compute the expected returns for the call and put.

   c.   For both options, compute initial values of Δ and B for the stock/safe asset replicating portfolio. Next, determine the *proportion* of funds invested in the replicating portfolio represented by stock and safe assets. Let w_S denote the proportion invested in stock and w_F the proportion invested in safe assets. The mathematics of leverage would suggest that the expected return of the replicating portfolio is $w_S(0.05) + w_F(0.01)$. Verify that the expected returns computed for the call and put in part "a" are consistent with the mathematics of leverage.

4.   A number of academic finance researchers have questioned the empirical validity of the Capital Asset Pricing Model. They think it does not fit the data of observed stock returns very well. But even a CAPM skeptic should accept the expected return for options calculated via the CAPM. Why?

5.   The following quote concerning the return potential from covered call writing was taken from the internet web site of megareturns.com:
   Write covered calls like the Pros and watch your money DOUBLE EVERY 60 TO 90 DAYS OR LESS!

   It is reasonable to interpret this quotation as a claim that the expected return from covered call writing is 100 percent every 60 to 90 days. Based on the CAPM-based analysis of expected returns and/or the mathematics of leverage as applied to option investing, what, if anything, is wrong with this claim?

9

Advanced Option Replication: Creating the Most Cost-effective Replicating Portfolio

9.1 Introduction

In this chapter I will show how exchange-traded options can be used in combination with the underlying stock and safe assets to replicate the pay-off structure of another option when there are more than two outcomes for the price of the underlying stock. When the analysis is applied to binomial outcomes that extend over long periods of time, the use of exchange-traded options in replication can serve as a substitute for stock/safe asset portfolio revisions that would otherwise be required at the end of each binomial period. As such, the use of exchange-traded options in replication in combination with the underlying stock and safe assets may reduce transaction costs and thereby may be a more cost-effective way to achieve a desired set of portfolio outcomes.

The initial analysis draws directly on the classic works of Arrow (1964) and Debreu (1959) who developed the theory of security pricing and replication in a world in which securities or portfolios are available for trading whose payoffs depend directly upon the realization of specific "states of nature." Such securities have since been termed "Arrow–Debreu" securities. The works of Arrow and Debreu provided great insight into the role of securities markets in the sharing of risks and the allocation of economic resources and helped both Arrow and Debreu to earn the Nobel Prize. However, their works have been viewed by some within the finance profession as having little practical relevance, since "real world" security and portfolio outcomes are not determined in terms of the realization of specific states of nature, and securities whose payoffs depend upon the realization of specific states do not exist. Later, Ross (1976), Rubinstein (1976) and Breeden and Litzenberger (1978), demonstrated that under certain ideal conditions, option markets serve the same role as Arrow–Debreu markets, and under more realistic conditions, option markets at least point us in the direction of the type of markets envisioned by Arrow and Debreu.

9.2 Replication when there are More than Two Outcomes for the Stock

The binomial model is based on the idea that a portfolio consisting of a certain combination of stock and safe assets can be constructed to replicate the two outcomes for an option over a single binomial period. More generally, when risk is characterized by two possible outcomes, any two securities with linearly independent outcomes can be combined in a portfolio to achieve any desired set of portfolio payoffs over the two states.[33]

> This same idea can be used when risk is characterized by more than two outcomes. As shown below, for each additional state or outcome, an additional security must be included in the replicating portfolio to achieve a desired portfolio payoff structure.

Consider a situation in which an underlying stock on which options are traded can take on m possible values after a specific period of time. If viewed within the context of the binomial model, the stock would take on m possible values after $m - 1$ binomial periods. But for now, it is not necessary to cast the analysis within a binomial framework. All that is necessary is that the stock can take on m values, whether these values evolve from an $m - 1$ period binomial process or by some other means.

Assume that m different linearly independent securities exist whose payoffs can be stated directly in terms of the m possible outcomes for the stock. One such security would be the stock itself. Another would be the safe asset; no matter which of m outcomes occurs for the stock, the safe asset produces the same value. Assume that the remaining $m - 2$ securities are exchange-traded options with linearly independent payoffs issued on the same stock.[34] I will now show how these m securities can be combined

---

33. Linear independence means that outcomes for one of the two securities cannot be stated as a linear function of the outcomes for the other security.
34. For example, assume the stock can take values of $100, $90, $80, and $70 at the end of the investment period. Also assume that call options on the same stock maturing at the end of the investment period with striking prices of $95, $92 and $85 are available for trading. In this situation, the call options with striking prices of $95 and $92 would not have linearly independent payoffs, since the payoffs in each state to the call with a striking price of $95 are simply $\frac{5}{8}$ of the payoffs of the call with a $92 striking price. Thus, the payoffs to either of these two call

in a portfolio to achieve any desired set of portfolio payoffs or to replicate the payoff structure of another option.

Let $X_{i,j}$ denote the payoff from one unit of security i in state j with $i = 1, 2, 3 \ldots m$ and $j = 1, 2, 3 \ldots m$. Also, let α_i denote the number of units of security i that are purchased. The idea is to determine the number of each security to purchase (or sell if α_i is negative) so that a specific desired set of payoffs is received in each state. Let Q_j denote the amount of money that the investor wants to receive in state j.

To determine the quantity of each security that must be purchased (or sold short) in connection with the replicating portfolio, the investor must solve the following system of linear equations:

$$\alpha_1 X_{1,1} + \alpha_2 X_{2,1} + \cdots + \alpha_3 X_{m,1} = Q_1$$
$$\alpha_1 X_{1,2} + \alpha_2 X_{2,2} + \cdots + \alpha_m X_{m,2} = Q_2$$
$$\vdots$$
$$\alpha_1 X_{1,m} + \alpha_2 X_{2,m} + \cdots + \alpha_m X_{m,m} = Q_m$$

An example

Assume that an underlying stock on which options are traded follows the binomial process shown below in figure 9.1. This is the same process assumed throughout chapter 3, the introductory chapter to binomial pricing.

Assume also that two European call options that mature at time 3 are available for trading. The first has a striking price of $150, and the striking price of the second is $100. Finally, assume that the risk-free rate of interest is 0.01 per binomial period. Therefore, a dollar invested in a safe asset at time zero will be worth $1.01^3 = 1.030301$ dollars after three binomial periods.

Using these four securities, an investor wants to create a portfolio that will have the same payoff structure after three binomial periods as a three-period call option with a striking price of $90. Table 9.1 summarizes the payoff structure of the four assets and the call option, or "target security," whose payoffs are to be replicated.

Denote the number of units of stock to purchase as α_1, the number of units of safe assets to purchase as α_2, the number of units of the call with a striking price of $150 as α_3 and the number of units of the call with a

---

options can be stated as a linear function of the payoffs to the other. However, the payoffs to the call option with a striking price of $85 are linearly independent of the payoffs to the other two options.

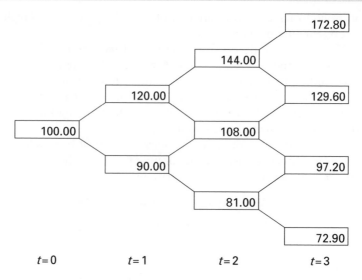

$t=0$ $t=1$ $t=2$ $t=3$

Figure 9.1 Binomial stock prices over three periods

Table 9.1 Security payoff structures

	Assets available for replicating portfolio				Target
State	Stock (1)	Safe asset (2)	Call with $K = \$150$ (3)	Call with $K = \$100$ (4)	Call with $K = \$90$
1	172.80	1.030301	22.80	72.80	82.80
2	129.60	1.030301	0	29.60	39.60
3	97.20	1.030301	0	0	7.20
4	72.90	1.030301	0	0	0

The payoff to the safe asset reflects investing $1 at an interest rate of 0.01 per period compounded for three periods. Values in parentheses are index numbers identifying each security to be used in the replicating portfolio.

striking price of \$100 as α_4. Then, to replicate the payoffs to the call option with a striking price of \$90, the investor must solve the following system of equations.

$$\alpha_1(172.80) + \alpha_2(1.030301) + \alpha_3(22.80) + \alpha_4(72.80) = 82.80$$

$$\alpha_1(129.60) + \alpha_2(1.030301) + \alpha_3(0) + \alpha_4(29.60) = 39.60$$

$$\alpha_1(97.20) + \alpha_2(1.030301) + \alpha_3(0) + \alpha_4(0) = 7.20$$

$$\alpha_1(72.90) + \alpha_2(1.030301) + \alpha_3(0) + \alpha_4(0) = 0$$

The solution to this system of equations is:

$$\alpha_1 = 0.29630$$

$$\alpha_2 = -20.96475$$

$$\alpha_3 = -0.12613$$

$$\alpha_4 = 0.77027$$

This solution indicates that the investor should purchase 0.29630 shares of stock, borrow $20.96475 for three periods at an interest rate of 1 percent per binomial period, write 0.12613 call options with a striking price of $150 and purchase 0.77027 calls with a striking price of $100. This combination of securities will then produce $82.80 in the first state, $39.60 in the second, $7.20 in the third, and $0.00 in the fourth state – precisely the payoffs of a call option with a striking price of $90.

The tradeoff between additional securities and portfolio revisions

In the standard binomial model, option replication is achieved over an n-period investment horizon by making an investment in the stock and safe asset in the initial state and then making $n - 1$ subsequent portfolio revisions. In the Arrow–Debreu model, replication is achieved *without revision* over an n-period binomial investment horizon by making an initial investment in the stock and safe asset along with $n - 1$ additional securities whose payoffs depend upon the ending outcomes for the stock.[35] In the three-period binomial example above, $n - 1 = 3 - 1 = 2$ additional securities beyond the stock and safe asset.

> As a general principle, each exchange-traded option used in replication reduces the number of required binomial-based portfolio revisions by one.

In the previous example, assume that the call option with the $100 striking price is not available, but the investor has access to the stock, safe asset and call option with a $150 striking price. These three securities could then be

---

35. In the binomial model, there will be $n + 1$ outcomes after n binomial periods. Therefore, within the context of the Arrow–Debreu model, $m = n + 1$. Since a total of m securities with linearly independent payoffs are needed for replication in the Arrow–Debreu model, if two of the m securities are the stock and safe asset, this leaves $m - 2 = (n + 1) - 2 = n - 1$ additional securities required for replication.

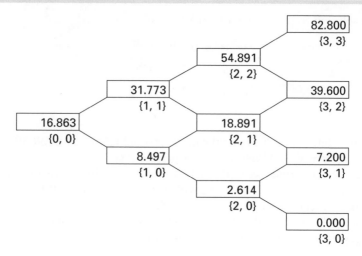

Figure 9.2 Pricing a three-period European call option with a $90 striking price. Riskless interest rate is 1 percent per binomial period

used to replicate the target call option with a $90 striking price, provided the investor is prepared to make one portfolio revision during the life of the replication program. This can be visualized by examining the entire binomial pricing tree for the target security in figure 9.2.

In this example, there are two ways the three securities can be used to replicate the payoffs of the target security. The first way is to use all three securities in combination to replicate the three possible outcomes for the target security as of the end of the second binomial period. Then, no matter which state occurs at time 2, the investor can use the money generated from the three-security portfolio, $54.891, $18.891, or $2.614, and form a new portfolio with any two of the three securities to replicate the payoffs to the target security in the final period.

The second approach would involve using any two of the three securities to replicate the payoffs of the target security at the end of time 1. For example, it is easily shown that an initial portfolio consisting of 0.776 shares of stock and $60.724 of borrowed funds will produce the same outcomes as the target security at time 1. Then, using the money generated at time 1 from the initial portfolio, either $31.773 in the up state or $8.497 in the down state, the investor can construct a portfolio using all three securities that will replicate the three possible outcomes as of time 3.[36]

---

36. It should be noted that after the initial up or down state occurs at time 1, only three of the original four states associated with time 3 can occur. For example, if state {1, 1} occurs at time 1, state {3, 0} cannot occur at time 3.

In actual option replication programs, portfolio revisions can be costly, and it is possible that a replication program that reduces the number of revisions by including additional exchange-traded options may be more cost effective.

The next section addresses the issue of creating the most cost-effective replicating portfolio by using exchange-traded options as a substitute for stock/safe asset portfolio revisions.

9.3 Creating the Most Cost-effective Replicating Portfolio

In Dennis and Rendleman (1995), an option replication model based on linear programming (LP) is developed that combines traditional binomial-based stock/safe asset option replication with the Arrow–Debreu approach described above. Dennis and Rendleman refer to the traditional approach as "time series" replication, since it requires portfolio revisions over time at the end of each binomial period. They refer to Arrow–Debreu replication as "cross-sectional" replication, since it involves using a cross section of securities whose payoffs are related to the underlying stock to form a replicating portfolio without the need for periodic portfolio revisions.

Linear programming is a mathematical optimization method in which a linear objective function is minimized (or maximized) while satisfying a number of pre-specified linear constraints. A classic example of LP is determining the lowest cost combination of foods in a diet that will satisfy a number of nutritional constraints. Similarly, LP can be used to determine the combination of foods in a diet that will minimize calorie intake while satisfying other nutritional constraints.

In the Dennis–Rendleman model, the objective is to minimize the upfront cost of establishing a replicating portfolio while ensuring that the portfolio will be self-financing and that target payoffs are met. The technical details of the Dennis–Rendleman model are very complex, and are not repeated here. Instead, a non-technical summary is provided along with illustrations of the model from the original paper.

Objective function

The objective in the Dennis–Rendleman model is to form the most cost-effective replicating portfolio possible using time series and cross-sectional replication in combination. In Dennis and Rendleman, transactions in stock and safe assets are subject to costs that can be summarized by the following linear cost function:

$$transaction\ cost_i = a_i \times (number\ of\ securities\ traded)$$
$$+\ b_i \times (value\ of\ securities\ traded)$$

where the subscript i denotes a specific security, and a_i and b_i are constants. Transaction costs for options are assumed to take the same form except that a_i is assumed to be zero.[37]

The objective in the Dennis–Rendleman model is to minimize the upfront cost of establishing the replicating portfolio. This objective function is summarized as follows:

Minimize: initial cost of securities purchased

– proceeds from initial short positions

+ transaction costs for initial long and short positions

– present value of over-financing

The first three items in the objective function represent the normal cost of establishing an initial portfolio position. The final item, the present value of over-financing, requires an explanation of the various constraints imposed in the model before it can be understood.

Position constraints

In the Dennis–Rendleman model, positions taken in options in the initial state are assumed to be fixed throughout the full term of the replication program. Only stock and safe asset positions can be changed over time. Also, positions in options are limited to those that mature on or prior to the end of the replication program.

Although the price of each option is known in the initial state and will be known on the date the option matures, it is not possible to know how each option will be priced between the initial and maturity states, since in any state prior to maturity, an option could be mispriced. Rather than estimate how mispricing in options might be resolved over time, Dennis and Rendleman simply assume that once option positions are established, they cannot be changed.

---

37.   Dennis and Rendleman make the assumption that $a_i = 0$ for options. Otherwise, the decision to exercise an option would be a function of the transaction cost.

Link constraints

Link constraints can be thought of as "housekeeping" or accounting constraints that keep track of position sizes over time. In the Dennis–Rendleman model, both the size and change in position size for each security must be known in each state. Knowing the size of each position is required so that once the replicating portfolio is liquidated at maturity, the linear program will know the portfolio's liquidation value. Knowing how position sizes change is required for computing transaction costs. Link constraints simply ensure that the size of a security position prior to a change plus the change equals the size after the change.

Target constraints

Target constraints ensure that in each state at the maturity of the replication program, the liquidation value of the replicating portfolio, after taking account of transaction costs, *equals or exceeds* the value of the target security in the same state. For example, suppose the target security should be worth $50 in a specific state. Then the Dennis–Rendleman model requires that the replicating program produce *at least* $50 in the same state. But what if $52 is produced?

In this case, the Dennis–Rendleman model would recognize that the replication program had been over-financed by $2. In addition, it would recognize a benefit to the investor to receiving the additional $2. But since the investor had not intended to receive the extra $2, he might not attribute a full $2 of value to receiving the extra funds.

If the LP model indicates in advance that the extra $2 will be produced in a specific state, the investor could arrange to sell a claim on the $2 to another investor at the beginning of the replication program. In the Dennis–Rendleman model the initial value of the claim is determined using the binomial model just like any other security. A proportional transaction cost is then assigned to initial value. For example, assume the binomial value of the extra $2 is $0.30 and a proportional transaction cost of 0.2 is assigned to this value. Then, the present value associated with the $2 of over-financing would be $0.30(1 − 0.2) = $0.24. The initial cost of the replicating program would then be reduced by this $0.24 amount.

Self-financing constraints

The Dennis–Rendleman model requires that the replication program be self-financing in every state. This means that the amount of money released from liquidating all or part of a security position in a given state must *equal or exceed* the amount of money needed to establish new security positions in the same state. If more money is released from the liquidation of security positions than is needed to establish new positions, over-financing will occur, and the benefit to the over-financing is computed the same way as described above.

Constraints that bring additional option-like characteristics to the replicating portfolio

As discussed in chapter 6, it is common practice to form a replicating portfolio that not only has immediate stock/safe asset risk-equivalency with a given option but also has other risk properties equivalent to that of the option being replicated. As discussed in chapter 6, immediate stock/safe asset risk equivalency is often referred to as "delta" equivalency. Option investors may also want to achieve gamma, and/or vega equivalency or equivalency in higher order partial derivatives. However, since these partial derivatives are zero for stock and safe assets, it is impossible to use these securities alone to achieve anything other than delta equivalency. To control for gamma, vega and other higher-order risk-equivalency, it is necessary to include exchange-traded options in the replicating portfolio.

The performance of the Dennis–Rendleman model as formulated depends critically on the user's estimate of the volatility of the underlying stock's returns. But if the volatility estimate is incorrect, portfolio outcomes will be subject to the type of error discussed in chapter 5. This error of volatility misestimation came back to haunt many option investors during the 1987 stock market crash when synthetic portfolio insurance programs using only stock and safe assets failed to deliver the downside protection that was expected.

The risk associated with volatility misestimation can be mitigated by including a constraint that equates the vega of the replicating portfolio to that of the target. This risk can be reduced further by also equating the second partial derivatives with respect to volatility. With these constraints, there should be little change in the value of the replicating portfolio if the actual volatility of the underlying stock turns out to be different from that which is expected.

An investor might also want to set the replicating portfolio's gamma to that of the target security. By doing so, the necessity of making frequent revisions to the security mix of the replicating portfolio should not be as critical.

Unlike the link, target and self-financing constraints, the Dennis–Rendleman model does not require the imposition of constraints designed to bring more option-like characteristics to the replicating portfolio. However, if constraints of this type can be imposed without significantly increasing the cost of the replicating portfolio, it would be prudent to include them.

9.4 Example Results

Dennis and Rendleman develop a set of option replication examples based on a common set of assumptions summarized in table 9.2.

Replication using stock and safe assets only

Table 9.3 summarizes the cost of replication of a one-year call option with a $100 striking price of $100 using stock and safe assets only for various levels of transaction costs for the stock and safe asset. In this table, the benefits associated with over-financing are ignored.

Table 9.2 Common assumptions in Dennis–Rendleman examples

Stock price	100
Interest rate	0.10 per year compounded annually
Volatility	0.20 per year
Maturity of target security	1 year
u	$e^{0.2/\sqrt{n}}$
d	$e^{-0.2/\sqrt{n}}$
$1 + r$	$1.10^{1/n}$
n	6

Table 9.3 Cost of replicating a 1-year call option using stock and safe assets only

Stock		Safe asset		
Fixed cost (a)	Proportional cost (b)	Fixed cost (a)	Proportional cost (b)	Cost of replication
0.00	0.00	0.0000	0.000	12.655
0.00	0.01	0.0000	0.000	14.849
0.06	0.01	0.0000	0.000	14.971
0.06	0.01	0.0000	0.005	15.898
0.06	0.01	0.0006	0.005	16.002

Stock price = $100; striking price of target = $100. The fixed cost for the safe asset is per dollar of investment at time zero. The fixed cost for stock is per share of stock.

The entries in the first row of table 9.3 indicate that in the absence of transaction costs, the cost of replicating the 1-year call option is $12.655. This is exactly the cost produced by the binomial model in the absence of transaction costs. Therefore, the binomial and Dennis–Rendleman models are internally consistent.

The table also indicates that for reasonable levels of transaction costs, the cost of replicating the payoffs to the call option increases dramatically. For example, in the last row, with reasonable levels of transaction costs assigned to both the stock and safe asset, the cost of replicating the payoffs to the call option is $16.002. Therefore, in the presence of such costs, the value of the option being replicated would have to exceed $16.002 before an arbitrage profit could be earned by purchasing the replicating portfolio and selling the call. Although not shown in this table, with the same level of transaction costs, the proceeds from replicating a writing position in the same option is $9.441. Therefore, if the option could be purchased for less than $9.441, an investor could earn a riskless arbitrage profit by purchasing the call option and selling the replicating portfolio for $9.441. In summary, if the market price for the option fell between $9.441 and $16.002, there would be no opportunity to earn a riskless arbitrage profit by taking a long or short position in the option.

> This suggests that the transaction costs associated with buying and selling stock and safe assets may make binomial and Black–Scholes-based riskless arbitrage prohibitively expense for all but the lowest cost professional investor.

Adding exchange-traded options to the replicating portfolio

The option replication example is now extended to include the use of the three options summarized in table 9.4 along with positions in stock and safe assets.

Note the at the first option is over-priced by 1 percent in relation to the binomial model, the second option in under-priced by 5 percent and the third option is under-priced by 40 percent.

Table 9.5 summarizes the cost and initial security mix for various replicating portfolios using stock, safe assets and various exchange-traded options.[38] The table shows how the cost of replication is reduced as the

---

38. The entries in tables 9.5 and 9.6 are equal to corresponding entries from Dennis–Rendleman divided by 0.98. This adjustment reflects that the Dennis–Rendleman analysis includes a transaction cost of 2 percent of the value of the target security that is not reflected here.

Table 9.4   Specification of option used in replicating portfolio

Option number	Type	Maturity in binomial periods	Striking price	Market value	Theoretical value	Mispricing (%)	Proportional cost (b)
1	call	4	100	9.546	9.452	+1	0.02
2	call	6	120	4.005	4.216	−5	0.02
3	put	6	90	0.984	1.640	−40	0.02

Table 9.5   Replication cost and initial security mix using stock, safe assets and exchange-traded options

Options used	Replication cost	Initial stock units	Initial safe asset units	Initial units option 1	Initial units option 2	Initial units option 3
Proportional cost to over financing = 1.0						
None	16.002	0.728	−57.804	0.000	0.000	0.000
1	15.704	0.470	−36.166	0.427	0.000	0.000
2	14.926	0.430	−32.295	0.000	0.897	0.000
3	14.967	0.993	−88.142	0.000	0.000	2.250
1 & 2	14.851	0.403	−30.173	0.087	0.805	0.000
1 & 3	14.967	0.993	−88.142	0.000	0.000	2.250
2 & 3	14.785	0.880	−77.200	0.000	0.196	1.790
1, 2 & 3	14.768	0.665	−56.130	0.042	0.486	0.935
Proportional cost to over-financing = 0.4						
None	16.002	0.728	−57.804	0.000	0.000	0.000
1	15.704	0.470	−36.166	0.427	0.000	0.000
2	14.905	0.412	−30.230	0.000	0.936	0.000
3	14.492	1.010	−90.353	0.000	0.000	3.035
1 & 2	14.848	0.377	−27.649	0.097	0.839	0.000
1 & 3	14.492	1.010	−90.353	0.000	0.000	3.035
2 & 3	14.492	1.010	−90.353	0.000	0.000	3.035
1, 2 & 3	14.492	1.010	−90.353	0.000	0.000	3.035

three options are made available individually, in pairs, and as a group of three.

Even though option (1) is over-priced, it always enters the replicating portfolio as a long position. A long position in this call displaces what would otherwise be a levered position in the stock that would be subject to revision with transaction costs. Apparently, the purchase of the call allows some of these transaction costs to be avoided at a lower overall net cost, even though the option itself is over-priced in relation to its standard binomial value.

Both panels of table 9.5 show a significant reduction in the cost of replication when options (1) and (2) are used individually. Even though option (3), is a put option and under-priced by 40 percent, its use in the upper panel option replication program is not quite as cost effective as option (2), call option that is only 5 percent under-priced. This results from the fact that a put option is not a good substitute for a levered stock position. In the upper panel, the lowest cost of replication is achieved when all three options can be used in the replicating portfolio.

The entries in the lower panel of table 9.5 are computed under the assumption that there is a cost reduction associated with over-financing. In addition to a lower cost of replication, some of the entries in the lower panel show a significantly different security mix for the replicating portfolio than corresponding entries in the upper panel. Interestingly, in the lower panel, having access to all three options does not reduce the cost of replication beyond the cost associated with using option (3) alone.

Equating partial derivatives with respect to volatility

Table 9.6 summarizes the effect of equating the first and second partial derivatives of the value of the replicating portfolio with respect to volatility to those of the target using the stock, safe asset and all three exchange-traded options. A comparison of the three panels of table 9.6 shows only a modest increase in the cost of replication when the constraints restricting the first and second partials to that of the target are added. Moreover, there is essentially no increase in cost for adding the constraint associated with the

Table 9.6 Replication cost and initial security mix using stock, safe assets and exchange-traded options with first and second partials with respect to volatility set to that of target

Over-financing cost	Replication cost	Initial stock units	Initial safe asset units	Initial units option 1	Initial units option 2	Initial units option 3
First and second partials ignored						
1.0	14.768	0.665	−56.130	0.042	0.486	0.935
0.4	14.492	1.010	−90.353	0.000	0.000	3.035
First partial set to that of target						
1.0	14.810	0.718	−60.714	0.011	0.367	0.935
0.4	14.768	0.740	−62.581	0.028	0.304	1.020
First and second partial set to that of target						
1.0	14.850	0.420	−31.917	0.073	0.811	0.076
0.4	14.838	0.408	−30.716	0.089	0.798	0.077

second partial beyond that of the first partial. Despite the almost negligible increase in cost, there is a significant change in the security mix as the two constraints are added. Although adding these constraints is extremely cost effective in this example, these results may not generalize.

Using the Dennis–Rendleman model to explain the volatility smile

Dennis (1996) employs the LP model to test the hypothesis that the *volatility smile* (see chapter 7) could occur under standard Black–Scholes assumptions in the presence of transaction costs. To test the hypothesis, Dennis determines the optimal method to replicate long and short positions in S&P 500 index options. For any traded option, an arbitrage opportunity would be present if the option's bid price is above the cost of replicating a long position. For example, if an option's bid price is $10, but the LP-based cost of replicating a long position is $9, an investor could purchase the replicating portfolio and simultaneously sell the option for $10, earning an arbitrage profit of $1 per share of underlying stock. Similarly, an arbitrage opportunity would be present if an option's ask price is below the proceeds available from an optimal LP-based short position.

Dennis tests his hypothesis using S&P 500 options on 30 randomly selected dates in 1993. To test for the presence of arbitrage opportunities, Dennis formulates an eight-period LP using the S&P 500 index, a safe asset and three to six options on the S&P. The LP is formulated to minimize up-front costs or, equivalently, maximize up-front proceeds, while ensuring that the portfolio payoff in every state is greater than or equal to zero. The LP assumes a proportional one-way transaction cost for the index and no transaction costs for options and the safe asset other than bid–asked spreads.

Dennis concludes that the one-way transaction cost for the index would have to be below 0.4 percent for an investor to earn an arbitrage profit based on pricing discrepancies among the options, stock and safe asset. However, since an eight-period binomial distribution is only a rough approximation to the lognormal distribution upon which the Black–Scholes model is based, arbitrage opportunities associated with the 0.4 percent transaction cost may not be riskless if stock prices are lognormally distributed. Using Monte Carlo simulations, Dennis determines that the one-way proportional transaction for the index would have to be less than 0.1 percent for the arbitrage strategy to be profitable over two-thirds of the time. As such, this study provides strong evidence that deviations from Black–Scholes pricing in actual exchange-traded options could be due to transaction costs alone.

9.5 Summary

This chapter shows how linear programming can be used to determine an optimal trading strategy to replicate the payoffs of a given target security. The program allows any number of exchange-traded options to be included in the replicating portfolio, along with stock and safe assets, and each can be subject to a linear transaction cost. In addition to reducing the cost of replication, the inclusion of exchange-traded options enables investors to bring certain option-like features to the replicating portfolio that are not possible using stock and safe assets alone. The linear program has been used to show that violations of Black–Scholes pricing, as revealed through the volatility smile, may not be exploitable as arbitrage opportunities unless transaction costs are very small.

REFERENCES

Arrow, K. J., "The Role of Securities in the Optimal Allocation of Risk Bearing." *Review of Economic Studies* 31 (April 1964), 91–6.
Breeden, D. T. and R. H. Litzenberger, "Prices of State-Contingent Claims Implicit in Option Prices." *Journal of Business* 51 (October 1978), 621–51.
Debreu, G., *Theory of Value*. John Wiley and Sons, New York, 1959.
Dennis, P. J., "Optimal No-Arbitrage Bounds on S&P500 Index Options and the Volatility Smile." Working paper, McIntire School of Commerce, The University of Virginia (September 4, 1996).
Dennis, P. and R. J. Rendleman, Jr., "An LP Approach to Synthetic Option Replication with Transaction Costs and Multiple Security Selection." *Advances in Futures and Options Research* 8 (1995), 53–84 (JAI Press, Inc., Greenwich, CT).
Ross, S. A., "Options and Efficiency." *Quarterly Journal of Economics* 90 (February 1976), 75–89.
Rubinstein, M., "The Valuation of Uncertain Income Streams and the Pricing of Options." *Bell Journal of Economics* 7 (Autumn 1976), 407–25.

RELATED WORK

Bensaid, B., J.P. Lesne, H. Pages, and J. Scheinkman, "Derivative Asset Pricing with Transaction Costs." *Mathematical Finance* 2 (April 1992), 63–86.
Boyle, P. and T. Vorst, "Option Replication in Discrete Time with Transaction Costs." *Journal of Finance* 47 (March 1992), 271–93.
Choie, K. S. and F. Novomestsky, "Replicating Long-term with Short-term Options." *Journal of Portfolio Management* 15 (Winter 1989), 17–19.
Edirisinghe, C., V. Naik and R. Uppal, "Optimal Replication of Options with Transactions Costs and Trading Restrictions." *Journal of Financial and Quantitative Analysis* 28 (March 1993), 117–38.

Garman, M. B, "An Algebra for Evaluating Hedge Portfolios." *Journal of Financial Economics* 3 (June 1976), 403–27.

Leland, H. E., "Option Pricing and Replication with Transaction Costs." *Journal of Finance* 40 (December 1985), 1283–301.

Rendleman, R. J., Jr. and T. J. O'Brein, "Volatility Misestimation in Option Replication Portfolio Insurance." *Financial Analysts Journal* 46 (May/June 1990), 61–70.

Ritchken, P. H., "On Option Pricing Bounds." *Journal of Finance* 40 (September 1985), 1219–33.

Ross, S. A, "Return, Risk and Arbitrage." Working paper 17-93a, Rodney White Center for Financial Research, University of Pennsylvania, Philadelphia PA (1973).

QUESTIONS AND PROBLEMS

This problem set is designed to show how any desired set of portfolio payoffs spanning N states can be created with N securities whose linearly independent payoffs span the same states.

You may use the file Arrow.xls, found on the website http://www. rendleman.com/book. The file contains a payoff matrix for a stock, with ending stock prices ranging from 0 to 10, call options on the stock with striking prices ranging from 1 to 9, and a safe asset. The matrix looks something like this:

		Security Payoffs									
		Call option with striking price of . . .									
Safe asset	Stock	1	2	3	4	5	6	7	8	9	Target
1	10	9	8	7	6	5	4	3	2	1	0
1	9	8	7	6	5	4	3	2	1	0	0
1	8	7	6	5	4	3	2	1	0	0	0
1	7	6	5	4	3	2	1	0	0	0	1
1	6	5	4	3	2	1	0	0	0	0	1
1	5	4	3	2	1	0	0	0	0	0	1
1	4	3	2	1	0	0	0	0	0	0	1
1	3	2	1	0	0	0	0	0	0	0	0
1	2	1	0	0	0	0	0	0	0	0	0
1	1	0	0	0	0	0	0	0	0	0	0
1	0	0	0	0	0	0	0	0	0	0	0

This table is best explained starting with the second column. This column gives a range of possible prices for a stock on which options are traded.

From top to bottom, the range is from 10 to 0. The third column shows the payoffs of a call option with a striking price of 1. Each of the next eight columns provide payoffs for call options of identical maturity with striking prices ranging from 2 to 9.

The first column provides state-dependent payoffs for a safe asset which promises to pay $1 at maturity. Note that the safe asset pays $1 in each state.

The last column, marked "target" shows the investor's desired payoffs in each state. In the example above, the investor would like to receive $1 if the stock price falls between 4 and 7 and zero otherwise.

Note that there are eleven states and eleven securities with linearly independent payoffs. Thus, using these eleven securities, one should be able to create any desired payoff structure.

General problem and solution method

Below you will be asked to determine the portfolio composition for several desired payoff structures. To determine any structure, you can simply change the entries in the target column of the Excel worksheet. However, see if you can first figure out each solution by hand. The number of units of each security necessary to achieve the target payoffs will appear in the solution section of the Excel worksheet.

1. Construct a portfolio that pays:
   a. $1 provided the stock price falls between $4 and $7 but zero otherwise.
   b. $0 if stock ≥ 7
      $1 if stock $= 6$
      $2 if stock $= 5$
      $1 if stock $= 4$
      $0 if stock ≤ 3
   c. $5 if stock ≤ 5 and an amount equal to the stock price if stock ≥ 6
   d. $5 if stock ≥ 5 and an amount equal to the stock price if stock ≤ 4
   e. For stock price from 10 to 0: payoffs of $1, -1, 1, -1$, etc.
   f. For stock price from 10 to 0: payoffs of $+1, -2, +3, -4, +5, -6, +7, -8, +9, -10, +11$
   g. For stock prices from 10 to 6: payoff $= 0$ For stock prices from 5 to 0: payoff $= 1, 2, 3, 4, 5$
   h. $0 if stock ≥ 6
      $1 if stock $= 5$
      $0 if stock ≤ 4
      How could the solution to part h be used to solve the other parts of this problem without actually going through the linear algebra?

2. What would happen to your algebraic solutions in question 1 if, in addition to the call options, put options with striking prices ranging from $1 to $9 were also available for trading?

3. Drawing on your solutions to question 1, discuss how options trading helps to improve the allocation of stock market risks beyond that available with stock and safe asset trading alone.

Problem 4 should only be assigned to advanced students who are comfortable with matrix algebra.

4. The purpose of this problem is to illustrate how desired portfolio payoff structures can be achieved using stock, safe assets and exchange-traded options in combination, even when there are an insufficient number of securities to span (cover) the relevant state-dependent outcomes.

Setup
Assume you can trade a single stock, safe assets, and a call option with a striking price of $100 on the same stock. The call option matures after three binomial periods. You would like to use these three securities to create the synthetic equivalent of a call option with a striking price of $90 that also matures in three binomial periods. A summary of the payoff structure of these three securities is shown below. This same data is also provided in an Excel worksheet entitled Dennis_Rjr.xls, found on the website http://www.rendleman.com/book.

Available securities					Target
				Call K=	Call K=
		Stock	Safe	100	90
		172.8	1	72.8	82.8
	144				
	120	44.99	129.6	1	29.6	39.6
100	23.07	108			
10.82	90	10.75	97.2	1	0	7.2
	3.90	81			
		0.00	72.9	1	0	0

$t = 0$	$t = 1$	$t = 2$	$t = 3$

	$r = 0.01$	
	$u = 1.2$	
	$d = 0.9$	$\pi = 0.3667$

Figure Q.1   Question 4

In figure Q.1 the second number in the tree, for example $10.82, represents the value of call option with striking price of $100.

Problem
Note that there are four state-dependent outcomes at time 3 but only three traded securities: the stock, safe asset and call with a striking

price of $100. Thus, it should not be possible to replicate the target security's payoffs by taking a position in the three traded securities and maintaining the position until time 3 without revision. However, in an effort to replicate the target security, it should be possible to take a position in the three traded securities while, simultaneously, planning to make one portfolio revision, either at time 1 or at time 2.

In an effort to replicate the time-3 payoffs of the target security, assume that you take an initial position among the three traded securities with the expectation of making a portfolio revision at time 1.

a.   What should the portfolio composition be in both the up and down states at time 1 and the value of the replicating portfolio in both states at time 1?

b.   Using the solution to part a, determine *an* initial portfolio composition that will produce the required funds at time 1. (There is actually more than one such portfolio that will accomplish this objective.)

   Now, assume that you plan to make your portfolio revisions at time 2, rather than at time 1.

c.   What should be the portfolio composition in the initial state?

d.   At time 2, assume the initial call option position is maintained and not revised. Determine what changes are necessary in the stock and safe asset positions for all three states at time 2 in order to replicate the time-3 payoffs of the target security.

A little help

The Excel file Arrow_Debreu.xls, found on the website http://www.rendleman.com/book, solves the four equations in four unknowns for the examples in section 9.2.

In problem 4 above, you will not need to solve four equations in four unknowns, but may need to solve three equations in three unknowns and/or two equations in two unknowns. Although Arrow_Debreu.xls is not set up for anything other than four equations, you can examine its structure to determine the Excel code necessary to solve general linear equation systems using matrix algebra.

Note, when you enter matrix algebra code in Excel, you must highlight the entire area in which you want to enter matrix algebra. Then, enter the matrix code, but do not put in the braces {} that you see in the code of the Arrow_Debreu.xls file. Instead, enter code such as = MMULT(MINVERSE(...etc.)), and when you are finished, press ctrl-shift-enter. This will enter the matrix algebra code for the entire highlighted region and put in the braces automatically.

If this all sounds confusing, go to Excel Help to learn how to code matrix algebra.

10

The Use of Exchange-traded Options in Asset Allocation

10.1   Introduction

> The most important decision made by an investor or portfolio manager is the allocation of funds among broad classes of financial assets.

In its simplest form, asset allocation involves deciding on the proportion of portfolio funds to allocate between safe and risky assets or how to appropriately lever a portfolio of risky assets through borrowing. In more advanced form, the decision can involve the allocation of funds across a wider range of asset groups such as domestic stocks, international stocks, long and short-term bonds, real estate, precious metals, foreign currencies, and so on.

The analysis in this chapter focuses on the most fundamental asset allocation problem of choosing the proportion of funds to allocate between risky and safe assets but modified to include the possibility of investing in an exchange-traded call or put option issued against the risky asset. If viewed within the context of an index portfolio of S&P 500-type assets, the allocation decision would involve choosing the proportion of wealth to allocate to the S&P, the proportion of wealth to allocate to safe assets (or borrowing, if the proportion in safe assets turns out to be negative), and the proportion to allocate to a call or put option on the S&P index.

10.2   Some Simple Allocation Rules Derived from Option Pricing Theory

Both the binomial and Black–Scholes option pricing models use option replication as a basis for determining equilibrium, or fair, option values.

Consider the binomial model. In any binomial state it is possible to form a portfolio, consisting of a positive or negative quantity of the underlying stock and a positive or negative quantity of safe assets, that will have the same value as the option in both the up and down states which immediately follow. However, if the stock–safe asset portfolio is to maintain its replication properties, the quantities of both assets must be changed in each binomial state. Nevertheless, by making appropriate changes to these quantities, one can employ a strategy of trading in the underlying stock and safe assets that should provide a payoff structure identical to that of the option. Inasmuch as the stock–safe asset strategy and the option have identical values in every state, the option's initial value should be the same as that of the replicating portfolio. The story behind the Black–Scholes model is the same, except that an infinite number of changes would have to be made to the stock–safe asset replicating portfolio to ensure that its value corresponds to that of the option at all times.

Consider a hypothetical investor in a binomial world who must allocate his portfolio funds among an S&P 500-type index fund, safe assets, and a single call option on the S&P. The theory of asset allocation requires that we know something about the investor's attitude toward risk (utility function) before we can determine how much of the investor's wealth should be allocated among various asset groups. However, without knowing anything about the investor's risk preferences, other than that he prefers more wealth to less, we can make some important general observations about portfolio choice involving stock, options and safe assets based on the binomial and Black–Scholes theories of option pricing.

> If options are properly priced,[39] and an investor is able to buy and sell securities costlessly at the end of every relevant trading period, options cannot improve portfolio outcomes beyond what could otherwise be achieved using stock and safe assets alone.

This is a very simple logical extension of option replication theory. If an option can be replicated using a stock–safe asset trading strategy, there is nothing to be gained by employing options in a portfolio that could not already be achieved using stock and safe assets alone.

This same principle can apply in other contexts. Suppose Leonardo DaVinci had only primary colors on his palate of paints when he painted the Mona Lisa. Could the Mona Lisa have been even more of a masterpiece if DaVinci had had access to more colors? The answer depends on both

---

39. Henceforth, properly priced means priced according to the binomial model in a binomial world or according to the Black–Scholes model in a Black–Scholes world, or more generally, priced according to any rational model of option pricing based on the theory of option replication.

DaVinci's ability to mix colors and the cost, in terms of wasted time, in doing so.

If DaVinci had been a master at mixing primary colors to achieve any desired color beyond the primaries, and he could do the mixing with sufficient speed so as not to lose the inspiration and emotional feeling reflected in the painting, then having a ready-mixed palate of non-primaries would have been of no use and could not have made the Mona Lisa a better painting. On the other hand, if DaVinci had not mastered the craft of paint mixing, and had only primaries at his disposal, perhaps the Mona Lisa might have been even better.

Using DaVinci as a point of departure, if there is something about stock–safe asset option replication that is the securities market-equivalent to DaVinci being unable to mix paint, or his inability to do so without losing his inspiration, then including options in the portfolio mix may enable an investor to achieve a superior portfolio than that which could be achieved with stock and safe assets alone. Thus, we must look to imperfections in securities markets or investor behaviors to find options to be useful in asset allocation. This leads to the following observation:

> Options that are priced fairly may improve portfolio outcomes over what would otherwise be an optimal allocation of stock and safe assets, provided that options reduce stock–safe asset trading costs or reduce constraints imposed on the investor, either directly through market structures, or indirectly through the investor's own rational choice.

Consider figure 10.1 (identical to figure 3.3) which illustrates the binomial replication strategy for a three-period call option with stock and striking prices equal to 100, $u = 1.2$, $d = 0.9$ and a riskless interest rate of 0.01 per binomial period. Note that the initial stock and safe asset replication quantities involve buying 0.63901 shares of stock at $100 per share and borrowing $53.079, for a net outlay of $63.901 − $53.079 = $10.822. Stated differently, the option replicating portfolio consists of investing the proportion $63.901/$10.822 = 5.90 in stock and −$53.079/$10.822 = −4.90 in safe assets. Thus, for each dollar invested in the option, the replicating portfolio consists of 5.90 dollars invested in stock and 4.90 dollars borrowed at the 0.01 riskless rate of interest.

Transaction costs

Consider an investor who does not have access to the options market. For every dollar of original portfolio funds, the investor would like to borrow an additional $4.90 to buy $5.90 in stock. Moreover, the investor wishes

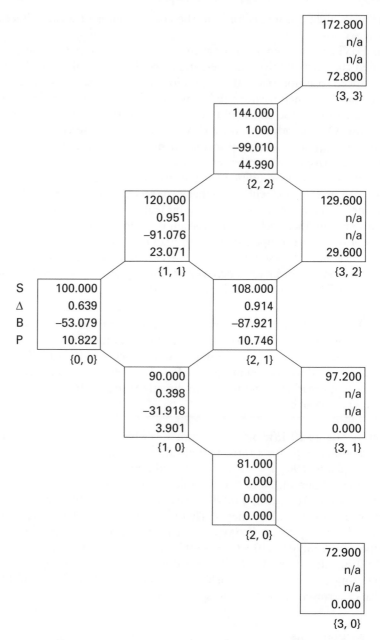

Figure 10.1 Pricing a three-period European call option with a $100 striking
price. Riskless interest rate is 1 percent per binomial period

to maintain these investment proportions at all times. Thus, at the end of each binomial period, whether the stock goes up or down, the investor wants to get back to the same relative proportions in stock and safe assets. At the same time, the portfolio revisions at the end of each binomial period that are required to get the portfolio back to $5.90 in stock per dollar of value are subject to transaction costs.

Now consider the purchase of the call option as a substitute for the initial highly levered stock portfolio. If the transaction costs associated with buying the option are less than those associated with establishing the levered stock position, the investor may want to start out investing in options as a substitute. (Note, if levered stock is a substitute for an option, then the option must be a substitute for levered stock.) However, the option will only serve as a perfect substitute for the levered stock position with constant portfolio proportions for one binomial period, not forever. For example, as shown in figure 10.1, if the stock goes up after the end of the first binomial period, the option will be equivalent in risk to 0.95123 shares of stock at $120 and borrowing $91.076, with a total value of $0.95123(\$120) - \$91.076 = \$23.071$. At this point the leverage-equivalent portfolio proportions are $0.95123(\$120)/\$23.071 = 4.95$ in stock and $-\$91.076/\$23.071 = -3.95$ in safe assets. If the investor wants to continue to maintain a portfolio proportion of 5.90 proportion in stock, the option is no longer equivalent to the desired leveraged stock portfolio. Therefore, additional funds must be borrowed and invested in stock to bring the portfolio's implicit stock–safe asset proportions back to 5.90 and −4.90. Nevertheless, with transaction costs, it may be cheaper to buy the call option initially and then make appropriate portfolio adjustments at the end of each binomial period than to maintain the leveraged stock portfolio using direct stock investment and leverage.

Borrowing constraints

Ordinary investors and portfolio managers are restricted in the amount they can borrow to buy stock through the Federal Reserve's Regulation T. Regulation T does not allow an ordinary investor to borrow more than his initial equity to purchase stocks. According to Regulation T, if an ordinary investor were to establish a brokerage account with $100,000, he could borrow another $100,000 to buy a total of $200,000 in stock, but that is all. Thus, the highest stock proportion permitted by Regulation T is 2.0.

Going back to the investor who would like to borrow $4.90 dollars per dollar of initial investment capital to purchase $5.90 in stock, Regulation T would not permit the investor to borrow a sufficient amount of funds to form his optimal portfolio. However, by purchasing the call option whose replication strategy is illustrated in figure 10.1, he can at least start out with an implicit amount of leverage equal to that which he finds optimal. Thus, the purchase of a call option enables the investor to obtain implied leverage beyond that allowed by Regulation T but without violating any laws.

Short selling constraints

When using a dynamic stock–safe asset trading strategy to replicate a long position in a put, the composition of the replicating portfolio consists of a short position in stock whose proceeds are used to partially fund a long position in the safe asset. In practice, however, it is almost impossible for an individual investor or portfolio manager to engage in such a strategy, since such investors cannot employ the proceeds of short sales for reinvestment.[40] In fact, margin rules require that an investor entering into a short stock position must have cash equity in his account equal to the value of stock in which the short position is taken. Moreover, stock exchange rules do not allow a short position in stock to be taken on a downtick.[41] Thus, despite the theoretical equivalence between a long position in a put and a replicating portfolio that involves short stock coupled with a long position in safe assets, investors who are unable to take short positions due to margin restrictions and uptick rules should find that put options expand their investment opportunities. As such, the ability to invest in exchange-traded puts could allow some investors to form portfolios with greater return potential than would otherwise be available with stock and safe asset investing alone.

Self-imposed constraints

According to standard finance theory, an investor determines how his wealth should be allocated among competing assets by choosing a portfolio mix that maximizes expected utility. Although few investors could describe the motivation behind their portfolio choices in terms of a mathematical

---

40. This is not entirely true. This statement applies to myself and most individual investors that I know. However, if I were very wealthy, and could potentially generate a large sum of commissions for my stock brokerage firm, the firm might cut a deal which would enable me to share in a portion of the interest that the brokerage firm would otherwise earn on the proceeds of my short sales. In contrast to individual investors, investment firms are able to short stock and reinvest the proceeds of the short sale.

41. Short sales can only be executed on an uptick or zero uptick. An uptick occurs when the transaction price for the short sale is greater than the price of the most recent transaction. A zero uptick occurs when the transaction price of the short sale is the same as the previous price, but the most recent change in price was positive.

utility function, financial economists believe that there are certain functions that do a reasonable job predicting how investors will make portfolio choices.

Consider an investor who makes portfolio choices based on an "isoelastic" utility function. The mathematical form of this utility function, shown later in equation 10.1, implies that such an investor cares about percentage changes in the value of his portfolio, rather than dollar changes, and would find a given percentage change in wealth, whether positive or negative, to provide the same level of satisfaction or dissatisfaction, regardless of his wealth level. Thus, "isoelastics" would obtain equal satisfaction going from $10,000 in wealth to $11,000 or $1,000,000 in wealth to $1,100,000. So if you think that way, you are an "isoelastic" whether you like it or not! But there is another property common to isoelastic choice; those who make portfolio choices based on isoelastic utility will avoid bankruptcy at all costs, or stated differently, will assign infinitely negative utility to the prospect of zero or negative wealth. This implies that investors of this type would avoid any type of leverage arrangement that would risk a zero or negative wealth outcome (i.e., bankruptcy). As such, isoelastic utility-maximizing investors may place self-imposed limits on the amounts they will borrow to buy risky assets.

For example, consider the binomial stock price dynamics shown in figure 10.1 in which the underlying stock returns either 1.2 or 0.9 dollars per dollar invested at the end of each binomial period. If the borrowing rate is 0.01 per binomial period, an investor who wishes to avoid bankruptcy would never borrow more than 8.1818 times his wealth at a 1 percent interest rate to invest the proportion 9.1818 of his wealth in stock. With these portfolio proportions, if the down state occurs, the value of the portfolio per dollar invested will be $9.1818(0.9) - $8.1818(1.01) = $0, and with greater leverage, the investor would end up with a negative value portfolio.

> As the binomial time interval becomes smaller, while holding the stock's mean return and standard deviation constant, it is less likely that an investor will incur a large loss over any single binomial period, and, therefore, the investor should be willing to use more leverage. In fact, if a binomial interval were infinitesimally small, there would be no risk of bankruptcy over any single binomial interval for any amount of leverage!

This same result can be generalized to a continuous-revision framework by assuming that any fixed length of time is partitioned into an infinite number of binomial intervals, with the up and down factors for the underlying stock chosen to hold the mean and standard deviation of the logarithmic stock returns constant over the fixed time period. From Chapter 4, we know that this type of binomial process approaches a lognormal distribution of stock returns when the number of binomial periods approaches infinity. Moreover, when the probabilities of up and down movements are equally likely, this convergence is very rapid. Therefore, . . .

if stock returns are lognormal, and an investor is able to continuously rebalance his portfolio, he can employ any amount of borrowing without risking ruin.

However, if the same investor were to borrow any amount of money to buy stock and maintain the position without revision over any fixed length of time, there would be a finite probability that the portfolio could end up with a zero or negative value. This leads to the following observation:

Any investor who assigns infinitely negative utility to outcomes of zero or negative wealth, and who believes stock returns are lognormal, will not borrow to buy stock if he cannot rebalance his portfolio continuously.

The rationale behind this observation is simple. If a portfolio strategy of borrowing to buy stock without revising the portfolio has a positive probability of resulting in infinitely negative utility, then the expected utility from such a strategy will be infinitely negative. As such, the investor would avoid taking a position in such a portfolio at all costs.

Why options enable investors to get around self-imposed borrowing constraints

As will be shown later in this chapter, it is relatively simple to determine the optimal allocation between stock and safe assets for an isoelastic utility maximizing investor who trades stock with lognormal returns and can make continuous revisions in his portfolio. As one might expect, the optimal proportion of wealth to hold in stock is an increasing function of the stock's expected return, that is, the higher the expected return, the more the investor will want to hold stock and reduce safe asset holdings. For a sufficiently high expected stock return, an investor who can continuously revise his portfolio could find it optimal to borrow to buy stock.

Unfortunately, if an investor is unable to revise his portfolio continuously and, instead, must maintain his stock and safe asset positions for a fixed length of time, the use of any borrowing would produce some risk of a zero or negative wealth outcome and, therefore, would be avoided. Suppose an isoelastic utility-maximizing investor would find it optimal to hold an all-stock portfolio, provided the expected return on the stock is 12 percent. If this same investor could not make continuous revisions to his portfolio, he would also choose an all-stock portfolio if the stock's expected return were 15 percent, 20 percent, or even 1000 percent. In these later cases, the self-imposed constraint against borrowing prevents the investor from taking advantage of the higher levels of expected return.

However, if the same investor is able to hold stock and buy a call option on the same stock or index, he can create limited liability leverage through the option without risking a zero or negative portfolio outcome. In the process, he can achieve a much higher level of expected utility when the stock's expected return is higher than would have been obtainable without access to call option investing.

How options help investors to get around self-imposed short selling constraints

For reasons mentioned earlier, institutional arrangements in the securities market make it very difficult to employ short selling to the extent that optimal portfolio allocation rules might imply. However, even if there were no uptick rules and restrictions against the reinvestment of short sale proceeds, isoelastic utility maximizing investors who do not have access to the options market and cannot rebalance their portfolios on a continuous basis would never sell stock short. Why? For the same reasons they would not borrow; short selling stock in any amount creates a risk of ruin. Thus, without options, . . .

> an isoelastic utility maximizing investor who cannot make continuous portfolio revisions would never short stock, no matter how pessimistic he might be about the stock's return prospects.

With options, however, an investor who is very pessimistic about a stock's return prospects can short the stock and buy a call option on the stock to provide insurance against an unanticipated increase in the stock's value. As such, . . .

> the ability to take an option position will enable a pessimistic isoelastic utility maximizing investor to achieve a higher level of expected utility than could be achieved with stock and safe assets alone.

10.3   The Mathematics of Continuous Time Portfolio Building Using Stock and Safe Assets

This section develops the mathematics of optimal stock and safe asset portfolio selection for an investor who can make continuous portfolio revisions and whose portfolio choices are based on maximizing an isoelastic utility function.[42]

Mathematically, isoelastic utility takes the following form:

$$U(H) = \frac{H^{1-\omega} - 1}{1 - \omega},$$

(10.1)

where $U(H)$ is the utility associated with a return per dollar invested of H, and ω is the investor's coefficient of relative risk aversion. Higher values of ω indicate a greater aversion to risk and would result in an investor making more conservative portfolio choices. Although not obvious from a simple inspection of equation 10.1, the limit of $U(H)$ as $\omega \to 1$ is $U(H) = \ln(H)$. Thus, logarithmic utility, a common function for illustrating portfolio choice under conditions of uncertainty, is a special case of isoelastic utility.

Optimal holdings

Consider an investor whose portfolio choices are characterized by isoelastic utility and who is faced with the problem of forming an optimal portfolio consisting of a single stock or stock index and a safe asset. The returns of the underlying stock are assumed to follow a lognormal distribution, and the investor can make continuous portfolio revisions. Thus, based on the analysis developed earlier, there would be no risk of ruin in a continuously revised leveraged portfolio and, therefore, no self-imposed constraint on borrowing. Although the mathematical details are omitted here, it can be shown that the optimal proportion of portfolio funds to hold in stock, q_S^*, and, implicitly, in safe assets, $1 - q_S^*$, is given by the following equation:

$$q_S^* = \frac{\mu_a + \frac{1}{2}\sigma_a^2 - r_a}{\omega \sigma_a^2},$$

(10.2)

---

42.   More detailed mathematics for all results obtained in this section can be found in Richard J. Rendleman, Jr., "Optimal Long Run Option Investment Strategies." *Financial Management* (Spring 1981), 61–76.

where μ_a is the stock's expected annual logarithmic or continuous return, σ_a^2 is the variance of the annual logarithmic return, and r_a is the continuously compounded annual risk-free rate of interest. As one might expect, equation 10.2 shows that optimal stock allocations increase with higher expected logarithmic return (μ_a), but decrease with higher return variance. The higher the interest rate, the more the investor would want to invest in safe assets rather than stock. Also, investors who are very risk averse, as measured by high values of ω, are inclined to put less money into stock.

Instantaneous expected returns and expected returns over longer time intervals

In equation 10.2, the term $\mu_a + \frac{1}{2}\sigma_a^2$ is sometimes referred to as the *stock's instantaneous expected return*, or the annualized expected return earned over an instantaneously small time interval. Although it is not obvious that the mean logarithmic return and logarithmic variance combine in this manner to produce an expected return, the following example using binomial outcomes as an approximation to a lognormal process illustrates why $\mu_a + \frac{1}{2}\sigma_a^2$ can be interpreted as an expected return.

Consider a stock whose returns follow a binomial process over the course of one year with $u = e^{0.10} = 1.10517$, $d = e^{-0.10} = 0.90484$. Assume that up and down returns are equally likely to occur. In this case, the expected logarithmic return, μ_a, is zero and the variance of the logarithmic return, σ_a^2, is 0.01. The expected (non-logarithmic) return is $0.5(0.10517) + 0.5(-0.09516) = 0.005003709$, or approximately one-half of 1 percent. Given the close relationship between the lognormal and binomial distributions, we can use $\mu_a + \frac{1}{2}\sigma_a^2$ to approximate the expected return:

$$\mu_a + \tfrac{1}{2}\sigma_a^2 = 0 + \tfrac{1}{2}(0.01) = 0.005000.$$

(10.3)

This corresponds to the actual binomial expected return to five significant digits. As the binomial time interval becomes infinitesimally small, these two expected returns converge in value. But even with the one-year binomial period of this example, which is far from instantaneous, the two measures of expected return are remarkably close.

Using the mathematics of compounding, if we allow the binomial process described above to evolve for n time periods (years), the expected return per dollar invested will be 1.005003709^n. For example, after 10 periods, the expected return per dollar invested is $1.005003709^{10} = 1.05118$. If stock returns are lognormal, it can be shown that the expected return per dollar invested after τ years is $e^{(\mu_a + (1/2)\sigma_a^2)\tau}$. Continuing with the same example with $\mu_a = 0$ and $\sigma_a^2 = 0.01$, the expected return per dollar invested after 10 years is $e^{(\mu_a + (1/2)\sigma_a^2)\tau} = e^{(0+0.01)10} = 1.05127$ which is quite close in value to the binomial-based expected return per dollar invested of 1.05118.

When is it optimal to hold an all-stock portfolio when continuous revision is possible?

One of the keys to understanding the use of options in "real world" optimal portfolio allocation is determining the conditions for which it would be optimal to hold an all-stock portfolio if an investor could reallocate stock and safe asset holdings continuously. Equation 10.2 shows the optimal proportion of assets to hold in stock. If q_S^* is set to 1 in equation 10.2, we obtain the conditions for which it is optimal to hold an all-stock portfolio. Making this substitution, an all-stock portfolio will be optimal when

$$\mu_a | (q_S^* = 1) = r_a + \sigma_a^2 \left(\omega - \tfrac{1}{2}\right).$$

$$(10.4)$$

(In equation 10.3, $\mu_S | (q_S^* = 1)$ denotes the mean logarithmic return of the stock, μ_a, under the condition that [or given that] the optimal proportion of portfolio funds to invest in stock, q_S^*, equals 1.) For the special case of logarithmic utility in which $\omega = 1$, an all-stock portfolio will be optimal when $\mu_a = r_a + \tfrac{1}{2}\sigma_a^2$. If we employ 0.05 as the one-year market rate of interest and 0.04 as the variance of annual logarithmic returns (a number which corresponds closely to the historical variance of returns for the S&P 500), an investor who maximizes logarithmic utility would find an all-stock portfolio to be optimal if $\mu_a = 0.05 + \tfrac{1}{2}(0.04) = 0.07$. Recognizing that the expected annual holding period return for lognormally distributed stock is $e^{(\mu_a + (1/2)\sigma_a^2)\tau} = e^{(0.07 + (1/2)(0.04))(1)} = 1.09418$, a logarithmic utility maximizer who can reallocate his portfolio continuously would find it optimal to hold nothing but stock if the expected stock return is 9.417 percent per year, compounded annually (or 9 percent per year compounded continuously).

Implications for optimal stock–safe asset allocation for the buy-and-hold investor

True continuous portfolio revision is not a viable investment alternative for any investor, although many professional investors such as floor traders and investment firms are in a position to make portfolio revisions frequently enough to approximate continuous revision. Thus, continuous-revision-based portfolio building rules may provide these types of investors with reasonable guidelines for determining optimal portfolio allocations.

On the other hand, . . .

> there are many investors for whom frequent portfolio rebalancing is not viable. These investors, such as individuals who hold stock positions for the "long run," or professional portfolio managers who take a long-term approach to investing, are perhaps better characterized as buy-and-hold investors.

For the purposes of this analysis, a buy-and-hold investor is defined as one who is considering using options in his portfolio and plans to hold all security positions without revision through the option's maturity date. Thus, if a buy-and-hold investor were considering the use of a six-month option in his portfolio, he would make his optimal portfolio allocation decision assuming that each stock, safe asset, and option position would be held without revision for six months.

Consider the stock–safe asset portfolio allocation problem of a buy-and-hold investor, ignoring, for the moment, the possibility of investing in options. The investor's portfolio allocation problem can be thought of as being identical to the continuous-time problem, except that the investor is constrained in the frequency of his trading. Thus, he must solve a portfolio selection problem that is more constrained than if continuous revision were allowed, and the fact that the problem is more constrained makes solving the problem more difficult. However, there is an important special-case solution that can be determined without resorting to any additional mathematics.

> As is well-known, and common sense, once you think about it, if the solution to an unconstrained (or less constrained) optimization problem is a feasible solution to a more constrained version of the same problem, it must also be the solution to the constrained problem. To see this principle in a different light, consider the problem of finding the most cost-effective means of traveling from Washington DC to New York City. Assume the solution is to travel by automobile, taking Interstate 95 through Maryland, Pennsylvania, and New Jersey. Now consider the same problem, modified by the constraint that you cannot travel through or over the state of California. Clearly, driving I-95 from DC to New York is a feasible solution to the second problem and, therefore, it must also be optimal. On the other hand, if one were not allowed to travel through or over the state of New Jersey, getting to New York would be more difficult and costly. In the latter case, the constraint, being binding, would result in an optimal solution with higher cost.

Getting back to portfolios, equation 10.3, repeated below, provides the expected logarithmic return of lognormally distributed stock for which an all-stock portfolio is optimal under continuous revision:

$$\mu_a|(q_S^* = 1) = r_a + \sigma_a^2 \left(\omega - \tfrac{1}{2}\right).$$

$$(10.3)$$

Since holding an all-stock portfolio is also a feasible solution for a buy-and-hold investor, when equation 10.3 holds, a buy-and-hold investor would also want to hold an all-stock portfolio. This leads to the following observation:

If stock returns are lognormal and $\mu_a = r_a + \sigma_a^2(\omega - \tfrac{1}{2})$, an investor who maximizes an isoelastic utility function characterized by a coefficient of relative risk aversion equal to ω will find it optimal to hold an all-stock portfolio, regardless of the frequency of his planned portfolio revisions.

If the expected logarithmic return is higher than that given by equation 10.3, an investor who can revise his portfolio continuously will find it optimal to borrow to buy stock. On the other hand, an isoelastic utility maximizing investor who takes a buy-and-hold approach to investing would not borrow, because he would want to avoid the possibility of a zero or negative portfolio outcome. Therefore, even if the expected logarithmic return is higher than that given by equation 10.3, a buy-and-hold investor, limited to investing in stock and safe assets, would not borrow.

Using options to improve the all-stock buy–hold solution

Earlier, it was established that if options are priced according to the Black–Scholes model, there would be no need to include them in a continuously revised stock–safe asset portfolio, since anything that could be accomplished with options could also be accomplished with stock and safe assets. On the other hand, an investor who is constrained to a buy-and-hold strategy might find that options could improve his portfolio outcomes, since options cannot be replicated with a buy-and-hold stock and safe asset position.

As mentioned earlier, a call option is economically equivalent to a limited liability leveraged position in stock. Therefore, a buy-and-hold investor who is optimistic about the stock would find investing in call options as a means of providing leverage without risking ruin. Therefore, ...

> If stock returns are lognormal, $\mu_a > r_a + \sigma_a^2 \left(\omega - \frac{1}{2} \right)$, and a buy-and-hold investor who maximizes isoelastic utility can choose from among stock, safe assets, and a Black–Scholes-priced call option on the stock, his optimal portfolio holdings will involve long positions in both the stock and the call option. Alternatively, using put–call parity, an economically equivalent position could be obtained by borrowing to buy the stock and purchasing a protective put to insure against zero or negative portfolio outcomes.

When is it optimal to hold an all-safe asset portfolio?

Following the analysis of the previous section, if it is optimal to hold an all-safe asset portfolio under continuous revision, it must also be optimal to hold an all safe-asset portfolio when one is constrained to buy-and-hold investing. Since holding all safe assets is feasible for a buy-and-hold investor, and is also the optimal solution to the less constrained continuous revision portfolio selection problem, it must also be the optimal solution for the more constrained buy-and-hold problem. By setting $q_S^* = 0$ in equation 10.2 and rearranging, the condition for which it is optimal for a continuous-time trader to invest all his money in safe assets is obtained:

$$\left(\mu_a + \tfrac{1}{2}\sigma_a^2 \right) \mid \left(q_S^* = 0 \right) = r_a.$$

(10.4)

From this relationship, the following observation can be made:

> If stock returns are lognormal and $\mu_a + \tfrac{1}{2}\sigma_a^2 = r_a$, an investor who maximizes an isoelastic utility function characterized by a coefficient of relative risk aversion equal to ω will find it optimal to hold an all-safe asset portfolio, regardless of the frequency of his planned portfolio revisions.

To better understand this relationship, recall that $\mu_a + \tfrac{1}{2}\sigma_a^2$ is the expected annualized instantaneous return of the stock. The statement above reflects that if the stock's expected return is equal to the riskless interest rate, one would have no incentive to invest in stock, since the returns of the stock are dominated in a risk–return sense by the riskless asset. This result holds regardless of the investor's attitude toward risk as measured by ω.

It is also the case that if the stock's instantaneous expected return is less than that of equation 10.4, an investor who is able to make continuous portfolio revisions would find it optimal to short the stock, investing the proceeds from the short sale in the safe asset. On the other hand, a buy-and-hold investor would not short the stock, because it would open up the possibility of a zero or negative portfolio outcome, an outcome to avoid at all costs. Therefore, if options were not available, a buy-and-hold investor who expects the stock's instantaneous return to be less than the riskless interest rate would put all his money in safe assets, no matter how pessimistic he might be.

Using options to improve the all-safe asset buy–hold solution

If the pessimistic investor is allowed to take a position in a call option, he could eliminate the unlimited risk in a short stock position by purchasing a call option and, thereby, achieve a higher level of expected utility than with stock and safe assets alone. Thus, when $\mu_a + \frac{1}{2}\sigma_a^2 < r_a$, the following observation can be made about the investor's optimal portfolio holdings:

> If stock returns are lognormal, $\mu_a + \frac{1}{2}\sigma_a^2 < r_a$, and a buy-and-hold isoelastic utility maximizing investor can choose from among stock, safe assets and a Black–Scholes-priced call option on the stock when selecting a portfolio, optimal holdings will consist of a short position in stock, a long position in safe assets, and a long position in a call option. Alternatively, using put–call parity, an economically equivalent portfolio would consist of long positions in safe assets and puts.

10.4 Examples of Optimal Portfolio Building Using Stock, Safe Assets, and Options

This section employs a set of examples to illustrate optimal asset allocations using a single stock or index, safe assets, and a single call option or put option issued on the stock or index. Both the put and call are assumed to be European and have the same striking price and maturity date.

> Since put–call parity ensures that investing in a call option, investing the present value of the option's striking price in safe assets and shorting the stock is equivalent to investing in a put, the optimal portfolio allocation using stock, safe assets, and either the call or the put implies an equivalent optimal portfolio involving the other option.

Table 10.1   Assumptions for optimal stock, safe-asset, and option portfolio

Stock price	$100
Option striking price	$120
Option maturity	1 year
Annual continuously compounded riskless rate of interest	0.03
Annual variance of logarithmic stock returns	0.06
Call option price	$4.285
Put option price	$20.738

The stock return is assumed to be lognormally distributed, and the optimal portfolio is assumed to be held without revision until the option's maturity date. Both the call and put prices are computed using the Black–Scholes model.

Therefore, optimal solutions for portfolios involving calls and puts are calculated separately. The optimization procedure is described in Rendleman (1981).

Optimal portfolios when options are fairly priced

Initially, optimal portfolio composition is examined when options are fairly priced. With lognormal stock returns, a fair price is the Black–Scholes price. Table 10.1 provides a summary of the assumptions upon which the analysis is based.

All examples are based on the maximization of a logarithmic utility function. Unlike more general isoelastic utility functions, expected logarithmic utility can be interpreted in a meaningful way by portfolio managers. A portfolio's expected logarithmic utility is equivalent to its expected continuously compounded rate of growth, sometimes referred to as its logarithmic return or growth rate. For example, a portfolio that has a logarithmic expected utility of 0.15 will have an expected continuously compounded rate of growth equal to 15 percent per year. Although I do not wish to imply that logarithmic utility is better than any other form of utility, it does have an interpretation to which most investors can relate.

Equation 10.3, repeated below, gives the condition for which an isoelastic utility maximizer would find it optimal to hold all stock in an optimal stock–safe asset-option portfolio, provided the option is priced according to the Black–Scholes model:

$$\mu_a| \left(q_s^* = 1\right) = r_a + \sigma_a^2 \left(\omega - \tfrac{1}{2}\right).$$

$$(10.3)$$

Table 10.2 Optimal portfolio mix with Black–Scholes pricing (stock's growth rate $\mu_a = 0.06$)

Security	Optimal buy–hold proportions		Optimal continuous revision proportions
	Using calls	Using puts	
Stock	1.0000	1.0000	1.0000
Call	0.0000	n/a	n/a
Put	n/a	0.0000	n/a
Safe asset	0.0000	0.0000	0.0000
Portfolio growth rate*	0.0600	0.0600	0.0600

*Expected logarithmic utility.
Stock's instantaneous expected return $\mu_a + \frac{1}{2}\sigma_a^2 = 0.09$.

With logarithmic utility ($\omega = 1$) and the riskless rate and variance parameters from table 10.1, the expected logarithmic return on the underlying stock or index which would cause an investor to want to hold an all-stock portfolio is:

$$\mu_a \mid \left(q_s^* = 1\right) = 0.03 + 0.06 \left(1 - \tfrac{1}{2}\right) = 0.06. \tag{10.4}$$

Alternatively, the instantaneous expected return, $\mu_a + \frac{1}{2}\sigma_a^2$, would be $0.06 + 0.06 \left(\frac{1}{2}\right) = 0.09$. Although we already know that under these conditions, the optimal portfolio is an all-stock portfolio, table 10.2 summarizes the solution to the optimal buy-and-hold stock–safe asset-option portfolio selection problem as found by the optimization algorithm of Rendleman (1981), as well as the solution to the same problem allowing for continuous portfolio revisions.

Table 10.2 illustrates what we should already know. If $\mu_a = 0.06$, the solutions to the buy-and-hold and continuous revision portfolio selection problems are the same; both problems result in an all-stock portfolio being optimal.

Table 10.3 provides optimal portfolio allocations when the expected logarithmic return for the stock is doubled from 0.06 to 0.12, while all the other parameters of the previous problem are kept the same. In this situation, the continuous-revision strategy calls for borrowing $1 per dollar of initial wealth and investing $2 in the stock or index. The growth rate, or expected logarithmic utility, associated with this portfolio is 0.15.

The buy-and-hold investor who uses call options in his portfolio will invest approximately 89 percent of his money in the stock while investing the remaining 11 percent in the call option. Alternatively, the investor would borrow 2.9632 dollars per dollar of wealth, and using the $2.9632

Table 10.3 Optimal portfolio mix with Black–Scholes pricing (stock's growth rate $\mu_a = 0.12$)

Security	Optimal buy–hold proportions		Optimal continuous revision proportions
	Using calls	Using puts	
Stock	0.8910	3.4355	2.0000
Call	0.1090	n/a	n/a
Put	n/a	0.5277	n/a
Safe asset	0.0000	−2.9632	−1.0000
Portfolio growth rate*	0.1403	0.1403	0.1500

*Expected logarithmic utility.
Stock's instantaneous expected return $\mu_a + \frac{1}{2}\sigma_a^2 = 0.15$.

plus his original $1, he would invest $3.4355 in the stock and $0.5277 in the put. In this case, the put options ensure that the levered stock portfolio will never sustain a zero or negative outcome. Using either the optimal call or put strategy, the portfolio growth rate (expected utility) is 0.1403.

Note that the 0.1403 growth rate associated with the optimal stock–safe asset-option portfolio is not as high as the 0.15 rate of growth that can be achieved with continuous revision. Nevertheless, this is a much higher rate of growth, or level of expected utility, than could be achieved by a buy-and-hold investor who does not have access to options. Without options, a buy-and-hold investor would not borrow; therefore, the maximum achievable growth rate is that of the stock itself, or 0.12. Thus, ...

> the use of options enables a buy-and-hold investor to achieve a significant improvement in expected utility and come much closer to the level of utility that would otherwise be available in the perfect world of continuous revision.

Table 10.4 shows optimal portfolio proportions if the expected growth rate for the stock or index is −0.10. In this situation, optimal continuous revision proportions involve shorting $1.6667 in stock per dollar of wealth and investing the proceeds of the short sale plus the initial dollar into safe assets. The resulting portfolio growth rate is 0.1133 or 11.33 percent.

The buy-and-hold investor will short $2.1864 per dollar of wealth in stock, which, along with the original $1, will provide $3.1864 to invest. $3.0927 of the $3.1864 is invested in safe assets with the remaining $0.0937 invested in the call. Alternatively, for each dollar of initial wealth, $0.4534 is invested in the put with the remainder invested in the

Table 10.4 Optimal portfolio mix with Black–Scholes pricing (stock's growth rate $\mu_a = -0.10$)

Security	Optimal buy–hold proportions		Optimal continuous revision proportions
	Using calls	Using puts	
Stock	−2.1864	0.0000	−1.6667
Call	0.0937	n/a	n/a
Put	n/a	0.4534	n/a
Safe asset	3.0927	0.5466	2.6667
Portfolio growth rate*	0.1075	0.1075	0.1133

*Expected logarithmic utility.
Stock's instantaneous expected return $\mu_a + \frac{1}{2}\sigma_a^2 = -0.07$.

safe assets. In both cases, the resulting portfolio growth rate is 0.1075. Note that this is quite close to the 0.1133 growth rate achievable under continuous revision and much higher than the 0.03 rate of growth that would result if the buy-and-hold investor did not have access to options. Why 0.03? Because the buy-and-hold investor would never risk ruin by shorting the stock, and, therefore, would invest all his funds in the safe asset that earns 3 percent compounded continuously.

Interestingly, I have experimented with many different inputs to this optimization model and have not come up with a single situation using Black–Scholes-priced options in which the popular strategy of covered call writing is optimal, that is buying stock and writing a call option against the stock in a 1 : 1 ratio. This leads to the conclusion that a buy-and-hold investor who has no expertise in identifying over-priced options, and, therefore, must trade options at fair market prices, would never find it optimal to engage in fully-covered call writing. No matter what his feeling might be about the growth prospects of the stock, there will always be a better option strategy.

Summary and implications regarding the use of fairly-priced options by buy-and-hold investors

The Black–Scholes[43] theory indicates that options are redundant securities in relation to stock and safe assets when investors can make costless and continuous portfolio revisions. In this framework, options that are

---

43. This discussion refers throughout to Black–Scholes pricing and the ability (or lack thereof) of investors to make continuous portfolio revisions. The discussion could also be cast in terms of binomial pricing and the ability (or lack thereof) to make

priced according to the Black–Scholes model cannot improve the portfolio prospects of any investor, regardless of his attitude toward risk. However, if investors are unable to make portfolio revisions as often as the Black–Scholes theory suggests, options priced according to the Black–Scholes model can improve return prospects beyond what would otherwise be available with stock and safe assets alone and, thereby, increase investor utility.

Since an option that is priced according to the Black–Scholes model is redundant relative to the particular continuous revision-based stock–safe asset trading strategy implied in its pricing, taking a position in the option is equivalent to engaging in that same continuous revision strategy. Given the economic characteristics of an option, its equivalent continuous revision-based stock–safe asset trading strategy will never involve rebalancing stock and safe assets back to constant proportions, a strategy which will provide the highest level of expected utility for an isoelastic utility maximizing investor. Nevertheless, the fact that an option is equivalent to some from of continuous revision-based stock–safe asset investing provides a buy-and-hold investor with an expanded set of stock–safe asset-equivalent payoff possibilities – the buy–hold outcomes directly available from stock and safe assets, and the continuous revision outcomes implied in the pricing of the option. Since an option expands the stock–safe asset-equivalent portfolio outcomes beyond those available from a simple buy-and-hold strategy, a buy-and-hold investor who has access to Black–Scholes-priced options can get closer to the level of expected utility associated with continuous portfolio revision. As a result, . . .

> options priced according to the Black–Scholes model, or more generally, options that are fairly priced, have the potential to significantly expand the investment opportunities of buy-and-hold investors and improve both the return prospects and utility levels associated with their portfolios.

Optimal portfolios using mispriced options

An investor who can buy and sell options which are either over-or under-priced relative to the Black–Scholes model could achieve infinite expected utility in an optimal continuous revision strategy by engaging in an infinite amount of riskless arbitrage. Therefore, with the continuous trading of

---

portfolio revisions at the end of each binomial period. References to the binomial model are omitted to avoid having to refer to both models throughout the discussion.

mispriced options, investors can achieve levels of expected utility infinitely higher than the levels available from optimal portfolios that employ stock and safe assets alone.

Although a buy-and-hold investor cannot achieve infinite expected utility by including mispriced options in his portfolio, the arbitrage profit implied in the pricing of an option can enable a buy-and-hold investor to achieve a level of expected utility significantly higher than the highest level available from a pure continuous revision-based strategy using stock and safe assets. One can think of a mispriced option as providing an investor the ability to purchase its equivalent continuous revision stock–safe asset portfolio at a discount or premium. If such a portfolio were priced fairly, it would not be preferred to an optimal stock–safe asset portfolio that is revised continuously to constant proportions. But if one could purchase the option-equivalent continuous revision portfolio at a discount, the purchase of such an option to ensure against extreme upside or downside risks in connection with a static buy-and-hold portfolio could easily dominate an optimal continuously revised stock–safe asset portfolio in terms of its expected utility. On the other hand, if the option-equivalent continuous revision portfolio sells for a premium, purchasing the option as insurance against extreme upside or downside risks would reduce the level of expected utility available to a buy-and-hold investor. With this as background, we now approach the same portfolio selection problem under the assumption that the option bought or sold in connection with a buy-and-hold strategy is mispriced relative to the Black–Scholes model.

Under-priced options

This analysis maintains all the assumptions of the previous section except that the call and put options are assumed to be priced as if the annual variance of logarithmic stock returns in 0.04 rather than 0.06. However, for the purposes of forming a portfolio that maximizes expected utility, the buy-and-hold investor continues to believe the variance is 0.06. Table 10.5 summarizes the results for the situation in which the stock's growth rate is 0.12, a situation that parallels table 10.3 using Black–Scholes pricing.

Compared with the solution shown in table 10.3, a significantly larger position is taken in the call option to take advantage of its limited liability leverage provided at a relatively inexpensive price ($2.767 per option compared with the Black–Scholes price of $4.285 in table 10.3). In contrast to the optimal solution of table 10.3, a small long position is also taken in safe assets. Note that the growth rate of the optimal buy-and-hold portfolio is 0.2101 compared with only 0.15 for an optimal continuously revised stock–safe asset portfolio. The put-equivalent buy–hold portfolio involves

Table 10.5 Optimal portfolio mix using under-priced options (stock's growth rate $\mu_a = 0.12$)

| Security | Optimal buy–hold proportions | | Optimal continuous revision proportions* |
	Using calls	Using puts	
Stock	0.6634	8.2477	2.0000
Call	0.2098	n/a	n/a
Put	n/a	1.4577	n/a
Safe asset	0.1270	−8.7054	−1.0000
Portfolio growth rate**	0.2101	0.2101	0.1500

Both the call and put option are priced as if the annual variance of logarithmic return is 0.04 rather than 0.06. This results in a call price of $2.767 and a put price of $19.220.

*Stock and safe assets only.

**Expected logarithmic utility.

Stock's instantaneous expected return $\mu_a + \frac{1}{2}\sigma_a^2 = 0.15$.

a substantially levered stock portfolio, $8.2477 invested in stock per dollar of wealth, with a substantial position in the put option ($1.4577 per dollar of wealth) to provide downside protection.

Table 10.6 summarizes optimal allocations for the situation in which the stock's growth rate is −0.10, a situation which parallels that which is summarized in table 10.4 with Black–Scholes pricing. Compared with table 10.4 results, the buy-and-hold solution with calls involves a substantially higher short position in stock protected by less expensive call options. The put-equivalent solution involves substantial borrowing to purchase a large number of puts (actually $0.8386/19.22 = 0.0436$, i.e., the put proportion divided by put price) per dollar invested and a lesser number of stock shares ($1.3505/100 = 0.013505$). The growth rate, or expected utility, of 0.1520 is significantly higher than the 0.1133 growth rate associated with an optimal continuously revised stock–bond portfolio.

Over-priced options

The analysis of optimal buy-and-hold portfolios using over-priced options parallels that using under-priced options, except that the call and put options are assumed to be priced with an annual variance of 0.08. This results in a call price of $5.653 and a put price of $22.1062. Table 10.7 summarizes optimal portfolio allocations for the situation in which the stock's growth rate is 0.12, a situation which parallels table 10.3 using Black–Scholes pricing.

Table 10.6 Optimal portfolio mix using under-priced options (stock's growth rate $\mu_a = -0.10$)

| Security | Optimal buy–hold proportions | | Optimal continuous revision proportions* |
	Using calls	Using puts	
Stock	−3.0120	1.3504	−1.6667
Call	0.1217	n/a	n/a
Put	n/a	0.8385	n/a
Safe asset	3.8913	−1.1889	2.6667
Portfolio growth rate**	0.1520	0.1520	0.1133

Both the call and put option are priced as if the annual variance of logarithmic returns is 0.04 rather than 0.06. This results in a call price of $2.767 and a put price of $19.220.
*Stock and safe assets only.
**Expected logarithmic utility.
Stock's instantaneous expected return $\mu_a + \frac{1}{2}\sigma_a^2 = -0.07$.

Table 10.7 Optimal portfolio mix using under-priced options (stock's growth rate $\mu_a = 0.12$)

| Security | Optimal buy–hold proportion | | Optimal continuous revision proportions* |
	Using calls	Using puts	
Stock	0.9734	1.4447	2.0000
Call	0.0266	n/a	n/a
Put	n/a	0.1042	n/a
Safe asset	0.0000	−0.5489	−1.0000
Portfolio growth rate**	0.1210	0.1210	0.1500

Both the call and put option are priced as if the annual variance of logarithmic returns is 0.08 rather than 0.06. This results in a call price of $5.653 and a put price of $22.106.
*Stock and safe assets only.
**Expected logarithmic utility.
Stock's instantaneous expected return $\mu_a + \frac{1}{2}\sigma_a^2 = 0.15$.

The buy-and-hold results in table 10.7 show a substantial reduction in expected utility, or portfolio growth, from that shown in table 10.3. In table 10.3, in which it is assumed that options are properly priced, the expected portfolio growth rate is 0.1403, but with over-priced options, the growth rate falls to 0.1210. The reason for this reduction in growth is that call options that are purchased to provide limited liability leverage,

Table 10.8 Optimal portfolio mix using under-priced options
(stock's growth rate $\mu_a = -0.10$)

| Security | Optimal buy–hold proportions | | Optimal continuous revision proportions* |
	Using calls	Using puts	
Stock	−1.7452	0.0000	−1.6667
Call	0.0988	n/a	n/a
Put	n/a	0.3685	n/a
Safe asset	2.6494	0.6135	2.6667
Portfolio growth rate**	0.0806	0.0806	0.1133

Both the call and put option are priced as if the annual variance of logarith-
mic returns is 0.08 rather than 0.06. This results in a call price of $5.653
and a put price of $22.106.
*Stock and safe assets only.
**Expected logarithmic utility.
Stock's instantaneous expected return $\mu_a + \frac{1}{2}\sigma_a = -0.07$.

or puts which are purchased to provide downside protection for a levered
stock position, are both very expensive. In fact, they are so expensive
that for all practical purposes, the 0.1210 growth rate is so close to the
0.1200 growth rate of an all-stock portfolio that it would probably not be
cost-effective to use options at all.

Similarly, as illustrated in table 10.8, when the investor is pessimistic
and anticipates a −0.10 growth rate for the stock, the use of over-
priced options in a buy-and-hold portfolio substantially reduces portfolio
expected utility or growth from that available with fairly priced options
(0.0806 vs. 0.1075). Under the pessimistic scenario, the call-based strategy still involves buying the call to protect a short position in the stock.
But since the call protection is expensive, less stock is shorted and fewer
calls are purchased.

With fairly-priced options, the put-based strategy consists of long positions in both the put and safe assets. Although purchasing over-priced puts
can still allow a buy-and-hold investor to take advantage of his pessimistic
outlook, the over-pricing prohibits him from taking full advantage, thereby
reducing his level of expected utility or portfolio growth. In this particular
case, however, the portfolio growth rate of 0.0806 is significantly greater
than the non-option buy-and-hold alternative of earning 0.03 in riskless
securities. Thus, despite having to use over-priced options, a buy-and-
hold investor can achieve a significant improvement in portfolio outcomes
compared with not using options at all.

Table 10.9 Analysis of option writing as an optimal strategy for a buy-and-hold investor who maximizes logarithmic utility

Stock growth rate	To induce any option writing		To induce fully-covered call writing	
	Implied variance	Portfolio growth rate	Implied variance	Portfolio growth rate
−0.06	0.1290	0.0300	0.2139	0.0539
0.00	0.0600	0.0600	0.1195	0.0512
0.03*	0.0593	0.0375	0.0821	0.0498
0.06**	0.0600	0.0600	0.0756	0.0666
0.12	0.0870	0.1200	0.1215	0.1352
0.18	0.1255	0.1800	0.1964	0.2095

*Continuously compounded riskless interest rate.
**Stock growth rate which causes all-stock portfolio to be optimal.

When does fully-covered call writing come into play?[44]

The foregoing examples examined a wide range of option pricing possibilities in connection with a wide range of stock growth forecasts. In no instance did option writing enter the optimal solution for a buy-and-hold investor. Generally, an optimistic buy-and-hold investor would like to borrow to buy stock if it were not for his utility-imposed constraint against risking ruin. But by purchasing calls along with stock, he can achieve leverage without risking a zero or negative portfolio outcome. Thus, even if calls are somewhat over-priced, they would still be attractive as a means of creating limited liability leverage.

Experiments with the optimization program show, however, that a point can be reached in the over-pricing of a call option at which the call is no longer attractive to hold. At this point and beyond, the writing of some calls becomes attractive, and at a higher level of mispricing, a buy-and-hold investor would find it optimal to allocate his entire portfolio to fully covered call writing.

The analysis summarized in table 10.9 shows how this can happen. In table 10.9, various growth rates are assumed for the underlying stock. Throughout the table it is assumed that the variance of logarithmic stock returns is 0.06. For each growth rate, two critical levels of implied variance in the pricing of the option are shown. The first level is the level that causes the buy-and-hold investor to allocate an infinitesimally small proportion of portfolio funds to call writing. The second level is that which causes the buy-and-hold investor to find fully covered call writing to be optimal.

---

44. This section draws on the analysis of covered call writing in Rendleman (2001).

Throughout, the option is assumed to have a striking price of $120 and a one-year maturity as in all previous examples.

Table 10.9 shows that options must be significantly over-priced for covered call writing to be an optimal strategy for either an extremely optimistic or pessimistic investor.

Stated differently, the call must be priced with an implied variance substantially higher than 0.06, the return variance assumed for the stock itself, for covered call writing to be optimal. Since, in the cases of extreme optimism or pessimism, the optimal strategy involving a fairly-priced call is to buy it, the option would have to be extremely over-priced to offset this tendency.

On the other hand, when the stock's growth rate falls between zero and 0.06 (the rate which would cause a buy-and-hold investor to hold an all-stock portfolio), the call option does not have to be nearly as over-priced to justify fully covered call writing. Using common brokerage terminology to characterize this situation, the stock might be said to be in a "trading range," a circumstance that is often used by brokers to justify a recommendation for a customer to engage in fully-covered call writing. Although the resulting growth rates associated with covered call writing are significantly higher than those available from stock (0.00, 0.03, or 0.06) or safe assets (0.03) alone, they are not substantially higher than those available from an optimal buy-and-hold strategy using stock and safe assets without options. Thus, ...

in order to justify covered call writing as an optimal strategy when a stock or index is trading within a "trading range," the call must be somewhat over-priced, and even then, the gains from fully covered writing are not large. Unless an investor is in a position to determine the extent of mispricing for an option he is prepared to write, chances are there will be a strategy involving the same assets which will provide superior outcomes.

10.5 Summary

In this chapter I show how options can be used to increase the level of expected utility (or the rate of portfolio growth, when utility is logarithmic) for an investor who is unable to rebalance his portfolio continuously, as is suggested by standard option pricing theory. If such an investor makes portfolio choices consistent with maximizing an *isoelastic* utility function, he will avoid any possibility of ruin. As such, he will not borrow to buy stock, nor will he sell stock short.

With access to options, however, a buy-and-hold investor can obtain the equivalent of limited liability leverage through the purchase of calls, and can also use calls to provide protection against an adverse price movement in a short stock position. Therefore, a buy-and-hold investor will find it optimal to dedicate a portion of his portfolio to a long position in calls, when he is optimistic about the stock's return prospects, and also take a long position in calls, to cover the risk of shorting stock, when he is pessimistic. Only when the investor is relatively neutral about the stock's return prospects is a strategy involving the writing of calls optimal. Interestingly, the very popular strategy of covered call writing can only be justified for an isoelastic utility maximizing buy-and-hold investor when calls are significantly over-priced.

If options are priced fairly, the level of utility associated with an optimal portfolio consisting of stock, a safe asset and an option on the stock cannot be used to obtain a level of utility as high as that attainable by an investor who can continuously revise a stock–safe asset portfolio. However, if options are mispriced, a buy-and-hold investor can often attain a higher level of utility using options than could be attained with a continuously revised stock–safe asset portfolio. Taken together, these results show that the limited liability leverage associated with options significantly expands the investment possibilities for a buy-and-hold investor, even when options are priced fairly. But when an investor has access to mispriced options, the potential to increase utility (or well-being), by including options as part of stock investing, is even greater.

REFERENCES

Black, F. and M. Scholes, "The Pricing of Options and Corporate Liabilities." *The Journal of Political Economy* 81, No. 3 (May/June 1973), 637–59.

Rendleman, R. J., Jr., "Optimal Long Run Option Investment Strategies." *Financial Management* (Spring 1981), 61–76.

Rendleman, R. J., Jr., "Covered Call Writing from an Expected Utility Perspective." *The Journal of Derivatives* 8 (Spring 2001), 63–75.

RELATED WORK

Carr, P. and D. Madan, "Optimal Positioning in Derivative Securities." *Quantitative Finance* 1 (January 2001), 19–37.

Haugh, M. B. and A. W. Lo, "Asset Allocation and Derivatives." *Quantitative Finance* 1 (January 2001), 45–72.

Rendleman, R. J., Jr. and R. W. McEnally "Assessing the Costs of Portfolio Insurance." *The Financial Analysts Journal* 43 (May/June 1987), 27–37.

QUESTIONS AND PROBLEMS

1. Assume options are priced according to the Black–Scholes model and the price of the underlying stock follows a lognormal distribution. Consider an optimal buy-and-hold portfolio consisting of a stock, a call or put option on the stock and safe assets. Why is the level of expected utility associated with this portfolio less than that associated with an optimal continuously revised portfolio involving the same stock, the same safe asset but no options.

2. Assume you are very pessimistic about the return prospects for a stock $(\mu_a + \frac{1}{2}\sigma_a^2 \ll r_a)$ and that you attempt to maximize a logarithmic utility function when forming a portfolio consisting of a single stock, a call option on the stock and a safe asset. Assume the option is priced according to the Black–Scholes model and the price of the underlying stock follows a lognormal distribution, why does the optimal position in a call option involve buying the call rather than writing the call?

3. Discuss the circumstances for which covered call writing would be an optimal strategy for a logarithmic utility maximizing buy-and-hold investor.

4. Drawing on the analysis of this chapter, why should the existence of active listed options exchanges increase the overall welfare of society?

5. Consider a stock, worth $100 per share, a European call on the same stock and a safe asset. The call matures in one year and has a striking price of $110. Its market price is $7.825 per share. The risk-free rate of interest is 5 percent per year compounded continuously.

   You have determined that an optimal portfolio consisting of the stock, call, and safe asset should consist of the proportion 0.811 invested in stock, 0.189 invested in the call, and 0.0 invested in the safe asset. Using put–call parity, determine the corresponding portfolio weights (proportions) for the same portfolio using a European put with the same striking price and maturity date rather than a call.

Pricing Interest Rate-dependent Financial Claims with Option Features

11.1 Background

If given the assignment of pricing a 2-year call option on a US government bond that matures in four years, would it be appropriate to use the Black–Scholes model or a similar binomial-type model as a basis for your analysis?

On the surface, it might appear that a Black–Scholes or binomial approach would be appropriate. After all, the call option is issued on an underlying asset whose value should be characterized by random movements over time. But, unlike a stock whose risks should increase with time, the price of a 4-year bond, although random, must eventually get back to par. Thus, even though the price of the bond may be very uncertain over the short run, over the long run, the price will be pulled to par systematically. As a result, option pricing models based on lognormal or binomial outcomes for the price of the underlying asset are inappropriate for valuing an option on the bond, and an entirely different approach to valutation must be taken.

A number of different models have been developed to deal with pricing of debt options. In contrast to stock option pricing, which relies almost exclusively on Black–Scholes-type pricing models, no one model has evolved as the "model of choice" for pricing debt options. Nevertheless, almost all models of debt option pricing are rooted in the three-step process of: (1) modeling the random character of interest rates; (2) using the distribution of interest rates to infer the distribution of price movements for the underlying debt instrument; and (3) using this distribution to value the option. Generally, the various models differ in how they characterize the randomness of interest rate behavior.

It should be noted that this same type of approach to valuation could be taken for stock options. With stock options, we could begin by assuming a random distribution for a company's earnings. Using this information, we could then infer how the price of the underlying stock should change over time, assuming some type of functional relationship between earnings and stock prices. Finally, using the inferred distribution for the price of the underlying stock, we could determine the option's price.

This represents an awkward approach to pricing, however, since we could assume a random distribution for stock prices to begin with. Moreover, unless we know the exact relationship between earnings and stock prices, we risk misspecifying the pricing dynamics for the stock and, in turn, for the option. Thus, when pricing stock options, we begin by assuming a random distribution for the price of the underlying asset rather than going back to one or more of its fundamental determinants. Unfortunately, we do not have the luxury of taking this approach to debt option pricing, since the natural pull to par keeps bond prices from conforming to any standard statistical distribution.

In an effort to deal with the unique problems associated with the pricing of debt options, two distinctly different classes of models have been developed. The first class, often referred to as *stochastic interest rate models*, is based on the assumption that movements in the underlying short-term rate of interest (or some other interest rate or set of rates) can be described by a pre-specified probability distribution. As in the three-step process mentioned above, the price process for the underlying bond is inferred from the interest rate process, and the option price is determined from the inferred bond price process.

There is a fundamental problem with this approach, however. It is entirely possible, and, in fact, quite likely that the price for the underlying bond which is inferred from the interest rate process will not equal the observed bond price. For example, the observed price for the bond might be $90 per $100 of par, while the bond price implied by the assumed interest rate model might be $93. In such a case, one would have little faith in the model value of the option when the same model produces a bond price that is off by $3.

Stochastic interest rate models not only produce values for the underlying bond, they can also produce theoretical values for the entire term structure of interest rates. Just as these models have a tendency to misprice the underlying bond, they are also likely to produce a theoretical term structure that differs from the observed term structure. Given the potential error in pricing both the underlying bond and the term structure of interest rates, there is likely to be equivalent error in pricing a debt-related option.

In 1986, Ho and Lee published a paper that introduced a second class of debt option pricing models known as *arbitrage-free stochastic term structure models*. In effect, these models take the observed term structure of interest rates as an input, along with estimates of its volatility structure, and determine the stochastic process for the short-term rate of interest that is implied by the observed term structure of interest rates and its estimated volatility structure. This information is then used to infer a distribution of values for the underlying bond, which, in turn, is used to price the option. By construction, models of this type produce theoretical values for riskless bonds that are consistent with observed prices in an arbitrage-free market.

We now turn our attention to stochastic interest rate models. Although these models have been made obsolete with the introduction of arbitrage-free stochastic term structure models, it is, nevertheless, instructive to understand pricing in this context before proceeding to the more advanced approach to pricing.

11.2   Stochastic Interest-Rate Models

This class of models will be illustrated using the binomial tree of 1-period riskless interest rates[45] shown in figure 11.1. In this example, there is no functional relationship between interest rates from one period to the next. For the purposes of the example, assume that each binomial period represents one year.

To maintain consistency between binomial-based interest rate models and binomial-based stock option pricing models, state designations indicate the number of times the value of the underlying asset, in this case a bond, goes up. Inasmuch as bond prices go up when interest rates go down, interest rates shown in figure 11.1 are inverted relative to the stock prices shown in the binomial trees of chapter 3; with interest rates, the lowest values are shown at the top of the tree. The 1-period interest rate at time t in state j is denoted as $r_{t,j}$.

Note that there is no consistent functional relationship between up and down values for the interest rate in figure 11.1. Although some stochastic interest rate models impose such a structure, this is not required.

Keeping the example as simple as possible, assume we want to price a European call option on a zero-coupon bond. The bond matures at time

---

45. Rendleman and Bartter (1980) developed a similar model which was later modified by Rendleman (1982) to reflect risk aversion. In contrast to the current example, however, the Rendleman-Bartter model imposes a very restrictive and somewhat unrealistic structure to the evolution of the short-term rate of interest.

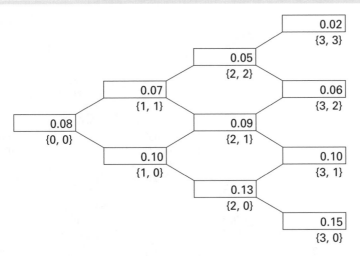

Figure 11.1 Example of binomial stochastic interest rate process

$t = 4$ with $100 par value. The option, with a striking price of $82, matures at the end of time 2.

With the interest rate structure of figure 11.1 along with an assumed value for the risk-adusted probability that bond prices will go up (and interest rates will go down), we can determine the price of the zero-coupon bond in each state.

As with the pricing of stock options, we begin at the end and work backwards, but in this case, the end is the maturity date of the zero-coupon bond. Since the bond has a par value of $100, its maturity value at time 4 will be $100, no matter what interest rate occurs.

Although the underlying zero-coupon bond is a 4-year bond today, it will be a 1-year bond three years from now. The entries in figure 11.1 show 1-year interest rates which, in turn, can be used to determine the prices of 1-year zero-coupon bonds at time 3. For example, if state $\{3,3\}$ occurs, the 1-year interst rate will be 0.02, implying that a $100 par 1-year zero-coupon bond will have a value of $100/1.02 = $98.04. Similarly, in state $\{3,2\}$, the value of a 1-year zero will be $100/1.06 = $94.34.

Figure 11.2 shows how the price of the 4-year zero-coupon bond and the call option will evolve over time. In the figure, D denotes the price of the bond and P denotes the corresponding value for the option. Prices in the figure are determined as if the risk-adjusted probability, π, associated with in an increase in the bond price (or decrease in interest rate) is 0.4. Thus, as in equation 3.3 in chapter 3, which determines how prices are related between periods in the original binomial pricing model, the hold

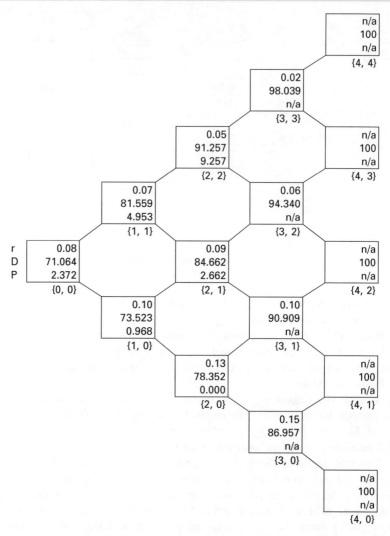

Figure 11.2 Pricing a 2-year call option on a 4-year zero-coupon bond. Strike = \$82, $\pi = 0.4$. Example calculations: $D_{h,2,1} = (\$94.340(0.4) + \$90.909(0.6))/1.09 = \$84.662$; $P_{h,1,1} = (\$9.257(0.4) + \$2.662(0.6))/1.07 = \$4.953$. r = interest rate, D = bono price, P = option price

value of the bond at time t is state j is given by:

$$D_{h,t,j} = \frac{D_{t+1,j+1}\pi + D_{t+1,j}(1-\pi)}{1+r_{t,j}},$$

$$(11.1)$$

and option hold values are determined in a similar fashion:

$$P_{h,t,j} = \frac{P_{t+1,j+1}\pi + P_{t+1,j}(1-\pi)}{1+r_{t,j}}$$

(11.2)

The only difference between these pricing equations and the original binomial pricing relationship in equation 3.3 is that the riskless rate of interest is not constant, but rather time- and state-dependent.

Unlike the original binomial model, π, in the debt option pricing model, must be specified by the user in order to infer the price dynamics for the underlying bond. If we were to assume a probability distribution of returns for the bond, as is done for the underlying stock in valuing stock options, we could infer the value of π. But since we do not know in advance how the bond's price will evolve, we must assume a value of π in order to infer the bond's price dynamics. Inasmuch as a value of π must be specified by the user, debt option pricing is inherently more difficult and subject to more error than stock option pricing.

When pricing debt options, it is often the case that the users of pricing models employ true probabilities when the models actually require risk-adjusted probabilities. In so doing, they are assuming implicitly that investors in debt markets are risk-neutral or that the risk in debt markets is not systematic and can be diversified away. Inasmuch as most financial economists agree that market prices are characterized by risk-averse investors and that interest rate risk can be significant, even in well-diversified holdings, error is introduced by treating π as if it were a true probability.

π can be shown to be a function of the probability if it is assumed that in each binomial period, all interest rate sensitive financial claims are priced to provide the same expected excess return per unit of risk as measured by the standard deviation of the security's return. That is, for any given binomial period, the difference between an interest-sensitive security's 1-period expected return and the 1-period riskless rate of interest, all divided by the standard deviation of the security's return, is equal to a common value for all interest-sensitive securities. Denoting this common value, often referred to as the market price of risk, as λ, Rendleman (1982) shows that the relationship between π and the true probability, θ, is given by:[46]

$$\pi = \theta - \lambda\sqrt{\theta(1-\theta)}$$

$$\lambda = \frac{\text{expected return} - r_{t,j}}{\text{standard deviation of return}} \qquad (11.3)$$

With estimates of θ and λ, one can estimate π as an input for pricing an interest-sensitive security. Alternatively, as in the calculation of an implied volatility, one could determine the value of π that is implied in the pricing of one or more debt options and use the implied value for valuing another related option. Unfortunately, unlike the pricing of options on stock, it is inappropriate to pre-specify the pricing dynamics for the underlying asset, and hence, the implied value of π cannot be extracted from the pricing of the underlying asset (or from its up and down factors).

How the various stochastic interest rate models differ in structure

Almost all stochastic interest rate models characterize interest rate behavior in terms of continuous probability distributions. The one exception is the model of Rendleman and Bartter (1980), which is cast within a binomial framework. Unlike the binomial example presented above, in the Rendleman–Bartter model, 1-period interest rates are related to each other in exactly the same way that binomial stock prices are related. In each period, the interest rate can go up or down by a constant percentage. In the limit, as the number of binomial periods becomes large, Rendleman and Bartter's interest rate process converges to a lognormal distribution. Financial researchers justifiably have objected to this model since it assumes the interest rate can become infinitely large, and there is no tendency for the interest rate to come back to a normal level.

Other representative models are those of Courtadon (1982), Vasicek (1977) and Cox, Ingersoll, and Ross (1985). The Courtadon model is like a continuous, or lognormal version of the model of Rendleman and Bartter, but one in which the mean drift in the interest rate is a function of the amount by which the rate exceeds or falls below a normal rate of interest. In the Courtadon model, the further the rate gets away from the normal rate, the more likely it is to change direction. This type of interest rate process is often referred to as a "mean-reverting diffusion process" because of the tendency for the interest rate to change direction.

Vasicek's model is similar to that of Courtadon except that the basic interest rate process is normal rather that lognormal. Like Courtadon, Vasicek

---

46. This relationship is also consistent with the analysis in the appendix to chapter 3.

also assumes mean reversion in the interest rate. Some have objected to Vasicek's model because it permits the interest rate to become negative.

The model of Cox, Ingersoll and Ross also is much like that of Courtadon except a "square root" mean-reverting diffusion process is assumed. In this type of model random changes in the rate of interest are proportional to the square root of the interest rate rather than to the level of the rate itself.

All of those models have theoretical or computational advantages over the others. But they all suffer from the common malady that the values of bonds they produce are almost certain to be different from observed prices. As such, in recent years there has been a tendency to abandon these models in favor of stochastic term structure models that, by construction, produce prices consistent with the observed term structure of interest rates. We now turn our attention to models of this type.

11.3   Arbitrage-free Stochastic Term Structure Models

In the previous section, the set of 1-year interest rates from figure 11.1 along with an assumed value of π of 0.4 were used to calculate price paths for a 4-year zero-coupon bond and for a 2-year option on the bond. With this same information set, one can also price zero-coupon bonds with maturities of one, two and three years and compute 1-year forward rates of interest between adjacent years.[47] These values are shown in table 11.1.

The entries in table 11.1 illustrate an important principle in pricing interest-sensitive securities. Any set of assumptions about the random values of interest rates and the value of π will produce a specific term structure of riskless zero-coupon bond prices and forward rates of interest. To the extent that these implied prices and forward rates are not consistent with the observed term structure, the model and/or its assumed input parameters must be misspecified.[48]

It should be noted that there are an infinite number of interest rate paths and values of π that will give rise to the same term structure. For

---

47. One-year forward rates between time $t-1$ and t are computed as the ratio of the price of the bond maturing at time $t-1$ to the price of the bond maturing at time t, and the price of any bond can be written as its $100 par value discounted at series of forward rates though its maturity date. For example, for the bond that matures at time 3 in table 11.1, $71.065 = \$100/((1.08)(1.0878)(1.0971))$.

48. Alternatively, one might assume that the model and its assumptions are correct, but the market has erred in determining the market prices.

Table 11.1   Prices of zero-coupon bonds (per $100 par) and implied forward interest rates

Maturity (t)	Bond price ($)	One-year forward interest Rate between times $t-1$ and t
1	92.593	0.0800
2	85.119	0.0878
3	77.591	0.0971
4	71.065	0.0918

One-year forward rates between time $t-1$ and t are computed as the ratio of the price of the bond maturing at time $t-1$ to the price of the bond maturing at time t.

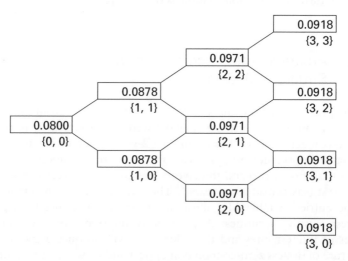

Figure 11.3   One-year interest rates that produce the same set of zero-coupon bond prices as in table 11.1

example, the 1-year interest rates in figure 11.3 will result in the same set of zero-coupon bond prices shown in figure 11.1.

The interest rates in figure 11.3 are simply the 1-year forward rates from table 11.1. By definition, they will produce the same set of bond prices as in table 11.1. Nevertheless, together table 11.1 and figure 11.3 illustrate an important point. Even if the assumed interest rate process produces a term structure of riskless bond prices consistent with observed prices, the pattern of interest rate volatility imbedded in that process may be entirely inappropriate if one's ultimate objective is to price an option. For example, the interest rate process shown in figure 11.3 has no volatility; all possible

1-year interest rates at any point in time are identical. Using these interest rates, it can be shown that the 2-year call option with an $82 strike price on a 4-year $100 par zero-coupon bond will have a value of $1.26 compared with $2.37 using the interest rate process of figure 11.1.

Arbitrage-free stochastic term structure models have been developed to avoid the types of problems encountered above. With models of this type, one determines the binomial process for the interest rate which is implied simultaneously by observed prices of zero-coupon bonds and a volatility structure for forward rates of interest (or bond prices) that has been pre-specified by the user. This process is then used to determine the price dynamics for the underlying bond on which an option is written and, finally, to determine the price dynamics for the option.

The analysis of stochastic term structure models begins with the model of Heath, Jarrow and Morton (1992). Although not the first model of this type, it is the most general and computationally intensive. The models of Ho and Lee (1986) and Black, Derman and Toy (1990) are developed as more simplified versions of the HJM model.

The Heath, Jarrow and Morton model

The model of Heath, Jarrow and Morton (HJM) is based on a general binomial process for the 1-period riskless rate of interest. Unlike the preceding binomial models, in HJM there is no requirement that the binomial tree of 1-period interest rates recombines. Thus, after n binomial periods, there are 2^n possible values for the interest rate.

Figure 11.4 shows the path for a generalized sequence of 1-period interest rates in a non-recombining binomial tree. Since the tree does not recombine, we must make a change in the way we define the various binomial states.

Notationally, the subscript k is used to define the *path* taken by the interest rate as of time t. The time and path designation $\{t, k\}$ denotes time t, path k where k can take on any value between 0 and $2^t - 1$.

The numerical values of the path designations are assigned in such a way as to indicate the sequence of events that has occurred through time t. This sequence is obtained by converting the path designation to an equivalent binary or base two value.

For example, consider the time and state path $\{t = 3, k = 5\}$. The binary equivalent of 5 is 101. In this binary value, the binary digit "1" represents an increase in bond prices (and a decrease in the interest rate), while the digit "0" represents a decrease in bond prices. Therefore, going from left to right, the binary path 101 indicates a sequence of bond price changes of up, down and up or interest rate changes of

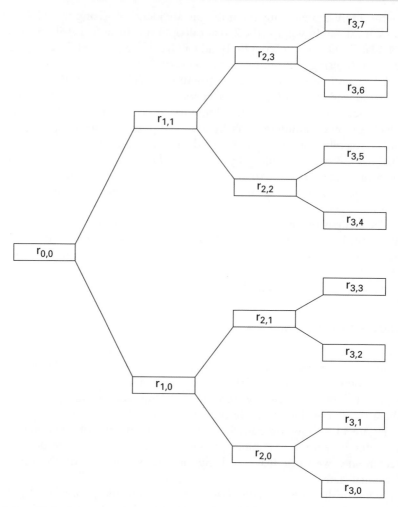

Figure 11.4 Interest rates in non-recombining binomial tree. $r_{t,k}$ denotes the 1-period interest rate at time t, path k. The binary equivalent of the path designation indicates the sequence of ups and downs in bond prices with the binary digit "1" indicating an increase in price and the digit "0" indicating a decrease

down, up and down. The highest path designation as of time 3 would be $k = 2^3 - 1 = 7$, or binary 111, indicating three successive increases in bond prices. The lowest value, $k = 0$, or binary 000, indicates three successive decreases.

The HJM model attempts to determine the various $r_{t,k}$ values, as shown in figure 11.4, that are implied in the observed pricing and estimated

Table 11.2 Price and volatility inputs for Heath–Jarrow–Morton example

Maturity (years)	Price ($)
Observed prices of $1 par value zero-coupon bonds	
1	0.92593
2	0.85446
3	0.78622
4	0.72090

Starting at time t, path k	Bond's maturity date	End-of-period volatility
Estimated information of yield volatility* for bonds maturing at times 2 through 4		
$t = 0, k = 0$	2	0.01852
	3	0.02081
	4	0.02182
$t = 1, k = 0$	3	0.01358
	4	0.01261
$t = 1, k = 1$	3	0.01422
	4	0.01657
$t = 2, k = 0$	4	0.01786
$t = 2, k = 1$	4	0.01370
$t = 2, k = 2$	4	0.01395
$t = 2, k = 3$	4	0.01449

*Standard deviation of continuously compounded annual yield as of the end of the period.

volatility structure of zero-coupon bond prices (or interest rates). Using the entries in figure 11.4 as a basis for analysis, note that there are a total of 15 interest rates that can possibly occur over the three binomial periods. Therefore, in order to infer the 15 interest rates from observed or estimated bond prices and volatility estimates, it is necessary to have 15 separate and independent pieces of information.

An example of such price and volatility information is contained in table 11.2. This information will be used as the basis for an example to illustrate how one would solve for implied 1-period future interest rates using the HJM model.

An example of extracting implied future rates of interest using the HJM model

We begin by observing the price of a 1-period zero-coupon bond. This price gives the initial 1-period riskless rate of interest. From table 11.2, the price of the 1-year zero-coupon bond is $0.92593 per $1 of par.

Therefore the 1-period riskless rate of interest is the solution to $0.92593 = 1/(1 + r_{0,0})$, or $r_{0,0} = 0.08$.

Next, we determine the prices in both the up and down states at time 1 for all bonds that mature after time 1. Before proceeding with these calculation, however, we must assume specific values for θ, the true probability that the interest rate will fall (and bond prices rise), and π, the corresponding risk-adjusted probability. For the purposes of this example, $\theta = 0.5$ and $\pi = 0.4$.

Let the price of any \$1 par zero-coupon bond at time t path k be denoted as $D_{t,k}$. Then, the relationship between the price at time t and $t + 1$ is given by:

$$
\begin{aligned}
D_{t,k} &= \frac{D_{t+1,2k+1}\pi + D_{t+1,2k}(1 - \pi)}{1 + r_{t,j}} \\
&= \frac{D_{t+1,2k} + \pi \left(D_{t+1,2k+1} - D_{t+1,2k} \right)}{1 + r_{t,k}}
\end{aligned}
$$

(11.4)

Note that in equation 11.4, the up state relative to time t, path k is time $t + 1$, path $2k + 1$, while the downstate is time $t + 1$, path $2k$. An examination of the path designations in figure 11.4 will verify this particular indexing method.

We also have estimated a value for the standard deviation of the zero-coupon yield, expressed as a continuously compounded rate, as of the end of each time t, for all bonds which mature after time $t + 2$. With $50:50$ probabilities associated with the interest rate going up or down in any period, it is easily shown that the standard deviation of any two binomial outcomes is one-half the difference in the two outcomes. Letting $\sigma_{t,k}$ denote the standard deviation of the zero-coupon yield as of the end of the period beginning at time t path k, the following expression is obtained for the standard deviation at time t, path k, in terms of the two possible price outcomes at time $t + 1$.

$$
\sigma_{t,k} = \frac{\ln \left(1/D_{t+1,2k}\right) - \ln \left(1/D_{t+1,2k+1}\right)}{2(m - [t + 1])}
$$

(11.5)

where m denotes the bond's maturity date, expressed in binomial periods.

Equations 11.4 and 11.5 can be solved simultaneously to determine $D_{t+1,2k+1}$ and $D_{t+1,2k}$, for any bond, given its price, $D_{t,k}$ and standard deviation, $\sigma_{t,k}$ as of time t, path k. Solution values as of time 1 for the prices of all bonds that mature after time 1 ($m > 1$) are given in table 11.3.

Note that the bond that matures at time 2 will be a 1-period bond as of the end of time 1. Therefore, the prices of this bond in the up and down

Table 11.3 Solution values for bond prices as of the end of time 1

Bond maturity date (year)	Price
Up state $\{t = 1, k = 1\}$	
2	0.94340
3	0.89185
4	0.84045
Down state $\{t = 1, k = 0\}$	
2	0.90909
3	0.82062
4	0.73731

states determine the 1-period rate of interest for both states. These rates are the solutions to the equations below:

$$0.94340 = \frac{1}{1 + r_{1,1}}; \quad r_{1,1} = 0.06$$

$$0.90909 = \frac{1}{1 + r_{1,0}}; \quad r_{1,0} = 0.10$$

We can apply the same computational method to determine all the remaining 1-period interest rates through time 3. We simply repeat the same general computations, but start in the up and down states at time 1 rather that at time 0. This will give us a set of bond-prices and the 1-period interest rate for all states at time 2. Continuing forward from time 2 and beyond, the entire set of future interest rates can be solved in terms of the initial set of observed bond prices and volatility estimates. The solution is shown in figure 11.5. Assuming ones ultimate objective is to price an option, once the path of future interest rates has been determined, one can determine the path for the underlying bond and the option using the same method described in section 11.2.

The Ho–Lee model

Although the HJM model is the most general stochastic term structure model, in a sense, it is too general. Given its path-dependent structure, there are 2^n possible interest rate paths after n periods, making it almost impossible to compute model values within a reasonable amount of time for values of n which exceed

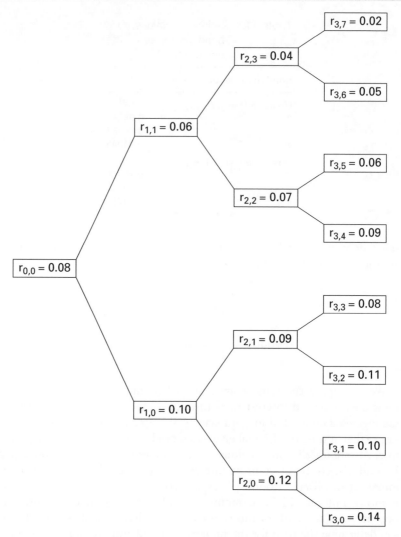

Figure 11.5 Solution values for 1-year riskless interest rates using price and volatility information from table 11.2

Box cont'd
20. Moreover, having to specify a state-dependent volatility structure for all zero-coupon bond prices or yields makes it difficult to determine an appropriate set of inputs for the model. Thus, there are advantages to simplifying the HJM structure in order to reduce the computational and input requirements.

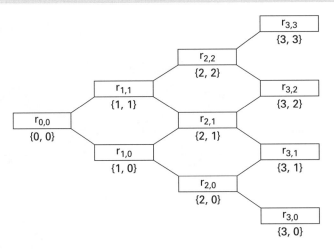

Figure 11.6 Binomial interest rates using the Ho–Lee model

The model of Ho and Lee (1986) assumes that interest rates evolve in a recombining fashion as shown in figure 11.6. Since there is no path-dependency, interest rate states are indexed by the subscript j, which indicates the number of decreases in the interest rate.

With a recombining interest rate tree, there are 10 possible interest rate outcomes over 4 periods. Thus, we need 10 pieces of information to solve for the implied rates. As in HJM, Ho and Lee use the observed prices of zero-coupon bonds maturing at times 1 through 4 as one source of pricing information. This leaves six additional pieces of information to solve for the 10 implied rates.

In the Ho–Lee model this additional information is supplied with one volatility parameter. In particular, it is assumed that the standard deviation of the 1-period zero-coupon yield, expressed as a continuously compounded rate, is the same in all adjacent states. Note from figure 11.6 that there are six adjacent pairs of states for which the standard deviation of the 1-period yield can be calculated. Thus, this assumption of constant volatility provides the additional six pieces of information necessary to extract the 10 implied 1-period rates.

The mathematics of the Ho–Lee model are complex. Nevertheless, assuming 50 : 50 probabilities associated with an increase or decrease in the interest rate, it can be shown that the 1-period interest rate at time t in state j is given by the following expression:

$$r_{t,j} = \frac{D(t)(\pi + [1 - \pi]\delta^t)}{D(t+1)\delta^{t-j}} - 1$$

$$\delta = e^{-2\phi_1(\tau/n)^{1.5}}$$

(11.6)

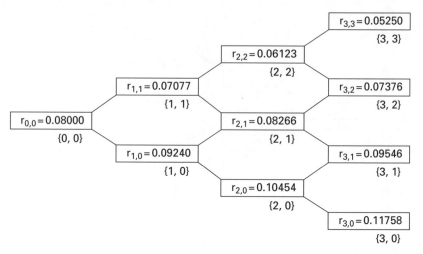

Figure 11.7 Solution to Ho–Lee example. Solution values based on: $D(1) =$ $\$0.92593$, $D(2) = \$0.85446$, $D(3) = \$0.78622$, $D(4) = \$0.72090$ and $\phi_1 = 0.01$

In equation 11.6, $D(t)$ denotes the observed price per dollar of a zero-coupon bond that matures at time t, ϕ_1 denotes the standard deviation of the logarithmic yield of a 1-year zero-coupon bond, assumed to be constant in all states, τ denotes the number of years until the maturity of the last bond used in the Ho–Lee analysis, and n denotes the number of binomial periods until the maturity of the last bond. As such, τ/n represents the length of one binomial period in years.

To illustrate the Ho–Lee model, assume the same set of initial bond prices as was used in the earlier HJM example: $D(1) = \$0.92593$, $D(2) = \$0.85446$, $D(3) = \$0.78622$, $D(4) = \$0.72090$. Also assume that the length of time between binomial periods is one year and that ϕ_1, the standard deviation of the logarithmic yield for a 1-year zero-coupon bond, is 0.01. Given these assumptions, figure 11.7 shows how the 1-year riskless rate of interest will evolve over the next three years.

Note that the standard deviation of the continuously compounded 1-year rate of interest is the same in all adjacent binomial states. For example, between adjacent states $\{1,1\}$ and $\{1,0\}$, the standard deviation is $0.5(\ln[1.09240] - \ln[1.07077]) = 0.01$. Between adjacent states $\{3,2\}$ and $\{3,1\}$, the standard deviation is also 0.01; $0.5(\ln[1.09546] - \ln[1.07376]) = 0.01$. One can easily verify that if the interest rates in figure 11.7 are used to price bonds with maturities of 1 to 4 years, the model prices will coincide exactly with the assumed set of observed prices.

The Black, Derman and Toy model

One problem with the Ho–Lee model is that it attempts to capture the entire volatility of riskless interest rates with only one volatility parameter. The Black–Derman–Toy (1990) (BDT) model overcomes this problem, to some extent, by allowing for a time-dependent volatility structure in interest rates.

Like Ho and Lee, BDT assume a recombining binomial structure for the riskless rate of interest. In their model, the ratio of all adjacent interest rates at any time, t, is assumed to equal a constant, α_t, specific to each time period. This results in a path structure for future 1-period rates as shown in figure 11.8.

The process followed by the short-term interest rate in the BDT model can be thought of the binomial-equivalent of a lognormal distribution with a time-dependent mean and volatility. With $50:50$ probabilities associated with up and down interest rate movements, it can be shown that $\alpha_t = e^{\sigma(r_t)/2}$, where $\sigma(r_t)$ denotes the standard deviation of the log of one plus the short-term interest rate at time t, r_t. The time-varying mean of the distribution is inferred from the observed term structure. Finding the various interest rates in the BDT tree requires solving a series of quadratic equations. Generally, this process is simplified by using iterative search. When both the mean and standard deviation are constant, the BDT model is equivalent to the model of Rendleman and Bartter (1980).

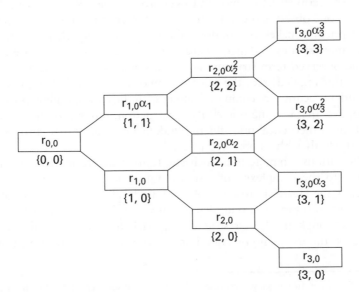

Figure 11.8 Binomial interest rates using Black–Derman–Toy model

11.4   Summary

Unlike stocks, whose risks increase with the passage of time, the prices of fixed income securities must eventually get back to par. As a result, a totally different approach to the pricing of options on fixed-income securities must be taken. Therefore, the binomial and Black–Scholes stock option pricing models are inappropriate for the pricing of options on debt securities.

Early models of option pricing for interest-dependent financial claims began by making assumptions about the stochastic properties of the risk-free rate of interest. When these models are cast within a binomial framework, values for the prices of an interest-dependent security can be computed or inferred for each interest rate state. Then, using standard arbitrage arguments, one can price an option on the same interest-dependent security in each state.

Taking this approach to pricing, the theoretical value of the underlying asset is a by-product of the pricing procedure. Ho and Lee (1986) were the first to recognize that the theoretical price so obtained is not likely to correspond with the observed price of the same instrument. As a result, option prices calculated with reference to an underlying asset whose theoretical price is incorrect are not likely to be of much value.

Ho and Lee, Heath, Jarrow, and Morton (1992), Black, Derman, and Toy (1990) and others have developed various versions of arbitrage-free stochastic term structure models to get around this problem. With these models, one observes the term structure of interest rates (or zero-coupon bond prices), makes assumptions about the volatility characteristics of future interest rates, and then calculates a binomial interest rate tree implied by the observed term structure and its assumed volatility characteristics. Using this implied tree, the price dynamics for the underlying interest-dependent security are computed, along with the corresponding prices for the option that is being priced. By construction, this approach to pricing produces a theoretical price for the underlying security that corresponds almost exactly with its observed price.[49]

The various arbitrage-free stochastic term structure models vary with respect to the complexity of assumed future interest volatility. At one extreme, the Heath, Jarrow and Morton model allows interest rate volatility to be both time and state-dependent in a non-recombining binomial tree. Although the least restrictive approach to modeling future interest rates, the use of non-recombining trees makes it impractical, from a

---

49. The theoretical price will correspond exactly if the security is priced without error relative to the observed term structure.

computational standpoint, to specify more than 20 or so binomial time periods.

At the other extreme, the Ho–Lee model assumes recombining binomial trees and constant interest rate volatility that is both time and state-independent. Therefore, when using the Ho–Lee model, it is impossible to price interest-dependent options under the assumption that interest rate volatility might increase or decrease with time or with the level of future interest rates. Although, the Ho–Lee model is computationally efficient compared with the Heath, Jarrow and Morton model, it lacks flexibility in modeling the future course of interest rates. The Black, Derman and Toy model allows interest rate volatility to vary with time but not with the level of interest rates. Other models, such as those developed by Hull and White (1990) and Jeffrey (1995), are also computationally efficient, but like the Ho–Lee and Black, Derman and Toy models, gain efficiency by restricting the extent to which future interest rate volatility can be specified.

REFERENCES

Black, F., E. Derman, and W. Toy, "A One-Factor Model of Interest Rates and Its Application to Treasury Bond Options." *Financial Analysts Journal* 46 (January/February 1990), 33–9.

Black, F. and M. Scholes, "The Pricing of Options and Corporate Liabilities." *The Journal of Political Economy* 81 (May/June 1973), 637–59.

Courtadon, G., "The Pricing of Options on Default-free Bonds." *Journal of Financial and Quantitative Analysis* 17 (March 1982), 75–100.

Cox,. J. C., J. E. Ingersoll, and S. A. Ross, "A Theory of the Term Structure of Interest Rates." *Econometrica* 53 (March 1985), 385–408.

Heath, D., R. A. Jarrow, and A. Morton, "Bond Pricing and the Term Structure of Interest Rates: A New Methodology for Contingent Claims Valuation." *Econometrica* 60 (January 1992), 77–105.

Ho, T. S. Y., and S.-B. Lee, "Term Structure Movements and Pricing Interest Rate Contingent Claims." *Journal of Finance* 41 (December 1986), 1011–29.

Hull, J. and A. White, "Pricing Interest Rate Derivative Securities." *Review of Financial Studies* 3 (Winter 1990), 573–92.

Jeffrey, A. M., "Single Factor Heath–Jarrow–Morton Term Structure Models Based on Markov Spot Interest Rate Dynamics." *Journal of Financial and Quantitative Analysis* 30 (December 1995), 619–42.

Rendleman, R. J., Jr., "Some Practical Problems in the Pricing of Debt Options." Working paper, (August 1982).

Rendleman, R. J., Jr. and B. J. Bartter, "The Pricing of Options on Debt Securities." *Journal of Financial and Quantitative Analysis* 15 (March 1980), 11–24.

Vasicek, O., "An Equilibrium Characterization of the Term Structure." *Journal of Financial Economics* 5 (November 1977), 177–88.

RELATED WORK

Rendleman, R. J., Jr., "First Derivatives National Bank: A Case Problem in the Management of Interest Rate Risk." *The Journal of Risk* 1, No. 3 (1999), 63–85.

QUESTIONS AND PROBLEMS

1. Which of the stochastic term structure models developed in this chapter must have been used to derive the set of 1-year riskless interest rates shown below? Why? As part of your "why," indicate how the interest rate structure of this model differs from that of the other two models, providing enough detail so that one would understand the general structure of each model.

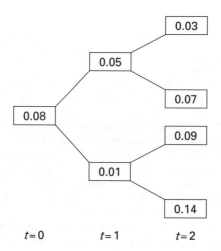

2. Using the binomial interest rate tree from question 1, Compute the price for a 1-year American call option on a 3-year $1,000 par value zero-coupon bond, assuming the call has a striking price of $830. For the purposes of this problem assume $\pi = 0.4$.

3. So that you are not working with the wrong numbers, assume the value of the 3-year bond in problem 2 is $785.93, the theoretical value of the call is $27.37, and the following payoffs to the 3-year bond and the call option can occur as of the end of the first binomial period.

Payoffs to 3-year bond and call option at
end of first binomial period

3-year bond	American call option
903.90	73.90
812.08	0.00

Assume the call option in problem 2 is not traded, but you want
to create its synthetic equivalent using the 3-year zero-coupon bond
and 1-year borrowing or lending at the 0.08 initial riskless rate of
interest. What is the appropriate dollar amount to invest in the 3-year
bond and in 1-year riskless securities to replicate the payoffs to the
option?

4. Assume the following binomial scenario for the 1-year risk-free rate of
interest.

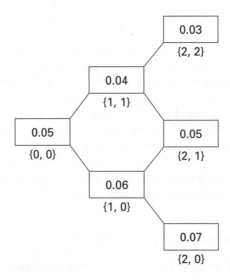

a. Determine the current term structure of 1-year forward interest
rates. For the purposes of this problem, assume $\pi = 0.4$.
b. Assume the true probability associated with an increase or decrease
in the 1-year interest rate is 0.5. Compute the expected 1-year
interest rate at time 1 and 2.
c. The expectations hypothesis of the term structure of interest
rates assumes that forward interest rates equal expected rates. Is

the expectations hypothesis consistent with pricing via stochastic interest rate and stochastic term structure models?

5. Using the binomial interest rate tree from problem 4, determine the theoretical value of a *3-year* mortgage that requires an annual end-of-year payment of $10,000. For the purposes of this problem, assume $\pi = 0.4$ and that the mortgage balance will amortize as in the table below. As with most conventional mortgages, the borrower has the right to pre-pay the mortgage at any time by paying the outstanding mortgage balance (plus accrued interest and principal).

Mortgage balance (Assuming 5% mortgage interest rate)	
Year 0 (today)	$27,232.48
Year 1	$18,594.10
Year 2	$9,523.81
Year 3	$0

6. The table below provides information about the prices of 1- and 2-year zero-coupon bonds and the estimated volatility, as of the end of year 1, for the bond maturing at the end of year 2. Using the binomial pricing framework, as applied to the Health–Jarrow–Morton model, assume that each binomial period represents one year.

    Determine the binomial tree for the 1-year interest rate through the end of the first year (in other words, for time 0 and time 1). For the purposes of this problem, assume that π, the risk-adjusted probability associated with an increase in bond prices (or decline in interest rates), is 0.4 and that the true probability is 0.5.

Price and volatility inputs for Heath–Jarrow–Morton model	
Observed prices of $1 par value zero-coupon bonds	
Maturity (years)	Price ($)
1	0.9090909
2	0.8333333
Estimated volatility for bond maturing at time 2	
Starting at time t, path k	$t = 0, k = 0$
End-of period standard deviation of continuously compounded yield	0.0322693

7. You observe the following prices, per $100 par, of zero-coupon Treasury securities:

Maturity (years)	Price per $100 par ($)
0.5	97.0874
1.0	94.0769
1.5	90.9835
2.0	87.8219

Using these prices, the assumption that the standard deviation of the continuously compounded yield of a 1-year Treasury security will be 0.01, and the assumption that $\pi = 0.4$, compute the interest rate tree for the 6-month rate of interest based on the Ho–Lee model through binomial time 3.

8. Discuss the primary conceptual difference between the Ho–Lee and Black, Derman and Toy models.

Introduction to Futures, Forward, and Swap Markets

12.1 Background

Up to this point, the focus of this book has been the pricing and management of financial risks using option contracts. In this chapter futures, forward, and swap contracts are introduced as additional tools for managing financial risks.

In 1865 the Chicago Board of Trade (CBOT) began trading futures contracts in agricultural grains. Up until 1972, futures contracts were written primarily on agricultural commodities, industrial commodities and precious metals. But in 1972, the Chicago Mercantile Exchange (CME) introduced futures on seven different currencies, marking the beginning of financial futures trading. In addition to futures on foreign exchange, the instruments to today's financial futures markets include contracts on broad-based stock market indices such as the S&P 500, contracts on more narrowly defined stock indices and industry groupings, futures contracts on US Treasury bonds and notes, Eurodollars, Treasury bills, the LIBOR rate, and many other interest rate-driven contracts too numerous to mention.

In the early 1980s, over-the-counter trading began in interest rate swaps, agreements in which two parties agree to swap a floating interest payment for a fixed payment, and soon expanded into currency swaps. According to the International Swap Dealers Association, as of June 30, 2000, interest rate and currency swaps on over $60 trillion of debt worldwide were outstanding. To appreciate the size of this market, $60 trillion is approximately five times the value of all the publicly traded stocks in the US. This book will focus on swaps of the simplest kind, known in the trade as "plain vanilla" swaps, although more complex interest rate and currency swap contracts can be created and tailored to the particular needs of the contracting parties. Details of swap markets and swap contracting are developed in chapter 16.

12.2   Forward Contracts

> Forward contracts are very similar in structure and function to futures contracts, but much simpler. Readers whose purpose is to get a feel for futures contracting without getting bogged down in technical details can treat futures as forward contracts without doing any significant damage. But readers who expect to be active users of futures markets need to know the technical differences between the two types of contracts and how these differences can affect futures pricing and the methods by which futures are used in hedging.

A forward contract is an agreement in which one party agrees to purchase a specified amount of an economic good at a specified price from another party at a future date or during some future period of time. The party who agrees to purchase the good is called the buyer and the party who agrees to sell is called the seller. The buyer is said to be *long* and the seller *short*. In a forward contract, both the buyer and seller are obligated to meet the terms of the contract. Although forward contracts may be partially guaranteed by collateral or the general credit worthiness of the parties, there are generally no formal mechanisms such as a clearing corporation or exchange to guarantee performance by both parties. By contrast, futures exchanges provide contract guarantees similar to those in the options market.

Most readers have engaged in forward contracting in their everyday lives. Anyone who has purchased an item COD has entered into a forward contract implicitly by agreeing to buy the item at a specified price at some time in the future. If you have ever ordered a new car with a special color or special accessories to be paid for at a pre-determined price at the time of delivery, you have entered into a forward contract. Technically, if you order a pizza for home delivery, you have entered into a forward contract. But perhaps the best example of forward contracting by ordinary individuals is agreeing to purchase a home listed by a real estate agent or offered for sale by a homeowner.

Purchase of a home as a forward contract

Assume the Smith family home has been listed for sale with a real estate agent at a price of $300,000. When the home is listed for sale, it is generally understood by the homeowner, the real estate agent and potential buyers that the title and purchase money will change hands two to three months after a contract to purchase the home has been signed. This time delay is necessary to allow the buyer to get his finances in order and to provide an opportunity for the seller to move.

A few days after the Smith home is listed, Mary Jones signs an agreement to buy the house for $300,000 in three months. In this instance, Ms Jones and the Smiths have entered into a forward contract. Ms Jones is the buyer, the Smiths are the seller, and the *forward price* is $300,000.

In this example it is important to note that if the sale price for the home is fair, the contract to which Ms Jones and the Smiths have entered should have no immediate value to either party. In a sense, the two parties have determined a fair price for a future exchange of title that will cause the contract itself to have a value of zero at the time the contract is signed. However, if the two parties had agreed to a sales price of $200,000, rather than the fair price of $300,000, the contract would have significant positive value to Ms Jones, the buyer, and significant negative value to the Smith's, since the contract allows Ms Jones to buy the house at a bargain price and forces the Smith's to sell their house at a price significantly below its fair value. On the other hand, if the price for the sale of the home were $400,000, the contract would have significant positive value to the Smith's and negative value to Ms Jones. But if $300,000 is a fair price, the contract itself, as a financial instrument, should have no value. There is a direct parallel to this type of contracting in futures markets. In futures markets, the futures price is the price for the future delivery of an underlying asset or commodity that causes the immediate value of the contract to be zero.

If you ever talk with a futures trader, you might hear him say something like "I just bought September corn futures at $2.25 per bushel." It sounds like something called corn futures was purchased at a price of $2.25 per bushel. In fact, nothing was purchased. Instead, the futures trader simply entered into an agreement to buy corn at a price of $2.25 in September. If the contract created by the agreement were offered for sale, its price would be zero. If the same terminology were applied to the signing of a contract to buy the Smith home, Mrs Jones might say "I just bought house futures for $300,000," but, again, nothing was purchased. Mrs Smith simply entered into a contract to buy the house and at the time the contract was signed; she had not actually bought the house.

Suppose the Smith home has been vacated at the time it is listed for sale. Assume further that Ms Jones is a wealthy lady with plenty of cash and that she can purchase the Smith home as soon as all legal matters can be worked out. In this instance, Ms Jones should be able to cut a deal with the Smith's for a price less than $300,000 to reflect that money will change hands approximately three months sooner than expected. If the 3-month rate of interest is 2 percent, the Smith's should be willing to accept $300,000/1.02 = $294,118, since with interest, receiving $294,118 immediately or $300,000 three months later are equivalent.

Using the vernacular of futures markets, $294,118 would be termed the *spot price*, which means the price for immediate delivery. The spot price is also referred to as the *cash* price. As we can see in this example, the forward (or futures) price should equal the spot price grossed up by the interest factor, 1.02. Although other things that can come into play in determining futures or forward prices in relation to spot prices, the interest factor, illustrated in this example, is the most important.

Other forward markets

One of the most significant forward markets is the market for foreign exchange. Most large money center banks do the bulk of their forward foreign exchange trading using forward contracts rather than futures contracts. In a typical forward transaction, a bank will enter into a contract with another financial institution or with a large corporation with good credit standing. As a result, there is not nearly the concern for credit risk as would be the case if individuals or small businesses were parties to the same transactions.

Forward contracts are also used extensively in the agricultural business. A grain farmer may contract with a firm that uses grain as an input to its production process or with a local grain elevator operator to lock in the price at which harvested grain will be sold in the future. But unlike foreign exchange transactions among money center banks and/or their large corporate customers, there is likely to be a significant element of credit risk in such contracting. As a result, futures markets in agricultural grains, which eliminate the credit risk to the contracting parties, play a very significant role in managing the risks associated with adverse price changes in agricultural commodities.

12.3   Futures Contracts, an Overview

Futures contracts are very similar in function to forward contracts. Like forwards, futures contracts represent agreements in which one party agrees to purchase a specified amount of an economic good at a specified price from another party at a future date or during some future period of time. Unlike forwards, futures contracts are created and traded on exchanges. They tend to be issued on homogenous commodities and financial assets for which there is significant national and worldwide interest. In today's futures markets, significant trading takes place in contracts for agricultural grains, precious metals, industrial commodities such as heating oil and natural gas, foreign currencies, Treasury bonds and notes, Eurodollars and various stock market indices.

Futures contracts are subject to special margining procedures that help to maintain the financial integrity of the markets. Consider, for example, the market for Euro futures. On December 6, 2000, the dollar/Euro exchange rate was $0.89 per Euro. One Euro futures contract, traded on the CME, calls for the delivery of 125,000 Euros, or $0.89 × 125,000 = $111,250 in Euros. On December 6, if one were to have entered into a single futures contract to either buy or sell Euros, exchange rules would have required an *initial margin* of $2,916 to be posted with a *futures commission merchant* (futures jargon for a futures broker). Margin amounts are subject to change at any moment. For example, if the market for Euros became very volatile, one could expect the CME to raise the margin requirement. Although more detail on margins will be provided later, one can think of initial margin as a good faith deposit that will eventually be returned to the investor when the contract is terminated, provided the investor does not default. It should be noted that both the long and short parties to the contract must post the same initial margin. Thus, ...

> it is inappropriate to think of the margin as the cost of the contract in the same way that one would think of an option premium as a contract cost. Even with margins, the initial cost of a futures contract is always zero.

The major futures exchanges

Table 12.1 lists the major futures exchanges in the United States, Europe and Asia. As can be seen in the table, these exchanges offer a wide variety of equity index and interest rate futures denominated in US dollars and major European and Asian currencies. Although futures markets began primarily as markets in agricultural products, the growth into the financial and energy arenas over the past 20 years has been so significant that volume in these contracts far surpasses that in the more traditional products. In addition to futures, the exchanges listed below also provide for trading in a large number of option contracts.

Table 12.1   Major US and international futures exchanges

	Primary futures products
US exchanges	
Chicago Board of Trade	Treasury bonds and notes, agricultural grains
Chicago Mercantile Exchange	S&P 500 Index, Eurodollars, currencies, livestock
New York Mercantile Exchange	Metals, petroleum, natural gas
International exchanges	
LIFFE (London)	European stock indices including FTSE 100, 3-month Euribor and other European-based interest rates
EUREX (Frankfurt, Zurich, Geneva)	European government bonds including 5-Year EURO-BOBL and 10-Year EURO-BUND, European stock indices including Dow Jones EURO STOXX and Dow Jones STOXX
MATIF (Paris)	EURO-based fixed income issues, European stock indices including stock indices including CAC 40 (French stocks)
SGX (Singapore)	Asian equity and interest rate futures

Examples of futures price quotations

Tables 12.2 to 12.5 show examples of settlement prices in various futures contracts as of December 7, 2000. Although settlement prices are similar to closing prices published daily for stocks, options and most other listed securities, they are not exactly the same. Instead, a settlement price represents what a committee of traders believes the closing futures contract price would be if the contract were to trade at or near the close of trading. These prices, in turn, are used to compute the amount of cash to transfer daily among futures brokerage firms to meet margin requirements.

Note the tendency for the futures price to increase with the maturity of the futures contract in the first three tables. Although the details of the theory of futures pricing will be developed later, this tendency is based on the interest factor, just as the price of a house listed with the expectation of being sold in three months would be greater than the price of the same house if it were sold today. It is also based on the assumption that the underlying commodity or asset on which the contract is written is easily stored without incurring significant costs or risking significant deterioration in the quantity of the asset or commodity being stored. This is why there is no apparent relationship between contract maturity and the futures price for the live cattle contract in table 12.5. One simply cannot store live cattle without incurring significant maintenance costs

Table 12.2   CME Euro FX futures settlement prices 12/07/00

Maturity month	Settlement price ($)
DEC00	0.8892
MAR01	0.8927
JUN01	0.8958
SEP01	0.8987
DEC01	0.9016

Contract is for 125,000 Euros. Price quote is dollars per Euro.
Source: www.cme.com.

Table 12.3   CBOT wheat futures settlement prices 12/07/00

Maturity month	Settlement price
DEC00	2546 = $2.5475
MAR01	2704 = $2.7050
MAY01	2814 = $2.8150
JUL01	2914 = $2.9150
SEP01	3014 = $3.0150
DEC01	3160 = $3.1600
JUL02	3340 = $3.3400
DEC02	3490 = $3.4900

Contract is for 5,000 bushels. First three digits
of price quote is cents per bushel. Right-most
digit is additional eights of a cent per bushel.
Source: www.cbot.com.

in the same way that a currency (Euro), stock portfolio (S&P index) or
agricultural grain (wheat) can be stored. As a result, the storage-based
theory of futures pricing does an excellent job explaining the relationship
between futures prices and contract maturity for contracts on storable commodities and assets but not for contracts on commodities that cannot be
stored.

The payoff structure of forward and futures contracts

Assume that the spot price of gold is $300 per Troy ounce and that
an investor enters into a forward contract to purchase 100 ounces of
gold in one year at a price of $315 per ounce. Table 12.6 illustrates the
payoff structure of the contract, provided the position in the contract is
maintained for the full year.

Table 12.4 CME S&P 500 futures settlement prices 12/07/00

Maturity month	Settlement price
DEC00	1,136.70
MAR01	1,156.50
JUN01	1,375.50
SEP01	1,394.00
DEC02	1,413.00
MAR02	1,436.00
JUN02	1,460.00
SEP02	1,484.00

Contract is for $250 times index value.
Source: www.cme.com.

Table 12.5 CME live cattle futures settlement prices 12/07/00

Maturity month	Settlement price
DEC00	76.425
FEB01	77.050
APR01	77.675
JUN01	73.700
AUG01	73.700

Contract is for 50,000 lbs. Price quote is cents per lb.
Source: www.cme.com.

Table 12.6 Payoffs to long position in gold forward contract with forward price of $315 per ounce

Spot price of gold in one year (per oz) ($)	Payoff to forward contract (per oz) ($)
345	30
335	20
325	10
315	0
305	−10
295	−20
285	−30

Table 12.7   Payoffs to short position in gold forward contract with forward price of $315 per ounce

Spot price of gold in one year (per oz) ($)	Payoff to short forward position (per oz) ($)
345	−30
335	−20
325	−10
315	0
305	10
295	20
285	30

Following the entries in table 12.6, suppose the price of gold in one year is $345 per ounce. Then a forward contract that requires an investor to buy gold for $315 per ounce, when the investor could immediately sell the gold for $345 per ounce, must be worth $345 − $315 = $30 per ounce, or $3,000 since the forward contract is for 100 ounces of gold. On the other hand, suppose the price of gold is $285 per ounce in one year. Since the contract requires the investor to buy gold for $315 per ounce that is otherwise worth only $285, the contract must have a value of $285 − $315 = −$30 per ounce, or minus $3,000 for the full 100 ounces. A negative value means that the investor would have to pay someone else $3,000 to assume the responsibilities of the contract.

Note that for all future gold prices greater than or equal to the forward price of $315, the payoffs to the forward contract are identical to those of a long position in a call option to buy gold for $315 per ounce. This correspondence is not maintained on the downside, however. For a call option with a striking price of $315, the payoff to the call is zero for all future gold prices below $315, but for the forward contract, the payoff is negative over this range. This illustrates an important connection between call options and forward contracts. A call option is like a forward contract for which all negative payoffs can be converted to zeros.[50]

As with options, the payoff to a short position in a forward contract is the negative of that of a long position. This is illustrated in table 12.7.

For future gold prices at maturity of $315 or below, the payoff to the forward contract is identical to that of a put with a striking price of $315. But for gold prices above $315, the payoff is negative. This illustrates that

---

50.   The conversion of negative values to zeros can be accomplished by purchasing a put. This then leads to another variation of the put–call parity equation, $call_E = $ long forward $+ \, put_E$.

a put option is like a short position in a forward contract for which the negative outcomes are converted to zeros.[51]

> Readers whose purpose is to gain a general understanding of derivative securities markets, rather than to become active derivatives users, can think of the payoff structure of forward and futures contracts as being identical. Little, if any, damage is done by ignoring the features of futures that make them different from forwards. But for those who may become active users of futures contracts, ignoring these differences can result in unanticipated gains and losses in the range of 2 to 3 percent of the value of the underlying commodity or asset, and depending on the size of positions taken, 2 to 3 percent can amount to millions of dollars. Therefore, it is important to develop the features of futures contracts that make them different from forwards and, in turn, affect their pricing and the way they are used in hedging and speculation.

12.4   Special Features of Futures Contracts

Price limits

Most futures contracts are subject to price limits that can be very complex, depending on the specific contract. For example, within a given day, the contract price for frozen pork belly futures, traded at the CME, cannot trade $0.03 above or below the previous day's settlement price. Therefore, if yesterday's settlement price for pork belly futures was $0.62 per pound, the contract prices for contracts made today must fall within the range of $0.59 to $0.65. If supply and demand conditions would otherwise cause pork belly futures prices to fall outside this range, the contract simply will not trade.

A futures contract is said to be trading *limit up* if the bid price for the contract is above the day's upper price limit. Similarly, a contract is said to be trading *limit down* if the offer price is below the day's lower price limit. When a contract is trading limit up or down, the market doesn't formally shut down, and the traders don't all go home, but no one is allowed to trade futures at a contract price outside the limits. Although there have been isolated incidents in which a futures contract has not traded for several days in a row, the exchanges will usually step in under these circumstances and

---

51. The conversion of negative values to zeros can be accomplished by purchasing a put. This then leads to another variation of the put–call parity equation, $put_E = short forward + call_E$.

change the limit amounts to reflect the new supply and demand dynamics of the market. Furthermore, some contracts call for automatic increases in limit increments when trading has been closed off for more than one day.

Some price limit specifications can be very complex. For example, for S&P 500 futures, price limits at the CME apply only on the downside. Moreover, they occur with a sliding scale applied within the day in increments of 2.5%, 5%, 10%, 15% and 20% from the preceding settlement price.

Whether price limits can be justified on sound economic grounds has been the subject of much debate. The primary reason given in justification of limits is to prevent panics, or to allow volatile markets to settle. According to this argument, if traders who might otherwise panic, are not allowed to trade, the prices that eventually do occur may more accurately reflect the true economics of the market.

Over the years there has been a tendency to liberalize price limits, and in some cases, eliminate them altogether. Typically, price limits in financial futures are not nearly as restrictive as those in agricultural commodities.

Daily settlement

Imagine how difficult it would be if the exchanges had to keep track of the contract price of every investor that transacts in a given futures contract. Therefore, to avoid keeping records of the futures price for every futures transaction, the exchanges use a process called daily settlement, or marking to the market, that effectively causes all participants in the market to be transacting at the same price at the end of each day. The process also helps to maintain the financial integrity of the market by enabling losses in futures contracts to be collected in small increments as they are occurring rather than waiting until a contract matures, or until a position is reversed, to collect losses. Here's how daily settlement works.

Going back to the gold futures example, assume the spot price of gold is $300 per ounce and the 1-year futures price is $315. Since each contract is for 100 ounces, one contract obligates the investor to buy or sell $31,500 in gold.

As of this writing, the initial margin for gold futures traded at the New York Mercantile Exchange (NYM), is $1,350. Therefore, both the buyer and seller of the futures would be required to post $1,350 with their brokers.

Assume that you enter into a long position in a single gold futures contract at a contract price of $315 on day 0. At that time, you would be required to post a $1,350 margin. The next day the settlement price rises by $2 per ounce from $315 to $317. Price changes over the remainder of the year are shown in table 12.8.

Table 12.8 Hypothetical settlement price in 1-year gold futures

Day	Futures price ($)	Change in futures price ($)	Cumulative change ($)
0	315	n/a	n/a
1	317	+2	+2
2	324	+7	+9
3	322	−2	+7
4–363	302	−20	−13
364	305	+3	−10
365	309	+4	−6

Even though you entered into a contract to buy gold at $315 per ounce, the next day your contract is re-written at a contract price of $317. To compensate you for agreeing to buy gold at a price $2 higher than your original contract price, the exchange gives you $2 per ounce, or $200. This $200 is credited to your brokerage account at the end of day 1, so at that point you would have $1,350+$200 = $1,550 in your account. Where does the $200 come from? It comes from investors who were short gold futures. Like you, their contract price is also reset to $317. But they have to pay the exchange $2 per ounce for having their selling price adjusted upward in their favor. At the end of day 1, an investor who established a short position on day zero would now have $1,350 − $200 = $1,150 in his brokerage account. To facilitate these money transfers, the exchanges transfer funds each night to and from member firms based on their net futures positions, and these funds, in turn, are distributed among the various customer accounts of the firms.

Now consider day 2 when the futures price rises by another $7 per ounce. As one who has a long position in the contract, your account will be credited with another $7 × 100 = $700 per ounce, and you will then be contracting to buy gold at $324. By contrast, anyone with a short position will lose $7 per ounce, but will have their contract price adjusted upward by the same amount. The investor with a short position established on day zero will now have only $1,350 − $200 − $700 = $450 in his account.

This brings us to a new kind of margin called *maintenance margin*. For NYM gold futures, the maintenance margin is $1,000 per contract. Note that the short investor has only $450 in his account, an amount that falls $550 below the maintenance margin level. Because his account balance is below the maintenance margin level, he will be required to bring his account balance back up to the level of the *initial margin*, not the maintenance margin level. If he has no other funds available with the brokerage firm, he will be requested to wire transfer $1,350−$450 = $900 per contract to the broker. If he is unable to respond to the request, and not a particularly good customer, the brokerage firm will close out his position and then seek the funds when the investor does become available.

Note that the long investor has $1,350 + $200 + $700 = $2,250 in his account, an amount that exceeds the initial margin by $900. Under these circumstances, he may take $900 out of his account, but may not remove the $1,350 initial margin until the position is closed. Generally, an investor may take out any funds in excess of the initial margin.

Suppose we step forward in time to day 365. On this day the futures price is $309 per ounce. We can safely assume that $309 is also the spot price of gold. Otherwise, investors could earn an immediate arbitrage profit by trading off the price discrepancies in the two markets. In a sense, when the futures contract matures, it becomes a spot contract rather than a futures contract.

By day 365 the gold futures price has gone up and down at least once, and perhaps many more times than are actually shown in the table. But no matter what path the price may take, at the end of day 365, both the long and short investors will be contracting to buy and sell gold at $309 per ounce. Over the 365-day period, the long investor will have paid his broker a net $6 per ounce, and the short investor would have received $6.

Note that if the long investor maintains his position until the last day, he will be required to buy gold at $309 per ounce. After adding the $6 he has paid his broker in daily settlement, the total amount paid for the gold is $309 + $6 = $315, the initial contract price. Similarly, the investor who is short will be required to sell gold for $309, but with the $6 he has received in daily settlement, he effectively sells gold for $315.

> When all is said and done, the investor who has a long position in gold futures effectively buys gold at $315 per ounce and the investor who is short effectively sells at $315. However the mechanics of how the $315 gets to be what it is are rather complex and not nearly as straightforward as agreeing to buy gold at $315 per ounce via a *forward* contract. But in both cases, the final result is the same or, as shown below, *almost* the same.

The difference between the effective contract prices for futures and forwards arises because of the ability to earn interest on gains credited to ones account through daily settlement and the necessity to pay interest (or possibly forego interest) on losses. If it were not for the interest factor, the final payoffs to futures and forward contracts would be economically equivalent. Going back to the example in table 12.8, if the long investor had to pay or forego $0.30 per ounce in interest over the 365-period, and the short investor earned interest of $0.30, the effective purchase price of gold for the long investor would be $309 + $6 + $0.30 = $315.30 as would be the seller's effective selling price.

> There can be a tendency for students to get bogged down in the nuances of the interest factor in daily marked-to-the-market gains and losses, and the nuances have produced a number of PhD dissertations. But, unless you plan to be an active user of futures markets taking large multi-million dollar positions, forget the interest factor and treat futures and forward contracting the same. Life will be a lot easier!

Cash settlement contracts

Futures contracts in gold and most other assets and commodities are what are known as *physical delivery* contracts. The term physical delivery means that one actually contracts to buy and take delivery (or sell, and make delivery) of the underlying asset or commodity. But some contracts are issued on assets, commodities or indices for which physical delivery is either impossible or very impractical. Perhaps the best example of this type of contract is the contract for the S&P 500 index.[52] Contracts for other indices as well as the Eurodollar also employ cash settlement to determine the final payoff to the contract.

An index is actually not a physical asset, but rather an indication of value. The S&P 500 index represents a scaled value of the total market capitalization of 500 stocks. Although one can assemble a portfolio that closely approximates the composition of the S&P, doing so without the use of fractional and odd lot shares is close to impossible, unless one has millions of dollars to work with. As a result, the Chicago Mercantile Exchange uses a process called *cash settlement* that provides a payoff structure to the contract identical to that which should occur with physical delivery. Here's how it works.

For the purposes of this illustration, refer back to table 12.8, but interpret it as illustrating daily settlement in the S&P contract rather than gold. Just like gold, the futures price from day zero through day 364 is determined by supply and demand. But on day 365 something different happens. With gold and other physical delivery contracts, the futures settlement price on

---

52. When the contract was initiated in the early 1980s, there was no practical way to trade the S&P 500 index directly. However, since the contract was introduced, S&P Depository Receipts (SPDRs) were developed as a means of investing in a small share of a much larger pool of funds invested in S&P stocks.

the final day is also determined by supply and demand, although a final price of anything other than the spot price will provide an arbitrage opportunity to investors. By contrast, the final settlement price of the S&P contract is set automatically to the *opening* value of the S&P 500 index on the contract's maturity date.[53] Therefore, in table 12.8, if the opening value of the index is $309 on day 365, the final cash settlement amount would be $4, reflecting a movement in the futures settlement price from $305 to $309 over the last two days.[54]

Again, using table 12.8 as a reference, consider the final payoff to one who goes long the S&P 500 contract. If an investor takes an initial long position at a futures price of $315 and maintains the position until maturity, he will have $6 taken out of his brokerage account. This is the same amount the investor would have lost if he had entered into a forward contract to buy the index at $315 and immediately sold the index at $309. With physical delivery, it would be almost impossible to actually buy and sell the index. But cash settlement provides the same end result using its simple settlement procedure.

Delivery options

Most futures contracts provide for the delivery of the underlying asset or commodity on non-standard terms. For example, the underlying asset for the Chicago Board of Trade's Treasury bond futures contract is a 30-year US Government Bond paying 6 percent interest annually. As of January, 2001, there were only a few 6 percent Treasury bonds or notes in existence, but none had a maturity of exactly 30 years. Obviously then, the exchange must provide for the delivery of bonds other than the standard 30-year 6 percent bond.

The Treasury bond contract actually allows any standard Treasury bond with 15 years to maturity or its first call date to be delivered. As of this writing, 34 such bonds were eligible for delivery. The terms of the contract also provide for an adjustment to the price received for the bond based on its coupon rate in relation to 6 percent. Bonds with coupon rates greater than 6 percent are delivered at a premium over the futures price, and bonds with coupons less than 6 percent are delivered at a discounted price,

---

53. The opening value is determined by using the opening price of each of the component stocks of the index. If a particular stock does not trade on the final day, it's most recent pervious price is used in computing the opening index value.
54. Cash settlement in the actual S&P 500 contract is based on 250 units of the index. Thus, in this example, the actual loss to one who took a long position in the contract would have been $6 \times 250 = \$1,500$.

with the discounts and premiums determined according to a published formula.[55]

Futures contracts on agricultural commodities typically provide for non-standard delivery with respect to time, quantity, quality and location. For example, delivery for the Chicago Board of Trade corn contract may take place any day on or before the second day following the last business day preceding the 15th calendar day of the delivery month. Corn with moisture content greater than 15 percent is not acceptable for delivery. If No. 2 yellow corn is delivered, the seller receives the most recent futures settlement price. Therefore, No. 2 yellow corn can be thought of as the standard grade. However, No. 1 yellow and No. 3 yellow corn are also deliverable. Since No. 1 is the highest grade, the seller receives a premium of 1.5 cents per bushel over the futures price when it is delivered. On the other hand, the seller receives the futures price less a 1.5-cent per bushel discount when No. 3 yellow corn is delivered.

Under the standard terms of the corn contract, corn is to be delivered to regular warehouses within the Chicago or Burns Harbor, Indiana switching districts. However, corn may also be delivered to regular warehouses within the Toledo, Ohio switching district at a 3-cent per bushel discount from the contract price and to the St. Louis-East St. Louis and Alton switching districts at a 7-cent per bushel premium.

Finally, the corn contract calls for the delivery of 5,000 bushels of corn. However, a variation in the quantity delivered of up to one percent in either direction is allowed.

> It is critical to understand that in futures markets, all options with respect to the time, location, quantity, and quality of the commodity or asset that is delivered are controlled by the seller. Since sellers are in control, they can be expected to make decisions with respect to these options that will be to their advantage. As a result, futures contracts do not trade according to their standard terms, but, instead, trade on the basis of the optimal delivery decisions that sellers are expected to make.

For teaching purposes, I like to explain futures contracts in terms of "large" and "fine" print. Although the corn contract is not actually written

---

55. The Chicago Board of Trade computes a conversion factor for each bond, computed as the present value of its remaining stream of payments per dollar of par, discounted at 6 percent per year compounded semi-annually. This computation is updated quarterly and published in tables available from the Board of Trade. The delivery price for each bond is determined by multiplying the futures settlement price by the bond's conversion factor.

in terms of large and fine print, if it were, the contract might read something like this.

Chicago Board of Trade Corn Futures Contract

This is a contract for the delivery of 5,000 bushels of No. 2 yellow corn to a regular warehouse within the Chicago or Burns Harbor, Indiana switching districts on the second day following the last business day preceding the 15th calendar day of the delivery month.

Exceptions to standard contract terms

1. The seller may deliver a quantity of corn that varies within one percent of 5,000 bushels in either direction.
2. No. 1 yellow corn may be delivered at a price of 1.5 cents above the contract price. No. 3 yellow corn may be delivered at a discount of 1.5 cents per bushel below the contract price.
3. Delivery may be made on any business day of the month on or prior to the second day following the last business day preceding the 15th calendar day of the delivery month.
4. Delivery may be made to regular warehouses within the Toledo, Ohio switching district at a 3-cent per bushel discount from the contract price and to the St. Louis, East St. Louis and Alton switching districts at a 7-cent per bushel premium.

Even though the large print indicates that the corn contract calls for the delivery of 5,000 bushels of No. 2 yellow corn to Chicago or Burns Harbor, Indiana, it might actually be optimal for sellers to deliver No. 1 yellow corn to St. Louis. Under these circumstances, the contract effectively becomes a contract in No. 1 St. Louis corn, and it will trade as if No. 1 yellow corn will be delivered to St. Louis.

Generally, the trading characteristics of No. 1 St. Louis corn and No. 2 Chicago corn are not likely to be significantly different. As a result, a corn farmer in North Carolina using the CBOT corn contract for hedging purposes is not likely to make a grave error by treating the contract as if No. 2 corn will be delivered to Chicago. However, a bond trader who hedges a fixed-income portfolio using the Treasury Bond futures contract expecting a 6 percent, 30-year bond to be delivered, when it is actually optimal to deliver a 15-year 8 percent bond, will grossly underestimate the volatility characteristics of the futures contract and likely make a serious error in hedging.

If there were no fine print in futures contracts, understanding futures markets would be relatively simple. Unfortunately, the fine print can make the analysis of some futures contracts much more complex than one would

Table 12.9 Spot and adjusted futures prices for corn during futures maturity month

Grade	Spot price ($)	Adjusted futures price ($)
No. 1 yellow	2.23/bu.	Futures price + 0.015
No. 2 yellow	2.20/bu.	Futures price
No. 3 yellow	2.16/bu.	Futures price − 0.015

expect by just looking at the standard terms. For example, the ability to deliver 34 different bonds to satisfy the terms of the Treasury bond contract, makes Treasury bond futures so complex that even the most knowledgeable users of the contract still do not completely understand it.

> Readers of this book whose objective is to gain a general understanding of futures markets, but do not expect to be active users of the markets, can ignore the fine print of most futures contracts. But those who expect to be active users must understand the fine print, or their trading in futures will almost certainly be doomed to failure.

Delivery options and the concept of "cheapest-to-deliver"

Consider table 12.9 which shows spot prices of Nos. 1 through 3 yellow corn along with the adjusted futures price for each grade. For the purposes of the entries in the table, it is assumed that the spot prices are observed during the maturity month of the corn contract. Based on the information in the table, which of the three grades of corn will be optimal to deliver, and what will be the futures price?

I have asked this question to my students for many years, and this is a typical response.

> Since the futures contract is for No. 2 yellow corn, and the futures and cash prices must converge in the futures maturity month, the futures price must be $2.20/bu., the cash price of No. 2 yellow corn.

Although this seems like a logically correct answer, in fact, it is wrong. Suppose the futures price were actually $2.20, as this answer suggests. A smart futures trader could buy No. 3 yellow corn for $2.16 per bushel, simultaneously sell a futures contract against the cash position, and immediately make notice of intention to deliver No. 3 yellow corn. When the corn is delivered, the trader would receive $2.20 − $0.015 = $2.185 per bushel for corn purchased at a price of $2.16, providing an immediate profit of $2.185 − $2.16 = $0.025 per bushel. To eliminate the possibility of this type of arbitrage, the futures price would have to fall to $2.175 per bushel. At this price, the adjusted futures price and the cash price of No. 3 yellow corn would be the same, and there would be no profit to be gained from this type of transaction. Moreover, there would be a loss at this futures price if the same type of transaction were attempted with the other two grades. For example, if No. 2 yellow corn were purchased in the cash market for $2.20 per bushel and sold immediately via the futures contract for $2.175, a loss of $0.025 per bushel would be incurred. Similarly, the same transaction in No. 1 yellow corn would produce a loss of $0.015 per bushel ($2.20 + $0.015 − $2.23 = −$0.015).

At this point, it is natural to ask why an investor could not undertake this same transaction in reverse and earn $0.015 per bushel in No. 1 corn? If this transaction could be accomplished, the investor would take a long position in the futures contract at $2.20, buy No. 1 yellow corn through the futures market at $2.20 + $0.015 = $2.215 per bushel and then sell the same corn in the cash market for $2.23, earning a profit of $0.015 per bushel.

The problem with this logic is that the investor who takes a long position in the futures contract has no control over which grade of corn is delivered. He cannot force a seller to deliver No. 1 yellow corn. Instead, he must wait for corn to be delivered to him, and in all likelihood, the corn delivered would be No. 3 grade.

Using the vernacular of futures markets, in this example, No. 3 yellow corn would be termed the "cheapest-to-deliver" grade of corn. Personally, I find the term "most-optimal-to-deliver" to be more descriptive, since an investor who has established a short position in corn futures would find it optimal to deliver No. 3.

Going back to the original problem described in table 12.9, here is a short-cut method to determine the futures price and the grade of corn that is cheapest-to-deliver. For each grade of corn, compute the futures price that equates the adjusted futures price for that grade to its respective cash price. For the three grades, we obtain:

$$
\begin{aligned}
\text{No. 1 yellow} \quad & \text{futures} + \$0.015 = \$2.23 \\
& \text{futures} = \$2.215 \\
\text{No. 2 yellow} \quad & \text{futures} + \$0.000 = \$2.20 \\
& \text{futures} = \$2.20 \\
\text{No. 3 yellow} \quad & \text{futures} - \$0.015 = \$2.16 \\
& \text{futures} = \$2.175
\end{aligned}
$$

Then, take the lowest of the computed futures prices.[56] In this example, the lowest futures price is $2.175, computed for No. 3 yellow corn. Therefore, No. 3 corn is the cheapest, or most optimal grade of corn to deliver. Note, if the futures price were any higher, one could profit by purchasing No. 3 yellow corn in the cash market, simultaneously selling the futures contract and giving immediate notice of delivery. Therefore, No. 3 yellow corn must be the cheapest-to-deliver grade, and the futures price will be $2.175.

In this example, if the differences in the cash market prices for corn were less than $0.015 per bushel, No. 1 yellow corn would be the cheapest-to-deliver grade, and if the cash market price differentials were exactly $0.015, any of the three grades would be equally attractive to deliver.

12.5   Summary

In this chapter, futures, forward, and swap contracts are introduced as additional derivative securities for managing financial risks. Futures and forward contracts are very similar. Both calls enable an investor to contract to buy or sell an underlying asset or commodity at a set price on a specific date or within a specific period of time. Generally, forward contracts are made directly between two contracting parties and are not subject to exchange guarantees. In contrast, futures contracts are subject to exchange guarantees, but due to daily settlement procedures, daily price limits and options relating to the quantity, quality, time, and location of delivery, tend to be more complex instruments.

Since over-the-counter trading began in interest rate and currency swaps in the early 1980s, the market has expanded to where there are now swaps outstanding on over $60 trillion of notional principal worldwide. Details on the mechanics, pricing and use of interest rate and currency swaps are developed in chapter 16.

QUESTIONS AND PROBLEMS

1. Assume the initial margin for gold futures is $3,000 per contract and the maintenance margin is $2,000. Each contract is for 100 Troy

---

56. In this example, it is assumed that we are in the maturity month of the futures contract. If the point of reference in time is prior to the futures maturity month, the cheapest, or most optimal grade to deliver will be that which provides the highest return from hedging, and the futures price will be that which causes the return from hedging the cheapest-to-deliver grade to equal the risk-free rate of interest. This concept will be developed further in chapter 15 in connection with Treasury bond futures.

ounces of gold. Today you take a position in one gold futures contract at a price of $300 per ounce. Tomorrow the settlement price (closing price) of gold futures is $292 per ounce. May you take money from your account or must you put money into your account? If so, how much?

2. Explain the difference between a physical delivery and cash settled futures contract. Why is it necessary to use cash settlement for certain contracts?

3. Yesterday the settlement price for December 2001 corn futures was $2.50 per bushel. The daily price limit for corn futures is 20 cents per bushel above or below the previous day's settlement. As precisely as possible, explain what would happen to trading today in December 2001 corn futures under the following circumstances.

   a. Bid price is $2.55, ask price is $2.57.
   b. Bid price is $2.69, ask price is $2.72.
   c. Bid price is $2.27, ask price is $2.29.

4. Assume that the standard terms for the wheat futures contract call for the delivery of medium-grade wheat but that high and low grades of wheat are also deliverable. The middle column of the table below shows how the delivery price will be adjusted in relation to the futures price for the various grades of wheat that can be delivered to satisfy the terms of the contract. The right-most column shows the current spot prices of wheat. Assuming the current month is the delivery month of the contract, what should be the futures price and which grade of wheat should be cheapest-to-deliver?

Adjustment to standard terms of wheat futures contract

Grade of wheat	Adjusted futures price per bushel ($)	Cash market price (spot price) per bushel ($)
High	Futures price + 0.05	2.53
Medium	Futures price + 0.00	2.50
Low	Futures price − 0.05	2.48

5. The party with a short position in a futures contract sometimes has options as to the quality of the asset or commodity that will be delivered, the location of delivery, the time of delivery and, within certain limits, the quantity that is delivered. Does the presence of these options cause the futures price to be higher, lower or the same as what the price would be without the options? Why?

6. Show that if the futures price of a commodity is greater than the spot price during the delivery period there is an arbitrage opportunity. Does an arbitrage opportunity exist if the futures price is less than the spot price? Explain your answer.

7. You have just taken a long position in a 1-year S&P 500 futures contract at a futures price of $1,300 per unit of the index and plan to maintain the position for a full year. For the purposes of this problem, assume that the futures position is marked to the market on a quarterly basis (every three months) rather than on a daily basis, as is the case with actual futures contracts. Assume that you can borrow at an interest rate of 1 percent per quarter and also earn 1 percent per quarter in safe assets. The table below shows how the futures price evolves during the year that you maintain your position.

S&P futures price	($)
Initial futures price	1,300
Futures price is 3 months	1,500
Futures price in 6 months	1,200
Futures price in 9 months	1,000
Futures price in 12 months	1,100

What will be your ultimate gain or loss in the contract, taking into account interest earned and paid on marked-to-market price changes? How does this gain or loss compare to that which would occur if the contract were a forward contract, not subject to daily marking to market, rather than a futures contract? To what extent is this difference a function of how the futures price gets to its final value?

Futures Pricing

13.1 Introduction

The focus of this chapter is on the determination of the futures price in relation to the spot price. In most texts, this is done from the perspective of hedging; the equilibrium futures price is that which causes the return from hedging the underlying commodity or asset to equal the risk-free rate. Through this approach, one not only learns how the futures price relates to the spot price, but also how futures are used in hedging. Unfortunately, much of the futures pricing story can be lost if the theory of futures pricing is developed from this perspective alone. Additional insight into pricing and the role of futures as an investment vehicle can be gained if the theory of pricing is also developed from the standpoint of the leverage-equivalence of futures and the spot-equivalence of futures held in conjunction with safe assets. Therefore, the theory of futures pricing is developed from three different angles, all of which lead to the same result. Through this approach the reader should gain a more general understanding of the role of futures contracts in expanding the investment alternatives of individuals and professional investors.

Initially, the theory of futures pricing is developed by showing that a long futures position is equivalent to borrowing the *full cost* of the underlying asset or commodity to buy the asset or commodity. This equivalence is summarized in equation 13.1 below.

$$futures \Rightarrow asset - safe$$

(13.1)

In equation 13.1, the term *futures* denotes taking a long position in a futures contract issued on one unit of the underlying asset or commodity.

The term *asset* denotes taking a long position in one unit of the underlying asset or commodity, the term *safe* denotes a long position in a safe asset *of equal value* to one unit of the underlying asset or commodity, and the negative sign in front of *safe* denotes borrowing the full value of the underlying asset or commodity. The symbol ⇒ means *is equivalent to*. Thus, equation 13.1 states that taking a long futures position is equivalent to buying the underlying asset or commodity by borrowing its full value.

Equations 13.2 and 13.3 follow as mathematical variations of 13.1. But each has its own story to tell while providing a different insight into futures pricing and the relationship among the futures contract, the underlying asset or commodity and leverage.

$$safe \Rightarrow asset - futures$$

$$(13.2)$$

$$asset \Rightarrow futures + safe$$

$$(13.3)$$

It is important to note that the theory of futures pricing as developed through equations 13.1 to 13.3 applies only to assets or commodities that are easily stored without incurring significant out-of-pocket costs or wastage. Accordingly, the theory will apply to financial assets such as currencies, Treasury securities and stock indices, to precious metals and to agricultural grains, but will not apply to contracts on live cattle and hogs or other commodities that cannot be stored.[57] Also, the theory of pricing, as developed below, applies to commodities or assets described in the "large print" of futures contracts. As such, it does not take account of the delivery options described in chapter 12. For some contracts, such as those issued on agricultural grains, modifying the theory to reflect the fine print is straightforward. For other contracts, such as Treasury Bond and Note futures, the fine print significantly complicates the analysis of pricing as well as the use of the contract for hedging and other investment purposes. But for now, these complications will be ignored, and the theory of futures pricing will be developed as if the futures contact is issued on a single grade of asset or commodity and there are no options associated with the contract with respect to quantity, time and place of delivery.

---

57. Although the theory can be modified to account for storage costs, typically the costs of storing and maintaining live cattle and hogs is so high that there is little relationship between spot and futures prices in these markets.

13.2   Futures Pricing with a Known Cash Payment from the Underlying Asset or Commodity

Assume that the current (spot) value of the S&P 500 index is $1,000 per unit of the index. Further, assume that the risk-free rate of interest for both borrowing and lending is 7 percent per year, compounded annually, and that the stocks in the index will collectively pay a dividend equivalent in value to $20 by the end of one year.[58] At this point in the analysis, it is assumed that there is no uncertainty with respect to the dividend amount, although in practice, the estimate of dividends on the S&P over a full year would be subject to risk. Using all three approaches to pricing, it will be shown that these assumptions lead to an equilibrium futures price of $1,050.

Pricing based on the leverage-equivalence of futures

Table 13.1 illustrates the payoff structures of two economically-equivalent investments. The first is a position in which one borrows $1,000 for a full year at 7 percent to buy one unit of the S&P index.[59] The second is a long position in the S&P futures contract held for a full year when the initial futures price is $1,050.

Table 13.1   Payoff table for borrowing to buy S&P 500 index versus long position in futures

Index value in one year ($)	+	Future value of dividend ($)	+	Loan payment ($)	=	Net ($)	Long futures ($)
1,250		20		−1,070		200	200
1,200		20		−1,070		150	150
1,150		20		−1,070		100	100
1,100		20		−1,070		50	50
1,050		20		−1,070		0	0
1,000		20		−1,070		−50	−50
950		20		−1,070		−100	−100

Spot price = $1,000; futures price = $1,050; dividend = $20; risk-free rate = 0.07.

---

58. Although most of the dividend paying stocks will have paid four quarterly dividends during the year, it is assumed that the total of all dividends paid, plus any interest earned on the dividends, will equal $20 in one year.
59. In practice, this could actually be accomplished by purchasing an S&P Depository Receipt (SPDR).

Table 13.2 Payoffs from borrowing to buy the index while simultaneously taking a short position in futures at a futures price of $1,060

Index value in one year ($)	Payoff from borrowing $1,000 to buy the index ($)	+	Payoff to short futures position ($)	=	Net position payoff ($)
1,250	200		−190		10
1,200	150		−140		10
1,150	100		−90		10
1,100	50		−40		10
1,050	0		−10		10
1,000	−50		60		10
950	−100		110		10

Spot price = $1,000; futures price = $1,060; future value of dividend = $20; risk-free rate = 0.07.

The entries in table 13.1 illustrate the equivalence of borrowing at 7 percent to buy the index and taking a long position in the futures contract. No matter what index value occurs in one year, the two provide equivalent payoffs. This would not be the case, however, if the futures price were different than $1,050. For example, if the futures price were $1,060, rather than $1,050, while the spot price, dividend and risk-free rate remained the same as the values in the table, all values in the "long futures" column would be $10 lower. Under such conditions, one could borrow $1,000 at 7 percent to buy the index while simultaneously taking a short position in the futures contract. This, in turn, would produce the payoff structure illustrated in table 13.2.

Table 13.2 indicates that if the futures price is $1,060, the position will produce a net payoff in one year of $10, no matter what ending value for the index occurs. Since the initial position requires no investment outlay, the $10 payoff represents a pure riskless arbitrage profit.[60] To prohibit riskless arbitrage gains from this type of transaction, the futures price can be no greater than $1,050. Although not illustrated, a riskless arbitrage profit could also be earned if the futures price were less than $1,050. In such a situation, the positions of table 13.2 would be reversed; the investor would short the index, invest the proceeds of the short sale in a safe asset earning 7 percent, while simultaneously taking a long position in the futures contract. This leads to the conclusion that the equilibrium futures price must be exactly $1,050.

---

60. In actual practice, an initial outlay equal to the initial margin for the futures contract would be required. However, this amount would be returned to the investor when the futures position is terminated, and therefore, a $10 arbitrage profit would still be earned.

More generally, the futures price must equal the spot price of the index grossed up by the interest factor, less the future value of dividends, or

$$F = spot(1 + i)^\tau - fv(div)$$

(13.4)

for stock index and other futures when the future value of the cash payment on the underlying asset or commodity, as of the futures maturity date, is a known quantity, $fv(div)$.

In equation 13.4, F denotes the futures contract price, i denotes the annual risk-free rate of interest stated on an annually compounded basis, τ denotes the number of years until the futures contract matures and $fv(div)$ denotes the future dollar value of dividends from the index expected to be accumulated as of the futures maturity date. Applying equation 13.4 to the example,

$$
\begin{aligned}
F &= spot(1 + i)^\tau - fv(div) \\
&= \$1,000(1.07)^1 - \$20 \\
&= \$1,050.
\end{aligned}
$$

The simultaneous determination of spot and futures prices

Before turning to the other two methods of futures pricing, it is useful to extend the leverage-equivalence theory of futures pricing to understand how spot and futures prices are jointly determined. Suppose it is morning, and the stock market is in a lull with everyone waiting to hear Federal Reserve Chairman Alan Greenspan's views on the state of the economy. The value of the S&P 500 is $1,000, just as in the above example, the future value of the S&P dividend is $20, the risk-free interest rate is 7 percent, and the contract price for one-year S&P futures is $1,050.

During the afternoon, Mr Greenspan announces that the Federal Reserve will cut interest rates, and this information is viewed as very bullish for the stock market. In fact it is so bullish, that you, and other investors like you, would like to borrow significant amounts of money to buy stocks such as those that comprise the S&P index. Unfortunately, due to regulation T margin requirements, which restrict the amount you can borrow to buy stock, you are unable to borrow as much as you would like.[61]

---

61. Regulation T prohibits an investor from borrowing no more than 50 percent of the value of marginable stocks in his brokerage account. As such, an investor

Moreover, even if you could borrow, you realize that the commissions and other transaction costs associated with buying a large number of individual stocks could be very high and significantly reduce the profit you would otherwise expect to earn by trading on Greenspan's announcement. As a result, you and others like you decide to take long positions in one-year S&P futures rather than buy stock outright.

Because of the sudden demand to go long, the contract price for S&P 500 futures rises immediately from $1,050 to $1,065 while leaving the index behind at $1,000. Clearly, based on the preceding analysis, the S&P futures and spot prices are out of line. So what should happen next? In all likelihood, Wall Street arbitrageurs and market makers will be the sellers of futures that you and others like you purchase. To protect their positions, the arbitrageurs and market makers will buy the index or buy portfolios of stocks that, statistically, are near equivalents to the index. In the process, the prices of the stocks will be bid up to reflect the bullishness of investors who had taken long futures positions. After the dust settles, if the futures price remains at $1,065, the spot price should have risen to a value, as calculated below, that enables equation 13.4 to be maintained.

$$F = spot(1 + i)^\tau - fv(div), \quad \text{or}$$

$$spot = \frac{F + fv(div)}{(1 + i)^\tau}$$

$$= \frac{\$1,065 + \$20}{1.07}$$

$$= \$1,014.02$$

This example illustrates that spot and futures prices are jointly determined. To think that futures traders simply wait to see what spot prices are before deciding the prices at which they will trade represents a fundamental misunderstanding of the markets. In fact, in many local grain markets, spot prices are quoted as so many cents per bushel above or below the futures price. But in any event, no matter which price adjusts first, when the futures and spot prices are in equilibrium in relation to each other, equation 13.4 must hold.[62]

---

with $100,000 in stocks, could borrow $50,000. Alternatively, an investor who wanted to buy stock worth $100,000, could invest $50,000 of his own money while borrowing another $50,000 from the brokerage firm.

62. More accurately, equation 13.4, or a conceptually-equivalent variation of the equation, must hold. A conceptually-equivalent variation would take account of

Table 13.3 Payoff table for heading the S&P 500 index with a short position in futures

Index value in one year ($)	+	Future value of dividend ($)	+	Short futures ($)	=	Net position value ($)
1,250		20		−200		1,070
1,200		20		−150		1,070
1,150		20		−100		1,070
1,100		20		−50		1,070
1,050		20		0		1,070
1,000		20		50		1,070
950		20		100		1,070

Spot price = $1,000; futures price = $1,050; future value of dividend = $20; risk-free rate = 0.07.

Futures pricing based on riskless hedging

The same futures pricing relationship can also be developed through the theory of riskless hedging, summarized mathematically in equation 13.2, *safe* ⇒ *asset* − *futures*. Equation 13.2 indicates that selling futures against a long position in the underlying asset or commodity can convert a risky investment into a safe investment. Like any security or portfolio with a certain outcome, the return on the underlying asset, when made riskless by hedging with futures, should equal the risk-free interest rate.

Continuing with the same assumptions of table 13.1, including a futures price of $1,050 for the S&P 500 index, table 13.3 illustrates the payoff structure to a long position in the S&P 500 index when hedged with futures. Note that when the long position in the index is established, the initial investment is $1,000, the value of one unit of the index. Selling futures against this position requires no additional investment outlay, so the total cost of the hedged position is $1,000. With a 7 percent interest rate, this hedged position should have a payoff of $1,000 × 1.07 = $1,070 if the futures price is in equilibrium relative to the spot value of the index. As illustrated in table 13.3, when the futures price is $1,050, the hedged position in the index will be worth exactly $1,070 in one year, thereby providing the investor a rate of return of 7 percent.

Mathematically, the equilibrium futures price is easily established from the theory of hedging. By hedging a long position in the underlying asset or commodity with a short position in futures, the total payoff to the hedged position held for τ years should be $1,000$(1 + i)^{\tau}$. There are two

different assumptions about the pattern and certainty of cash (dividend) payments and costs of storage, although for the S&P, the cost of storage should be zero. Nevertheless, such variations would still lead to a direct relationship between the spot and futures prices but in slightly different mathematical form. Some of these forms will be developed later in this chapter.

components to this payoff, F, the final payoff to the asset or commodity locked in by selling futures and $fv(div)$, the future value of dividends. Therefore, in equilibrium, the following pricing relationship must hold:

$$spot(1 + i)^\tau = F + fv(div),$$

$$(13.5)$$

which leads to

$$F = spot(1 + i)^\tau - fv(div),$$

the equilibrium spot/futures pricing relationship as expressed in equation 13.4.

Futures pricing based on creating a synthetic long position in the underlying asset or commodity by taking simultaneous long positions in the safe asset and futures

Equation 13.3, *asset* $\Rightarrow$ *futures* + *safe*, states that a long position in a futures contract issued on one unit of the underlying commodity (or asset) plus investing the dollar value of one unit of the commodity in a safe asset will provide a payoff structure identical to that of the underlying commodity. This is illustrated in table 13.4 which compares the payoffs to a long position in one-year S&P futures, held in conjunction with $1,000 invested at 7 percent, to the payoffs to the index held long. As with the previous examples, the initial value of the index is assumed to be $1,000, and the futures price is $1,050.

Table 13.4   Payoffs to a long position in 1-year S&P futures held in conjunction with $1,000 invested at 7 percent

Index value in one year ($)	+	Future value of dividend ($)	=	Total payoff to being long ($) the index ($)	Long futures	+	Long safe asset ($)	=	Total of long futures and long safe asset ($)
1,250		20		1,270	200		1,070		1,270
1,200		20		1,220	150		1,070		1,220
1,150		20		1,170	100		1,070		1,170
1,100		20		1,120	50		1,070		1,120
1,050		20		1070	0		1,070		1,070
1,000		20		1,020	−50		1,070		1,020
950		20		970	−100		1,070		970

Spot price = $1,000; futures price = $1,050; future value of dividend = $20; risk-free rate = 0.07.

Note that if the futures price were $X less than $1,050, all the dollar amounts in the long futures column of table 13.4 would be $X higher. This, in turn, would also make the total value in the right-most column $X higher. Under such conditions, taking a long futures position and investing in the safe asset would provide a payoff $X higher than the index itself for every possible value of the index. Similarly, if the futures price were $Y higher than $1,050, taking a long futures position and investing in the safe asset would provide a payoff $Y lower than the index, no matter what value of the index occurs. Therefore, to maintain pricing equilibrium among the futures, the index and safe asset, the futures price must be $1,050, the same value given by equation 13.4.

The investment advisory firm, Smith Breeden Associates, Inc., uses a slight variation in the futures–safe asset investment strategy summarized in table 13.4 to produce a portfolio designed to outperform the S&P 500 index in its Stock Market Plus mutual fund and Equity Market Plus institutional fund which collectively include several billion dollars under management. Interestingly, Smith Breeden's expertise is in the fixed income area and in particular, investing in mortgage-backed securities. Through its expertise, Smith Breeden believes it can produce a relatively safe return of 50 to 125 basis points per year above conventional fixed income investments.[63] In terms of the example above, when the risk-free interest rate is 7 percent, Smith Breeden would expect to earn 7.50 to 8.25 percent with little risk in its managed fixed income portfolio. To produce index returns in excess of S&P returns, Smith Breeden's strategy is to take a long position in S&P 500 futures in conjunction with its managed fixed income portfolio, hedged to zero interest rate risk. Assuming Smith Breeden could earn a return of 8 percent on its fixed income portfolio in what is otherwise a 7 percent risk-free rate environment, the outcomes from its enhanced index portfolio would be as summarized in the right-hand panel of table 13.5.

Note that this strategy produces a portfolio value $10 higher than the S&P (with dividends) in every state. Stated differently, the return from this strategy is always one percentage point greater than the S&P return. More generally, if Smith Breeden is able to earn an excess fixed income return, it can transform this excess return into an excess return relative to the S&P index by overlaying long S&P futures on its managed fixed income fund. Interestingly, with this strategy, Smith Breeden needs no expertise in stock picking to offer excess stock returns – but it does need expertise.

---

63. The term "basis point" is used by fixed income investors to indicate one hundredth of a percentage point. This estimate was obtained from Smith Breeden's website at http://www.smithbreeden.com/dsam/enh2.htm.

Table 13.5 Payoffs to a long position in 1-year S&P futures held in conjunction with $1,000 invested in a managed fixed income fund earning 8 percent in a 7 percent interest rate environment

Index value in one year ($)	Future value of + dividend ($)	Total value of = index investment ($)	Long futures ($)	Long managed fixed income + fund ($)	Total of long futures and long managed income = fund ($)
1,250	20	1,270	200	1,080	1,280
1,200	20	1,220	150	1,080	1,230
1,150	20	1,170	100	1,080	1,180
1,100	20	1,120	50	1,080	1,130
1,050	20	1070	0	1,080	1,080
1,000	20	1,020	−50	1,080	1,030
950	20	970	−100	1,080	980

Spot price = $1,000; futures price = $1,050; future value of dividend = $20; risk-free rate = 0.07. Return from managed fixed income fund = 0.08.

Extension of pricing theory to Treasury Bond futures

In the previous sections, the S&P index was assumed to pay a known dividend over the life of the futures contract. To the extent that the dividend would not be known with certainty, there would be some slight error in equation 13.4.

Unlike the pricing of S&P futures, assuming a known dividend or similar cash payment in the pricing of Treasury Bond futures would be an absolutely correct assumption, since interest payments on Treasury securities are fixed by contract. Consider an example for which the Treasury Bond futures contract calls for the delivery of a 30-year 6 percent government bond, and no other bonds can be substituted. Also assume that interest on Treasury bonds is paid semi-annually, with the first two payments of $3 per $100 par being made in exactly 6 and 12 months. Finally, assume that the yield curve is flat at 7 percent per year compounded annually, equivalent to 6.882 percent compounded semi-annually, or 6.882/2 = 3.441 percent every six months. This implies a current price for the 30-year 6 percent bond of $87.872 per $100 par.[64] What should be the 1-year Treasury

---

64. The price is computed by discounting 60 semi-annual interest payments of $3 per $100 par at 3.441 percent per six months and also discounting the par value of $100 to be received in 30 years, or 60 6-month periods, at the same rate.

Bond futures price? Applying equation 13.4,

$$F = spot(1 + i)^{\tau} - fv(interest)$$
$$= \$87.872(1.07)^{1} - (\$3[1.03441] + \$3)$$
$$= \$94.023 - (\$3.103 + \$3)$$
$$= \$87.923.$$

Let's see if this answer makes sense in terms of the hedging-based theory of futures pricing. Suppose you bought the 6 percent 30-year bond for $87.872 and simultaneously took a short position in one-year futures at a contract price of $87.92. In one year, you would have locked in a $87.92 selling price for the bond while earning $3(1.03441) + $3 = $6.103 in accumulated interest. Thus the total investment value locked in after one year would be $87.923 + $6.103 = $94.026. Given an initial investment of $87.872, your return per dollar invested would be $94.026/$87.872 = 1.07, or 7 percent, the risk-free rate of interest. Therefore, you would have earned exactly the correct return for an investment whose outcome in one year is certain.

Presently, over 30 different bonds can be delivered in conjunction with the Treasury Bond contract. Therefore, determining the futures price for the actual Treasury Bond contract is not nearly as simple. Nevertheless, as we shall see in chapter 15, making the same type of futures price calculation as in the example above for each deliverable bond is a critical step in determining the bond that is cheapest to deliver and, ultimately, the equilibrium futures price.

13.3 Futures Pricing when the Cash Payment to the Underlying Asset or Commodity is Proportional to its Ending Value

Stock index futures

When determining the futures price for certain assets or commodities, an assumption that the cash payment is proportional to the asset or commodity's ending value may be more appropriate than an assumption of a fixed cash payment. In fact, this is probably a better assumption when pricing stock index futures. Although many companies with stock in an index may have announced upcoming quarterly dividends, projecting the exact dollar values of dividends beyond the first quarter would, at best, be an educated guess. Perhaps a more appropriate assumption would be that the future value of dividends, as of the futures maturity date, would be a fixed percentage of whatever the index value turns out to be. For example, if it is generally believed that stocks in the S&P index will pay a weighted dividend of 1.7 percent annually, one might assume a future dividend amount of 0.017 times the ending index value.

Currency futures

For currencies, a fixed percentage of ending value is an exact representation of how the cash payment should evolve. To understand this concept, consider an American investor who buys British Pounds, purchasing £100,000 at a price of $1.50/£ for an initial investment cost of $150,000. Unless the investor plans to spend the British Pounds immediately, he will hold them. Although he could hide the £100,000 in his mattress, he is more likely to invest the Pounds to earn interest.

Assume the investor purchases £100,000 in risk-free securities in the UK earning 9 percent for one year. After one year, he will have £100,000(1.09) = £109,000. If he then converts the Pounds back to dollars, he will have £109,000 times the $/£ exchange rate in one year. For the purposes of this example, assume the exchange rate turns out to be $2.00/£. Therefore, after converting Pounds back to dollars, the investor will have £109,000($2.00/£) = $218,000, which can be broken down mathematically as follows:

$$£100,000(1.09)($2.00/£) = $200,000(1.09)$$
$$= $200,000 + 0.09($200,000).$$

The second line in the set of equations above indicates that the value of the investment after one year is the value of the original £100,000 converted to dollars plus 9 percent of this same value.

In the example above, when the investor buys £100,000 and invests the Pounds to earn 9 percent, he does not know that the $/£ exchange rate will be $2.00/£ after one year. Therefore, his investment in Pounds will be subject to risk in the fluctuations in the $/£ exchange rate. However, the investor can eliminate this risk by selling futures against his British Pound investment.

Let $F_{\$/£}$ denote the futures price quoted as dollars per Pound. By selling futures against his original investment in Pounds, and also against the Pounds expected to be earned as interest, the investor can lock in £109,000$F_{\$/£}$ dollars after one year.

For the purpose of determining the equilibrium futures price, we need to determine the value of $F_{\$/£}$ that will enable the investor to earn the US risk-free rate of interest on his original investment. Recall that he originally purchased £100,000 at a price of $1.50/£, requiring a total investment outlay of \$150,000. Assume, as in the previous examples, that the US risk-free rate of interest is 7 percent. Then, the equilibrium futures price is the value of $F_{\$/£}$ for which £109,000$F_{\$/£}$/\$150,000 = 1.07 or F = \$1.472.

More generally, let $spot_{\$/£}$ denote the initial \$/£ exchange rate, $i_\$$ the annual interest rate to be earned by investing US dollars and $i_£$ the annual interest rate to be earned by investing British Pounds. Then, an initial investment in one Pound would cost $spot_{\$/£}$. If this Pound were invested to earn a rate of return of $i_£$, this investment would increase to $(1+i_£)^\tau$ Pounds after τ years. The dollar value of the $(1 + i_£)^\tau$ Pounds can be locked in by selling futures maturing in τ years at a price of $F_{\$/£}$, producing a risk-free payoff of $F_{\$/£}(1+i_£)^\tau$. If the futures price is in equilibrium, the annualized return from investing $spot_{\$/£}$ dollars and locking in $F_{\$/£}(1+i_£)^\tau$ dollars by selling futures should be $i_\$$, the US risk-free rate of interest. Therefore, in equilibrium, $F_{\$/£}(1 + i_£)^\tau/spot_{\$/£} = (1 + i_\$)^\tau$, which gives the following equilibrium futures price.

$$F_{\$/£} = spot_{\$/£} \left(\frac{1 + i_\$}{1 + i_£} \right)^\tau$$

(13.6)

> Equation 13.6 is the *interest rate parity equation*, well-known to students of international finance and economics.

If we interpret the symbol £ to denote any non-US currency, rather than restricting ourselves to the British Pound, the equation states that the relationship between the spot and futures exchanges rates depends upon the relative values of the interest rates in the two countries. If the domestic (\$) interest rate is higher than the foreign (£) interest rate, the futures exchange rate should exceed the spot exchange rate. But if the domestic interest rate is lower, the futures exchange rate should fall below the spot rate.

Table 13.6 illustrates how well the interest rate parity equation held up on August 22, 1998 for futures in the British Pound, Canadian Dollar, Deutschemark and Japanese Yen, all maturing on June 16, 1999. For the purposes of making the calculations in the table, I was unable to find foreign interest rates for money market instruments maturing on or around June 16. Therefore, for the calculations, I used one-year interest rates, and assumed that if rates for instruments maturing on June 16 could have been obtained, the annualized June 16 rates would have been close to the one-year rates. The theoretical futures exchange rate for British Pounds

Table 13.6 Spot/futures price relationship at approximately 2:20 pm, August 11, 1998

Currency	Spot exchange rate	1-year interest rate	Futures maturing on June 16, 1999	
			Actual futures price	Theoretical futures price
British Pound	1.6322	7.057	1.6080	1.6059
Canadian Dollar	0.6577	5.333	0.6577	0.6561
Deutschemark	0.5621	3.603	0.5708	0.5686
Japanese Yen	0.6791	0.370	0.7086	0.7056
US Dollar		5.116		

Spot exchange and interest rates were taken from Bloomberg web site. Futures prices were taken from the web site of the Chicago Mercantile Exchange.

was calculated as follows:

$$F_{\$/£} = spot_{\$/£} \left(\frac{1 + i_\$}{1 + i_£} \right)^{\tau}$$

$$= 1.6322 \left(\frac{1.05116}{1.07057} \right)^{306/365}$$

$$= 1.6059,$$

and calculations for the other currencies followed analogously.

Notice the close correspondence between the actual and theoretical futures prices. Also note that futures exchange rates are higher than spot rates for the Deutschemark and Japanese yen, the two currencies for which the foreign interest rate is below the US rate. For the British Pound, the futures exchange rate is below the spot rate, as theory would suggest, reflecting that the £ interest rate of 7.057 percent is significantly above the 5.116 interest rate in the US. Interestingly, the spot and futures exchange rates for the Canadian Dollar are identical, which is consistent with interest rates in the two countries being almost identical (5.333 and 5.116 percent).

Extending the price theory to stock index and other futures contracts

The components of the interest rate parity theory, as stated in equation 13.6, can be reinterpreted and applied to the pricing of stock index and other futures, provided the cash payment on the underlying asset or commodity is expected to be a known fraction of its ending value.

Recall in equation 13.6, $i_£$ denotes the rate of interest in British Pounds (or, more generally, in the foreign currency). It also represents the number of new British Pounds, per Pound originally invested, that the investor will have after one year.

Suppose an investor purchases one unit of the S&P index, anticipating a cash dividend in one year of q_{div} times the value of the index. After receiving the cash, the investor could purchase q_{div} new index units, bringing his unit total units to $1 + q_{div}$. Therefore, a cash dividend equal to a constant, q_{div}, times the ending value of the index is economically equivalent to a dividend paid in q_{div} new units of the index rather than in cash. Thus, an investor who buys one unit of the index, holds it for a year, earns a cash dividend and uses the dividend to buy q_{div} new units will end up with $1 + q_{div}$ index units, just as the investor in British Pounds will end up with $1 + i_£$ Pounds. If we substitute $1 + q_{div}$ for $1 + i_£$, $1 + i$ for $1 + i_$$, F for $F_{$/£}$ and *spot* for $spot_{$/£}$ in equation 13.6, the following pricing relationship for stock index and similar futures is obtained, where the cash payment on the underlying asset or commodity is expected to equal a constant, q_{div}, times the ending value of the same asset or commodity.

$$F = spot \left(\frac{1+i}{1+q_{div}} \right)^\tau$$

(13.7)

for stock index and other futures when the cash payment is q_{div} times the ending value of the underlying asset or commodity.

If you are typical of many students I have taught in the past, you might be asking, "Professor, which equation should I use for pricing stock index futures, equation 13.4 or equation 13.7?" As a practical matter, it probably doesn't make much difference. Consider the initial example when the spot value of the index was $1,000 and a $20 dividend as of the one-year futures maturity date was projected. Using equation 13.4, the theoretical futures price was

$$F = spot(1 + i)^\tau - fv(div)$$
$$= \$1,000(1.07)^1 - \$20$$
$$= \$1,050.$$

Suppose this same pricing problem were solved using equation 13.7, assuming $q_{div} = 20/1{,}000 = 0.02$. Then, the futures price would be

$$F = spot \left(\frac{1+i}{1+q_{div}} \right)^{\tau}$$

$$= \$1{,}000 \left(\frac{1.07}{1.02} \right)^{1}$$

$$= \$1{,}049.02,$$

an amount not much different from $1,050. In fact, if you thought the announced upcoming quarterly dividend is more accurately described in terms of fixed dollars but that successive dividends might be described more accurately as a fixed proportion of the ending index value, then the futures price should fall somewhere between $1,049.02 and $1,050. But unless you plan to be an active stock index futures trader, there is no need to lose any sleep over these differences.

13.4   How are Expectations of Future Prices Reflected in Futures Contract Prices?

It is common to view the futures price as an estimate of the expected future price of the underlying asset or commodity. For storable assets and commodities, this is clearly a mistake. From equations 13.4, and 13.6 and 13.7, we can see that the futures price equals the spot price adjusted by an interest and dividend (or cash payment) factor. The expected value of the future price does not enter into the pricing equation.

Although not immediately evident from the pricing equations, the futures price *can* be thought of as the *certainty-equivalent* of the expected future price. In financial economics, a certainty-equivalent is a value, which if received with certainty, is considered to be equivalent to receiving an alternative uncertain outcome.

Consider the binomial option pricing equation.

$$P_{h,t,j} = \frac{P_{t+1,j+1}\pi + P_{t+1,j}(1-\pi)}{1+r}$$

$$\pi = \frac{1+r-d}{u-d}.$$

As discussed in chapter 3, π is the risk-adjusted probability associated with an increase in the stock price. As such, the numerator of the equation can be interpreted as the risk-adjusted expected value of the end-of-period option value, that is, the expected value calculated with risk-adjusted probabilities rather than true probabilities. This is just another way of saying that the risk-adjusted expected value is the certainty-equivalent of the option's end-of-period value. Once this value is calculated, it is adjusted for time by discounting at the risk-free rate to get us from the future to the present. Similarly, once the certainty-equivalent future value of any asset or commodity is established (plus any cash to be received), this value is discounted at the risk-free rate to obtain the spot price. For assets or commodities with futures contracts, this certainty-equivalent price is the futures price.

So which comes first, the spot price or the futures price? As in the earlier discussion of how S&P index and futures prices adjust to new information, spot and futures prices are determined jointly. But once the adjustment has been made, and you know either of the two prices, the other is implied. To the extent that the futures price represents a risk-adjusted expected value, and the spot price is the discounted present value of this same risk-adjusted value, the spot price contains the same expectation of future value as that imbedded in the futures price. Therefore, . . .

> if you observe the spot price, all the information you need about future expected prices is imbedded in that price, and looking to the futures market for additional information about the future would be double counting. Thus, for storable assets and commodities, futures prices contain no more information about the future than spot prices.

For non-storables, the futures price still represents the risk-adjusted expected value, but since the asset or commodity cannot be stored, there is no way to transform the information about the future to the present through arbitrage. Therefore, the futures price may contain more information about prices in the future than is contained in spot prices. Nevertheless, even for a non-storable commodity, the futures price represents a risk-adjusted expected price, not an actual expected price.

Standard finance theories of risk and return, such as the Capital Asset Pricing Model, indicate that assets or commodities whose returns are positively correlated with the returns of the market portfolio of all assets, should have expected returns in excess of the risk-free rate. Equivalently, for such assets or commodities, risk-adjusted expected future prices should be less than their corresponding non-risk-adjusted expected values. Therefore, following standard finance theory, futures prices should be less than expected future prices for commodities or assets whose returns are positively correlated with the overall market. However, for a commodity such as gold, whose return is often viewed as having a negative correlation with the market portfolio, the futures price could exceed the expected price in the future. Notwithstanding the above, if a commodity or asset can be stored, even if finance theory suggests a relationship between the futures price and the expected price in the future, the same relationship should be reflected in the spot price.

13.5 Summary

In this chapter the theory of futures pricing is approached from three different perspectives. The first is the equivalence between a long futures position and a leveraged position in the underlying asset or commodity. The second is the equivalence between a safe asset and a long position in the underlying asset or commodity hedged by a short position in futures. The third is the equivalence between a long position in the underlying asset or commodity and long positions in safe assets and futures. All three approaches lead to the same futures/spot pricing relationship, but each provides a different insight into pricing and the role of futures as an investment vehicle. The theory suggests that spot and futures prices of storable assets and commodities are jointly determined. Therefore, neither price contains unique information that is not reflected in the other.

QUESTIONS AND PROBLEMS

1. The current value of the S&P 500 index is 1,300. The riskless rate of interest is 6 percent per year compounded annually. As a rough approximation, you expect the stocks in the index to pay dividends, which when reinvested with interest, will equal $10 six months from now. Compute the equilibrium futures price for the S&P futures contract maturing in exactly six months.

2. A 1-year forward contract on gold is entered into when the spot price of gold is $200 per ounce and the risk-free rate of interest is 5 percent per year, compounded annually.

   a. What is the theoretical forward price?
   b. What is the initial dollar value of the forward contract, that is, the value of the contract as a financial instrument?
   c. Six months later, the price of gold falls to $180 per ounce and the risk-free interest rate is still 5 percent. What is the new value of the old forward contract referred to in parts a and b?

3. The 3-month interest rates in the UK and the US are 4 percent and 9 percent per annum, respectively, with continuous compounding.

The spot price of the British Pound is $1.45/£. What should be the futures price for a contract deliverable in three months?

4. ZAI, a US firm, is a major player in foreign currency markets. Today ZAI can borrow or lend US dollars at a rate of 5 percent per year compounded annually. ZAI can also borrow or lend British Pounds (£) at a rate of 7 percent per year compounded annually. The spot exchange rate for British Pounds is $1.60/£, and the 1-year futures exchange rate is $1.56/£.

   ZAI believes there is a price discrepancy between the spot and futures exchange rates that can be exploited to earn a riskless arbitrage profit. ZAI begins its arbitrage transaction by borrowing £1,000,000 at 7 percent. Describe the remaining part of the arbitrage transaction, and calculate the profit ZAI can expect to earn 1 year from today.

5. Consider a futures contract issued on a specific 3-year Treasury note. The note pays interest of 4 percent every six months. In today's market, all Treasury bonds and notes yield 6 percent per year compounded semi-annually, or 3 percent every six months. Compute the 6-month futures price per $100 par.

6. You have been given $260,000,000 to manage with an objective of providing an overall portfolio beta of 0.5 measured against the S&P 500 index. Presently, the value of the S&P index is $1,300 per unit of the index. The price of 1-year S&P futures is $1,378 per unit of the index, reflecting a risk-free interest rate of 6 percent per year compounded annually and no dividends.

   How could you use futures contracts to achieve your portfolio objective without investing in stocks at all?

7. According to table 13.6, what is the *expected* $/£ exchange rate on June 16, 1999? Explain.

8. Yesterday the S&P 500 index closed at 1,340. Today, immediately before the opening of trading on the New York stock exchange, 1-year S&P futures are trading at 1,397.25. The 1-year riskless rate of interest is 5 percent per year compounded annually. The expected annual dividend yield for the S&P index is 1.5 percent of its current value. What is your best estimate of today's opening value for the S&P index?

9. Assume that the standard terms for the wheat futures contract call for the delivery of medium-grade wheat but that high and low grades of wheat are also deliverable. The middle column of the table below shows how the delivery price will be adjusted in relation to the futures price (FP) for the various grades of wheat that can be delivered to satisfy the terms of the contract. The right-most column shows the current spot prices of wheat. Assume that the price differences shown in the final column have been in effect for years and are expected to continue into the indefinite future.

The riskless interest rate is 6 percent per year compounded annually, and carrying charges for storing wheat are zero, regardless of grade. Compute the equilibrium 1-year futures price for wheat.

Adjustment to standard terms of wheat futures contract

Grade of wheat	Adjusted futures price per bushel ($)	Cash market price (spot price) per bushel ($)
High	FP + 0.05	2.56
Medium	FP + 0.00	2.50
Low	FP − 0.05	2.43

14

Hedging with Futures

14.1 Introduction

One of the primary functions of futures contracts is hedging. Farmers or farming organizations that can produce agricultural grains efficiently, but have little expertise in predicting future grain prices, can take short positions in grain futures to lock in the selling prices of the grains they have planted and expect to harvest. Firms like Kelloggs and Ralston Purina that use grains as production inputs can take long positions in grain futures to lock the future purchase prices of these inputs. Fixed-income portfolio managers often use Treasury Bond futures to reduce the duration, or effective maturity of bond portfolios, thereby reducing exposure to adverse changes in long-term interest rates. The list of potential hedging applications goes on and on.

The theory of hedging, as it relates to the pricing of futures, has already been introduced in chapter 13. The present chapter extends this theory to include certain aspects of the mathematics of hedging not obvious from the previous discussion.[65]

The mathematics of futures hedging is usually approached in one of two ways. The first hedging method is what I call *unit* or *forward-based* hedging. This method represents the common-sense approach and the approach that has been used up to this point in the book. Technically, however, this approach is applicable only to hedging with forward contracts. The second approach is what I call *tailed* or *futures-based* hedging. This approach will result in slightly lower hedging quantities than unit-based hedges. But like several other futures-related concepts developed in this book, if your objective is simply to gain a general understanding of futures markets without

---

65. The material on the mathematics of hedging draws heavily from Rendleman (1993).

getting bogged down in details, no harm will be done if you think of futures hedging in terms of the unit or forward-based approach. However, if you plan to be an active user of futures markets, it is important that you understand the difference between hedging with futures and hedging with forward contracts. Although the difference in the hedging quantities using the two methods can be small, when applied to large positions, the dollar value of hedging errors can be significant.

14.2 Unit-based Hedging

The gold contract traded at the New York Mercantile Exchange calls for the delivery of 100 Troy ounces of gold. Using the logic of unit-based hedging, if you want to hedge 100 Troy ounces of gold, you would need to sell one contract. Similarly, the Chicago Board of Trade wheat contract calls for the delivery of 5,000 bushels of wheat. Therefore, if you want to hedge 100,000 bushels, you would need to sell $100,000/5,000 = 20$ wheat contracts. Generally, the unit-based hedging quantity, Q_{unit} is given by:

$$Q_{unit} = \frac{\text{units to be hedged}}{\text{units per contract}}.$$

$$(14.1)$$

Some hedging problems are denominated more naturally in dollars, but can be converted easily to units. For example, assume that the S&P 500 index is currently quoted at $1,000. The Chicago Mercantile Exchange S&P 500 futures contract is based on the implicit delivery of 250 units of the S&P index using cash settlement. The contract price for 1-year S&P futures is $1,070. You want to use S&P 500 futures to hedge the risk in a $200,000,000 S&P index fund.

Using the logic of unit-based hedging, we must determine how many units of the S&P are represented by the index fund. Since the S&P 500 index is currently quoted at $1,000, the index fund is equivalent to $200,000,000/\$1,000 = 200,000$ "units" of the index. Since each futures contract is for 250 units, the hedging quantity is given by:

$$Q_{unit} = \frac{\text{units to be hedged}}{\text{units per contract}} = \frac{200,000}{250} = 800 \text{ contracts.}$$

Suppose the portfolio being hedged is not an S&P index fund, but, instead, is a well-diversified portfolio with a beta of 1.5 in relation to the S&P. In this case, the portfolio is *equivalent in risk* to $1.5 \times 200,000 = 300,000$ units of the S&P index. Therefore, the hedging quantity is:

$$Q_{unit} = \frac{\text{units to be hedged}}{\text{units per contract}} = \frac{300,000}{250} = 1,200 \text{ contracts.}$$

Note that the futures contract price of $1,070 never came into play in determining the hedging quantity.

Consider an American aircraft manufacturing company that contracts with Rolls-Royce to purchase jet engines one year from today at a price of £50,000,000. Although the American company could wait for a year and pay £50,000,000 at a dollar-equivalent value that reflects the $/£ exchange rate in one year, the company might want to lock in the dollar cost of the jet engines in advance. Assume the spot exchange rate is $1.50/£, and the 1-year futures price for British Pounds is $1.4725/£, reflecting interest rates of 7 and 9 percent in the US and UK, respectively.[66] Since each futures contract is for 62,500 British Pounds, the unit-based hedging quantity is:

$$Q_{unit} = \frac{\text{units to be hedged}}{\text{units per contract}} = \frac{50,000,000}{62,500} = 800 \text{ contracts.}$$

Note that with this hedge, the American company must take a long position in futures at a contract price of $1.4725/£, since it wants to lock in the price it pays for British Pounds in the future. Using the vernacular of futures markets, this type of hedge is called a *long hedge*, since the futures component of the hedge involves a long position. Similarly, a hedge involving a short position in futures, such as that taken by a farmer to lock in the selling price of his grain harvest, is called a *short hedge*.

14.3   Tailed or Futures-based Hedging

Technically, the hedging quantities computed above would be correct if the contracts used for hedging were forward contracts rather than futures contracts. However, if futures contracts are used, a "tailing" adjustment must be made to account for the difference between forward and futures contracting.

Tailing the hedge

To understand tailing, refer back to the gold hedging example. Using unit-based hedging logic, we determined that if one wanted to hedge the price

---

66. From equation 13.6, $F_{\$/£} = spot_{\$/£}((1 + i_\$)/(1 + i_£))^\tau = (\$1.50/£) \times (1.07/1.09)^1 = \$1.4725/£.$

risk associated with 100 Troy ounces of gold, one would need to sell one gold futures contract computed as follows:

$$Q_{unit} = \frac{\text{units to be hedged}}{\text{units per contract}} = \frac{100}{100} = 1 \text{ contract.}$$

Assume that the riskless interest rate is 7 percent per year compounded annually, the spot price of gold is $400 per ounce and the contract price for a 1-year futures contract is $400(1.07) = $428, reflecting no carrying charges other than an interest cost. By selling one 1-year futures contract against a 100-ounce gold position, one would expect to lock in a value of $428 per ounce or $428 × 100 = $42,800 for the gold position one year from today.

Assume that the futures price falls immediately to $418 per ounce from $428 after the initial short futures position is taken. In this case the hedger would receive immediate cash credit of $428 − $418 = $10 per ounce or ($10/oz.) × 100 oz. = $1,000 in his futures brokerage account. Assuming he can earn interest at a rate of 7 percent on the $1,000, the cash credit of $1,000 will grow to $1,070 in one year.[67]

To keep the analysis simple, assume that the futures price never changes again over the year. Then, the futures price will be $418 per ounce at maturity, and the cash price of gold will also be $418, since the futures and spot prices must converge on the futures maturity date. In this case, the hedger could sell his gold for $418 × 100 = $41,800 and cash out of his futures position for $1,070, bringing the total value of the position to $41,800 + $1,000 = $42,870. Thus, the hedger will end up with $42,870 rather than the $42,800 that had been expected. Although this results in a pleasant surprise, it is not exactly what the hedger had anticipated. Moreover, if the futures price had risen to $438, rather than having fallen to $418, the hedger would have incurred an immediate loss of $1,000 in his futures account. After financing this loss at 7 percent for a year, the total loss in the futures position would have been $1,070. Therefore, after one year, the total value of the hedged position would have been $438 × 100 − $1,070 = $42,730, or $70 short of the $42,800 that had been anticipated.

Note that after accounting for interest, any immediate gain or loss in the futures position will become larger by a factor of 1.07 after one year. But ideally, if the futures price moves up or down by $10 per ounce, the

---

67. Technically, marking to the market occurs on a daily basis rather than immediately. Therefore, interest would actually accrue for only 364 days of a 365-day year, resulting in $1,000 × 1.07$^{364/365}$ = $1,069.80.

ultimate gain or loss in the futures position should be $10 per ounce, or $1,000, rather than $1,070. This can be accomplished by selling $1/1.07 = 0.9346$ contracts, or more generally, by reducing the number of contracts one would sell under unit-based hedging by a factor of 0.9346. Thus, if unit-based hedging calls for selling 1,000 gold futures contracts, after adjusting for tailing, one should sell $1,000 \times 0.9346 = 934.60$ or 935 contracts, after rounding up.

The forgoing analysis assumes that the futures price never changes after the initial movement from $428 to $418. But even if the futures price *does* change over the course of the year, as it most certainly will, the initial $10 change will *contribute* $10 \times 1.07 = 10.70 per ounce to the value of the final futures balance. Therefore, if the hedger would like the $10 change to contribute exactly $10 per ounce to the final balance in the futures account, he must sell $1/1.07 = 0.9346$ contracts for every contract that he would otherwise sell based on unit hedging. Or more generally, if the hedger would like an immediate futures price change of $X per ounce to translate into exactly $X per ounce on the futures maturity date, he must sell $1/1.07 = 0.9346$ times the unit-based hedging quantity, no matter what the change in the futures price turns out to be.

It is important to note that as time passes, the interest factor will be reduced, and the hedging quantity must be increased. For example, assume that unit-based hedging calls for selling 1,000 gold futures contracts, but after adjusting for tailing, $1,000/1.07 = 934.58$ or 935 1-year futures contracts are sold. In six days, the same futures contract will have only 359 days remaining, so, technically, one should be short $1,000/1.07^{359/365} = 935.62$, or 936 contracts after rounding up. Therefore, one additional contract should be sold after the sixth day. Six days later, with 353 days remaining on the contract, $1,000/1.07^{353/365} = 936.66$ contracts would be needed, or 937 contracts after rounding. Therefore, another contract would need to be sold to maintain the tailed-based hedge.

With tailing, all the hedging quantities computed in the unit-based hedging examples of the previous section should be adjusted by the interest factor. However, in each case, the hedging quantities should be adjusted upward over time as the interest factor gets closer to 1.0. Letting τ denote the number of years remaining over the life of the futures contract and i denote the risk-free interest rate, the tailed-based hedging quantity becomes:

$$Q_{tailed} = \left(\frac{\text{units to be hedged}}{\text{units per contract}} \right) \left(\frac{1}{[1 + i]^{\tau}} \right)$$

$$= \frac{Q_{unit}}{(1 + i)^{\tau}}$$

(14.2)

A second method for computing the futures-based hedging quantity

Futures hedging quantities can also be computed on the basis of simple calculus. Consider a situation in which you want to hedge the immediate price risk of an asset or commodity with a value of *spot* dollars per unit using futures with a contract price of F dollars per unit. Assume that the relationship between the spot and futures price is:

$$F = spot(1 + i)^\tau,$$

reflecting no dividend or other cash income from the underlying asset or commodity.

The objective in hedging should be to choose a quantity of futures to sell so that any change in the value of the spot position will be offset by an equal but opposite change in the value of the futures position. Thus, you must choose a quantity of futures contracts to sell, denoted as $Q_{futures}$, such that

$$Q_{futures} \times \Delta F \times units\ per\ contract = \Delta spot \times units\ hedged, \quad or$$

$$Q_{futures} = \left(\frac{units\ hedged}{units\ per\ contract} \right) \left(\frac{\Delta spot}{\Delta F} \right).$$

From the spot/futures pricing relationship, $F = spot(1+i)^\tau$, which implies

$$\Delta F = \Delta S(1 + i)^\tau.$$

Therefore, one must sell the following number of contracts to hedge one unit of the asset or commodity:

$$
\begin{aligned}
Q_{futures} &= \left(\frac{units\ hedged}{units\ per\ contract} \right) \left(\frac{\Delta spot}{\Delta F} \right) \\
&= \left(\frac{units\ hedged}{units\ per\ contract} \right) \left(\frac{\Delta spot}{\Delta spot[1 + i]^\tau} \right) \\
&= \left(\frac{units\ hedged}{units\ per\ contract} \right) \left(\frac{1}{[1 + i]^\tau} \right) \\
&= \frac{Q_{unit}}{(1 + i)^\tau}.
\end{aligned}
$$

$$(14.3)$$

> This is the same hedging quantity obtained with tailed-based hedging. Therefore, adjusting this quantity for tailing would be double counting.

I have seen several treatments of hedging that compute this quantity and then divide by $(1 + i)^\tau$ to reflect tailing. But this is a mistake. The only hedging quantity that should be "tailed" is one based on unit hedging.

How to avoid double counting

Note that the hedging quantity above can be stated as:

$$Q_{futures} = \left(\frac{units\ hedged}{units\ per\ contract} \right) \left(\frac{1}{[1 + i]^\tau} \right) \quad \text{or as}$$

$$Q_{futures} = \left(\frac{units\ hedged}{units\ per\ contract} \right) \left(\frac{spot}{F} \right),$$

since $F = spot(1 + i)^\tau$. Therefore, the two hedging formulas,

$$Q_{futures} = \left(\frac{units\ hedged}{units\ per\ contract} \right) \left(\frac{1}{[1 + i]^\tau} \right) \quad \text{and}$$

$$Q_{futures} = \left(\frac{units\ hedged}{units\ per\ contract} \right) \left(\frac{spot}{F} \right),$$

both lead to the same hedging quantity.[68] Generally, if a hedging formula contains the interest factor $1/(1 + i)^\tau$, the hedge has been adjusted for tailing. Similarly, if the hedging formula does not contain an interest factor,

---

68. The analysis that led to $Q_{futures} = (units\ hedged/units\ per\ contract)(1/[1 + i]^\tau)$ assumes no cash income from the underlying asset or commodity. It can be shown that if the underlying asset earns cash income q_{div} times the asset's ending value, the tailed hedging quantity for hedging one unit of the asset is $Q_{tailed} = (units\ hedged/units\ per\ contract)((1 + q_{div})/(1 + i))^\tau$ and $Q_{futures} = (units\ hedged/\ units\ per\ contract)((1 + q_{div})/(1 + i))^\tau = (units\ hedged/units\ per\ contract)(spot/F)$. (Also, the unit-based hedging quantity is $Q_{unit} = (units\ hedged/units\ per\ contract)\ (1 + q_{div})^\tau$, so, again, the tailed quantity is the unit quantity divided by $[1 + i]^\tau$.) If the underlying asset earns a fixed cash dividend with future value, $fv(div)$, the tailed hedging quantity is $Q_{tailed} = (units\ hedged/units\ per\ contract)(1/[1 + i]^\tau)$ and $Q_{futures} = (units\ hedged/units\ per\ contract)(1/[1 + i]^\tau) = (units\ hedged/units\ per\ contract)(spot/(F + fv[div]))$.

but does include the futures price, such as

$$Q_{futures} = \left(\frac{units\ hedged}{units\ per\ contract} \right) \left(\frac{spot}{F} \right) \quad \text{or}$$

$$Q_{futures} = \left(\frac{units\ hedged}{units\ per\ contract} \right) \left(\frac{spot}{F + fv[div]} \right)$$

(see footnote 68), the hedging quantity reflects tailing implicity. Therefore, multiplying such a hedging quantity by $1/(1+i)^\tau$ would double-count the "tail."

An example of avoiding double counting

This example will extend the unit-based portfolio hedging example using S&P 500 index futures. In the example, the S&P 500 index is currently quoted at $1,000 per unit. The S&P 500 futures contract is based on the implicit delivery of 250 units of the S&P index using cash settlement. The contract price for 1-year S&P futures is $1,070 per unit or $1,070 × 250 = $267,500 for the actual contract. To keep the example simple, assume that stocks in the S&P 500 index do not pay dividends. Therefore, the risk-free rate implied in the relationship between the spot price of $1,000 and futures price of $1,070 is 7 percent. The S&P 500 futures contract will be used to hedge the risk in a $200,000,000 portfolio with a beta of 1.5 in relation to the S&P 500 index.

For this type of hedging problem, most texts indicate the following hedging quantity:

$$Q_{futures} = \beta \left(\frac{portfolio\ value}{total\ futures\ price} \right)$$

$$= 1.5 \left(\frac{\$200,000,000}{\$267,500} \right)$$

$$= 1,121$$

Note that this is the same quantity determined earlier, using unit-based hedging,

$$Q_{unit} = \frac{units\ to\ be\ hedged}{units\ per\ contract} = \frac{300,000}{250} = 1,200\ \text{contracts},$$

times the interest factor, $1/1.07$, to adjust for tailing, or $1,200/1.07 = 1,121$. Thus, if we were to compute the hedging quantity as $Q_{futures} = \beta(portfolio\ value/total\ futures\ price) = 1,121$, and then divide this quantity by 1.07, we would be double counting the tailing adjustment.

14.4 Cross Hedging

A *cross hedge* is a hedge that uses a futures contract to hedge an asset or commodity different from that which underlies the futures contract. Hedging a $200,000,000 stock portfolio with a beta of 1.5 using S&P 500 futures is a good example of a cross hedge. The portfolio does not have the same composition as the S&P 500, yet the S&P contract can be used to hedge the market component of the portfolio's risk. Nevertheless, after hedging the portfolio's exposure to market risk, there is still some risk that portfolio's return will be higher or lower than expected. If the portfolio performs exactly as expected, given that its market risk exposure has been removed, the return from hedging should equal the risk-free rate. However, if it performs X percent better (or worse) than expected, the return from hedging should equal the risk-free rate $+X$ percent. Therefore, this hedge, like other cross hedges, is not perfect, but it should expose the asset or commodity being hedged to much less price risk than if it had not been hedged.

The basis and basis risk

> Futures traders use the term *basis risk* to refer to the risk that the price of a commodity or asset being hedged will not eventually converge to the futures price.

Mathematically, the *basis* is defined as follows:

$$basis = spot\ price\ of\ asset\ or\ commodity\ being\ hedged - futures\ price.$$

(14.4)

This definition recognizes that the asset or commodity being hedged may not be exactly the same as that which underlies the futures contract. For example, the basis for the Chicago Board of Trade corn contract would be different for North Carolina corn than for corn grown in Illinois.

As a futures contract approaches its maturity date, the basis for the asset or commodity that underlies the contract should approach zero. However, for other assets or commodities, the final basis could end up higher or lower than zero, depending upon the correlation between the price of what is being hedged and the price of the asset or commodity that underlies the futures contract.

Futures traders who engage in cross hedging often refer to their positions as being *long the basis* or as speculating on the basis. Since the basis is typically a negative amount that should eventually approach a value close to zero, one should expect the basis in a cross hedge to eventually get larger, or less negative. This is the rationale for the term *long the basis.*

An example of cross hedging foreign currency

Suppose you want to hedge a commitment to purchase 1,000,000,000 Czech Krona (CK), but cannot find a bank that will sell a forward contract in Krona of sufficient quantity on favorable terms to carry out the hedge. Moreover, none of the futures markets trade contracts on Czech Krona. Therefore, if you want to hedge the commitment to purchase Krona, you would have to engage in a cross hedge, most likely one involving a long position in futures of a different currency.

Common sense tells us that using futures on the Mexican Peso is not likely to result in an effective hedge. However, it is quite possible that changes in the value of Krona are highly correlated with changes in the values of other European currencies on which futures are traded.

In theory, you should find an alternate currency whose returns are the most highly correlated with Czech Krona. For the purposes of this example, assume the most correlated currency is the Deutschemark. You would then regress returns, or percentage changes in the Krona, against returns in the Deutschemark. Suppose this regression indicated that on average, Krona returns equal a constant plus 1.2 times the Deutschemark return. Assume the current exchange rates are $0.025/CK and $0.50/DM. Based on this information, how should you hedge the commitment to purchase CK1,000,000,000?

The futures contract in Deutschemarks, traded at the Chicago Mercantile Exchange is for 125,000 D-Marks. Note that the exchange rates $0.025/CK and $0.50/DM imply a DM/CK exchange rate of ($0.025/CK)/($0.50/DM) = DM0.05/CK. Therefore, if the returns of Deutschemarks and Czech Krona moved in parallel, CK1,000,000,000 would be equivalent in risk to (CK1,000,000,000)(DM0.05/CK) = DM50,000,000. But with the Czech Krona assumed to be 1.2 times as volatile as the Deutschemark, the CK1,000,000,000 is the risk-equivalent of DM50,000,000 × 1.2 = DM60,000,000. Since one futures contract will hedge 125,000 D-Marks, you would need to take a long position in (DM60,000,000)/(DM125,000/contract) = 480 Deutschemark futures contracts. This quantity represents a unit-based quantity, so, technically, it should be tailed to create the best possible hedge.

In this example, as well as the example involving the hedging of returns of a stock portfolio with a beta of 1.5, the hedges are only as good as the predicted relationship between the asset or commodity being hedged and that which underlies the hedging instrument.[69] A portfolio beta of 1.5, based on a regression of past returns, or a currency beta of 1.2, also calculated with past returns, may not necessarily hold up over future time periods. Therefore, I am not suggesting that one use slope coefficients from simple regressions of past return series to predict future return relationships, although this might be a good starting point. With today's computational power and the development of sophisticated statistical techniques, there are better ways to predict future return relationships than using slope coefficients from ordinary least squares regressions. Nevertheless, from a conceptual standpoint, this is the type of information one would need for executing effective cross hedges using futures.

14.5 Summary

This chapter develops the theory of unit-based hedging, tailed hedging and cross hedging. Unit-based hedging represents the common sense approach to hedging and is equivalent to hedging with forward contracts. According to unit-based hedging, if one wants to hedge a position in 1,000 Troy ounces of gold, and each gold futures contract is for 100 ounces, then a short position in 1,000/100 = 10 futures is needed. Unfortunately, the ability to earn interest on daily marked-to-the market futures gains and the necessity to pay or to forego interest on daily losses can cause the hedged position's final payoff per ounce to differ from the futures price. This problem can be corrected, however, using a process called tailing that takes account of the interest factor over the life of the hedge.

---

69. Many texts develop the concept of the optimal hedge ratio, originally attributable to Ederington (1979). This ratio is that which minimizes the sum of the squared hedging errors, and it turns out to be exactly the same as the regression coefficients that have been used in the hedging examples of this chapter. From this theory, the measure of potential hedging effectiveness is the R^2 that results from such a regression. If you understand that a stock portfolio with an S&P-based beta of 1.5 is equivalent in risk to 1.5 times as many dollars invested in the S&P, and should be hedged accordingly, you implicitly understand the concept of optimal hedging.

Cross hedges involve the use of futures to hedge the price risk of an asset or commodity different from that which underlies the contract. The ability to engage in effective cross hedging depends upon the correlation between the two assets or commodities. If the correlation is high, the hedge is likely to be more effective. Examples of cross hedging include the use of S&P 500 futures to hedge the market risk in a non-S&P stock portfolio, the use of grain futures to hedge the price risk at harvest for a farmer or farming organization located a significant distance from the designated delivery points of the futures contract and the use of currency futures to hedge the exchange risk in another currency with undeveloped or illiquid forward markets.

REFERENCES

Ederington, L, "The Hedging Performance of New Futures Markets." *The Journal of Finance* 34 (September 1979), 229–63.
Rendleman, R. J., Jr., "A Reconciliation of Potentially Conflicting Approaches to Hedging with Futures." *Advances in Futures and Options Research* 6 (1993), 81–92.

QUESTIONS AND PROBLEMS

1. Six months from now in October 2001, Mid-West, Inc., a major corporate farming organization, expects to harvest 10,000,000 bushels of wheat. Each wheat futures contract is for 5,000 bushels. The spot price of wheat is $3.00 per bushel and the October futures price is $3.09 per bushel. Using unit-based hedging, how can Mid-West lock in the selling price of its expected wheat harvest?

2. On August 11, 2001 you enter into a contract to purchase Rolls-Royce jet engines at a price of 100,000,000 British Pounds on June 15, 2002. The current exchange rate is $1.750 per Pound. The June futures price is $1.7333 per Pound, reflecting that interest of 5 percent and 6 percent can be earned between August 11 and June 15 in the US and UK; respectively (that is, $1.7333 = $1.75[1.05/1.06]). Each futures contract is for 62,500 British Pounds. Using *unit and tailed-based hedging*, how can you use futures to lock in the US dollar cost of the contract?

3. You manage a portfolio that holds a bond denominated in Euros scheduled to pay 120,000,000 Euros in one year. The current exchange rate is $0.9000 per Euro. The contract price for 1-year Euro futures is $0.9171, reflecting 1-year dollar and Euro interest rates of 7 percent and 5 percent, respectively. Each futures contract is for 125,000 Euros. Using *unit and tailed-based hedging*, how can you use futures to lock

in the amount received from the bond in US dollars one year from now?

4. You are managing a stock portfolio worth $260,000,000. The portfolio has a beta of 0.8 measured against the S&P 500 index.

You have become very bearish about stocks, and would like to sell all of the stocks in the portfolio and invest the proceeds in Treasury bills. However, you have been told that you can do the equivalent by using S&P 500 futures without even touching the stocks.

Presently, the value of the S&P index is $1,300 per unit of the index. The price of 1-year S&P futures is $1,365 per unit of the index, and each contract is based on the cash settlement of 250 index units.

a. What unit-based transaction involving futures would be the near-equivalent to selling your stocks and investing the proceeds in Treasury bills? Be as precise as possible, indicating the size of your hedging position and whether you should be long or short.

b. What risk, if any, is there that this transaction will not be equivalent to selling your stocks and investing the proceeds in Treasury bills?

15

Interest Rate Futures

15.1   Introduction

Futures issued on interest-sensitive financial assets, usually referred to as *interest rate futures*, and interest rate swaps, described in the next chapter, are among the most important financial instruments for managing interest rate risk. Consider a commercial bank that holds interest-sensitive assets and liabilities. The bank's current asset/liability mix may reflect a desire among its officials to position the bank to become more profitable in the event that interest rates fall. As such, one would expect the average maturity of the bank's interest-sensitive assets to be longer than that of its interest-sensitive liabilities.

Suppose the same officials suddenly change their interest rate forecast, believing that interest rates will rise. The change in beliefs, coupled with the bank's interest rate risk exposure, imply the expectation of lower profits or even losses for the bank. If the bank could reduce the maturity of its loan portfolio and/or increase the maturity of its deposits, it could reduce the risk associated with an adverse change in interest rates. But making such changes immediately would be extremely difficult if the bank were to focus its efforts entirely on changing loan and deposit maturities. However, by taking an appropriate position in interest rate futures, the bank could immediately fix its exposure problem without directly altering its loan or deposit portfolios.

The primary futures contracts for accomplishing changes of this type in dollar-denominated portfolios are the 3-month Eurodollar contract, traded at the Chicago Mercantile Exchange and the Treasury Bond and Note contracts offered by the Chicago Board of Trade. The 3-month Euribor contract, offered

To properly manage the interest rate risk exposure of a fixed-income
portfolio or a financial institution such as a commercial bank, one must
be able to measure the portfolio's or institution's sensitivity to changes
in interest rates and to also estimate the interest rate sensitivity of potential instruments, such as financial futures and interest rate swaps, used
to manage this risk. *Duration* is one of the primary analytical tools used
by fixed-income professionals for estimating and managing interest rate
risk. Therefore, before turning to descriptions of specific financial futures
contracts, I will develop the mathematics and theory of duration.

15.2 Duration: An Analytical Tool for Measuring and Managing Interest Rate Risk

Duration as a measure of effective maturity

Duration, as originally formulated by Fredrick McCauley (1938), is a
measure of the effective maturity of a fixed-income security such as a
government bond or a portfolio comprised of a number of fixed-income
instruments. But since McCauley's formulation, it has been shown that
duration is also directly related to the change in the security's price that
should accompany a change in interest rates. As such, duration can be
used to estimate the sensitivity of a fixed-income portfolio and its potential
hedging instruments to changes in interest rates and to formulate a hedging plan to help meet a portfolio manager's goal with respect to interest
rate risk exposure.

The mathematical definition of a bond or fixed-income portfolio's
duration is as follows:

$$duration = \sum_{k=1}^{m} t_k w_k,$$

$$(15.1)$$

where t_k denotes the time of the bond's kth cash payment, m denotes
the number of payments, and w_k denotes the proportion of the bond's
total present value contributed by the kth payment. From equation 15.1,
duration is the sum of the times of each cash payment weighted by the

70. Like the London Interbank Offered Rate (LIBOR), which is denominated in
dollars, Euribor is an Interbank Offered Rate denominated in Euros.

proportion of total value attributable to the payment. As such, it represents a weighted average time to maturity. Note that the duration of a bond that makes a single payment, such as a zero-coupon bond, will be the time of the single payment. However, a coupon-paying bond will have a duration less than that of the time of its final payment, since the times of the coupon payments received prior to the final payment and their respective valuation weights are part of the overall weighted average.

Table 15.1 provides an example of the duration calculation for a bond maturing in 3.5 years that pays interest of 8 percent per year in two semi-annual installments. In this example, it is assumed that the bond is being priced to yield 6 percent per year compounded continuously.

In this example, the bond's price is $105.937 per $100 par. $3.882 of this value is attributable to the first interest payment, received in 0.5 years, so the time of payment, 0.5, is weighted by $3.882/$105.937 = 0.0366 in the computation of the bond's duration. Similarly, $3.767 of the bond's value is attributable to the $4 interest payment to be received in 1.0 years. Therefore, 1.0 is weighted by $3.767/$105.937 = 0.0356 in the duration calculation. Even though the bond is technically a 3.5-year bond, the payment received in 3.5 years is weighted by $84.301/$105.937 = 0.7958, so the bond's overall weighted time of payment is less than 3.5 years. Summing all the weighted times produces a duration of 3.1337 years. Using McCauley's notion of effective maturity, this bond has an effective maturity of 3.1337 years, the same as a zero-coupon bond that makes a lump sum payment in exactly 3.1337 years.

Some students seem to have trouble with the idea that a 3.5-year bond could have an effective maturity of anything other than 3.5 years. If you are also having trouble with this concept, look back at table 15.1 and think of the payment stream, not as that of a 3.5-year bond, but, instead, as that of a portfolio of zero-coupon bonds. The first zero pays $4 at time 0.5. The second pays $4 at time 1.0 and so on, with the final zero paying $104 at time 3.5. In this context, the portfolio's effective maturity reflects the maturity of its various component securities with the most valuable getting the most weight in the effective maturity calculation. Using the portfolio concept, the zero-coupon bond that pays $104 in 3.5 years comprises 79.58 percent of the portfolio's value and, therefore, gets 79.58 percent of the weight in the effective maturity calculation. With 3.66 percent of the total value, the bond paying $4 at time 0.5 gets 3.66 percent of the weight, and so on. Since the 3.5-year 8 percent bond is economically equivalent to portfolio of zeros, it must have the same duration.

Table 15.1 Calculation of duration for a 3.5-year bond paying interest of 8 percent annually and yielding 6 percent per year compounded continuously

k (payment number)	1	2	3	4	5	6	7	Total
t_k (time of payment in years)	0.5	1	1.5	2	2.5	3	3.5	
Payment amount ($)	4	4	4	4	4	4	104	
PV of payment ($)	3.882	3.767	3.656	3.548	3.443	3.341	84.301	105.937
Proportion of total value	0.0366	0.0356	0.0345	0.0335	0.0325	0.0315	0.7958	1.000
Proportion $\times t_k$	0.0183	0.0356	0.0518	0.0670	0.0812	0.0946	2.7852	3.1337

Present value of bond payments = $105.937. Duration = 3.1337 years.

Duration as a measure of sensitivity to interest rate changes

Taking a mathematical derivative is the standard method for determining how the value of a function changes when one of its components changes. This notion can be applied to the pricing of a bond to determine how its price should change when its yield changes.[71] Let $P_{full} = P_{quoted} + A$, where P_{quoted} is the quoted price of a bond, A is accrued interest and P_{full} is the bond's full price, the sum of the quoted price and accrued interest, which represents the amount that one must actually pay to buy the bond.[72] The bond's continuously compounded annual yield, denoted as y, is the discount rate that sets the present value of the stream of bond payments, discounted at y, to the full price. For a bond with \$100 par value, the full price becomes:[73]

$$P_{full} = \sum_{k=1}^{m} \left(\frac{C}{2} \right) e^{-yt_k} + 100e^{-yt_m},$$

(15.2)

where C is the bond's annual coupon per \$100 par and k is an index of integers $1, 2, \ldots, m$ that is incremented by one every six months. This formulation reflects that an interest payment of $C/2$ is made twice a year.

By taking the derivative of the bond's full price with respect to its yield, one can determine how much the bond's full value should change with an

---

71. A bond's *yield* is the same as its internal rate of return. As such, it is the discount rate that equates the present value of the bond's stream of payments to its purchase price.
72. Typically, bonds are priced using the accrued interest convention in which the total amount paid for a bond is a quoted price plus accrued interest. Methods for calculating accrued interest can be slightly different for different types of bonds. However, regardless of the method by which accrued interest is calculated, the total of accrued interest and the quoted price should be the same, since this total is the amount that one must actually pay for the bond. For analytical purposes, it is best to think of the full price, which should reflect the present value of the bond's stream of future payments, as being determined first, with the quoted price being what is left after subtracting accrued interest. Slight errors can be made in duration calculations and in hedging if the quoted and full prices are used interchangeably.
73. Some readers may be concerned about the use of continuous compounding in the formulation of the bond's price. Without going into the details, compared with the use of annual or semi-annual compounding, the mathematics of duration are *much* easier using continuous interest, especially when dealing with cash payments that do not line up precisely in equal time increments. Note that the bond price as formulated in equation 15.2 would be the same for any time intervals represented by the values of t_k. In contrast, formulating the price of a bond, and its duration, when cash payments are not made in regular integer units of time is very tedious. Therefore, I use continuous interest throughout this chapter in an effort to keep things as simple as possible.

instantaneous change in the yield.

$$\frac{dP_{full}}{dy} = -\left(\sum_{k=1}^{m} t_k \left[\frac{C}{2} \right] e^{-yt_k} + t_m 100 e^{-yt_m} \right)$$

(15.3)

Dividing both sides of equation 15.3 by the full price, P_{full}, gives:

$$\frac{dP_{full}/P_{full}}{dy} = -\left(\frac{\sum_{k=1}^{m} t_k [C/2] e^{-yt_k} + t_m 100 e^{-yt_m}}{P_{full}} \right)$$

$$= -duration$$

(15.4)

Note that the term in parenthesis in equation 15.4 represents the sum of the cash payment times, t_k, multiplied by the proportion of present value attributed to each bond payment. As such, the term in parenthesis is the bond's duration. Therefore, duration can be interpreted as the negative of the instantaneous proportional change in the bond's full value per unit change in yield, or

$$duration = -\frac{dP_{full}/P_{full}}{dy}.$$

(15.5)

The term $(dP_{full}/P_{full})/dy$ is negative, reflecting that bond prices fall when their yields rise. By multiplying the numerator and denominator of the right-hand-side of equation 15.5 by 100, duration can also be interpreted as the negative of the instantaneous *percentage* change in price per unit change in yield *measured in percentage terms*.

To illustrate this concept, go back to the 3.5-year bond in table 15.1 with duration calculated as 3.1337. The table shows that the bond's price is $105.937 per $100 par, calculated as the present value of the bond's stream of payments discounted at 6 percent per year compounded continuously. Although not shown in the table, if the same stream of payments were discounted at 7 percent with continuous compounding, the bond's full price would be $102.672, which represents a reduction in value of 100($102.672 − $105.937)/$105.937 = −3.08 percent. This −3.08 percent difference corresponds very closely with the 3.1337 percent reduction predicted by duration. (Remember, duration is the negative of the percentage change in price per 100 basis point change in yield.) But like option deltas, changes in mathematical function values predicted

Table 15.2 Effects of coupon and maturity on duration

Annual coupon		Maturity in years				
		5	10	15	20	30
0	Price	74.08	54.88	40.66	30.12	16.53
	Duration	*5.00*	*10.00*	*15.00*	*20.00*	*30.00*
2	Price	82.59	69.70	60.14	53.07	43.94
	Duration	*4.76*	*8.88*	*12.29*	*14.94*	*18.13*
4	Price	91.10	84.51	79.63	76.01	71.35
	Duration	*4.56*	*8.16*	*10.91*	*12.92*	*15.38*
6	Price	99.61	99.33	99.11	98.96	98.75
	Duration	*4.39*	*7.65*	*10.07*	*11.86*	*14.16*
8	Price	108.12	114.14	118.60	121.90	126.16
	Duration	*4.25*	*7.28*	*9.51*	*11.19*	*13.47*
10	Price	116.63	128.96	138.09	144.85	153.57
	Duration	*4.13*	*6.99*	*9.10*	*10.73*	*13.02*

All table entries are calculated assuming a yield of 6 percent per year compounded continuously. The shaded area represents bonds within the general coupon and maturity range eligible for delivery in connection with the Treasury Bond futures contract.

by derivatives are only exact for infinitesimally small changes in function components. Therefore, one should not expect the bond's price to be exactly 3.1337 percent lower with a 7 percent yield but, instead, *approximately* 3.1337 percent lower.[74]

Table 15.2 shows prices per $100 par and durations for bonds with various maturity and coupon combinations based on a 6 percent continuous yield. Consistent with equation 15.1, all zero-coupon bonds have durations equal to their actual maturity. Also, for a given maturity, as the coupon is increased, the duration declines, since a greater proportion of the bond's total cash flow is received prior to its maturity date. For example, a 30-year zero-coupon bond has a duration of 30 years, but a 10 percent 30-year bond has a duration of only 13.02 years. Even though the latter bond matures in 30 years, it should have roughly the same sensitivity to interest rate changes as a zero-coupon bond that matures in 13 years.

The shaded area of table 15.2 represents bonds within the general coupon and maturity range eligible for delivery in connection with the

---

74. The approximation error increases for larger Δy because duration is not constant for all values of y. This phenomenon is known to bond traders as *convexity*.

Treasury Bond futures contract.[75] Durations within this area are as high as 15.38 for the 4 percent 30-year bond and as low as 9.10 for the 10 percent 15-year bond. The ratio of these durations, $9.10/15.38 = 0.592$, indicates that the interest sensitivity of the 15-year bond should be only 59.2 percent of that of the 30-year bond.

Suppose the market is pricing the Treasury Bond futures contract as if the 30-year 4 percent bond will be delivered, but, unknowingly, you hedge a fixed-income portfolio with Treasury Bond futures thinking that the 15-year 10 percent bond will be delivered. Under these circumstances, you will have grossly underestimated the interest sensitivity of the futures contract and constructed a hedge that could expose the portfolio to significant risk in the event of an adverse interest rate change.

> It is extremely important that users of Treasury Bond and related futures contracts be able to determine which of the eligible bonds will serve as the delivery vehicle for the contract (that is, which bond will be cheapest to deliver), since the futures contract will mimic the risk of this bond and not that of the other eligible bonds. The analysis in section 15.3 shows how the bond that is cheapest to deliver can be identified.

Duration-based hedging

It can be shown that the duration of a fixed-income portfolio is a weighted average of the durations of its component securities. For example, from table 15.2, the durations of the 6 percent 15-year and 4 percent 5-year bonds are 10.07 and 4.56 years, respectively. Therefore, the duration of a portfolio invested 60 percent in the first bond and 40 percent in the second is $0.6(10.07) + 0.4(4.56) = 7.87$.

Let dur_P denote the duration of a portfolio and dur_H the duration of a financial instrument, such as an interest rate futures contract, used to hedge the portfolio's interest rate risk. Similarly, let V_P denote the value of the portfolio and V_H the value of the asset that underlies the hedging instrument.[76] Also, let y_P and y_H be the respective yields of the portfolio

---

75. Presently, bonds eligible for delivery have coupons ranging from 5.25 percent to 9.125 percent.
76. Suppose a 1-year Treasury Bond futures contract is the hedging instrument and it has been determined that a bond with 15 years until maturity at the time the futures contract matures will be cheapest-to-deliver. Presently, this same bond would have a 16-year maturity. For the purposes of calculating the duration of the futures contract, 15 years is the relevant maturity for the underlying bond.

and hedging instrument. Applying equation 15.5 to discrete value and yield changes, ΔV_P and Δy_P,

$$dur_P \approx -\frac{\Delta V_P / V_P}{\Delta y_P}$$

$$(15.6)$$

and

$$dur_H \approx -\frac{\Delta V_H / V_H}{\Delta y_H}.$$

$$(15.7)$$

Rearranging equation 15.6 gives:

$$-dur_P V_P \Delta y_P \approx \Delta V_P$$

$$(15.8)$$

and for equation 15.7:

$$-dur_H V_H \Delta y_H \approx \Delta V_H$$

$$(15.9)$$

The objective in hedging is to take a position in the hedging instrument of sufficient quantity so that any change in the value of the portfolio is offset by an equal but opposite change in the value of the hedging instrument. Mathematically, this means that if the hedge is properly executed for a portfolio in which one is long, a short position in the hedging instrument should be taken of sufficient quantity such that, $\Delta V_H = \Delta V_P$. This quantity can be found by equating the left-hand-sides of equations 15.8 and 15.9.

$$-dur_H V_H \Delta y_H \approx -dur_P V_P \Delta y_P.$$

$$(15.10)$$

Rearranging equation 15.10 gives:

$$V_H \approx \left(\frac{dur_P}{dur_H} \right) \left(\frac{\Delta y_P}{\Delta y_H} \right) V_P.$$

$$(15.11)$$

For the moment, assume $\Delta y_P / \Delta y_H = 1$, which means that any change in interest rates will produce the same change in yield for the portfolio and hedging instrument. Then the portfolio will be hedged, or *immunized* against an adverse change in interest rates, if the dollar value of the hedging instrument times its duration is equal to the value of the portfolio times its duration (equation 15.10). This implies that the portfolio will be immunized if $V_H = (dur_P/dur_H)V_P$ (equation 15.11).

The expression dur_P/dur_H can be thought of as an interest rate "beta." It is a measure of the interest-sensitivity of the portfolio in relation to that of the hedging instrument, just as a stock portfolio's S&P-based beta is a measure of its risk sensitivity in relation to the S&P. Thus, if the two duration values indicate that the portfolio is twice as sensitive to interest rate changes as the hedging instrument, the dollar commitment to a short position in the hedging instrument should be twice that of the portfolio being hedged.[77]

The expression $V_H = (dur_P/dur_H)V_P$ serves as the basis for many duration-based treatments of interest immunization. However, for this expression to be valid, $\Delta y_P/\Delta y_H$ must equal 1.0. This means that any change in interest rates is expected to produce the same change in yield for the portfolio and the hedging instrument.

One way to ensure that $\Delta y_P/\Delta y_H$ is approximately equal to 1.0 is to choose a hedging instrument with approximately the same effective maturity as the portfolio being hedged. Regardless of the initial shape of the yield curve, or any new shape resulting from a subsequent change in interest rates, if the effective maturities of the portfolio and its hedging instrument are approximately the same, the changes in their yields resulting from an overall change in interest rates also should be approximately the same. Under these circumstances, little damage would be done by using $V_H = (dur_P/dur_H)V_P$ as the basis for a hedge.

> If the effective maturities of the portfolio and hedging instrument are significantly different, choosing an appropriate value of $\Delta y_P/\Delta y_H$ can be extremely difficult, and assuming $\Delta y_P/\Delta y_H = 1$ doesn't solve the problem.

Figure 15.1 illustrates the potential danger of assuming $\Delta y_P/\Delta y_H = 1$ in duration-based hedging. In the figure, a portfolio with duration of approximately six years is being hedged with a financial instrument of approximately 10 years duration. Assume that the yield curve at the time the hedge is initiated is the downward sloping dotted curve that starts at a 1-year yield of 7 percent and that the second dotted curve represents a

---

77. Technically, when one takes a long or short position in a futures contract, the out-of-pocket investment is zero. However, recall from chapter 13 that a futures contract is economically equivalent to a leveraged position in the underlying asset or commodity. Therefore, when used in connection with a futures contract, the term V_H refers not to the value of the contract itself, but instead, to the value of the asset or commodity that underlies the contract.

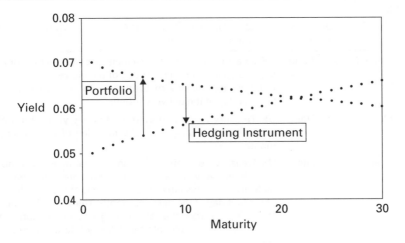

Figure 15.1 Zero-coupon yield curves

new yield curve that occurs while the hedge is being maintained. Note that the new curve has a different shape; it is upward sloping rather than downward sloping. As a result, the change in yield for the hedging instrument is about $\frac{2}{3}$ that of the portfolio. Therefore, a duration-based hedge carried out under the assumption that $\Delta y_P / \Delta y_H = 1$ would be under-hedged by a factor of $\frac{2}{3}$. However, if a hedging instrument with approximately the same effective maturity as the portfolio were used, the change in yield of the two would be approximately the same, regardless of how the shape of the yield curve might change.

15.3   Treasury Bond and Note Futures

The 30-year Treasury Bond and 10-, 5- and 2-year Treasury Note contracts, offered by the Chicago Board of Trade, provide a wide range of effective maturities for hedging and/or speculating in interest rate risk. Moreover, each contract provides the seller with a significant amount of flexibility with respect to the bonds or notes that can be delivered to satisfy the terms of the contract. Table 15.3 summarizes the bonds and notes eligible for delivery in connection with these four contracts.

For each contract, the futures invoice price, or the actual amount of money paid by the buyer to the seller, is the futures settlement price times a *conversion factor* plus accrued interest. The conversion factor is the present value of the remaining stream of payments, per $1 of par, of the bond or

Table 15.3   Bonds and notes eligible for delivery in connection with Treasury Bond and Note futures contracts

30-Year Treasury Bond	US Treasury bonds that, if callable, are not callable for at least 15 years from the first day of the delivery month or, if not callable, have a maturity of at least 15 years from the first day of the delivery month.
10-Year Treasury Note	US Treasury notes maturing at least $6\frac{1}{2}$ years, but not more than 10 years, from the first day of the delivery month.
5-Year Treasury Note	US Treasury notes that have an original maturity of not more than five years and three months and a remaining maturity of not less than four years and three months as of the first day of the delivery month. The 5-year Treasury Notes issued after the last trading day of the contract month will not be eligible for delivery into that month's contract.
2-Year Treasury Note	US Treasury notes that have an original maturity of not more than five years and three months and a remaining maturity of not less than one year and nine months from the first day of the delivery month but not more than two years from the last day of the delivery month.

Source: the contract specifications section of the Chicago Board of Trade's web site, www.cbot.com.

note that is delivered, discounted at a rate of 6 percent per year with semi-annual compounding (or 3 percent every six months), and the accrued interest is the interest amount accrued for that same bond or note. Using the 6 percent discounting method, a bond or note that pays 6 percent annual interest will have a conversion factor of 1.0. Therefore, if a 6 percent bond or note is delivered, the seller will receive the futures settlement price without adjustment plus accrued interest. If the annual coupon rate is less than 6 percent, the conversion factor will be less than 1.0. Therefore, the adjusted futures price will be less than the settlement price. Similarly, if a bond or note with an annual coupon rate greater than 6 percent is delivered, the seller will receive the futures settlement price times a quantity greater than 1.0, plus accrued interest.

This method of adjusting the futures price is designed to make all eligible bonds and notes equally attractive to deliver in a market in which all bonds and notes, regardless of maturity, yield 6 percent per year with semi-annual compounding. In markets other than this, which will be 99.99 percent of the time, a specific bond or note will be the most economical to deliver, and as such, the futures price should reflect the price action in this particular bond or note. The analysis that follows shows how one can determine the bond that is most economical to deliver in connection with the Treasury

Bond contract. A parallel analysis for Treasury notes would be identical except that Treasury securities of shorter maturity would be eligible for delivery.

Although prices for Treasury Bond and Notes are quoted on a $100 par basis, each futures contract actually calls for the delivery of a bond or note of $100,000 par value. Therefore, a quoted futures price of $80 would correspond to an actual futures price of $80,000.

How to determine the Treasury Bond that is cheapest to deliver

At present, there are over 30 Treasury bonds eligible for delivery in connection with the Treasury Bond futures contract, but only one of these bonds will be the cheapest to deliver. Table 15.4 summarizes an analysis for determining the bond that is cheapest to deliver among three eligible candidates under three different interest rate scenarios. In the next section, the same type of analysis is extended and applied to the 33 bonds eligible for delivery in connection with the June, 2001 futures contract.

The three bonds eligible for delivery in table 15.4 are distinctly different. The first bond is a 30-year bond with a 4 percent annual coupon. The second is a 21-year bond with a 6 percent coupon, and the third is a 15.5-year bond with a 8-percent coupon. Although the durations of the three bonds are not shown in the table, the first has the longest duration, since it has the longest actual maturity and the lowest coupon rate. By contrast, the third bond, with the shortest maturity and highest coupon rate, has the shortest duration.

The futures contract is assumed to mature in exactly six months. To keep the analysis simple, each of the three bonds is assumed to make a semi-annual interest payment in exactly six months. Therefore, for the purposes of the analysis, it is not necessary to deal with accrued interest either today, when a bond might be purchased, or six months from now, when the futures contract matures.

In the upper panel of table 15.4, the market rate of interest is assumed to reflect a flat yield curve at 7 percent per year compounded semi-annually. Each bond price listed in the column, "Bond's current market price," is computed as the present value of the bond's remaining stream of payments discounted at 7 percent per year compounded semi-annually (or 3.5 percent every six months). For example, the price for the 30-year 4 percent bond is computed as follows.

$$62.58 = \frac{2}{1.035^1} + \frac{2}{1.035^2} + \cdots + \frac{2}{1.035^{60}} + \frac{100}{1.035^{60}}$$

Table 15.4 Determining bond that is cheapest to deliver in connection with 6-month Treasury bond futures contract

Current maturity	Bond maturity at futures maturity date	Annual coupon (%)	Bond's current market price	Futures price	×	Conv. factor	=	Adjusted futures price	Hedged return	Futures price to yield hedged return equal to market rate of interest
Market interest rate = 7% per year										
30.0	29.5	4	$62.58	$86.591		0.7249		$62.77	0.0350	$86.591
21.0	20.5	6	89.08	86.591		1.0000		86.59	0.0057	89.200
15.5	15.0	8	109.37	86.591		1.1960		103.56	−0.0165	91.301
Market interest rate = 6% per year										
30.0	29.5	4	$72.32	$100.000		0.7249		72.49	0.0300	$100.000
21.0	20.5	6	100.00	100.000		1.0000		100.00	0.0300	100.000
15.5	15.0	8	120.00	100.000		1.1960		119.60	0.0300	100.000
Market interest rate = 5% per year										
30.0	29.5	4	$84.55	$109.862		0.7249		$79.64	−0.0343	$116.781
21.0	20.5	6	112.91	109.862		1.0000		109.86	−0.0004	112.733
15.5	15.0	8	132.09	109.862		1.1960		131.40	0.0250	109.862

All prices per $100 par. All market interest rates assume semi-annual compounding. For example, 7% per year with semi-annual compounding is equivalent to 3.5 percent every six months. All hedged returns are 6-month returns. Conversion factors are computed as of the maturity date of the futures contract. Bonds in italicized rows are the cheapest to deliver.

The last column, labeled "Futures price to yield hedged return equal to market interest rate," is the most critical column in the table. The futures price shown in this column is the equilibrium futures price that would result if the bond in question were the *only* bond eligible for delivery. For example, assume that the first bond is purchased for $62.58 while simultaneously taking a short position in the 6-month futures contract at a futures price of F. Since the price received for the bond through the sale of futures will equal the futures price, times the bond's conversion factor, 0.7249, and half of the $4 annual coupon, or $2 will also be received in six months, the total value locked in by selling futures is $F(0.7249) +$ $2. Therefore, the return per dollar invested over the 6-month period is $(F(0.7249) + \$2)/\$62.58$. Since a riskless hedge of this type should earn the risk-free rate of interest, or 3.5 percent per six months, the equilibrium futures price is the solution to $(F(0.7249) + \$2)/\$62.58 = 1.035$, or $F = \$86.591$. Similar calculations are also made for the other two bonds. If the second bond were the only bond eligible for delivery, the futures price would be $89.200, and if the third bond were the only eligible bond, the futures price would be $91.301.

Given that all three bonds can be delivered to satisfy the terms of the futures contract, the equilibrium futures price must be the lowest of these three values, or

$$F = \min (\$86.591, \$89.200, \$91.301) = \$86.591.$$

Why? Because if the futures price were any higher, the return from hedging the first bond would be greater than the market rate of interest. The column in table 15.4 labeled "Hedged return" shows the return from hedging each of the three bonds, provided the futures price is $86.591. Note that only the first bond earns the market rate of interest when hedged; the returns from hedging the other two bonds are significantly lower.

Some readers may think there is an arbitrage opportunity available to an investor who uses one of the other two bonds to put on the hedged position in reverse. For example, the return from taking a long position in the third bond and locking in its selling price by selling futures is −1.65 percent per six months. If the position were reversed, one could short the third bond and, hopefully, lock in its purchase price in six months by taking a long position in the futures contract. This would be the equivalent to borrowing money at −1.65 percent! Since the money borrowed could be employed to earn a positive return, this would seem like a sure way to make some fast money.

The problem with this logic is that it fails to recognize that the party who is long the futures contract has no control over which bond is actually delivered. Under the circumstances summarized by the first panel of table 15.4, it would be irrational for the party who is short the futures contract to deliver the third bond. As a result, the anticipated return from using the third bond in connection with a reverse hedge should never materialize.

In the second panel of table 15.4, the market rate of interest is assumed to be 6 percent per year with semi-annual compounding. Note that with a 6 percent interest rate, the futures price that will cause each bond to earn the market rate of interest when hedged is $100 for each bond. Therefore, any of the three bonds would be equally attractive to deliver.

In the third panel, the market rate of interest is 5 percent per year with semi-annual compounding. In this case, the futures price will be $109.862, and it will be optimal to deliver the third bond. This analysis leads to an approximate rule of thumb for determining the bond that is cheapest-to-deliver.

A simple way to determine the Treasury Bond that will be cheapest to deliver

1. When interest rates are above 6 percent, the eligible bond with the longest effective maturity will be optimal to deliver.
2. When interest rates are exactly 6 percent, any eligible bond will be equally-attractive to deliver.
3. When interest rates are below 6 percent, the eligible bond with the shortest effective maturity will be optimal to deliver.

Determining the cheapest-to-deliver bond for an actual futures contract

Table 15.5 summarizes an analysis of the cheapest-to-deliver bond, as of the close of trading on February 13, 2001, for the Treasury Bond futures contract maturing on June 21, 2001. The futures settlement price on February 13, was $103.9375. The analysis of table 15.5 shows the annualized return from hedging, with continuous compounding, for each of 33 bonds eligible for delivery in connection with the June 2001 contract. At the time of the analysis, the yield-to-maturity for each of the 33 bonds fell within the range of 5.54 to 5.64 percent, with semi-annual compounding.

Each bond is assumed to be purchased at the quoted ask price plus accrued interest, calculated on the basis of February 14, 2001 settlement. For US Government bonds, accrued interest is calculated as:

accrued interest

$$= \left(\frac{C}{2} \right) \left(\frac{Exact\ days\ from\ last\ payment\ to\ settlement\ date}{Exact\ days\ from\ last\ payment\ to\ next\ payment} \right)$$

For example, for the first bond listed in the table, the 8.125 percent bond maturing on 8/15/19, interest payments are made on February 15 and August 15 of each year. Therefore, the accrued interest for this bond, as of February 14, 2001, is

$$accrued\ interest = \left(\frac{8.125}{2}\right)\left(\frac{183}{184}\right) = 4.040,$$

reflecting 184 days from August 15, 2000 to February 15, 2001 and 183 days from August 15, 2000 to February 14, 2001.

Using Chicago Board of Trade Rule 1836.01, conversion factors are calculated for each bond based on time to maturity in complete three month increments (in other words, 15 years and 5 months = 15 years and one-quarter) from the first day of the delivery month. The conversion factor is the present value of the bond's stream of payments, discounted at 6 percent per year with semi-annual compounding (or at 3 percent every six months), less accrued interest. When a bond's time to maturity is an integer number of 6-month periods, the conversion factor is $(C/200)((1 - 1.03^{-m})/0.03) + (1/1.03^m)$, where C is the annual coupon per $100 par and m is the number of payment times remaining on the bond. If the first of m payments is to be received in three months, the conversion factor is $(C/200 + (C/200)((1 - 1.03^{-m+1})/0.03) + (1/1.03^{m-1})/\sqrt{1.03}) - (C/400)$. All conversion factors shown in table 15.5 were verified against those provided by the Bloomberg system in a similar analysis computed in real time.

The annual return shown in the next-to-last column of table 15.5 is the annualized return, with continuous compounding, from purchasing the bond at its full price and locking in the value shown in the column "Total locked in," which reflects the sum of the adjusted futures price (futures price × conversion factor), accrued interest and any coupon received between February 14 and June 21, plus interest on the coupon, accumulated at a rate of 5 percent per year compounded continuously. All bonds listed in the table are shown in the descending order of this return.

Since interest rates were less than 6 percent on February 13, the rule of thumb for determining the cheapest-to-deliver bond indicates that the bond with the shortest effective maturity should provide the highest return from hedging, and therefore, be identified as cheapest-to-deliver. Consistent with this rule of thumb, note that the bonds listed at the top of the table are generally those with the shortest durations. However, there is a group of short-duration bonds near the middle of the table, whose hedging returns are not consistent with the rule. There are three possible explanations for why these bonds do not provide higher returns from hedging.

Table 15.5 Analysis of cheapest-to-deliver bond for June 2001 Treasury Bond futures using closing prices on February 13, 2001

Annual coupon (%)	Maturity date	Bond's quoted price	Initial accrued interest	Bond's full price	Conv. factor	Conv. factor× futures price	Futures accrued interest	Interim coupon with interest	Total locked in	Annual return (%)	Duration
8.125	08/15/19	128.838	4.040	132.878	1.232	128.048	2.828	4.133	135.009	4.573	11.01
8.750	08/15/20	137.031	4.351	141.382	1.309	136.082	3.046	4.451	143.579	4.431	11.20
7.875	02/15/21	126.969	3.916	130.885	1.214	126.162	2.741	4.006	132.909	4.411	11.11
8.125	08/15/21	130.313	4.040	134.353	1.246	129.464	2.828	4.133	136.425	4.399	11.67
8.875	02/15/19	137.063	4.413	141.476	1.309	136.042	3.089	4.515	143.645	4.374	10.22
8.500	02/15/20	133.688	4.227	137.914	1.277	132.738	2.959	4.324	140.020	4.355	10.63
8.750	05/15/20	136.813	2.200	139.012	1.307	135.835	0.880	4.397	141.112	4.309	10.82
7.125	02/15/23	118.688	3.543	122.231	1.135	117.958	2.480	3.625	124.063	4.276	11.92
8.125	05/15/21	130.156	2.042	132.199	1.244	129.280	0.817	4.083	134.180	4.276	11.28
8.000	11/15/21	128.969	2.011	130.980	1.232	128.103	0.804	4.020	132.928	4.242	11.47
7.250	08/15/22	120.125	3.605	123.730	1.148	119.334	2.523	3.688	125.546	4.186	12.23
8.875	08/15/17	135.563	4.413	139.976	1.293	134.400	3.089	4.515	142.004	4.135	10.13
9.000	11/15/18	138.281	2.262	140.544	1.319	137.145	0.905	4.523	142.573	4.120	10.28
9.125	05/15/18	139.125	2.294	141.419	1.327	137.944	0.917	4.586	143.447	4.092	10.08
7.625	11/15/22	124.938	1.917	126.854	1.194	124.058	0.767	3.832	128.656	4.054	11.87
6.250	08/15/23	107.781	3.108	110.889	1.030	107.089	2.175	3.179	112.443	4.000	12.88
8.750	05/15/17	134.000	2.200	136.200	1.278	132.784	0.880	4.397	138.061	3.901	9.81
7.500	11/15/16	120.344	1.885	122.229	1.148	119.359	0.754	3.769	123.882	3.861	9.93
7.625	02/15/25	126.063	3.792	129.854	1.203	125.071	2.654	3.879	131.604	3.846	12.29

7.500	11/15/24	124.313	1.885	126.198	1.187	123.334	0.754	3.769	127.857	3.755	12.45
6.875	08/15/25	116.375	3.419	119.794	1.111	115.427	2.393	3.497	121.317	3.632	13.20
6.750	08/15/26	115.031	3.357	118.388	1.096	113.966	2.349	3.434	119.749	3.286	13.50
6.000	02/15/26	104.906	2.984	107.890	1.000	103.938	2.088	3.052	109.078	3.148	13.15
6.625	02/15/27	113.500	3.294	116.794	1.081	112.367	2.306	3.370	118.043	3.055	13.13
6.500	11/15/26	111.750	1.634	113.384	1.064	110.640	0.654	3.267	114.560	2.965	13.31
6.375	08/15/27	110.219	3.170	113.389	1.049	109.037	2.219	3.243	114.499	2.799	13.90
6.125	11/15/27	106.844	1.540	108.383	1.016	105.632	0.616	3.078	109.326	2.489	13.70
5.500	08/15/28	98.406	2.735	101.141	0.934	97.031	1.914	2.798	101.744	1.707	14.55
5.250	11/15/28	94.969	1.320	96.289	0.900	93.530	0.528	2.638	96.696	1.214	14.38
5.250	02/15/29	95.000	2.611	97.611	0.900	93.502	1.827	2.671	98.000	1.143	14.24
6.125	08/15/29	107.688	3.046	110.733	1.017	105.689	2.132	3.116	110.937	0.528	14.50
6.250	05/15/30	110.125	1.571	111.696	1.034	107.465	0.628	3.141	111.234	−1.191	14.25
5.375	02/15/31	99.250	2.673	101.923	0.914	95.003	1.871	2.734	99.609	−6.601	14.76

Futures price = $103.9375 per $100 par. All futures and bond prices were taken from the February 14, 2001 issue of *The Wall Street Journal*. Initial accrued interest is based on February 14 settlement. Futures accrued interest is based on June 21 maturity and June 21 settlement. Using Chicago Board of Trade Rule 1836.01, conversion factors are calculated based on time to maturity in complete three month increments (i.e., 15 years and 5 months = 15 years and one-quarter) from the first day of the delivery month. The annual return shown in the next-to-last column is the annualized return, with continuous compounding, from purchasing the bond at its full price and locking in the value shown in the column "Total locked in," which reflects the sum of the adjusted futures price, accrued interest and any coupon received between February 14 and June 22, plus interest on the coupon, accumulated at a rate of 5 percent per year compounded continuously. Duration values are calculated based on each bond's yield-to-maturity, taking into account the exact times of each cash flow.

First, these bonds may be slightly mispriced in relation to the other bonds listed in the table. Second, the rule of thumb for determining the cheapest-to-deliver bond is based on an assumption of a flat yield curve, which is almost never observed in practice. Third, the rule of thumb requires that conversion factors be updated daily, but in practice, conversion factors are updated only every three months.

Additional considerations

The preceding analysis is based on an implicit assumption that the market rate of interest is above or below 6 percent and that it can be expected to stay in that range over the lives of the futures contracts. Otherwise, there is a possibility that the bond that appears optimal or cheapest-to-deliver will change. This gets to be a particularly important factor when the market rate of interest is close to 6 percent as it was in February 2001, in which case a subsequent change in interest rates to a level above or below 6 percent would be a distinct possibility. In such a market, the futures price will reflect the probabilities associated with interest rates rising above or falling below 6 percent. Market professionals who use the Treasury Bond futures contract understand this and are likely to use the Heath–Jarrow–Morton (1992), Black–Derman–Toy (1990) or related models to determine the equilibrium futures price and model its trading characteristics. But for the purposes of this chapter, I will not develop that level of detail and will proceed as if an analysis such as that summarized in table 15.4 can be used to determine the Treasury bond that is cheapest to deliver.

Why determining the cheapest-to-deliver bond is so important

Determining the bond that is cheapest-to-deliver is very important because the Treasury Bond futures contract will trade as if it is issued on that particular bond and will take on its risk characteristics. If the market rate of interest is above 6 percent, this bond should be a bond of relatively long duration and a high degree of interest rate sensitivity in relation to other bonds. In contrast, if the market rate of interest is below 6 percent, this bond should be one of relatively short duration with less sensitivity to interest rate changes in relation to that of other eligible bonds. This, in turn, implies that the interest sensitivity of the futures contract itself will be a function of the level of the market rate of interest in relation to 6 percent.

15.4   Eurodollar Futures

Three-month Eurodollar futures, traded at the Chicago Mercantile Exchange, are the most actively traded futures used in managing short-term dollar-denominated interest rate risk. Each contract is for a hypothetical 3-month Eurodollar deposit with a maturity value of $1,000,000 (par). The exchange uses a cash settlement procedure to determine the contract's final settlement value based on the British Bankers Association Interest Settlement Rate for 3-month dollar deposits at 11:00 am London time on the contract's last trading day. The cash market offered rate for 3-month Eurodollar time deposits (or LIBOR) is subtracted from 100.00 to determine the contract's final settlement price per $100 par.

The method by which Eurodollar futures prices are quoted implies a duration of approximately 93 days for the contract. Here is how the price quotation method works.

Suppose that today, several months prior to the maturity of the 3-month Eurodollar contract, futures are trading as if the Eurodollar contract rate is 8 percent. Then the Eurodollar futures contract would be *quoted* at a price of $100 − $8 = $92 per $100 par. But as far as ones brokerage account is concerned, the futures price is actually $100 − $8(90/360) = $98, reflecting that 8 percent is an annual rate with quarterly compounding. Note, this is not an error. *A quoted price of $92 really means $98.*

Assume that tomorrow, Eurodollar futures trade as if the Eurodollar contract rate is 9 percent. Then tomorrow's quoted price would be $100 − $9 = $91, implying a mark-to-market value of $100 − $9(90/360) = $97.75. Thus, if the contract rate goes up by 1 percentage point, the mark-to-market value of the futures position will decline by $0.25 per $100 par, or 100($0.25/$98) = 0.255 percent relative to the initial mark-to-market value. Since duration is the negative of the percentage change in a security's value per 100 basis-point change in yield, this percentage change corresponds to a duration of approximately 0.255 × 365 = 93 days.[78]

In practical applications, it may be easier to think of the Eurodollar contract as being issued on a Eurodollar deposit with an immediate value of $100 (or $1,000,000) rather than at a value discounted from $100. In this case, the $0.25 price change represents a 0.25 percent change in relation to $100. This, in turn, gives an implied duration of 0.25 × 365 ≈ 91 days. Thus, if you think of each contract as being issued on Eurodollars with $1,000,000 of present value, use 91 days, or $\frac{1}{4}$ year, as the contract duration. On the other hand, if you think of the value of the Eurodollars in

---

78. Technically, *duration* $= -(dP_{full}/P_{full})/dy$ is based on a continuously compounded yield rather than the quarterly compounded yield imbedded in the pricing of Eurodollar futures. Nevertheless, 8 percent per year compounded quarterly is so close to 8 percent per year compounded continuously, that little, if any, practical error is introduced in the computation of the 93-day duration. Moreover, the final duration number would be close to 93 days for most interest rates that one might reasonably expect to occur.

terms of a discount from $1,000,000, use a duration of 93 days. In either case, the quantity *duration × value* will be the same. Therefore, both methods will lead to the same predicted change in value resulting from a change in interest rates, since, from equation 15.9, $\Delta V_H \approx -dur_H V_H \Delta y_H$.

15.5 Duration-based Hedging with Treasury Bond, Treasury Note and Eurodollar Futures

Mathematics

Equation 15.11, rearranged below in terms of the value of the hedging instrument, V_H, summarizes the mathematics of duration-based immunization.

$$V_H \approx V_P \left(\frac{dur_P}{dur_H} \right) \left(\frac{\Delta y_P}{\Delta y_H} \right).$$

(15.12)

If the hedging instrument is a futures contract, the value of the hedging instrument, V_H, can be broken down as $V_H = contracts \times F$, where *contracts* is the number of futures contracts sold, and F is the actual un-scaled futures price.[79] Substituting $V_H = contracts \times F$ into equation 15.12, substituting the subscript F for H to denote that the hedging instrument is a futures contract, and solving for the number of contracts yields:

$$contracts \approx \left(\frac{V_P}{F} \right) \left(\frac{dur_P}{dur_F} \right) \left(\frac{\Delta y_P}{\Delta y_F} \right).$$

(15.13)

It should be noted that the hedging quantity of equation 15.13 is implicitly tailed, since it is derived from calculus-based futures hedging principles. Adjusting this quantity for an interest factor to reflect tailing would be double counting.

As is evident from equation 15.13, the hedging quantity requires an estimate of the duration of the futures contract. Earlier, it was shown that $dur_F = 93$ for the Eurodollar contract. For Treasury Bond and Note futures, duration should reflect the duration of the cheapest-to-deliver bond. Although little damage is done by assuming dur_F is the same as the duration of the cheapest-to-deliver bond, technically, this is not correct.

---

79. If Treasury bond futures are quoted at $80, the un-scaled futures price would be $80,000, since each contract is for a Treasury bond with $100,000 par value.

To obtain the correct duration for Treasury Bond and Note futures, let dur^*_{CTD} denote the duration of the cheapest-to-deliver bond *computed as of the futures maturity date*. This calculation reflects the present value of the bond's stream of payments to be received from the futures maturity date forward, discounted back to the futures maturity date rather than to the present date. Also, let A^*_{CTD} denote accrued interest for the cheapest-to-deliver bond as of the futures maturity date. For consistency, A^*_{CTD} is computed with the same par value as the futures contract. Finally, let $conv^*_{CTD}$ denote the conversion factor for the cheapest-to-deliver bond computed as of the futures maturity date. Then, according to Clarke (1992) and Rendleman (1999),[80]

$$dur_F = \frac{(conv^*_{CTD}F + A^*_{CTD})dur^*_{CDT}}{conv^*_{CTD}F}$$

(15.14)

Although equation 15.13 represents the standard way of expressing the number of contracts required in a duration-based hedge, by substituting the value of dur_F from equation 15.14, the number of contracts can be re-expressed as follows.

$$contracts \approx \left(\frac{V_P}{conv^*_{CTD}F + A^*_{CTD}}\right)\left(\frac{dur_P}{dur^*_{CDT}}\right)\left(\frac{\Delta y_P}{\Delta y_F}\right)conv^*_{CTD}.$$

(15.15)

An interesting and important special case arises from equation 15.15. Suppose the portfolio being hedged is $100,000 par value of the cheapest-to-deliver bond. Moreover, assume that the hedge is being constructed to lock in the value of the cheapest-to-deliver bond as of its maturity

---

80. To understand equation 15.14, let $P^*_{full,CTD} - A^*_{CTD} = P^*_{quoted,CTD} = conv^*_{CDT}F$, where $P^*_{full,CTD}$ represents the present value of the cheapest-to-deliver bond's stream of payments to be received from the futures maturity date forward, discounted back to the futures maturity date. Also, note that dur^*_{CTD} is the duration of the cheapest-to-deliver bond computed on the basis of the bond's projected *full* price. Applying equation 15.5, $dur^*_{CTD} = -((dP^*_{full,CDT}/P^*_{full,CDT})/dy)$, or $dur^*_{CTD}P^*_{full,CDT} = -(dP^*_{full,CDT}/dy)$. Define dur_F as the projected duration of the cheapest-to-deliver-bond based on its *quoted* price, $P^*_{quoted,CTD} = P^*_{full,CTD} - A^*_{CTD} = conv^*_{CDT}F$, rather than its full price. Then, $dur_F = -((dP^*_{quoted,CDT}/P^*_{quoted,CDT})/dy)$ and $dur_F P^*_{quoted,CDT} = -(dP^*_{quoted,CDT}/dy)$. Since a change in interest rates should produce the same dollar changes in the quoted and full prices, $dP^*_{quoted,CDT}/dy = dP^*_{full,CDT}/dy$, which implies $dur_F P^*_{quoted,CDT} = dur^*_{CTD}P^*_{full,CDT}$. Rearranging this final expression yields $dur_F = (dur^*_{CTD}P^*_{full,CDT}/P^*_{quoted,CDT}) = ((conv^*_{CTD}F + A^*_{CTD})dur^*_{CDT}/conv^*_{CTD}F)$.

date rather than to prevent the bond's immediate value from changing. Then the relevant portfolio duration is $dur_P = dur^*_{CDT}$. Also, $\Delta y_P = \Delta y_F$, since the portfolio and futures yields will be one in the same. Substituting $dur_P = dur^*_{CDT}$ and $\Delta y_P = \Delta y_F$ into equation 15.15 yields $contracts \approx (V_P/(conv^*_{CTD}F + A^*_{CTD}))conv^*_{CTD}$. Assume the bond makes no interest payments prior to the futures maturity date. Then $V_P/(conv^*_{CTD}F + A^*_{CTD})$, the ratio of the bond's present value to the value locked in at maturity, must represent the present value of $1 to be received as of the futures maturity date, discounted at the risk-free rate. Therefore, the hedging quantity $contracts \approx (V_P/(conv^*_{CTD}F + A^*_{CTD}))conv^*_{CTD}$ can be interpreted as the conversion factor, $conv^*_{CTD}$, adjusted for tailing. The bottom line? Ignoring tailing, locking in the value of $100,000 par value of the cheapest-to-deliver bond requires $conv^*_{CTD}$ Treasury Bond or Note contracts. Many who see this relationship for the first time are surprised by the result, thinking the number of contracts should be one. The following analysis should shed light on why $conv^*_{CTD}$ is, in fact, the correct quantity.

Assume we are very close to the maturity date of the Treasury Bond futures contract and a bond with a conversion factor of 1.2 has been identified as cheapest-to-deliver. Further, assume that the price of this bond is $120 per $100 par, the futures settlement price is $100 per $100 par and there is no accrued interest.

Tomorrow, the price of the cheapest-to-deliver bond decreases to $118.80. To prevent arbitrage, the adjusted futures price must decrease to this value, implying a new futures price of $99 such that $99 × 1.2 = $118.80.

Suppose you hold $100,000 par value of this bond. When the bond's price changes from $120 to $118.80, you will lose $120,000 − $118,800 = $1,200. Suppose you short one futures contract to hedge your bond position. When the futures price changes from $100 to $99, you will have $100,000 − $99,000 = $1,000 credited to your brokerage account, but this is not enough to make up for the $1,200 loss in your long bond position. To create a gain in the futures account that will fully cover your loss, 1.2 futures must be shorted, not 1.0. Then, if the futures gain is $1,000 per contract short, your total gain will be $1,000 × 1.2 = $1,200.

A portfolio hedging example

Assume you are responsible for managing the interest rate risk exposure of the bond trading desk of a large commercial bank that employs many bond traders. Each is given certain limits regarding the total size of his position, but within these size restrictions, each trader is allowed to act as

Table 15.6 Summary of bond and note positions held by bank

Maturity in years	Annual coupon	Market value ($MM)	Proportion of portfolio value	Duration	Weighted duration*
21	8	600	0.600	12.042	7.225
30	5	300	0.300	15.841	4.752
8	7	400	0.400	6.379	2.551
13	4	−100	−0.100	10.094	−1.009
24	9	−200	−0.200	12.698	−2.540
Overall portfolio		1,000			10.980

Futures price = $109.862. Negative market values indicate short positions.
*For each bond, weighted duration is duration times its proportion of portfolio value. The sum of the weighted durations gives the duration for the overall portfolio.
Market yield = 0.05.

an individual entrepreneur. When a trader believes interest rates will fall, he may take an aggressive long position in bonds, and when he believes interest rates will rise, he may take an aggressive short position.

At any moment, some bond traders may be long, others may be short, and the risks of some traders may cancel out. However, even after pooling the risks, the collective contribution of the bond traders' positions to the bank's overall rate risk exposure can be significant.

It is the bank's policy to maintain neutrality in its interest rate risk exposure without requiring that traders individually hedge against potential changes in interest rates. As a result, it is your job to neutralize the trading desk's interest rate risk exposure by using interest rate futures to bring the duration of the overall portfolio to zero.

Presently, the yield curve is flat with all Treasury bonds and notes being priced to yield 5 percent per year with semi-annual compounding. Table 15.6 summarizes the long and short positions in Treasury bonds and notes currently held by the various traders of the bank.

As indicated in table 15.6, the total value of the bank's portfolio is $1 billion, reflecting long positions, with a total value of $1.3 billion, less short positions with a total value of $0.3 billion. The portfolio's duration, calculated as a weighted average of the durations of its component security positions, is 10.980 years.

To keep the analysis relatively simple, assume that the three bonds shown in table 15.4 are the only bonds eligible for delivery in connection with the 6-month Treasury Bond futures contract, and as indicated in the third panel of the table, the 8 percent bond maturing in 15.5 years is the cheapest bond to deliver. As indicated in the third panel of table 15.4, the futures price is $109.862 per $100 par. Consistent with the analysis of table 15.4, no accrued interest on the cheapest-to-deliver bond will be due on the futures maturity date. Although not shown in the table, the duration of the cheapest-to-deliver bond is 10.007, and the duration of this same bond, projected as of the futures maturity date, is 9.581 years. For the purposes of computing futures duration, $dur^*_{CTD} = 9.581$. We now have most of the information required to compute the number of Treasury Bond futures contracts to sell. Using equation 15.13,

$$contracts \approx \left(\frac{V_P}{F}\right)\left(\frac{dur_P}{dur_F}\right)\left(\frac{\Delta y_P}{\Delta y_F}\right)$$

$$\approx \left(\frac{\$1,000\text{MM}}{\$109,862}\right)\left(\frac{10.980}{9.581}\right)\left(\frac{\Delta y_P}{\Delta y_F}\right)$$

$$\approx 10,431\left(\frac{\Delta y_P}{\Delta y_F}\right)$$

$$dur_F = \frac{(conv^*_{CTD}F + A^*_{CTD})dur^*_{CDT}}{conv^*_{CTD}F}$$

$$= \frac{(conv^*_{CTD}F + 0)(9.581)}{conv^*_{CTD}F} = 9.581$$

As indicated above, the size of the short position in 6-month Treasury Bond futures required to hedge the bank's interest rate risk exposure is $10,431 \times (\Delta y_P/\Delta y_F)$ contracts. Technically, this is an incomplete answer, since it requires estimating $\Delta y_P/\Delta y_F$. Although it is common practice to assume $\Delta y_P/\Delta y_F = 1$, such an assumption, when applied arbitrarily, can lead to very serious hedging errors. In the case of this problem, however, assuming $\Delta y_P/\Delta y_F = 1$ is not likely to do serious damage, since the effective maturities (durations) of the portfolio and its hedging instrument are almost the same. However, if the effective maturities had been significantly different, estimating $\Delta y_P/\Delta y_F$, or at least being aware of the consequences of assuming $\Delta y_P/\Delta y_F = 1$, would be a critical component to the analysis.

The effectiveness of this hedge can be verified by determining how the value of the hedged portfolio would change, given an immediate change in its yield. Table 15.7 shows how the value of the original portfolio holdings and the value of the futures position would change if the market yield were to change from 5 to 6 percent and 4 percent. With an increase in yield from 5 to 6 percent, the original portfolio should decrease in value from $1 billion to $0.90149 billion. At the same time, however, the futures price should decline from $109,862 to $100,000.[81] Therefore, with a short position in 10,431 contracts, the portfolio should gain $10,431(\$109,862 - \$100,000) = \$0.10287$ billion in value, bringing its

---

81. This can be verified from the middle panel of table 15.4.

Table 15.7   New portfolio values, given an immediate change in yield

Maturity in years	Annual coupon	Market value ($MM)	New value, including short position in 10,431 Treasury Bond futures
Market yield = 0.06			
21	8	535.00	new value = $901.49MM + 10.431M
30	5	258.49	×($109.862M − $100M)
8	7	376.03	= $901.49MM + $102.87MM
13	4	−90.72	= $1,004.36MM
21	8	−177.31	
Overall portfolio		901.49	
New futures price = $100.000			
Market yield = 0.04			
21	8	676.72	new value = $1,117.08MM + 10.431M
30	5	352.14	×($109.862M − $121.064M)
8	7	425.87	= $1,117.08MM − $116.85MM
13	4	−110.47	= $1,000.23MM
21	8	−227.18	
Overall portfolio		1,117.08	
New futures price = $121.064			

total value to $0.90149 + $0.10287 = $1.00436 billion. Thus, if the market yield changes from 5 percent to 6 percent, there should be very little change in the portfolio's value. Similarly, if the yield falls to 4 percent, the value of the original position should increase to $1.11708 billion while the futures position loses $0.11685 billion, for a net value of $1.00023 billion.[82] Again, if the portfolio is properly hedged, a very significant change in yield should lead to very little change in the portfolio's value.

In the forgoing problem, the bank's net interest rate risk exposure is hedged using only the 30-year Treasury Bond futures contract. However, a careful examination of the components of the bank's portfolio indicates that a more effective hedge might be carried out using two or more different interest rate futures contracts. For example, the bank holds a long position in an 8-year bond with a 7 percent coupon and a short position in a 13-year , 4 percent bond, both of which have much shorter maturities than any of the other bonds in the portfolio. It is likely that a better hedge could be constructed if these positions were hedged separately using shorter-term 10-year Treasury Note futures rather than 30-year Treasury Bond futures. Similarly, if any of the bank's holdings included long or short positions in very short-term Treasury notes or bills, it would be best

---

82. The new futures price is computed using the same type of analysis as table 15.4 with a yield of 4 percent.

to hedge these positions with short-term instruments such as futures on Eurodollars or 2-year Treasury notes.

15.6   The Wild-card Play

The possibility of exceuting the *wild-card* play in connection with Treasury Bond and Note futures can significantly affect the pricing and trading characteristics of these contracts. Readers whose purpose is to gain a general understanding of interest rate futures can skip this section. However, those who expect to be involved with the trading of Treasury Bond or Note futures need to understand the wild-card play and how it can affect the way these futures contracts trade.

Trading in Treasury Bond and Note futures ceases on the eighth business day before the end of the maturiy month. On that day, or on any prior business day of the delivery month, the seller may give notice of intention to make delivery. When notice of delivery is made, it is at the settlement price established as of the close of futures trading at 2:00 pm CST on the same day. Interestingly, however, Treasury bonds and notes continue to trade until 4:00 pm CST, and notice of intention to deliver may be made at any time prior to 8:00 pm CST.

Suppose you hold a postion in $1,000,000 par value of the cheapest-to-deliver bond during the delivery month, and this bond has a conversion factor of 1.2. Since the number of contracts required for hedging a postion in the cheapest-to-deliver bond is its conversion factor per $100,000 par value, you hedge the $1,000,000 in par value by selling 12 contracts. Ignoring accrued interest, the futures price times the conversion factor should equal the price of this same bond. Assume the 2:00 pm futures settlement price is $100 per $100 par and the price of the cheapest-to-deliver bond at 2:00 pm is $100 \times 1.2 = $120.

Although this represent an extreme move, assume that after 2:00 pm, but before 4:00 pm, the price of the cheapest-to-deliver bond falls from $120 to $110. In light of the provisions of the futures contract, is there anything you could do as futures trader to take advantage of this $10 price change?

You could earn an immediate profit by providing your broker with notice of intention to deliver at the 2:00 pm settlement price on all 12 contracts for which you are short. Note that this requires delivery of $1,200,000 par value of the cheapest-to-deliver bond or any of 30-plus other bonds eligible for delivery. You satisfy $1,000,000 par value of the delivery requirement by delivering the $1,000,000 par value bond that you hold. Note that no profit is made from this transaction. However, you still need to deliver bonds with an additonal $200,000 in par value. This can be accomplished by purchasing $200,000 par value of the cheapest-to-deliver bond at the new market price of $110 and delivering this bond. When the bond is delivered you will receive the futures settlement price of $100, established at 2:00 pm, times the conversion factor of 1.2, or $120 per $100 par. Therefore, your profit will be $120 − $110 = $10 per $100 par, or $20,000. You just made $20,000 via the wild-card play!

Although this example is based on an extreme price change, it is clear that the potential to make the wild-card play is present between 2:00 and 4:00 pm of any trading day of the delivery month. On some days, making the play could be marginally profitable, but waiting to make the play on another day might have an even higher expected profit. Although one could use an option-pricing framework to place a value on the play, it is not developed here.

It should be noted, however, that the potential profit from making the wild-card play is the highest for bonds with the highest conversion factors. In the example above, there would have been no profit from the wild-card play if the conversion factor for the delivered bond had been 1.0. On the other hand, the profit would have been $50,000, rather than $20,000, if the delivered bond's conversion factor had been 1.5 rather than 1.2.[83] This leads to the following conclusion.

> If there are two or more bonds eligible for delivery in connection with the Treasury Bond contract, all of which give comparable direct returns from hedging, the bond with the highest conversion factor should provide the highest overall expected return from hedging, after taking into account both the direct return from hedging and the potential to make the wild-card play. As such, this bond will be the most attractive to hedge, and, therfore, cheapest-to-deliver.

15.7 Long-term vs. Short-term Hedging with Treasury Bond and Note Futures

Hedging theory suggests that securities required for the implentation of a riskless hedge should be priced so that the hedge earns the risk-free rate of interest. Applying this concept to Treasury Bond and Note futures, while recognizing the complexities of the contracts, one can conclude that one

---

83. Some may consider the possibility of doing the play in reverse if the conversion factor of the delivered bond is less than 1.0. However, doing a reverse wild-card play requires control of the contract by a party who has a long position in futures, and, therefore, is infeasible.

should earn a *risk-adjusted* expected return equal to the risk-free rate when hedging *optimally* with Treasury Bond or Note futures. Part of this return may come as a sure direct return from hedging. Another part may come from the wild-card play. A final part may come about as a result of a shift in interest rates above or below 6 percent causing a significant change in the bond that would otherwise be cheapest-to-deliver. Although the returns of these last two components are uncertain, the overall expected return from an optimal hedge, after adjusting for the risk of the last two components, should equal the risk-free rate.

From the analysis of the cheapest-to-deliver bond, summarized in tables 15.4 and 15.5, one can observe that the return from hedging a bond other than that which has been identified as cheapest-to-deliver, can be substantially below the risk-free rate. Moreover, one can extrapolate from this analysis to conclude that the return from hedging a portfolio of bonds most of which are not likely to be the cheapest-to-deliver, can be substantially below the risk-free rate. For example, if one were to maintain a short position in 10,431 6-month Treasury Bond futures contracts for a full six months to hedge the portfolio described in table 15.6, one should expect to earn a return substantially less than the risk-free rate, since this portfolio is not the cheapest-to-deliver bond.

This does not mean, however, that Treasury Bond and Note futures cannot be used effectively to provide a quick fix against a potential adverse change in interest rates. In the example involving the bank trading desk, the short position in 10,431 Treasury Bond contracts should help immunize the bank against any immediate risk associated with a change in interest rates. Stated differently, bank officials shouldn't lose sleep over interest rate risk exposure if a short position in 10,431 contracts is taken. However, if they plan to sleep as long as Rip Van Winkle before removing their hedge, they are likely to wake up having lost a lot of money. The bottom line . . .

> use Treasury Bond and Note futures to accomplish a short-term fix in interest rate risk exposure, but do not use these same contracts as vehicles for hedging long-term.

15.8 Summary

Interest rate futures are among the most important financial instruments for managing interest rate risk. Among available contracts, 30-year Treasury Bond and 10-year and 5-year Treasury Note futures tend to be the contracts of choice for managing long to intermediate-term interest rate risk. Short-term risk typically is managed using Eurodollar futures.

Due to the ability to deliver a large number of bonds or notes to satisfy the terms of Treasury Bond and Note contracts, the possibility of engaging in the wild-card play, and the potential for interest rate changes to affect the bond that is cheapest-to-deliver, these contracts are extremely complex. Nevertheless, if the latter two complicating factors are ignored, it is possible to determine the bond or note that will be cheapest to deliver and to use the mathematics of duration to determine the number of Treasury Bond or Note futures contracts required to hedge or otherwise manage the interest rate risk of a fixed-income portfolio. But given that these factors do exist, duration-based hedging quantities using Treasury Bond and Note futures serve only as approximations. These problems can be substantially overcome by using interest rate swaps, described in the next chapter, as alternative vehicles for managing the risks associated with adverse interest rate changes.

REFERENCES

Black, F., E. Derman, and W. Toy, "A One-Factor Model of Interest Rates and its Application to Treasury Bond Options." *Financial Analysts Journal* 46 (January/February 1990), 33–9.

Clarke, R. G., *Options and Futures: A Tutorial*, The Research Foundation of The Institute of Chartered Financial Analysts, Charlottesville, VA, (1992).

Heath, D., R. A. Jarrow, and A. Morton, "Bond Pricing and the Term Structure of Interest Rates: A New Methodology for Contingent Claims Valuation." *Econometrica* 60 (January 1992), 77–105.

McCauley, F., *Some Theoretical Problems Suggested by the Movement of Interest Rates, Bond Yields, and Stock Prices in the U.S. Since 1856*, National Bureau of Economic Research, New York, (1938).

Rendleman, R. J., Jr., "Duration-Based Hedging with Treasury Bond Futures." *The Journal of Fixed Income* 9 (June 1999), 84–91.

QUESTIONS AND PROBLEMS

1. The risk-free market rate of interest is 9 percent per year compounded semi-annually for all default-free debt instruments, regardless of maturiy. (In other words, the yield curve is flat.) Assume a Treasury bond that matures in exactly 16 years and pays interest at a rate of 11 percent per year, or 5.5 percent every six months, is the only bond eligible for delivery in connection with the 6-month Treasury Bond futures contract. As of the maturity date of the futures contract, the conversion factor for this bond will be 1.500, calculated as the present value per dollar of par of the remaining 15.5 years of

interest and principal payments, using a discount rate of 6 percent with semi-annual compounding.

With a market rate of interest of 9 percent per year compounded semi-annually, the 16-year 11 percent coupon bond has a market price of $116.79 per $100 of par.

Compute the equilibrium futures price for the 6-month Treasury Bond futures contract.

2. Assume that a 30-year bond with a 3 percent annual coupon and a 21-year bond with a 6 percent annual coupon are also eligible for delivery. (Again, interest is paid semi-annually for both bonds.) Compute the equilibrium futures price for the 6-month Treasury Bond futures contract.

3. As interest rates change, so will the futures price and the prices of all three bonds. The interest rate risk characteristics of the futures contract will parallel those of which of the three bonds? Explain.

4. Assume that the three bonds shown in the table below are the only bonds eligible for delivery in connection with the 6-month Treasury Bond futures contract.

Bonds eligible for delivery

Years until maturity	Annual coupon rate (%)	Current market price	Conversion factor in six months
28	4.00	85.02	0.7323
21	6.50	119.37	1.0585
17	9.00	145.45	1.3115

The current market rate of interest is 5 percent per year compounded semi-annually, and the yield curve is flat. The futures price is $110.244 per $100 par.

You are managing a $500,000,000 fixed-income portfolio, but would like to hedge its immediate interest rate risk exposure by selling an appropriate number of Treasury Bond futures contracts. The durations for your portfolio and the projected durations for the three bonds eligible for delivery are given in the table below.

Portfolio/Bond	Duration (years)
Your portfolio	11.000
28-year, 4.00%	15.833
21-year, 6.50%	12.194
17-year, 9.00%	9.985

Based on this information, determine the number of Treasury Bond futures contracts that must be sold in order to immunize your portfolio against an immediate change in interest rates.

5. Extending problem No. 4, assume that $100,000,000 of the $500,000,000 portfolio is invested in 1-year zero-coupon Treasury bond. Assume, further, that the portfolio can also be hedged with 90-day Eurodollar futures maturing in one year or with 5-year Treasury Note futures maturing in six months. Presently, the contract price for 5-year Treasury Note futures is $103.955 per $100 par, and the contract is trading as if the current 5-year, 7 percent coupon note will be delivered in six months. The duration for this Treasury note, projected six months from now, is 3.575 years.

   a. Compute the duration of the $400,000,000 portion of the portfoio that is not invested in a 1-year zero-coupon bond.

   b. Formulate a plan for immunizing the entire portfolio against an immediate adverse change in interest rates that will best utilize the available futures contracts.

6. Discuss the following. "As the market rate of interest gets closer to a flat yield curve at 6 percent with semi-annual compounding, the use of Treasury Bond and Note futures as hedging vehicles becomes more risky."

7. You have performed an analysis to determine the cheapest-to-deliver bond in connection with the Treasury Bond futures contract, similar to that summarized in table 15.5. You rank the annualized returns from hedging all 30+ available bonds from highest to lowest, and your analysis shows that bonds A, B and C, shown below, produce the highest annalized hedging returns.

Bond	Conversion factor	Annualized return from hedging (%)
A	0.9000	7.00
B	1.0000	6.95
C	1.4000	6.90

Assume the market rate of interest is 8 percent.

   a. How can it be possible for the highest return from hedging to be 7 percent in what is otherwise an 8 percent market?

   b. Which of the three bonds, A, B, or C, is likely to drive the market for Treasury Bond futures? Carefully explain.

16

Swap Markets

16.1 Introduction

The market for interest rate swaps began in the early 1980s, primarily as a means to lower the interest cost of corporate debt. Although a limited number of swaps are traded on various options and futures exchanges, the market for swaps is primarily an over-the-counter market dominated by large commercial banks and investment banking firms.

> According to a survey of the International Swap Dealers Association, by June 30, 2000, there was over $60 trillion in notional principal outstanding worldwide in interest rate and currency swaps.

Although the original motivation for swaps was the lowering of interest costs, today swaps are used primarily as tools for managing interest rate and currency risks. In fact, as will be shown in subsequent analysis, the apparent reduction of interest cost results from a misunderstanding of swap mathematics. It is quite possible that one can enter into a swap transaction thinking that interest costs will be reduced only to find that the actual interest cost is much higher than expected.

16.2 The Mechanics of Plain-vanilla Interest Rate Swaps

Introduction

A plain vanilla interest rate swap is a contract in which one party agrees to make a fixed interest-like payment on a certain notional principal amount

Table 16.1   5-year borrowing terms for parties A and B

Party	Fixed rate	Floating rate
A	6.40	LIBOR + 0.50
B	5.50	LIBOR + 0.00
Quality spread (A−B)	0.90	0.50

Quality spread differential = 0.90 − 0.50 = 0.40.

while the counterparty to the transaction agrees to make a floating payment on the same principal amount over the same period of time. It is customary for the floating payment to equal the LIBOR[84] rate established at the beginning of each payment period times the notional principal amount. Typically, the party that makes the fixed payment will have a floating-rate loan outstanding of a comparable principal amount and maturity. By combining its swap and loan payments, this party effectively converts its floating-rate loan to a fixed-rate loan. Similarly, the party that makes a floating payment typically will have a fixed-rate loan outstanding of comparable size and maturity. For this party, the swap has the effect of converting the fixed-rate loan to a floating-rate loan. Presumably, the interest costs of these converted loans will be lower than if the two parties had taken out the loans directly. Often bank loans and swaps are packaged together as a means of reducing interest costs relative to a direct loan.

Consider the situation describing borrowing terms for parties A and B summarized in table 16.1. If party A borrows for five years at a fixed rate of interest, it must pay 6.40 percent per year, but for the same type of loan, party B must pay only 5.50 percent. The difference between these two rates, 0.90 percent, or 90 basis points, is called the *fixed-rate quality spread*.

Similarly, if party A borrows the same sum at a floating rate for five years, it must pay LIBOR plus 50 basis points, but party B must pay only LIBOR. The difference between the rates, 50 basis points, is the *floating rate-quality spread*. The difference between the fixed and floating rate-quality spreads, which in this case is 0.90 − 0.50 = 0.40, or 40 basis points, is called the *quality spread differential*. As will be shown below, ...

whenever the quality spread differential is non-zero, it is possible to construct an interest rate swap between the two parties that will appear to provide an interest savings to both. The following is an example of such a swap.

---

84. LIBOR is the London Interbank Offered Rate. It represents the cost of short-term funds for commercial banks and corporations of the highest credit quality.

An example of a swap that appears to provide interest savings to both parties

Using the logic of swap mathematics, party A is said to have a *comparative advantage* relative to party B in the floating-rate market, or less of a disadvantage, since it pays only 50 basis points interest more than B. Similarly, party B is said to have a comparative advantage in the fixed-rate market, since it pays a full 90 basis points less than A. For the purposes of constructing this example, assume that both parties borrow initially in the market for which they have a comparative advantage. Therefore, party A takes out a 5-year floating-rate loan at LIBOR + 0.50 and party B takes out a 5-year fixed-rate loan at 5.50 percent as indicated in table 16.1. However, for strategic reasons, which could involve the management of interest rate risk exposures, each of the two parties would prefer to take out a loan of the opposite type. Thus, although party A borrows at a floating rate, it would prefer to borrow at a fixed rate and party B, with fixed-rate debt, would prefer to borrow at a floating rate.

Both parties can accomplish their borrowing objectives by entering into a 5-year interest rate swap. According to the terms of the swap, party A agrees to make a fixed payment to party B in the amount of 5.72 percent per year on a specified notional principal amount. Simultaneously, party B agrees to pay party A the LIBOR rate in effect at the beginning of each payment period on the same notional amount. Table 16.2 summarizes the total interest cost to both parties after taking into account the interest owed on their original debt obligations plus the cash flows expected by both in connection with the swap.

After adding the net cash payment from the swap against the interest on its original loan, party A makes a net payment of 6.22 percent. As a result, it effectively converts its floating-rate loan to a 6.22 percent fixed-rate loan. Note that 6.22 percent is 18 basis points less than the 6.40 percent interest cost required by A if it were to take out a fixed-rate loan directly. Thus, party A sees the swap as not only converting its debt from a floating rate to fixed,

Table 16.2 Net cash flows in plain vanilla interest rate swap

Party	Interest on original loan	Pays in swap	Receives in swap	Net payment
A	LIBOR + 0.50%	5.72%	LIBOR	LIBOR + 0.50% + 5.72% − LIBOR = 6.22%
B	5.50%	LIBOR	5.72%	5.50% + LIBOR − 5.72% = LIBOR − 0.22%

Interest savings to A = 6.40% − 6.22% = 0.18%.
Interest savings to B = LIBOR − (LIBOR − 0.22%) = 0.22%.

but also as reducing its fixed-rate interest cost. Similarly, through the swap, party B converts its fixed-rate debt to floating-rate debt and is able to save 22 basis points (b.p.) in its floating-rate interest cost. Together, the total interest savings to both parties is $18b.p. + 22b.p. = 40b.p.$, an amount that corresponds to the quality spread differential shown in table 16.1. As it turns out, no matter how the terms of the swap are constructed, the total amount of apparent interest savings to both parties will equal the quality spread differential, which, in this case, is 40 basis points.

Although not reflected in the above example, it is standard practice to net swap payments. Applying this procedure to the example, if the LIBOR rate exceeds 5.72 percent, party B must pay party A the difference between the two rates while party A pays nothing to B. On the other hand, if the LIBOR rate is less than 5.72 percent, party A must pay B the difference between the two rates, and B would pay nothing. The net effect is the same as if A were to pay B 5.72 percent and B were to pay A the LIBOR rate.

How can both parties reduce their interest costs?

> A swap transaction represents a zero-sum game between the two counterparties. As with all zero-sum games, any amount gained by one party must come at the direct expense of the other party. So how can both parties benefit by entering into a swap? It appears as if they are creating value out of thin air!

A careful examination of the original loan terms in table 16.1 reveals the answer.[85] According to table 16.1, if party B were to take out a floating-rate loan, its interest cost would be the LIBOR rate. This is, essentially, the lowest floating rate available to corporate borrowers and an indication that the borrower is of the highest credit quality. For the purposes of this example, assume that any amount loaned to party B is risk-free, whether the debt is floating or fixed rate, and there is no chance that party B will default on its debt or swap obligations.

---

85. A more detailed and analytical treatment of this problem can be found in Cooper and Mello (1991) and in Rendleman (1993a, 1993b). These papers show that a non-zero quality spread differential, such as that shown in table 16.1, can be a natural outcome of equilibrium pricing when the debt and swap payments of one or both parties is subject to default risk. In simple terms, the mathematics of floating and fixed-rate default risk are different, and there is no reason for quality spreads for the two types of loans to be the same. The fact that the two spreads are different does not imply an inefficiency in pricing that can be exploited by the two contracting parties.

On the other hand, party A must pay an interest premium for fixed or floating-rate debt, presumably to reflect the default risk that a lender faces when loaning money to A. Thus, one can assume that there is some small chance that A will be unable to meet its debt and swap obligations.

Suppose that over the lives of the two loans and the swap, all goes well and both parties are able to meet their debt and swap obligations. Then the effective interest costs to both parties will be exactly as indicated in the last column of table 16.2. Party A will save 18 basis points in interest and party B will save 22 basis points.

Assume, instead, that party A runs into difficulty and is unable to meet its debt and swap obligations. For example, assume that A is unable to pay B the 5.72 percent owed in connection with the swap at a time when the LIBOR rate is 4.00 percent. In this case, party B, which has borrowed at a rate of 5.50 percent, must still pay 5.50 percent in interest on its original loan while receiving nothing in connection with the swap. Thus, B's net interest cost will be 5.50 percent at a time when it would have expected a net cost of LIBOR $-$ 0.22 percent, or 3.78 percent. In this situation, B ends up paying $5.50 - 3.78 = 1.72$ percent more than would be indicated by the terms of the swap.

Since B is a default-free party, A does not have to worry about receiving the payments promised by B. Therefore, A can treat the net interest cost of 6.22 percent shown in the last column of table 16.2 as a sure thing, or at least a sure thing in the sense the total of its net interest costs cannot exceed 6.22 percent. In contrast, party B should look at the LIBOR $-$ 0.22 percent net interest cost of table 16.2 as a best-case scenario, knowing that if party A defaults on its swap obligation, B could end up paying a much higher rate of interest.

Using a financial intermediary

In the early days of swaps, corporations would set up contracts between each other similar to that described above. Each party would make regular swap payments to the other, or make a net payment, depending upon the relationship between the fixed and floating rates. No third party or intermediary would be involved.

As the market for swaps developed, however, commercial banks and investment banking firms became active players and now serve as principals and/or agents in connection with most swap transactions. By extending the above example, we can see how a financial intermediary might be involved as principal in a swap transaction.

Suppose that parties A and B do not transact with each other, but instead, transact directly with a commercial bank. As such, A enters into a swap with the bank in which A makes a fixed payment and receives a floating

Table 16.3 Net cash flows in plain vanilla interest rate swaps with bank serving as principal

Party	Interest on original loan	Pays in + swap	Receives − in swap	Net = payment
A	LIBOR + 0.50%	5.75% to bank	LIBOR from bank	6.25%
B	5.50%	LIBOR to bank	5.70% from bank	LIBOR − 0.20%
Bank		LIBOR to A	5.75 from A	0.05%
		5.70 to B	LIBOR from B	

Interest savings to A = 6.40% − 6.25% = 0.15%
Interest savings to B = LIBOR − (LIBOR − 0.20%) = 0.20%
Profit to bank = 0.05%.

payment from the bank. At approximately the same time, B enters into a swap with the bank in which it makes a floating payment and receives a fixed payment. In order for the bank to make a profit on the two transactions, the terms of the two swaps are adjusted slightly. According to the adjusted terms, A pays the bank 5.75 percent while receiving the LIBOR rate from the bank, and B pays the LIBOR rate to the bank while receiving 5.70 percent. In all likelihood, neither party A nor B knows that the other has entered into a swap with the bank. Each transacts directly with the bank, and the fact that the bank may be involved with other transactions should be irrelevant to A and B. Table 16.3 summarizes the net cash flows to all three parties.[86]

In this situation, the terms of the two swaps allow the bank to earn a profit of 0.05 percent, provided that neither party A nor party B defaults on its swap obligation. Note that the collective interest savings to A and B plus the profit to the bank is 40 basis points, the same as the quality spread differential shown in table 16.1.

Does the presence of the bank allow parties A and B to both realize interest savings? If the bank is a commercial bank subject to federal deposit insurance, both parties can view the payments promised by the bank as being as good as gold. Since party B is contracting directly with the bank, it does not have to worry about the creditworthiness of party A. Therefore, as long as the bank can be expected to pay B what is promised, B can view its interest savings as a sure thing. Similarly, A can view its savings as a sure thing. So who loses?

---

86. It is typical for a bank to enter into a swap with one party without immediately finding another party to do the other side of the swap. This practice is called *warehousing*. Such a bank will manage its overall interest rate risk exposure by entering into additional swaps with different terms or by entering into transactions in interest rate futures or other interest-sensitive derivative securities.

With deposit insurance, the US Government is not likely to allow the bank to default on its swap obligations, and in all likelihood, will make good on all the bank's deposits and swap contracts. In fact, this is exactly what happened in 1991 when Bank of New England failed. At the time, the bank was one of the most significant participants in the swap market, but when the bank failed, the government guaranteed its entire $7 billion swap book. In this case, both its shareholders and the American public bore the cost of guaranteeing Bank of New England's swap payments.

So who wins and who loses in swap transactions? Swaps represent a zero-sum-game, but not necessarily just between the two counterparties. Among all parties involved, the expected profit must be zero. But it is entirely possible that the losing party may be you and I, especially when one of the counterparties is a commercial bank. So from the perspective of the counterparties alone, it is possible to create value out of thin air by exploiting the implicit government guarantee of commercial bank liabilities. Whether this is a good thing for society as a whole is open to debate.[87]

16.3 Pricing Default-free Interest Rate Swaps

This section addresses two questions. First, once a default-free swap is issued and outstanding, what is its fair value? Second, what should be the initial terms of a default-free swap to make it a fair contract for both parties?

In answering both of these questions it is assumed that the swap's fixed and floating payments are made every six months and that the first set of swap payments are scheduled to occur in exactly six months. Although it is typical for a swap's floating payments to be tied to the LIBOR rate, it is assumed, initially, that each floating payment is equal to the 6-month Treasury bill rate in effect at the beginning of each payment period. After establishing how the swap should be structured within this framework, the terms of the swap are modified to reflect LIBOR-based pricing.

The value of the swap for which one is scheduled to receive a floating payment and make a fixed payment is given as follows:

$$swap\ value = PV\,(floating\ payments) - PV\,(fixed\ payments)$$

$$(16.1)$$

87. This issue is developed further in Rendleman (1993a), pp. 29–31 and in Rendleman (1993b), pp. 50–3.

Although principal, or par value, is not exchanged at the termination of an interest-rate swap, the mathematics of swap pricing are simplified if a payment of *par*, assumed to be made at the termination of the swap and standardized to a value of $100, is added to both present value terms in equation 16.1. Since $100 appears in both terms, adding this value to both, which amounts to adding $100 and subtracting $100, does not change the value of the swap. With this adjustment, the value of the swap becomes:

$$swap\ value = PV(floating\ payments + \$100)$$
$$- PV(fixed\ payments + \$100).$$

$$(16.2)$$

The first component of the swap value is the present value of a stream of floating-rate payments per $100 par plus the present value of a $100 payment at the termination date of the swap. The second component is the present value of a stream of fixed-rate payments per $100 par plus the present value of a $100 payment received on the swap's termination date. Evaluating the second component, $PV(fixed\ payments + \$100)$, amounts to discounting the stream of fixed payments plus par at the prevailing term structure of risk-free forward interest rates. But determining $PV(floating\ payments + \$100)$ requires an entirely different method of valuation, since all but the first of the series of floating payments will not be known in advance.

To understand how to evaluate $PV(floating\ payments + \$100)$, assume that the initial Treasury bill rate is 4 percent per six months. Since the floating rate to be paid at the end of each 6-month period is assumed to equal the 6-month Treasury bill rate in effect at the beginning of each period, the initial floating payment will be $4 per $100 par.

Rather than using present value discounting, $PV(floating\ payments + \$100)$ is evaluated using a replication argument similar to that employed in earlier valuation methods. Below, I describe how the series of floating payments plus par can be replicated by making a series of investments in Treasury bills. Since the Treasury bill series will have a payoff structure identical to that of the swap's floating payments (plus par at the end), $PV(floating\ payments + \$100)$ must equal the value of the investment outlay required for the Treasury bill series.

To understand the replication argument, assume that you invest $100 in a 6-month Treasury bill scheduled to earn 8 percent with semi-annual compounding or 4 percent for the 6-month period. You also plan to reinvest $100 at the end of each subsequent 6-month period at whatever the Treasury bill rate happens to be and plan to terminate this series of investments after m 6-month periods which corresponds to the maturity date of the swap. Let $\tilde{R}_t$ denote the 6-month Treasury bill rate in effect as of

Table 16.4 Cash flows from series of Treasury bill investments designed to replicate floating-rate payments plus par

6-month period	Cash received	+ Cash reinvested	= Net cash received
1	$4 + \$100 = \$104$	$100	$4
2	$\tilde{R}_2(\$100) + \$100$	$100	$\tilde{R}_2(\$100)$
3	$\tilde{R}_3(\$100) + \$100$	$100	$\tilde{R}_3(\$100)$
.	.	.	.
.	.	.	.
.	.	.	.
m	$\tilde{R}_m(\$100) + \$100$	$0	$\tilde{R}_m(\$100) + \$100$

the beginning of the tth 6-month period. (The squiggle over the symbol R is called a tilde and is standard mathematical notation for indicating an amount whose value is random or unknown in advance.) Table 16.4 summarizes the series of cash flows that will be received from this series of Treasury bill investments.

Note that the net cash received, shown in the final column, is exactly the same as the floating payments to be received from the swap, with par value of $100 added at the end. Therefore, *PV (floating payments + $100)* must equal the initial cost of the investment that produces the cash flows of the final column. This cost is $100, or par, since it is the amount that must be invested initially to get the program started. After the initial Treasury bill is purchased, the investment takes care of itself, and no further cash outlay is required. Therefore,[88]

$$PV\,(\textit{floating payments} + \$100) = \$100$$

$$(16.3)$$

---

88. This very important pricing relationship can be used, not only for swap pricing, but also for the pricing of any default-free instrument that has a floating-rate component to its payment stream. For example, suppose a bank wants to price a default-free loan for which the interest payment equals the Treasury bill rate plus 100 basis points, or 50 basis points per six months. The value of this loan, per $100 par, can be broken down into two components, *PV (floating rate + $100) + PV* $(0.005 \times \$100$ *every six months*) $= \$100 + PV(0.005 \times \$100$ *every six months*). If there are additional features to the loan, such as a maximum or minimum value that the floating rate can attain, these features can be valued separately using option pricing theory and then added to the base amount, $100 + PV(0.005 \times \$100$ *every six months*). An application of this concept is provided in Rendleman (1999).

Substituting $100 for PV (*floating payments* + $100) into equation 16.2 gives the following value for the swap, assuming one receives a floating payment and makes a fixed payment.[89]

$$swap\ value = \$100 - PV(fixed\ payments + \$100)$$

(16.4)

Although one can use standard present value discounting to evaluate PV (*fixed payments* + $100), its use can be somewhat problematic when the yield curve is not flat. Therefore, I will take a slightly different, but equivalent, approach to evaluate PV (*fixed payments* + $100).

The term PV (*fixed payments* + $100) can be thought of as having an annuity component and a lump sum component. For example, if a 5-year swap calls for an annual payment of 9 percent, or 4.5 percent every six months, the annuity component would be $4.50 per $100 par every six months for five years and the lump sum component would be $100 received in five years.

In introductory finance, students are taught to look at present value tables in the back of the book to determine the present value of an annuity of $1 per period and the present value of a lump sum payment of $1 and to apply these values to the annuity and lump sum amounts. I will use this same approach, but I will not get annuity and lump sum present values from the back of a book, but instead, from prices in the bond market.

To see how this works, let PVA_m denote the present value of an annuity of $1 to be received at the end of m 6-month periods and PVL_m denote the present value of $1 to be received at the end of period m. Also, let $bond_j^m$ denote the price of m-period bond j that pays interest of C_j dollars per year per $100 par. Then, the prices of any two m-period bonds, denoted as bonds 1 and 2, with distinctly different annual coupons, C_1 and C_2, can be written as:

$$bond_1^m = \left(\frac{C_1}{2}\right) PVA_m + \$100\ PVL_m$$

(16.5)

$$bond_2^m = \left(\frac{C_2}{2}\right) PVA_m + \$100\ PVL_m$$

(16.6)

---

89. If the first swap payment is scheduled to be made in less than three months, then PV (*floating payments* + $100) equals the present value of the first floating payment per $100 par plus the present value of $100, assumed to be received at the same time. For example, assume that the first floating payment occurs in three months and is $4 per $100 par. Also, assume that a 3-month treasury bill is presently priced at $0.9810 per dollar of par. Then PV (*floating payments* + $100) = $104(0.981) = $102.024.

Table 16.5 Prices of Treasury securities maturing on 2/15/06 for settlement on 2/15/01

Annual coupon rate	Bid price	Ask price	Average of bid and ask
9.375	118.6875	118.8125	118.750
5.625	102.5000	102.5625	102.53125

Solving equations 16.5 and 16.6 simultaneously for PVA_m and PVL_m yields:[90]

$$PVA_m = 2 \left(\frac{bond_1^m - bond_2^m}{C_1 - C_2} \right)$$

(16.7)

$$PVL_m = \frac{C_1 bond_2^m - C_2 bond_1^m}{100(C_1 - C_2)}$$

(16.8)

An example of default-free swap pricing

Consider the following 5-year default-free swap to be priced on February 14, 2001. One party to the swap must make an annual fixed payment of 9 percent, or 4.5 percent every six months, while the counter-party must pay the 6-month Treasury bill rate in effect at the beginning of each 6-month period. The swap will be valued from the perspective of the party that receives float and pays fixed, and, therefore, equation 16.4 applies. If approached from the opposite perspective, the value of the swap would be the negative of the value given by equation 16.4.

On February 14, 2001, there were two Treasury bonds or notes out-standing with February 15, 2006 maturities. These securities would be scheduled to make interest payments every February 15 and August 15. Since a bond purchased on February 14 would be settled, or paid for, the next day, its price on February 14 can be thought of as the February 15 price, and from that point on, there would be exactly six months between the bond's remaining payments. These Treasury securities and their prices are summarized in table 16.5.

Substituting the coupon rates and averages of the bid and ask prices into equations 16.7 and 16.8 gives the following annuity and lump sum present

---

90. If full prices (quoted price plus accrued interest) are used in equations 16.7 and 16.8, they will correctly determine the annuity and lump sum factors, even if the time to the first coupon payment is not six months.

value factors:

$$PVA_m = 2\left(\frac{118.750 - 102.53125}{9.375 - 5.625}\right) = 8.65$$

$$PVL_m = \frac{9.375(102.53125) - 5.625(118.75)}{100(9.375 - 5.625)} = 0.78203$$

Applying these present value factors to the 5-year annuity of 4.5 percent per six months and the lump sum of $100 after five years yields the following value for the present value of the swap's fixed payments plus par:

$$PV\,(fixed\,payments + \$100) = \$4.50(8.65) + \$100(0.78203)$$
$$= \$117.208.$$

Substituting this value into equation 16.4, gives the value of the swap per $100 par.

$$swap\,value = PV\,(floating\,payments + \$100)$$
$$- PV\,(fixed\,payments + \$100)$$
$$= \$100 - \$117.208$$
$$= -\$17.208$$

Determining the initial terms for the swap

Like a futures contract, when a swap contract is written, the terms of the swap should be structured so that it has no immediate value to either party. Stated differently, neither party should have to make a payment to the other as an inducement to enter into the swap. Assuming the floating side of the swap is tied to the Treasury bill rate, the fixed payment that causes the present value of the swap to equal zero is that which causes $PV\,(fixed\,payments + \$100)$ to equal $100. Using the vernacular of bond traders, the annual rate of fixed payment that causes the present value of a stream of m fixed payments plus par to equal $100 is called the *par yield*.[91]

Let C_{par} denote the annual coupon per $100 par that causes a bond to sell for par. Then, the par yield, or coupon per $100 par, of a bond that

---

91. The annual yield-to-maturity, with semi-annual compounding, of a bond that sells for par value is its coupon rate. The *par yield*, which refers to the annual yield-to-maturity that causes a bond to sell for its par value, will, therefore, equal the bond's annual coupon rate.

makes m semi-annual interest payments plus a return of principal at the end is the solution to

$$\$100 = \left(\frac{C_{par}}{2}\right) PVA_m + \$100 \, PVL_m,$$

or

$$C_{par} = \frac{\$200 - \$200 \, PVL_m}{PVA_m}.$$

(16.9)

Using the same bond prices in table 16.5 to determine the annuity and lump sum present value factors, the 5-year par yield on February 15, 2001 would be

$$C_{par} = \frac{\$200 - \$200(0.78203)}{8.65}$$

$$= 5.0398.$$

Therefore, if one had entered into a 5-year default-free swap on February 14, 2001 with the floating rate tied to the Treasury bill rate, the fixed side of the swap should have been 5.0398 percent per year, or 2.5199 percent every six months.

Adjusting initial swap terms for LIBOR-based pricing

The foregoing analysis is based on the assumption that the floating side of the swap is equal to the 6-month Treasury bill rate in effect at the beginning of each payment period. In practice, however, the floating side is almost always tied to LIBOR rather than the Treasury bill rate. At the same time, however, the terms for the fixed side of a swap are quoted by traders as a number of basis points in excess of the Treasury-based par yield. This creates an "apples and oranges" problem in which the methods for quoting the floating and fixed sides of swaps are inconsistent. Therefore, the method of swap pricing developed earlier must be adjusted to reflect the convention of quoting the floating side of a swap in terms of LIBOR and the fixed side in terms of the US Treasury par yield.

The 6-month LIBOR rate is the rate on 6-month Eurodollar deposits. Therefore, the adjustment for LIBOR can be accomplished by discounting all fixed and floating-rate cash flows using Eurodollar rates rather than US Treasury rates. As with Treasury-based discounting, with Eurodollar-based discounting the present value of a swap's LIBOR-based floating payments, plus par at the termination of the swap, is par.

> To find the fixed payment that makes the swap a fair contract for both parties, one must determine the fixed rate for which the Eurodollar-based discounted present value of fixed payments plus par also equals par. This is simply the par yield of a Eurodollar-denominated bond of comparable maturity to the swap.

By convention, Eurodollar yields are quoted with an assumption of annual compounding, whereas Treasury yields are quoted with an assumption of semi-annual compounding. Therefore, the Eurodollar-based yield must be converted to a semi-annual equivalent to make it comparable to a Treasury yield. Letting y_{annual} and y_{semi} denote a yield with annual compounding and its semi-annual compounding equivalent,

$$y_{semi} = 2\left(\sqrt{1 + y_{annual}} - 1\right).$$

(16.10)

The data in table 16.6 illustrate this adjustment using price quotations for a 5-year swap, 5-year Treasury Notes and 5-year Eurodollar deposits on February 14, 2001. Column C of the table indicates that the semi-annual compounding equivalent of the 5-year Eurodollar par yield is 5.73 percent. This corresponds exactly to the quote of 5.73 percent for the fixed side of a LIBOR-based swap. Note that 5.73 percent is 0.69 percent, or 69 basis points, in excess of the 5-year Treasury par yield. Thus, at the time, a swap dealer would have quoted 5.73 percent for the fixed side of the swap or 69 basis points over the Treasury par yield.

Pricing an existing LIBOR-based swap

Consider a swap that was issued originally as a 10-year swap but on February 14, 2001 has exactly five years remaining. According to its original terms, the swap calls for a floating payment equal to the beginning of period 6-month LIBOR rate and a fixed payment of 10 percent annually, or 5 percent every six months.

There are two ways that the pricing of this swap can be approached. Using Eurodollar-based discounting, the present value of the floating side of the swap plus par per $100 of par equals $100. Then, the value of a swap for which a floating payment is received and a fixed amount is paid is $100 minus the Eurodollar-based present value of the ten remaining fixed payment of $5 per $100 par plus $100 par at the end of five years.

Table 16.6 5-year quotes for Treasury securities, Eurodollars and swaps
February 14, 2001

(A) 5-year Treasury par yield with semi-annual compounding	(B) 5-year Eurodollar par yield with annual compounding	(C) 5-year Eurodollar par yield with semi-annual compounding	(D) Fixed side of LIBOR-based 5-year swap	(E) Swap spread over 5-year Treasury par yield (D) − (A)
5.04%	5.81%	5.73%	5.73%	0.69%

Sources: (A) Calculated based on *Wall Street Journal* quotations; (B) Bloomberg; (C) calculated using equation 16.10; (D) Datastream.

Alternatively, the same pricing problem can be approached using Treasury-based discounting. Note from table 16.6 that as of February 14, 2001, the fixed side of a newly issued LIBOR-based swap is 0.69 percent higher than what the fixed side would have been if the swap's floating payment had been tied to the Treasury bill rate rather than the LIBOR rate. Therefore, for the purposes of pricing an existing swap using Treasury-based discounting, 0.69 percent should be subtracted from the swap's annual fixed payment, implying that the annual fixed payment should be adjusted to 10 percent minus 0.69 percent or 9.31 percent. Using the previously-determined Treasury-based annuity and lump sum present value factors for February 14, 2001,

$$swap\ value = PV\,(floating\ payments + \$100)$$
$$- PV\,(fixed\ payments + \$100)$$
$$= \$100 - \left(\left[\frac{\$9.31}{2} \right] 8.65 + \$100[0.78203] \right)$$
$$= \$100 - \$118.47$$
$$= -\$18.47$$

16.4 Calculating the Duration of an Interest Rate Swap

One of the primary purposes for swap contracting is the management of interest rate risk. Therefore, it is important that one be able to calculate the durations of newly issued and preexisting swaps. For the purposes of this section, it is assumed that swaps are default-free.

Calculating the duration of a newly issued swap is complicated by the fact that when the swap is issued, its value is zero. This problem can be overcome, however, by breaking the swap into two separate components, the first being the swap's fixed payment plus par at the end and the second its floating payments plus par. The durations of these two components can then be calculated separately, and each can be treated as two separate security holdings, one long and one short, in a larger fixed-income portfolio. This same approach can also be applied to pre-existing swaps, even though their values are not likely to be zero. To avoid developing two methodologies for calculating swap duration, the approach of evaluating the durations of the fixed and floating sides separately will be applied to both types of swaps.

For the purposes of calculating swap durations, I will assume Treasury-based pricing. Therefore, if the floating side of the swap is actually tied to the LIBOR rate, the swap's annual fixed payment must be adjusted by subtracting the current spread between the semi-annual Eurodollar and Treasury par yields from the swap's actual annual payment, and the duration of the swap's fixed side must be calculated on the basis of this adjusted payment.

> Calculating the duration of the floating side of a swap, plus par at the end, is straightforward. The duration is simply the time, in years, to the first floating swap payment. Why? Because the entire floating-rate stream plus par at the end can be replicated by purchasing a Treasury bill that matures on the date of the first swap payment. Therefore, the duration of a swap's floating side plus par at the end is the Treasury bill's time to maturity. For a newly issued swap, the duration will be six months, or 0.5 years.
>
> Calculating the duration of a swap's fixed side, plus par at the end, is also straightforward. The duration should be calculated just like that of a Treasury bond with the same stream of fixed payments.

An example of duration-based portfolio management with swaps

The example from chapter 15 of a bank engaging in duration-based fixed-income portfolio management is extended to include a swap as part of the portfolio and the use of a swap, rather than Treasury Bond futures, to immunize the portfolio against an immediate adverse change in interest rates. In the example, the yield curve is flat with all Treasury bonds and notes being priced to yield 5 percent per year with semi-annual compounding. Table 16.7 summarizes the bank's portfolio holdings modified to

Table 16.7 Summary of portfolio positions

Bond positions					
Maturity in years	Annual coupon	Market value ($MM)	Proportion of total portfolio value	Duration	Weighted duration*
21	8	600	0.750	12.042	9.032
30	5	300	0.375	15.841	5.940
8	7	400	0.500	6.379	3.189
13	4	−100	−0.125	10.094	−1.262
24	9	−200	−0.250	12.698	−3.175
Total bond value		1,000			
Swap floating payments plus par		500	0.625	0.500	0.313
Swap fixed payments plus par		−700	−0.875	7.090	−6.204
Total portfolio value		800			7.834

Market yield = 0.05.
*For each portfolio position, weighted duration is duration times its proportion of portfolio value. The sum of the weighted durations gives the duration for the overall portfolio. The swap has a notational principal amount of $500MM and a term of 10 years. The swap's initial floating payment is $2.50 per $100 par, or $12,500,000 and its annual fixed payment is $10.1318 per $100 par or $50,659,000.

include a 10-year swap with a notional principal amount of $500MM. The swap contract calls for the bank to make a fixed payment of 10.1318 percent annually while receiving the beginning-of-period 6-month Treasury bill rate.[92]

Notice that the fixed and floating sides of the swap are broken out separately in the summary of the bank's holdings. The floating side of the swap, plus par at the swap's termination date, has a value of $500MM and a duration of 0.5 years. The value of the fixed side of the swap, plus par at termination, is −$700MM, and its duration is 7.090 years. The inclusion of the swap, with a value of −$200MM, brings the portfolio's value to $800MM and its duration to 7.834 years.

Assume that the bank wishes to immunize the portfolio against an adverse change in interest rates by taking a position in a newly-issued swap in sufficient quantity to bring the portfolio's duration to zero. Note that the duration of the portfolio is 7.834 years. Since the portfolio has a positive duration, the new swap position should be one with negative duration, which implies that the new swap should be structured so that the bank receives a floating payment and makes a fixed payment.

---

92. 10.1318 percent was chosen conveniently to cause the net value of the swap to be exactly −$200MM.

Table 16.8 New portfolio values, given an immediate change in yield

Market yield = 0.06 (bonds)			Market yield = 0.04 (bonds)		
Maturity in years	Annual coupon	Market value ($MM)	Maturity in years	Annual coupon	Market value ($MM)
21	8	535.00	21	8	676.72
30	5	258.49	30	5	352.14
8	7	376.03	8	7	425.87
13	4	−90.72	13	4	−110.47
21	8	−177.31	21	8	−227.18
Total bond value		901.49	Total bond value		1,117.08
Original swap float + par		497.57	Original swap float + par		502.45
Original swap fixed + par		−653.68	Original swap fixed + par		−750.66
New swap float + par		719.68	New swap float + par		726.74
New swap fixed + par		−661.95	New swap fixed + par		−791.58
Total portfolio value		803.11	Total portfolio value		804.03

Assume that the bank has an opportunity to take a large position in a 12-year swap that calls for the bank to make a series of fixed payments and receive a series of floating payments tied to the Treasury bill rate. Since the yield curve is flat at 5 percent, the 12-year par yield should be 5 percent, which, in turn, defines the annual fixed payment for a newly issued swap. It can be shown that the duration of a 12-year 5 percent bond with semi-annual payments is 9.166 years. If the portfolio is immunized under the assumption that $\Delta y_P / \Delta y_H = 1$, the notional principal amount of the new swap, denoted as *notional*, should be chosen such that

$$dur_P V_P = dur_H V_H$$

$$\$800\text{MM}(7.834) = notional(9.166) - notional(0.5),$$

reflecting that the duration of the floating side of the swap, plus par at the end, is 0.5 years, and the duration of the swap's fixed side, plus par at the end, is 9.166 years.[93] Solving for the notional principal amount,

$$notional = \$723.19\text{MM}.$$

The effectiveness of this hedge can be verified by determining how the value of the hedged portfolio would change, given an immediate change in its yield. Table 16.8 shows how the value of the original portfolio

---

93. Using the notation from chapter 15, dur_P and dur_H denote the duration of the portfolio and hedging instrument, respectively, V_P and V_H denote their respective values y_P and y_H denote their respective yields.

holdings and the value of the newly issued swap would change if the market yield were to change from 5 percent to 6 percent and 4 percent. With an increase in yield from 5 percent to 6 percent, the original portfolio should decrease in value from $800 million to $901.49 + $497.57 − $653.68 = $745.38 million. At the same time, however, the value of the new swap should increase in value to $719.68 − $661.95 = $57.73 million, bringing the total value of the portfolio to $745.38 + $57.73 = $803.11 million. Therefore, if the market yield changes from 5 percent to 6 percent, there should be very little change in the portfolio's value. Similarly, if the yield falls to 4 percent, the value of the original position should increase to $1,117.08 + $502.45 − $750.66 = $868.87 million while the new swap loses $791.58 − $726.74 = $64.84 million, for a net value of $868.87 − $64.84 = $804.03 million. Again, if the portfolio is properly hedged, a very significant change in yield should lead to very little change in the portfolio's value.

The impact of LIBOR pricing on duration-based hedging

The foregoing analysis assumes that a change in the spread between Eurodollar and Treasury yields does not accompany a change in interest rates. If there is no change in the spread, the duration-based hedge should be accurate. However, if the spread does change, the ultimate hedging outcome will be subject to risk.

It should be noted that the spread between Eurodollar and Treasury yields reflects the very small degree of default risk associated with Eurodollar investments in relation to Treasuries. As investors perceive an increase in default risk, the spread should increase. A decrease in perceived default risk should be accompanied by a reduction in the spread.

> The potential for a change in the credit spread can actually work to the advantage of the portfolio being hedged if high-grade corporate bonds or bank loans are held in the portfolio rather than Treasury securities. Since these assets should also be subject to a change in the credit spread, the value change associated with a change in spread for both the assets being hedged and the hedging vehicle could be partially offsetting.

16.5   Currency Swaps

Plain vanilla currency swaps, sometimes referred to as *fixed-for-fixed* currency swaps, are used to convert loans or fixed-income investments

Table 16.9 5-year fixed-rate borrowing terms for US and British firm

Firm	US Dollar rate (%)	Rate in British pounds (%)
US	5.50	7.20
British	6.00	6.50

denominated in one currency to a loan or investment of equivalent value denominated in another currency.

> Since most firms are able to borrow on more favorable terms in their home currency than in a foreign currency, if a domestic and foreign firm enter into a currency swap, each can take advantage of the other's power to borrow in its home currency and, thereby, reduce its foreign borrowing cost.

Consider the following example involving a US and British firm. Both are considered to be of the highest credit quality when borrowing in their home currency. For strategic reasons, the US firm would like to borrow British Pounds, perhaps to offset the currency risk that it faces with assets whose future cash flows are denominated in British Pounds. Similarly, the British firm would like to borrow US dollars. However, due to inefficiencies in cross-border borrowing, neither firm can borrow in the other's currency on terms that reflect its true credit quality. Table 16.9 summarizes the terms for 5-year fixed-rate borrowing for the two firms.

Assume that the spot exchange rate is $1.50/£. The US firm borrows $150,000,000 in US dollars for five years at 5.50 percent. At the same time, the British firm borrows £100,000,000 at 6.50 percent. At the current exchange rate of $1.50/£, the two principal amounts are equivalent.

After borrowing these amounts, the two firms enter into a fixed-for-fixed currency swap in which the initial principal amounts are exchanged, the ending principal amounts are also exchanged, and each agrees to make payments each year to the other equal to the other's interest payment. (In contrast to interest rate swaps, it is common practice to exchange principal at the initial and termination dates of currency swaps.) Table 16.10 summarizes the net cash flows of the two parties after borrowing in their home currency and entering into the swap transaction.

Through the swap, the US firm effectively borrows £100,000,000 at a rate of 6.5 percent. At the same time, the British firm effectively borrows $150,000,000 at a rate of 5.5 percent. The ability to enter into the swap eliminates the inefficiency in cross-border borrowing for the two

Table 16.10   Net cash flows (in $millions) in fixed-for-fixed currency swap

Party	Principal received on original loan	Pays in swap	Receives in swap	Net amount received
At the beginning				
US	$150	$150	£100	$150 − $150 + £100 = £100
British	£100	£100	$150	£100 − £100 + $150 = $150

Party	Interest payment on original loan	Pays in swap	Receives in swap	Net annual payment
Each year				
US	0.055 × $150 = $8.25	£6.5	$8.25	$8.25 + £6.5 − $8.25 = £6.5
British	0.065 × £100 = £6.5	$8.25	£6.5	£6.5 + $8.25 − £6.5 = $8.25

Party	Principal paid on original loan	Pays in swap	Receives in swap	Net amount paid
At the end				
US	$150	£100	$150	$150 + £100 − $150 = £100
British	£100	$150	£100	£100 + $150 − £100 = $150

parties, and as such, *does* create value for both, provided the next-best alternative for each is to borrow in foreign currency at the rates shown in table 16.9.

Valuing currency swaps

The valuation of currency swaps is approached from the perspective that US dollars and British Pounds are exchanged in the swap and the swap is valued in terms of dollars. Consider the swap in the above example. The US firm pays $150,000,000 up front, receives $8.25 million (5.5 percent) each year plus $150,000,000 at the termination of the swap. This is the same series of cash flows that would occur if the US firm had purchased a $150,000,000 5-year bond paying interest at 5.50 percent per year. At the same time, the US firm receives £100,000,000 up front, pays

£6.5 million (6.5 percent) each year plus £100,000,000 at the termination of the swap. This is the same set of cash flows that would occur if the US firm had shorted a £100,000,000 5-year bond that pays interest in British Pounds at 6.5 percent per year. Clearly, then, the value of the swap must be the present value of the dollar-denominated interest and principal to be received, evaluated at US interest rates, denoted as $PV_\$(\$\ interest\ and\ principal)$, less the present value of British Pound-denominated interest and principal to be paid, evaluated at British interest rates, denoted as $PV_\pounds(\pounds\ interest\ and\ principal)$. But since this second value is denominated in British Pounds, it must be converted to dollars by multiplying by the spot $/£ exchange rate. Thus, the dollar value of a swap to receive dollars and pay Pounds is:

$$swap\ value = PV_\$(\$\ interest\ and\ principal)$$
$$- PV_\pounds(\pounds\ interest\ and\ principal)spot_{\$/\pounds}.$$

(16.11)

To illustrate equation 16.11, assume that a pre-existing swap with exactly two years remaining until its maturity date. The swap calls for $9 million to be received every six months plus $300 million in two years. This implies a dollar-denominated coupon rate 6 percent per year with semi-annual payments. At the same time, £8.8 million is to be paid every six months plus $220 in two years. This implies a Pound-denominated coupon rate of 8 percent per year with payments made semi-annually. As in the previous example, assume that the current US rate of interest is 5.5 percent per year with semi-annual compounding (or 2.75 percent every six months), the current rate of interest in the UK is 6.5 percent per year compounded semi-annually (or 3.25 percent every six months), and the spot exchange rate is $1.50/£. Then, the value of the swap in $millions is:

$$swap\ value = \frac{\$9}{1.0275} + \frac{\$9}{1.0275^2} + \frac{\$9}{1.0275^3} + \frac{\$309}{1.0275^4}$$
$$- \left(\frac{\pounds 8.8}{1.0325} + \frac{\pounds 8.8}{1.0325^2} + \frac{\pounds 8.8}{1.0325^3} + \frac{\pounds 228.8}{1.0325^4} \right)(\$1.50/\pounds)$$
$$= \$302.80 - (\pounds 226.10)(\$1.50/\pounds)$$
$$= \$302.80 - \$339.15 = -\$36.35$$

Although this swap may have been issued initially to have zero value to both parties, changes in interest and exchange rates has caused the swap to now have a negative value to the US firm.

The relationship between currency swaps and forward contracting

Consider the example of the 5-year currency swap whose cash flows are summarized in table 16.10. After an exchange of principal, the US firm agrees to pay the British firm £6.5 million (6.5 percent) per year plus £100 in five years at the termination of the swap. At the same time, the US firm will be receiving $8.25 million (5.5 percent) per year and $150 at the termination of the swap. As the theory of swap pricing suggest, this is equivalent to purchasing a 5.5 percent US bond with $150 million in notional principal and shorting a 6.5 percent British bond with £100 million in notional principal. But rather than shorting the 6.5 percent British bond, the US firm could also enter into a series of forward contracts that would require the purchase of £6.5 million each year, or £3.25 million every six months, and £100 at the end of five years. Therefore, for the US firm, the swap is equivalent to buying a 5.5 percent US bond with $150 million in notional principal and simultaneously entering into a series of forward contracts to purchase £3.25 every six months plus £100 in five years.

Although the combination of purchasing the US bond and entering into a series of forward contracts to purchase British Pounds may be equivalent to the swap, it may not be as cost-effective. Presumably, if the firm has entered into the currency swap rather than the forward contract-based transaction, it has determined that the swap is less costly. Nevertheless, it is important for firms considering a currency swap to recognize the equivalency between the swap and the alternative transaction involving forward contracting and to enter into the swap only when it makes sense from a cost perspective.

16.6 Summary

The market for interest rate swaps began in the early 1980s primarily as a means to reduce the interest cost of corporate debt. It is easy to show, however, that this cost reduction can be illusory, especially if one party to the contract is subject to a significant amount of credit risk. Despite the illusion, interest rate swaps can be used very effectively as a means of managing interest rate risk.

As with Treasury Bond and Note futures, it is possible to estimate the duration of a swap contract and to use this information for the purpose of hedging or managing the interest rate risk of a fixed-income portfolio. But it should be noted that swap terms typically provide for a floating payment based on the LIBOR rate rather than a Treasury rate. As a result, swap values should correlate more highly with high-grade corporate bond and bank loan values than Treasury bond values.

Currency swaps can be used to reduce the interest cost associated with borrowing in a foreign currency, especially if there are cross-border inefficiencies in the pricing of corporate loans. In essence, a currency swap allows one party to borrow at the other's home currency-denominated interest rate and, thereby, reduce the potential inefficiencies in cross-border borrowing.

REFERENCES

Cooper, I. and A. S. Mello, "The Default Risk of Swaps." *The Journal of Finance* 46 (June 1991), 597–620.

Rendleman, R. J. Jr., "How Risks are Shared in Interest Rate Swaps." *Journal of Financial Services Research* 7 (1993a), 5–34.

Rendleman, R. J. Jr., "Share and Share Unlike." *Risk* (February 1993b), 50–3.

Rendleman, R. J. Jr., "First Derivatives National Bank: A Case Problem in the Management of Interest Rate Risk." *The Journal of Risk* 1 (1999), 63–85.

QUESTIONS AND PROBLEMS

1. Companies X and Y have been offered the following annual interest rates with semi-annual compounding on $5 million 6-year loans:

Company	Fixed rate (%)	Floating rate
X	6.0	LIBOR
Y	6.5	LIBOR + 0.2%

Company X borrows initially at a fixed rate but would like to have a floating-rate loan. Company Y borrows initially at a floating rate but would like a fixed-rate loan. Design a swap between the two parties that will net each the same amount of apparent interest rate savings for the types of loans they prefer.

2. You observe the following prices for US Treasury bonds.

Bond prices per $100 Par

Maturity (Years)	Coupon	Price
0.5	0	97.00
1.0	0	94.00
1.5	0	91.00
2.0	0	89.00
2.5	8	86.00

   a. Determine the fair annual fixed rate per $100 of notional principal for a default-free 2.5-year swap in which one receives a fixed payment every six months and makes a floating payment equal to the 6-month Treasury interest rate times the swap's notional principal amount.

   b. Determine the value of a default-free 2.0-year swap for which one receives a fixed rate of 4.5% annually and pays the 6-month LIBOR rate. For the purposes of this problem, assume the current spread between the 2-year Eurodollar par yield and the 2-year Treasury par yield is 40 basis points.

   c. Assume that swap in part (a) involves a notional principal amount of $1,000,000 and that the swap is held as part of a larger portfolio. The remaining portion of the portfolio has a market value of $5,000,000 and a duration of six years. What is the duration of the entire portfolio?

3. Dogwood National Bank (DNB) holds a 2-year default-free fixed-for-fixed currency swap with a notional principal amount of $10,000,000. According to the terms of the swap, DNB must make semi-annual payments in US dollars at an annual rate of 10.0 percent on the notional principal amount. At the same time, DNB is scheduled to receive semi-annual payments in Euros (not Eurodollars) at an annual rate of 9 percent.

     Assume that the risk-free dollar- and Euro-denominated market rates of interest are 6 percent and 4 percent, respectively, with semi-annual compounding. The current exchange rate is $0.92 per Euro. Determine the value of DNB's position in the currency swap.

Index